Steps in Composition

Eighth Edition

Lynn Quitman Troyka | Jerrold Nudelman

Upper Saddle River, New Jersey 07458

Library of Congress Cataloging-in-Publication Data

Troyka, Lynn Quitman
Steps in composition/Lynn Quitman Troyka, Jerrold Nudelman.—8th ed.
p. cm.
Includes index.
ISBN 0-13-110069-6
1. English language—Rhetoric. 2. English language—Grammar—Problems, exercises, etc.
3. College readers. I. Nudelman, Jerrold II. Title.
PE1408.T697 2004
808'042—dc22 2003062445

Editor in Chief: Leah Jewell
Senior Acquisitions Editor: Craig Campanella
Editorial Assistant: Joan Polk
Director, Production and Manufacturing: Barbara Kittle
Production Editor: Joan E. Foley
Production Assistant: Marlene Gassler
Copyeditor: Kathryn Graehl
Permissions Coordinator: Ron Fox
Text Permissions Specialist: Stacey Keomany
Assistant Manufacturing Manager: Mary Ann Gloriande
Prepress and Manufacturing Buyer: Brian Mackey
Director, Marketing: Beth Mejia
Senior Marketing Manager: Rachel Falk
Marketing Assistant: Adam Laitman
Media Production Manager: Lynn Pearlman
Media Editor: Christy Schaack
Director, Image Resource Center: Melinda Reo
Image Rights and Permissions Manager: Zina Arabia
Image Permissions Coordinator: Lisa Amato
Director, Creative Design: Leslie Osher
Art Director: Anne B. Nieglos
Interior and Cover Designer: Kathy Mystkowska
Cover Art: "Cityscape with Yellow Windows," Paul Klee. 1919. Stadtische Komposition mit Gelben Fenstern. Gouache auf Butten, auf Karton aufgezogen Ulmer Museum-Stiftung. Sammlung Kurt Fried.

This book was set in 10/12 New Baskerville by Pine Tree Composition, Inc., and was printed and bound by LSC Communications.

For permission to use copyrighted material, grateful acknowledgment is made to the copyright holders on page xix, which is considered an extension of this copyright page.

Pearson Education LTD.
Pearson Education Singapore, Pte. Ltd
Pearson Education, Canada, Ltd
Pearson Education–Japan
Pearson Education Australia PTY, Limited
Pearson Education North Asia Ltd
Pearson Educación de Mexico, S.A.de C.V.
Pearson Education Malaysia, Pte. Ltd
Pearson Education, Upper Saddle River, NJ

21 17
ISBN 0-13-110069-6 (student ed.)
ISBN 0-13-184473-3 (instructor ed.)

Dedicated to our parents,
Belle and Sidney Quitman
Frances and Henry Nudelman

CONTENTS

PREFACE

This eighth edition of *Steps in Composition* continues to reflect our conviction that writing is a lively, engaging activity that helps students to fulfill their personal and professional goals. Our approach to teaching writing is both practical and pedagogically sound. To encourage student success, we use a number of essential elements:

- Engaging visuals elicit responses as each chapter begins.
- Contemporary, thought-provoking reading selections on the same theme as the visuals stimulate critical thinking and promote effective reading skills.
- Comprehensive discussions of rhetoric, grammar, mechanics, vocabulary building, and spelling provide jargon-free explanations and clear examples.
- Frequent Try It Out mini-exercises throughout the instructional material help students to reinforce their learning as they go along.
- Exercises are sequenced from basic practice to participatory applications, a research-based progression that transfers well to actual writing.
- Informative, entertaining exercise content includes news items with universal themes and fascinating facts to keep student interest high.
- Numerous charts help students use the text as an out-of-class reference tool.
- Extensive lists of topics for writing both paragraphs and essays stimulate student writing on a variety of contemporary issues.

To ensure that *Steps in Composition* remains both current and comprehensive, this eighth edition has been expanded to include thirteen chapters and several new features:

- Chapters 12 and 13 contain detailed information on all nine major patterns of essay development: description, narration, exemplification, process, comparison/contrast, classification, cause/effect, definition, and argumentation. Each rhetorical mode is illustrated with three model essays and is supported by guided writing exercises that give students the opportunity to reinforce learning.
- Five of the thirteen essays are new and are accompanied by new Reading Survey questions and vocabulary materials.
- The new design enhances the text's usefulness as a reference tool. The pages in all grammar and rhetoric sections are bordered in blue, to help students find these important materials in a chapter. In addition, a boldface heading now introduces each grammar rule or rhetorical concept, making it easier for students to retrieve information on a page.

We retain the features added to our previous revisions and continue to use the same chapter organization and instructional framework, one that offers an integration of writing instruction with reading, vocabulary building, and spelling. All thirteen chapters feature:

SPRINGBOARDS TO THINKING. Photographs, cartoons, graphs, advertisements, and an artwork—accompanied by stimulating questions—get students' thinking started on a contemporary issue that forms each chapter's theme. In this edition, themes range from road rage to race relations, from gender issues to troubled families.

ESSAY. Lively discussions of thought-provoking topics focus on each chapter's theme. Several new essays are included together with some of our favorites from the previous edition. Among the authors represented in this eighth edition are Dave Barry, Ellen Goodman, Alice Walker, Martin Gottfried, Anna Quindlen, and Wally Lamb.

READING SURVEY. Questions center on main ideas, major details, inferences, and opinions. This sequence is designed to move students toward critical reading skills by leading them from literal meaning to inferential reasoning to evaluative thinking.

VOCABULARY BUILDING. Words from each chapter's essay are clustered around each chapter's theme. In this eighth edition, students learn and practice, for example, the vocabulary of self-image, of today's adolescent subculture, of a violent society. Simple, functional definitions are given within a context, and exercises encourage inductive thinking. For supplementary practice or quizzes, our *Instructor's Resource Manual* offers additional exercises for all lessons.

SPELLING. Lessons on spelling rules or patterns are accompanied by exercises that force students to focus on the individual letters in a word. An alphabetical list of spelling demons in Appendix III serves as an easy reference for students who want to check the spelling of a troublesome word.

KEY STEPS IN GRAMMAR OR RHETORIC. These sections, the heart of each chapter, cover skill areas central to successful writing. Clear, functional explanations are used while complicated terminology and minor rules are avoided. Spaced throughout are brief Try It Out exercises to reinforce learning in smaller steps than the chapter's culminating exercises permit. To enhance the transfer of learning from an exercise to an actual piece of writing, the exercise sequence provides participatory experiences. That is, never do students merely put checkmarks next to correct answers; instead, students complete, rewrite, create, or otherwise become directly involved with the skill. For use as supplementary practice or quizzes, a collection of additional exercises on all key grammar and rhetoric topics can be found in our *Instructor's Resource Manual.* The grammatical and rhetorical skills included in this eighth edition are:

- Using the writing process and prewriting strategies
- Determining purposes for writing
- Identifying an audience
- Writing effective topic sentences
- Developing paragraphs with full details and in logical order
- Revising a paragraph
- Writing mature, rich sentences rather than sentence fragments, comma splices, or run-ons
- Using correct verb forms
- Using pronouns correctly
- Applying paragraph principles to the expository essay—with special attention to finding a writing topic, drafting a thesis statement, forming main body ideas, and writing introductory and concluding paragraphs
- Revising an essay
- Using all marks of punctuation correctly
- Writing a unified essay
- Using the appropriate word
- Using parallelism and modifiers correctly
- Writing an essay that follows one of the nine major patterns of development: description, narration, exemplification, process, comparison/contrast, classification, cause/effect, definition, and argumentation

The order in this text is flexible. Chapters can be used in whatever sequence suits personal needs and preferences. Material can be omitted, rearranged, or added without interfering with underlying pedagogical principles. The *Instructor's Resource Manual* includes sample syllabi showing how to modify the organization of *Steps in Composition* to fit a variety of course outlines.

REFRESHER. This final exercise of the chapter, derived from the chapter's theme, invites students to apply their learning acquired in this and previous chapters. This exercise appears in a handwriting typeface to symbolize the need for correction.

SPRINGBOARDS TO WRITING. This long list of suggested topics for paragraphs and essays is based on each chapter's theme. Presented in the context of the writing process, the topics offer students the opportunity to explore their thinking as well as to practice their skills.

THE SUPPLEMENTS

To supplement this eighth edition of *Steps in Composition,* many materials, for both instructor and student, are available:

- An *Instructor's Edition* includes all exercise answers; information about using the Reading Survey sections; a collection of recommended teaching techniques and teacher-designed classroom materials; and an extensive list of audio-visual materials that can enliven a composition class. ISBN 0-13-184473-3.
- The *Instructor's Resource Manual* contains two comprehensive diagnostic tests; additional exercises for all vocabulary, rhetoric, and grammar sections of the text; a collection of transparency masters that are coordinated with the text; sample syllabi; essay reading-level information; study guides for the Florida and Texas state competency exams; Study Aids charts; and an individualized study program to help students monitor their progress. Contact your local Prentice Hall representative for a copy of this valuable resource. ISBN 0-13-047515-7.
- The Companion Website™ <www.prenhall.com/troyka>. This free website for students provides additional thematically-arranged readings online. For each reading, students can answer Before You Read and Reading Survey questions. There are also self-grading vocabulary quizzes, paragraph editing exercises, and writing prompts for each selection.
- PH WORDS. An Internet-based course management program, PH WORDS gives English instructors the ability to measure and track students' mastery of the elements of writing from the writing process, to patterns of development, to grammar. Covering over 100 topics, PH WORDS allows students to work on their specific areas of weakness, freeing up class time for instructors. Sold at a discount when packaged with *Steps in Composition.* Visit <www.prenhall.com/phwords> for more information. Package ISBN 0-13-105381-7.
- *The New American Webster Handy College Dictionary.* Available free to students when packaged with *Steps in Composition,* this dictionary has over 1.5 million Signet copies in print and over 115,000 definitions, including current phrases, slang, and scientific terms. It offers more than 1,500 new words, with over 200 not found in any other competing dictionary, and features boxed inserts on etymologies and language.
- *The Prentice Hall ESL Workbook* (ISBN 0-13-092323-0). Available free to students when packaged with *Steps in Composition,* this 138-page workbook is divided into seven major units, providing explanations and exercises in the most challenging grammar topics for non-native speakers. With over 80 exercise sets, this guide provides ample instruction and practice in nouns, articles, verbs, modifiers, pronouns, prepositions, and sentence structure.

- *The Prentice Hall Grammar Workbook* (ISBN 0-13-092321-4). Available free to students when packaged with *Steps in Composition,* this 21-chapter workbook is a comprehensive source of additional grammar, punctuation, and mechanics instruction. Each chapter provides ample explanation, examples, and exercise sets. The exercises contain enough variety to ensure a student's mastery of each concept.
- *The Prentice Hall TASP Writing Study Guide* (ISBN 0-13-041585-5). Available free to students when packaged with *Steps in Composition,* this guide prepares students for the writing portion of the Texas Academic Skills Program test. In addition, it familiarizes the reader with the elements of the test and provides strategies for success. There are exercises for each part of the exam and then a full-length practice test with answer key so that students can gauge their own progress.
- *The Prentice Hall Florida Exit Test Study Guide for Writing* (ISBN 0-13-111652-5). Free when packaged with *Steps in Composition,* this guide prepares students for the writing section of the Florida Exit Test. It also acquaints readers with the parts of the test and provides strategies for success.
- *The Prentice Hall Writing Skills Test Bank* (ISBN 0-13-111628-2). Available in fall 2003, this printed test bank will include hundreds of additional exercises for instructors to give students. Covering many of the basic skills of writing, including the writing process, methods of development, and grammar, *The Prentice Hall Writing Skills Test Bank* can be used with any text as a source of extra practice or quizzes.
- Research Navigator™. Research Navigator™ is the one-stop research solution—complete with extensive help on the research process and three exclusive databases including EBSCO's *ContentSelect*™ Academic Journal Database, *The New York Times* Search-by-Subject Archive, and *Best of the Web* Link Library. Take a Web tour <http://www.researchnavigator.com>. Your students get FREE ACCESS to Research Navigator™ when you package *Steps in Composition* with our exclusive *Evaluating Online Resources: English 2004 Guide.* The ISBN for the Guide is 0-13-184085-1.

To order any of these supplements or packages, please contact your local Prentice Hall sales representative or call Faculty Services at 1-800-526-0485.

Acknowledgments

While preparing the eighth edition, we benefited from the many warm comments and helpful suggestions given to us by students and teachers throughout the country. Most especially, we thank Nancy-Laurel Pettersen of Queensborough Community College for her many fine contributions to the new chapters on the patterns of essay development. We are fortunate that four talented writers—Keith Gramegna, Kulikam Messiah Justin, Carol L. Skolnick, and James Wanless—provided several of the model essays in these chapters. Throughout the revision process, we also benefited greatly from the generous help and advice provided by Alvin H. Schlosser of Queensborough Community College.

For their incisive reviews of this book, we are grateful to Catherine Gould Barrows of Orangeburg-Calhoun Technical College, Thomas G. Beery of Lima Technical College, Stacey Fitzpatrick of Ivy Tech State College, Heather K. Foote of Denver Technical College, Wendy Jean Frandsen of Vance-Granville Community College, Paulette Longmore of Essex County College, Jamie Moore of Scottsdale Community College, and Harvey Rubinstein of Hudson County Community College.

At Prentice Hall we had the privilege of working with a number of talented, hard-working people. Craig Campanella, senior English editor, supervised this project with unfailing optimism, enthusiasm, and patience. Joan Foley, production editor, demonstrated considerable skill and tact as she guided this project to its completion. Joan Polk, editorial assistant, offered her support whenever we were faced with problems. Kathryn Graehl copyedited our work with great care and sensitivity, and Kathy Mystkowska created a handsome new design that reinforces our pedagogical concepts. Indeed, each person has understood and facilitated our goal of producing a text that respects students and helps them fulfill their potentials as writers.

LYNN QUITMAN TROYKA
JERROLD NUDELMAN

CREDITS

Chapter 1

SPRINGBOARDS TO THINKING

For informal, not written, response . . . to stimulate your thinking

1. What is the message of the cartoon above?

2. Do many drivers feel that their cars are actually assault weapons? Explain.

3. Why do some people who are usually polite and mild-mannered become angry, rude, and inconsiderate when they are behind the wheel?

4. What is the message of the advertisement on the opposite page?

5. Can children be influenced toward violence if they see drivers threatening other motorists? Explain. What other effects does such road rage have on our society and on everyone's quality of life?

Rambos of the Road

Martin Gottfried

(1) The car pulled up and its driver glared at us with such sullen intensity, such hatred, that I was truly afraid for our lives. Except for the Mohawk haircut he didn't have, he looked like Robert De Niro in *Taxi Driver*, the sort of young man who, delirious for notoriety, might kill a president.
(2) He was glaring because we had passed him and for that affront he pursued us to the next stoplight so as to express his indignation and affirm his masculinity. I was with two women and, believe it, was afraid for all three of us. It was nearly midnight and we were in a small, sleeping town with no other cars on the road.
(3) When the light turned green, I raced ahead, knowing it was foolish and that I was not in a movie. He didn't merely follow; he chased, and with his headlights turned off. No matter what sudden turn I took, he followed. My passengers were silent. I knew they were alarmed, and I prayed that I wouldn't be called upon to protect them. In that cheerful frame of mind, I turned off my own lights so I couldn't be followed. It was lunacy. I was responding to a crazy *as* a crazy.
(4) "I'll just drive to the police station," I finally said, and as if those were the magic words, he disappeared.
(5) It seems to me that there has recently been an epidemic of auto macho—a competition perceived and expressed in driving. People fight it out over parking spaces. They bully into line at the gas pump. A toll booth becomes a signal for elbowing fenders. And beetle-eyed drivers hunch over their steering wheels, squeezing the rims, glowering, preparing the excuse of not having seen you as they muscle you off the road. Approaching a highway on an entrance ramp recently, I was strong-armed by a trailer truck, so immense that its driver all but blew me away by blasting his horn. The behemoth was just inches from my hopelessly mismatched coupe when I fled for the safety of the shoulder.
(6) And this is happening on city streets, too. A New York taxi driver told me that "intimidation is the name of the game. Drive as if you're deaf and blind. You don't hear the other guy's horn and you sure as hell don't see him."
(7) The odd thing is that long before I was even able to drive, it seemed to me that people were at their finest and most civilized when in their cars. They seemed so orderly and considerate, so reasonable, staying in the right-hand lane unless passing, signaling all intentions. In those days you really eased into

highway traffic, and the long, neat rows of cars seemed mobile testimony to the sanity of most people. Perhaps memory fails, perhaps there were always testy drivers, perhaps—but everyone didn't give you the finger.

(8) A most amazing example of driver rage occurred recently at the Manhattan end of the Lincoln Tunnel. We were four cars abreast, stopped at a traffic light. And there was no moving even when the light had changed. A bus had stopped in the cross traffic, blocking our paths: it was a normal-for-New-York-City gridlock. Perhaps impatient, perhaps late for important appointments, three of us nonetheless accepted what, after all, we could not alter. One, however, would not. He would not be helpless. He would go where he was going even if he couldn't get there. A Wall Street type in suit and tie, he got out of his car and strode toward the bus, rapping smartly on its doors. When they opened, he exchanged words with the driver. The doors folded shut. He then stepped in front of the bus, took hold of one of its large windshield wipers and broke it.

(9) The bus doors reopened and the driver appeared, apparently giving the fellow a good piece of his mind. If so, the lecture was wasted, for the man started his car and proceeded to drive directly *into the bus.* He rammed it. Even though the point at which he struck the bus, the folding doors, was its most vulnerable point, ramming the side of a bus with your car has to rank very high on a futility index. My first thought was that it had to be a rental car.

(10) To tell the truth, I could not believe my eyes. The bus driver opened his doors as much as they could be opened and he stepped directly onto the hood of the attacking car, jumping up and down with both his feet. He then retreated into the bus, closing the doors behind him. Obviously a man of action, the car driver backed up and rammed the bus again. How this exercise in absurdity would have been resolved none of us will ever know, for at that point the traffic unclogged and the bus moved on. And the rest of us, we passives of the world, proceeded, our cars crossing a field of battle as if nothing untoward had happened.

(11) It is tempting to blame such belligerent, uncivil and even neurotic behavior on the nuts of the world, but in our cars we all become a little crazy. How many of us speed up when a driver signals his intention of pulling in front of us? Are we resentful and anxious to pass him? How many of us try to squeeze in or race along the shoulder of a lane merger? We may not jump on hoods, but driving the gantlet, we seethe, cursing not so silently in the safety of our steel bodies on wheels—fortresses for cowards.

(12) What is it within us that gives birth to such antisocial behavior and why, all of a sudden, have so many drivers gone around the bend? My friend Joel Katz, a Manhattan psychiatrist, calls it "a Rambo pattern. People are running around thinking the American way is to take the law into your own hands when anyone does anything wrong. And what constitutes 'wrong'? Anything that cramps your style."

(13) It seems to me that it is a new America we see on the road now. It has the mentality of a hoodlum and the backbone of a coward. The car is its weapon and hiding place, and it is still a symbol even in this. Road Rambos no longer bespeak a self-reliant, civil people tooling around in family cruisers. In fact, there aren't families in these machines that charge headlong with their brights on in broad daylight, demanding we get out of their way. Bullies are loners, and they have perverted our liberty of the open road into drivers' license. They represent an America that derides the values of decency and good manners, then roam the highways riding shotgun and shrieking freedom. By allowing this to happen, the rest of us approve.

Reading Survey

1. MAIN IDEA

What is the central theme of this essay?

2. MAJOR DETAILS

a. What examples of "auto macho" does the author give?
b. According to the author, how did drivers behave long before he was able to drive?
c. What is the "Rambo pattern"?

3. INFERENCES

a. Read paragraph 9 again. Why did the author think "that it had to be a rental car"?
b. Read paragraph 11 again. Why does the author call cars "fortresses for cowards"?

4. OPINIONS

a. Do you agree with the author that "in our cars we all become a little crazy"? Explain your point of view.
b. Answer the author's questions: "What is it within us that gives birth to such antisocial behavior and why, all of a sudden, have so many drivers gone around the bend?"

Vocabulary Building

Lesson One: The Vocabulary of Road Rage, Part I

The essay "Rambos of the Road" by Martin Gottfried includes words that are useful when you are discussing road rage.

glared (paragraph 1)
sullen (1)
delirious (1)
notoriety (1)
affront (2)
indignation (2)
intimidation (6)
mobile (7)
testy (7)
vulnerable (9)

People who display road rage have often **glared**—stared angrily—at other drivers.

People who display road rage may be in a **sullen**—gloomy and disagreeable—mood.

People who display road rage may even drive as if they are **delirious**—wildly excited or even crazy.

People who display road rage sometimes earn **notoriety**—a wide and unfavorable reputation—for their bad driving.

People who display road rage may consider everyone else's bad driving an **affront**—insult—to themselves.

People who display road rage tend to act with **indignation**—anger over something that is unfair—when another car passes them.

People who display road rage usually rely on **intimidation**—the use of frightening threats—to get through heavy traffic.

People who display road rage tend to use their cars as **mobile**—movable—weapons.

People who display road rage are often **testy**—impatient and easily annoyed—for no reason.

People who display road rage may see other cars as **vulnerable**—open to attack—targets for their anger.

EXERCISE 1A: Match each sentence with a vocabulary word from this lesson.

1. The President declared that the nation would not give in to the dictator's frightening threats. — 1. ____________________

2. After my parents turned down my demand for a new car, I was in a gloomy and disagreeable mood for several days. — 2. ____________________

3. Because the soldiers were caught in an open space without cover, they were open to attack. — 3. ____________________

4. As the police led the convicted murderer away, the victim's wife shot angry looks at him. 4. ____________________

5. After I broke my leg, I used a wheelchair so that I could move around easily. 5. ____________________

6. When the gangster gunned down two FBI agents, he became famous. 6. ____________________

7. The teenage girls at the 'Nsync concert became so wildly excited that they almost seemed to be going crazy. 7. ____________________

8. My boss is extremely difficult to work for because he is very impatient and everything seems to annoy him. 8. ____________________

9. The accountant reacted angrily to the false charge that she had stolen the money. 9. ____________________

10. When my mother refused to attend my wedding, I was really insulted. 10. ____________________

Lesson Two: ***The Vocabulary of Road Rage, Part II***

The essay "Rambos of the Road" by Martin Gottfried includes more words that are useful when you are discussing road rage.

untoward (paragraph 10)	**seethe** (11)
belligerent (11)	**antisocial** (12)
uncivil (11)	**bespeak** (13)
neurotic (11)	**perverted** (13)
resentful (11)	**deride** (13)

People who display road rage may not see anything wrong with their **untoward**—improper—behavior.

People who display road rage tend to take a **belligerent**—warlike—attitude toward other drivers.

People who display road rage may not care that others think their driving is **uncivil**—rude or impolite.

People who display road rage may even behave as if they are **neurotic**—mentally or emotionally unsteady.

People who display road rage seem to be **resentful**—angered by some insult or injury—when anyone gets in their way.
People who display road rage may **seethe**—boil with anger—when another driver cuts them off.
People who display road rage do not seem to realize that their behavior is **anti-social**—unfriendly toward others and against the basic principles of society.
People who display road rage **bespeak**—indicate or show signs of—a society that is under strain.
People who display road rage have **perverted**—misused or moved away from what is morally right—their right to drive.
People who display road rage may even **deride**—show a lack of respect by laughing at—polite drivers.

EXERCISE 1B: Match each sentence with a vocabulary word from this lesson.

1. The football players took to the field as if they were going into battle. 1. ______________________
2. Your behavior is rude and impolite. 2. ______________________
3. If you continue to call me a liar, I'm going to become angry. 3. ______________________
4. After Chuck dyed his hair purple, his classmates started to make fun of him. 4. ______________________
5. A high dropout rate and poor test scores are signs of a school system in trouble. 5. ______________________
6. When the governor paid for his vacation with taxpayers' money, he misused his power. 6. ______________________
7. Millie is afraid to leave her house because she is mentally and emotionally unsteady. 7. ______________________
8. Carl is such an unfriendly person that he enjoys shouting four-letter words at anyone who comes near him. 8. ______________________
9. If you take off your clothes in the middle of the street, you will probably be arrested for your improper behavior. 9. ______________________
10. I am boiling with anger because my landlord raised my rent by $75. 10. ______________________

SPELLING

Methods to Improve Your Spelling

Although there are no particular rules to help you learn the Spelling Demons listed in Appendix III, there are some helpful techniques for memorizing these words and any others that you find troublesome.

I **Keep an Individual Spelling List.**

II **Enlarge the Trouble Spot.**

III **Use the Dictionary.**

IV **Learn the Proper Pronunciation.**

V **Divide the Word into Parts.**

VI **Use Flashcards.**

VII **Use Memory Tricks.**

Read each of these suggestions and then try each one out for yourself. Through practice, you will become skilled at using the techniques you favor.

I. Keep an Individual Spelling List. Use the last page of a school notebook for your spelling list. Each time you misspell a word, add it to the list. Go back over these words in your spare time; it may be during lunchtime or on the bus in the morning. The point is to make your word study a habit. After you have about fifteen words on your list, look at the types of errors you consistently make. Most people make certain kinds of spelling mistakes, and you can probably diagnose your particular kind: it could be double letters, or vowels (using an *i* for an *e* and vice versa), or vowel combinations, or confusion of *v* and *f*. If a clear pattern of kinds of mistakes is not obvious, ask your instructor to take a look. Sometimes another observer can see tendencies that you might miss.

II. Enlarge the Trouble Spot. If you forget the *d* in *knowledge*, then enlarge the *d* when you write the word on your spelling list. Do the same with the second *c* in *conscious* as a reminder of your trouble spot.

knowleDge consCious

III. Use the Dictionary. When you write, keep a dictionary nearby so you can quickly look up any problem words that you may want to use. It is important to find the correct spelling of a word *before* you actually write it; each time you write a word incorrectly, you reinforce the misspelling in your mind. Some students complain, "I need to know how to spell the word in order to find it in the dictionary, so what's the use?" Actually, you usually have a fairly good idea of how to spell the problem word: The confusion is centered in just one or two syllables, not the whole word. Thus, the search is not that difficult. When you look at the word, note that it is separated into syllables, so it should be easy for you to see clearly the part that was causing you trouble. After you have looked up a word often enough, you will find that you have learned to spell it.

IV. Learn the Proper Pronunciation. Many words are misspelled because they are pronounced incorrectly. If you omit letters from words when you say them—such as quan*ti*ty and proba*bl*y—you are sure to do the same when you write them. If you add an *e* to *athletic* and *disastrous* when you speak, you will add the *e* when you write. Pronouncing *children* as *childern* will lead to writing it the same way. When you are not sure how a word is pronounced, listen to it carefully whenever you hear it. Check the pronunciation in the dictionary or, if you are still not clear on the pronunciation of a certain word, ask someone you can trust.

V. Divide the Word into Parts. Identify compound words, roots, suffixes, and prefixes. Then divide the word into smaller parts that are easier to spell. For example, *knowledge* can be divided into *know* and *ledge; considerably* can be divided into *consider* and *ably.*

VI. Use Flashcards. Instead of using a spelling list, you may prefer to use the flashcard method. Write the troublesome word—in large letters—on one side of a 3″ × 5″ index card. Concentrate on the word for a few minutes, and then turn the card over. When you can visualize the word on the blank side of the card, you have mastered it. As an alternative method, use one side of an index card for the word and the other side for its definition. When you want to study the word, first read the definition; then spell the word that goes with it, and turn the card over to check your spelling.

VII. Use Memory Tricks. Sometimes it is helpful to use memory tricks to learn a word. To memorize *business,* you might remember that bus*in*ess is no *sin.* You would surely remember to put the *w* in *knowledge* if you realized that a person with knowledge must kno*w* a great deal. To memorize *stationery* remember that paper is station*er*y and that you st*a*nd still when you are station*a*ry.

EXERCISE 1C: Follow the directions for each item.

1. In each of the following Demons, circle the letter or letters that are likely to cause you trouble. Then copy the word in the space provided, enlarging the trouble spot so that it stands out as a reminder.

   a. enough ______________________________

   b. guard ______________________________

   c. guilty ______________________________

   d. taught ______________________________

   e. those ______________________________

   f. wrong ______________________________

2. Each of the following Demons contains one or more smaller words in its spelling. Using one of these smaller words and the original Demon, compose a sentence that will help you to associate the two.

   Example: *courtesy* We must show *court*esy in *court*.

   a. against ______________________________

   b. architect ______________________________

   c. background ______________________________

   d. enjoy ______________________________

   e. interest ______________________________

   f. lawyer ______________________________

   g. maybe ______________________________

   h. signal ______________________________

3. With the aid of a dictionary, divide these Demons into syllables.

   a. athlete ______________________________

   b. permanent ______________________________

   c. philosophy ______________________________

   d. simply ______________________________

   e. university ______________________________

   f. writing ______________________________

4. Using each set of Demons given below, create a complete sentence that makes sense.

   a. financial, disastrous, prepare ______________________________

   ____

   ____

   b. handle, responsibility, influence ______________________________

   ____

   ____

   c. survive, character, situation ______________________________

   ____

   ____

   d. alcohol, minimum, citizen ______________________________

   ____

   ____

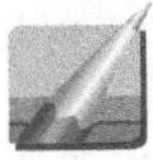

The Writing Process

You will be writing many paragraphs and essays for your English classes and for your other subjects. When you write, your goal is to get your message across to your reader as effectively as possible. To achieve this goal, you will benefit from understanding that *writing is a process.* The writing process consists of specific steps that help all writers, including professional writers, produce writing that is clear, correct, and interesting to read.

Writing involves much more than picking up a pen and expecting words to flow perfectly onto paper. Most professional writers plan, write, and rewrite many drafts of a piece of writing before they consider it finished. As a student writer, you can expect that many of your writing assignments will demand similar amounts of time and patience.

TRY IT OUT

DRAWING ON YOUR PREVIOUS EXPERIENCES IN WRITING FOR CLASS, THINK ABOUT THE STEPS YOU USUALLY GO THROUGH FROM THE TIME YOU ARE GIVEN AN ASSIGNMENT UNTIL THE TIME YOU HAND IT IN. LIST YOUR STEPS AS COMPLETELY AS YOU CAN. USE YOUR OWN PAPER FOR THIS ASSIGNMENT.

Experts who have studied what people do when they write have found that the writing process usually consists of five steps. Here they are, as they apply to writing assignments, whether you have chosen your own topic or the topic has been assigned.

FIVE-STEP WRITING PROCESS

STEP 1: *Prewriting.* In this step, you think and plan for your writing. To do this, you explore your ideas about your topic, gather additional information, and begin to organize your material. For help, see Prewriting Techniques, pages 17–22.

STEP 2: *Drafting.* In this step, you write using the ideas and plans you developed during your prewriting. As you do, you keep in mind your purpose for writing: Do you want to inform the reader? Do you want to persuade the reader? Or do you want to entertain the reader? (For more information on the purposes for writing, see pages 23–30.) You also refine your organization into a structure suitable for a paragraph or an essay. Here you are involved with the content of your ideas, not with your grammar, punctuation, or spelling. Now you have a first draft.

STEP 3: *Revising.* In this step, you read over what you have written, decide what ideas need to be improved so that you have as good a paragraph or essay as possible, and—most important—rewrite your draft to achieve the improvements you want. When rewriting, you add new points that need to be made or more specific details that better support the points you are making, or you drop some ideas that do not belong, and you rearrange the material you have. As you make these revisions, you are guided by the needs and expectations of your audience. (For more information on audience, see pages 31–39.) Now you have a second draft, which you should revise the same way you did your first. When you have a draft that is well developed and logically organized, you begin revising for style. At this point, you concentrate on your choice of words and sentence structure as you work to make your sentences flow smoothly and to establish the appropriate tone for your audience. You should continue to revise all further drafts until you are satisfied with the outcome. For help with revising, see pages 79–88 and 311–22.

STEP 4: *Editing.* In this step, you check thoroughly to make sure that your grammar, punctuation, and spelling are correct. While editing, you should keep this textbook and a dictionary handy to use as quick reference tools.

STEP 5: *Proofreading.* In this step, you carefully reread the copy you intend to hand in. Be sure that you have no errors that you previously overlooked, and be sure that your handwriting is legible or typing is neat. For help with proofreading, see pages 135–37.

Rarely are these five steps as entirely separate from one another as this list implies. Writing moves forward, but it also sweeps backward as the writer tries to work out the best content, form, and language for fulfilling a particular assignment. For example, while prewriting, a writer might draft a few sentences or a few pages to discover fresh ideas that will help with further planning; or while drafting, a writer might go back to use some prewriting techniques for the purpose of expanding ideas and finding additional details to support key points; or while revising, a writer might edit a grammar or spelling mistake that interferes with clarity. Nevertheless, these five steps in the writing process offer a useful sequence that will help you work efficiently.

TRY IT OUT

LOOK BACK AT THE LIST OF YOUR OWN WRITING STEPS, WHICH YOU DREW UP FOR THE PREVIOUS TRY IT OUT (PAGE 14). COMPARE THE SIMILARITIES AND DIFFERENCES BETWEEN YOUR LIST AND THE FIVE-STEP WRITING PROCESS JUST DESCRIBED. USE YOUR OWN PAPER FOR THIS ASSIGNMENT.

When experienced writers move from step to step in the writing process, they allow themselves time, from as little as a half hour to as much as a day or two, to put their work aside. When they come back to it, they have a fresh outlook and can make new connections and see new possibilities for improvement.

Understanding the writing process can help you in two ways. First, you will always remember that you are not finished just because your first draft is complete. Second, you will have a technique to avoid getting stuck at any step. For example, if your drafting is stalled after the first paragraph, or if you cannot think of more supporting details needed for your revision, you can use some of the prewriting techniques explained on pages 17–22 to search for new ideas.

TRY IT OUT

WRITE A BRIEF ANSWER TO EACH QUESTION. USE YOUR OWN PAPER FOR THIS ASSIGNMENT.

1. You have made what seem to be some good plans for your writing assignment, but you have not started writing. Is this the best time to check a point concerning punctuation? Why or why not?
2. You have reached the middle of your first draft, and your plans from prewriting do not seem to be working anymore. Should you check the spelling of what you have written, or should you try some more prewriting activities? Explain.
3. You have finished writing a first draft of your assignment. Is this the best time to start thinking about revising? Why or why not?
4. You have just finished checking your grammar. Is this the best time to see if your ideas are fully and clearly presented? Why or why not?
5. You have finished editing for grammar, punctuation, and spelling. Is your paper ready to be handed in? Why or why not?

As you work with each step in the writing process, you will find specific help in this book. Some sections guide you in finding ideas to write about, others deal with the structure and content of paragraphs and essays, others concentrate on grammar and punctuation, and others teach about proofreading. This book gives you many opportunities to practice as you go along. Whenever you want to know where to find specific information, consult the table of contents in the front of this book, or for a detailed breakdown of all the subjects covered, consult the General Index in the back.

 Prewriting Techniques

Prewriting techniques help you think of ideas to use in your writing. If you have trouble getting started, if you find that you run out of ideas in the middle of your writing, or if you feel that your ideas are not worthy of your reader's attention, prewriting techniques will help you. These techniques stimulate your mind to come up with good ideas. Most thinking for writing is conscious, but these techniques also draw on your ability to "get lost in thinking" and thereby to discover new ideas and fresh insights. Here are five useful prewriting techniques.

I Keeping a Journal

II Writing Nonstop

III Writing Nonstop with a Focus

IV Brainstorming and Making Lists

V Making a Subject Map

I. Keeping a Journal. Keeping a journal requires you to think on paper about matters of interest to you. It means writing every day, or as many days as you can manage or as are required by your instructor. Always write for as long as possible, but consider fifteen minutes a minimum for each journal session. Use a special notebook for your journal. Start each day's entry with the date. You can write about anything you wish: your reactions to what you are learning in class, your ideas about what is going on in the world, your observations about people, your feelings, or whatever else is on your mind. A journal, however, is not a diary of events in which you record merely what time you got up, what the weather was like, what you ate, and what you did all day. You can be personal if you wish, but you do not have to be. Your writing style can be relaxed and informal.

If at times you cannot think of anything to write in your journal, try answering any of the following questions.

How do you feel about writing? Why? How do you feel about taking a composition class? Why?

Did you ever have an unpopular opinion or belief? Explain. What made you have this opinion or belief? Do you still hold this view? Why or why not? What, if anything, happened as a result of your holding this point of view?

What are your family's attitudes concerning money? Sex? Religion? Marriage? Work? This country? Some other aspect of life? At what specific times have the members of your family displayed these attitudes? Do you agree with these attitudes? Why or why not?

What specific places make you feel happy? Sad? Lonely? Afraid? Fully alive? Depressed? What is it about each place that makes you feel as you do? Do other people react to these places in the same ways that you do? Why or why not?

What do you think your life will be like in ten years? What kind of work (if any) do you expect to be doing? What do you think your family life will be like? What particular interests might you have? What special accomplishments do you hope to achieve? What specific actions will you have to take to make these predictions come true? How would you feel if they did not come true?

You will be the main reader of your journal. It will give you a record of how your fluency in writing moves along. Also, it will be a collection of your thoughts on various subjects. If you remember to record ideas that interest you as they come to mind, your journal can be a sourcebook when you are looking for ideas for your writing assignments. Your instructor also might want to read your journal, depending on the policy in your class.

TRY IT OUT

BUY A NOTEBOOK TO USE AS YOUR JOURNAL. START USING IT BY WRITING YOUR FIRST ENTRY. WRITE FOR AT LEAST FIFTEEN MINUTES.

II. Writing Nonstop. Sometimes called *freewriting,* nonstop writing means writing without stopping for at least ten minutes at a time. (Set a timer or alarm clock so that you do not stop even to look at the time.) Do not lift your pen from the paper. Never stop. Keep your hand moving across the page. Even if your wrist begins to hurt, do not stop; after a few sessions, your muscles will get stronger. Change nothing you have written. Do not be concerned here about grammar, punctuation, or spelling. Write about whatever is on your mind. If you cannot think of anything, write about not being able to think of anything to write about.

Nonstop writing is a warm-up activity designed to help you loosen up. Eventually your mind and body will feel at ease when your pen moves rapidly across a page, when your words flow freely, and when you become completely involved in the act of writing.

You can also perform this exercise on a computer. Try it with the monitor dimmed so you will not be tempted to rewrite as you go along.

TRY IT OUT

SET A TIMER OR ALARM CLOCK TO GO OFF IN TEN MINUTES. WRITE NONSTOP FOR TEN MINUTES.

III. Writing Nonstop with a Focus. To write nonstop with a focus, you choose a topic to write about before you get started, and you focus on that topic only. You can use the topic of your next writing assignment or any topic that interests you. Get down whatever you know and then make mental associations, sometimes called *free associations,* to the topic. Write down whatever comes to mind without thinking about whether it relates or not.

After ten minutes, stop and read what you have written. Choose one sentence that particularly interests you from all that you have written and underline it. Now use the content of that sentence as the focus for your next ten minutes of nonstop writing. Here is one student's focused nonstop writing on the topic *work,* with one underlined sentence that became the focus of the student's next nonstop writing.

> Work is such a bore. I hate it. I never seem to get into it. My mother says it is good experience, but I still don't like it. When I go to work, I am a teller in a bank, and sometimes it can get so boring that I go to sleep. I wish I had an exciting job to go to. I also wish when I get up to go to work that I would be happy. A job that is exciting every minute of the day. I also want to be rich and successful. I don't want to have any problems on the job. I want to be my own boss. I want to be happily married, have kids, and have a great job. <u>You have to like work.</u> It has to be something you want and like, not something boring that you cannot get into. For example, being a flight attendant I think would be very exciting. I think those people just love their jobs. That is what I want. This better end very soon. This better end very soon. I know someone who loves his job and would not give it up for anything. He is so happy; his family is happy too. And I think that's what counts the most, being happy with your job. Having a nice family to go home to every day would be nice too.

Jean Bianchi
Student

Jean used the sentence "You have to like work" as the focus for her second round of nonstop writing. She wrote about liking work that pays well, that keeps her mind occupied, and that gives her an opportunity to meet new people.

The second round of nonstop writing gives you the chance to focus closely on the aspect of your topic covered in the sentence you have underlined. Write nonstop again. Do not censor. Allow your mental associations to flow freely. Later, when you read back over your focused nonstop writing, you will often be pleasantly surprised to find interesting ideas and fresh perspectives. One warning: At times you will not find interesting material when you read your focused nonstop writing. Be patient with yourself. Once you get your mind into the habit of searching for ideas, the results will be more fruitful.

TRY IT OUT

CHOOSE A TOPIC TO FOCUS ON. SET A TIMER OR ALARM CLOCK TO GO OFF IN TEN MINUTES. WRITE NONSTOP ON YOUR TOPIC FOR TEN MINUTES. READ WHAT YOU HAVE WRITTEN. UNDERLINE A SENTENCE THAT PARTICULARLY INTERESTS YOU. AGAIN SET A TIMER OR ALARM CLOCK TO GO OFF IN TEN MINUTES. NOW WRITE NONSTOP, FOCUSING ON THE CONTENT OF THE SENTENCE YOU CHOOSE.

IV. Brainstorming and Making Lists. When you *brainstorm,* you first jot down a list of ideas about all aspects of a topic. The ideas can be in whatever form in which they come to mind: words, phrases, questions, or sentences. After you have compiled a fairly long list of items, you group together the items that seem to belong together. Sometimes one item fits into more than one group, and sometimes an item fits into no group and has to be dropped.

On the topic *television,* here is one student's brainstorming list.

BRAINSTORMING ON THE TOPIC OF TELEVISION

set in every house
children's cartoons
entertaining
educational
lots of violence
isn't realistic
waste of time
baseball
ads, ads, ads
news
dumb programs
love stories
football
brings people together
arguments over what to watch
soap operas
makes me lazy
great programs
watch too much
tennis
isolates people
set in every room
informative
VCR's are popular
cable TV
assumes everyone is stupid

Now the student groups items together.

GROUPING ITEMS FROM THE BRAINSTORMED LIST

I
assumes everyone is stupid
waste of time
dumb programs
makes me lazy
ads, ads, ads
isn't realistic

II
children's cartoons
love stories
soap operas
news
ads, ads, ads
football
baseball
tennis

III
brings people together
isolates people
arguments over what to watch

IV
set in every house
set in every room
VCR's are popular
cable TV

V
educational
entertaining
informative

Now choose one group that particularly interests you *and* that will give you sufficient material for your assignment. Because the chances are that no one group is long enough to give you all the material you need, you now have to brainstorm to expand the list with specifics.

Using this system, the student decides that he wants to write on group I. The student then brainstorms to expand the list. By asking of the items the journalist's questions, *who, what, when, where, why, how,* the student comes up with the names of specific actors and writers, the names of specific programs and advertisements, statistics about how often advertisements are shown, descriptions of the plots of specific programs, and so on. In addition, the student relates the items to the five senses: *sight, smell, taste, hearing,* and *touch.* For example, the student mentions that laugh tracks go off when nothing is really funny, characters wear clothing that they obviously cannot afford, and products do not taste or smell the way they are advertised. Then the student looks over all the material and decides on a main point for the writing assignment.

TRY IT OUT

BRAINSTORM ON THE TOPIC *HEALTH*. FIRST, JOT DOWN EVERYTHING THAT COMES TO MIND. SECOND, LOOK OVER YOUR JOTTINGS AND GROUP RELATED ITEMS TOGETHER. THIRD, CHOOSE ONE OF THE GROUPS AND EXPAND IT BY ASKING THE JOURNALIST'S QUESTIONS AND BY THINKING ABOUT THE FIVE SENSES. FINALLY, DECIDE ON A TENTATIVE TITLE SUITABLE FOR THE EXPANDED LIST YOU HAVE DEVELOPED.

V. Making a Subject Map. Making a subject map means brainstorming about your topic by drawing an informal chart that shows the connections among your ideas.

Because a subject map illustrates the relationships among ideas, it organizes your material and gives you an informal outline of the points you want to make. On the topic *music,* here is one student's subject map. The student started with the word *music* in the center of her map; she then branched out to her main associations with her related material.

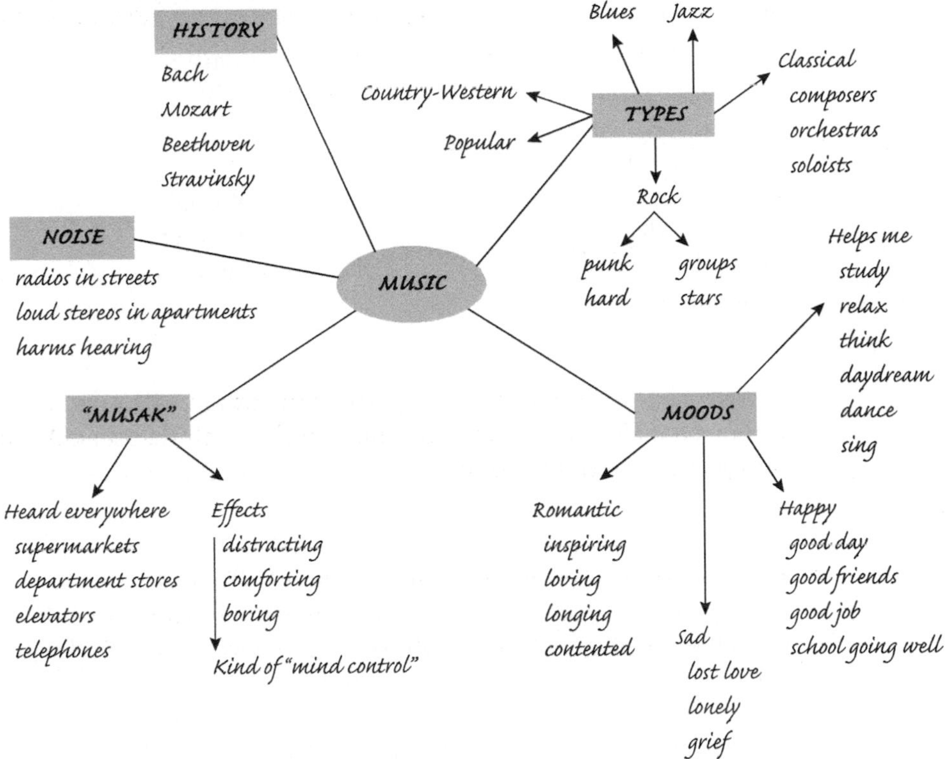

After you have drawn a subject map, look it over to see which areas seem to be fruitful for further development. For example, this student found that the area of "moods" was open to further development. She then drew a more focused subject map. Finally, after thinking about her second map, she made up this tentative title for her writing assignment: "Music Influences People's Moods."

TRY IT OUT

DRAW A SUBJECT MAP ON THE TOPIC *FOOD.* LOOK AT YOUR MAP AND CHOOSE ONE AREA THAT YOU THINK IS FRUITFUL FOR FURTHER DEVELOPMENT. DRAW ANOTHER SUBJECT MAP ABOUT THAT AREA. NOW DECIDE ON A TITLE SUITABLE FOR A WRITING ASSIGNMENT.

Purposes for Writing

As you gather and organize the ideas for your topic, you should keep one very important question in mind: Why am I writing this paper? The obvious answer is that you want to please your instructor and get a good grade in the course. However, you will probably not achieve these goals unless you first establish a clear purpose for each piece of writing that you produce. Most good writing fulfills one of these four major purposes.

I To Express Yourself

II To Inform

III To Persuade

IV To Entertain

Having a specific purpose for a piece of writing will help you select the most appropriate ideas for your topic and determine the most effective way to present those ideas to the reader.

I. To Express Yourself. You record your personal feelings and experiences in a diary, journal, poem, or even song lyrics. You do this type of writing primarily for your own enjoyment. Notice how the journal entry below expresses the writer's personal feelings.

> Boy, am I ticked off! I just found out that Dad is paying for all of Gary's school expenses. How come I had to pay for everything (books, tuition, etc.) out of my puny paycheck from Key Food? But not the prince! He gets whatever he wants without lifting a finger: his own TV set, stereo, telephone. No wonder he's spoiled rotten. I didn't have any of those things when I was his age. Carol is always complaining about the same thing happening with her little sister. She gets new clothes, CD's, even expensive jewelry. I read somewhere that it's common for parents to spoil the youngest kid in the family. I wonder why. In the end, both kids get hurt.

Lynette Saunders
Student

TRY IT OUT

1. Why did the student write this journal entry?
2. If the student wanted to expand this entry to make it more suitable for others to read, what changes should she make in the material? What new information should she add?

II. To Inform. You provide specific information to help educate the reader about a topic. You might explain how something happened, how something works, or why a problem exists. When instructors ask you to do this type of writing, they are often trying to determine how well you understand the topic yourself. Notice how the paragraph below provides specific information to inform the reader.

The different physical characteristics of each race of people in this world have developed over thousands of years, usually as a result of adaptation to climate. The Eskimos, for example, have thick, fatty upper eyelids to prevent the eyeballs from freezing in the extremely cold weather of the far north. Although Arabs have no special eye characteristics, many have long, high-arched noses that are suited to desert living: Before the dry desert air gets to the delicate tissue of the lungs, the air is humidified in the Arabs' long nasal passages. The East African Masai have their own special characteristics. The Masai are unusually tall and thin so that more sweat evaporation is possible to cool the skin in the tremendous heat. Physical characteristics, then, not only make people look interesting and special but may also help them survive in difficult climates.

TRY IT OUT

1. What is the topic of this paragraph?
2. What specific information does the writer provide to inform the reader about this topic?

III. To Persuade. You use sound reasoning and solid evidence to convince the reader to agree with your point of view on an issue that has more than one side to it. Your goal is to influence people to change their minds or take a particular action. Persuasive writing comes in many forms: advertisements, newspaper editorials, letters to the editor, movie reviews, and argument essays. (For more information about arguing an opinion, see pages 597–607.) Notice how the paragraph below provides specific reasons and evidence to try to persuade the reader.

People should avoid eating white bread. The problem starts at the mill where wheat is ground into flour. During the milling process, the outer shell of the wheat (bran) is removed to speed up the preparation of the bread, and the kernel of the wheat (germ) is removed to prolong the freshness of the bread. This procedure destroys proteins and vitamins, especially the B complex vitamins and vitamin E. With the bran removed, the flour also lacks the roughage that people need for healthy digestion. At the baking plant, some vitamins and minerals may be added back to the flour, but major B vitamins and amino acids are not. The flour is then mixed with fats that may have been combined with hydrogen to slow down spoilage; these treated fats prevent the body from using whatever nutrients are in the bread. To delay spoilage still further, an artificial substance such as calcium propionate is added to the dough; calcium propionate is made from the same chemicals that are used in athlete's foot remedies and can cause allergic reactions in those eating the bread. After coming from the oven, the bread is shipped to the marketplace—fresh but tasteless, nutritionally poor, and potentially dangerous.

TRY IT OUT

1. What is the writer of this paragraph trying to persuade the reader to believe?
2. What specific reasons and evidence does the writer provide to support this point of view?

IV. To Entertain. You might use humor, romance, or suspense as the basis for a poem, short story, play, or novel. Your main goal is to create enjoyment for the reader. Notice how the paragraph below tries to entertain the reader.

On the first day of my ancient history class, I was pleasantly surprised to find myself seated next to the college football team's star quarterback. As the professor launched into a lengthy and boring lecture on William the Conquerer, my handsome classmate and I started flirting with each other shamelessly. Finally, about halfway through the class, he drew a "#" on a piece of scrap paper and passed it to me. Delighted, I quickly wrote down my telephone number and passed it back to him. Looking down at my response, he seemed puzzled for a moment. Then he drew another "#" sign, this time adding an *X* to the upper left-hand corner. He had wanted to play tick-tack-toe!

TRY IT OUT

1. What is entertaining about this paragraph?
2. What types of writing do you find entertaining to read?

You will write more effectively and successfully if you always identify the major purpose for each piece of writing you undertake. For example, if your instructor asks you to explain the history of rap music, he or she expects you to write a paper that will inform the reader. If, instead, you explain why you think that rap music is terrible or wonderful, you are trying to persuade the reader. If you misunderstand the major purpose of the assignment, you cannot fulfill your instructor's expectations. Whenever you are not sure of the guiding purpose for a particular assignment, discuss it with your instructor before you begin writing.

If an assignment does not indicate a major purpose, choose one that seems appropriate for the topic. Making a choice can help you focus clearly on your intended approach to the topic. As you write and explore your ideas about the topic, you might find that you need to switch to another purpose. Switching away from a starting purpose is a common experience for writers, so do not be surprised if it happens to you. As you gain experience as a writer, you will become more skillful at determining a suitable purpose from the start.

TRY IT OUT

WHAT IS THE MAIN PURPOSE FOR EACH WRITING ASSIGNMENT GIVEN BELOW?

1. Explain how to be a successful college student.
2. In your journal, discuss your personal feelings about taking an English class.
3. Describe a humorous incident that happened while you were on a date or a family outing.
4. Write about whether or not the use of marijuana should be legalized.

Once you have identified your purpose, you must then provide the type of information needed to achieve that goal. Notice that the next paragraph does not accomplish its purpose.

> All beer advertising should be banned from television. In the last year, beer companies spent about $640 million advertising their products on TV. As a result, viewers are constantly being reminded that Budweiser is the "king of beers" and Miller Lite has "that light, refreshing taste." These slogans are accompanied by lively music and scenes filled with happy people enjoying cold, frosty glasses of beer at a party, a baseball game, or the local tavern. Such images send the clear message that beer is not only a thirst quencher but also an important ingredient for having a good time. Apparently these commercials are highly effective, for the average American drinks more than 16 gallons of beer annually. Advertisements for hard liquor were banned from television many years ago. Even though beer contains only about one-tenth of the alcohol content of liquor, all beer commercials should be removed from the airwaves too.

TRY IT OUT

1. What is the major purpose for the paragraph above?
2. Why doesn't the paragraph fulfill that purpose?
3. What does the paragraph need to fulfill its purpose?

EXERCISE 1D: For each of the ten items given below, answer these questions:

a. What is the major purpose for the writing assignment?
b. What could be used to fulfill the purpose of the assignment?

1. Explain why people should or should not have big families.
2. Tell a funny story about something that happened to a member of your family.
3. Write a brief history of your family.
4. In your journal, discuss your personal feelings about your family.

5. Explain how to save money when buying a new car.
6. Argue for or against buying a foreign-made car.
7. Discuss whether or not it is a good idea to lend money to a friend.
8. Describe the best ways to make new friends.
9. Compare baseball with the popular British game cricket.
10. Explain why you think baseball is a better game than cricket.

EXERCISE 1E: For each of the five items given below, answer these questions:

a. What is the main purpose for the writing assignment?
b. Does the paragraph fulfill that purpose? If it does not, why not?
c. If the paragraph does not fulfill its purpose, what would help it succeed?

1. Assignment: Explain why your favorite fast-food restaurant is better than the others.

   Wendy's is better than any of the other fast-food chains. When Dave Thomas founded Wendy's, he named it for his daughter. The food served is similar to what is on the menu at either McDonald's or Burger King: hamburgers, french fries, various salads, chicken sandwiches, and a variety of beverages. When I eat at Wendy's, I usually have the all-you-can-eat salad bar, a bowl of chili, and a large Coke to wash it all down. The prices are about the same at all of the major fast-food chains. These restaurants are always competing with each other on price. Just recently, for example, McDonald's started to advertise hamburgers for 99 cents. Within a few days, both Wendy's and Burger King were selling hamburgers for 99 cents too. Shortly after McDonald's introduced Egg McMuffins, the other fast-food chains also created breakfast menus. The best thing that McDonald's has on its menu is the Chicken McNuggets, which are very tasty and come with several kinds of dipping sauces. But Wendy's is still my favorite place to eat.

2. Assignment: Describe the major benefits of the U.S. space program.

   Many materials originally created for the U.S. space program are now being used to improve the quality of our everyday lives. Unfortunately, these technological advances come at a very high price. Indeed, one space shuttle flight costs as much as $1 billion of our tax money, and the yearly budget for the entire program runs about $6 billion. How can we justify spending that money at a time when communities are struggling to maintain their public school systems, when the nation's crime rate is at an all-time high, and when approximately 2 million Americans are homeless? Yes, the space shuttle program has given us long-lasting batteries that power hand-held computers and strong but lightweight metals that make automobiles more fuel efficient. But imagine how many teachers and police officers could be hired and how much new housing could be built with $6 billion a year. Or perhaps we could use that money to reduce the national debt that is crippling our economy. We should fund the space program only after we have dealt effectively with the serious problems that are troubling our society.

3. Assignment: Argue for or against the use of fireworks.

Most people should not be allowed to use fireworks. The evidence clearly supports this point of view. Last year more than 12,200 Americans, most of them under age fifteen, were seriously injured while playing with fireworks. The injuries included first-degree burns, deep wounds, and the loss of fingers and toes. Over 400 people lost sight in one or both eyes. My twelve-year-old niece, Donna, was one of these victims. While she was playing with a seemingly harmless sparkler, some sparks flew into her face and left her blind in her right eye. Obviously, fireworks are dangerous. Yet many communities still allow them to be sold to anyone looking for a few thrills. Although some communities have banned fireworks, residents need only travel to nearby areas to purchase them legally. Searching for excitement, these people are usually too young and irresponsible to understand the very real possibility of being permanently injured. To stop this senseless maiming, the federal government should ban the use of fireworks by anyone other than a professional who is specially trained to handle these explosives safely.

4. Assignment: Explain why it is or is not a good idea to use credit cards.

Credit cards are great to use and fairly easy to get. The easiest ones for young people to obtain are those issued by department stores. As a teenager with a good part-time job, I had no trouble getting credit cards from J. C. Penney and Sears. Whenever I charged something, I made sure to pay the bill quickly. In that way I managed to prove that I could handle money responsibly. As a result, I was then able to open charge accounts with other stores and with gasoline companies. Now that I have a full-time job and an excellent credit rating, I regularly receive invitations in the mail to accept credit from banks offering Visa and MasterCard. Another way to build a credit history is to apply for a secured credit card, which requires people to keep a certain amount of money on deposit in the bank issuing the card. Once someone has proved worthy of being given credit, that person can obtain cards without putting up security. Whichever method a person uses to get credit cards, he or she will find that they are a great convenience.

5. Assignment: Write about something that is not fair in today's society.

Fat people are discriminated against in the workplace. According to a government study, many employers assume that fat workers will do their jobs slowly and will be sick frequently. Because of these false assumptions, personnel directors are often reluctant to hire people who are more than 20 percent overweight. In addition, fat people earn an average of $4,000 less than thin people do in similar jobs. My own experience as a 295-pound man supports these findings. Although I graduated at the top of my accounting class, classmates with much lower grades than mine were offered jobs long before I was. After I eventually found employment, I worked hard to prove myself, received excellent job evaluations, and never missed a day of work in over four years. Yet during that time, several less qualified co-workers were promoted over me. When I complained to my boss, he explained apologetically that a higher position would require me to deal directly with the company's clients and I simply did not fit the corporate image. In disgust, I quit and am now hunting for another job. I hope that when I find one, my new boss will realize that fat people can be productive and energetic members of the work force.

Audience

Whenever you write, your goal is to communicate effectively with the people who are going to read what you write. These readers are considered your audience. Sometimes your audience might include specific people such as your classmates, your instructor, your friends, your family, or your boss. At other times, you might be writing for the general public that reads your local newspaper.

As you write, ask yourself: Who will read this? How much do they already know about my topic? What are their attitudes about my topic? The answers to these questions can help you identify your audience. (For additional help with identifying your audience, refer to the Pointers for Identifying an Audience on page 35.) Once you have analyzed your audience, you will be better able to decide on the content, vocabulary, and tone that are most suitable for your paper. For help with these decisions, review the guidelines below.

I How Audience Affects Content

II How Audience Affects Vocabulary

III How Audience Affects Tone

I. How Audience Affects Content. When you are having a conversation with someone, that person may ask you to clarify a point you are trying to make. However, when someone is reading a piece of your writing, he or she usually does not have the opportunity to ask you questions. Therefore, as you gather your ideas for a paper, you need to anticipate what your audience does and does not know about your subject. Let's say, for example, that you are writing about how to get enough money to pay for college. In your paper, you might discuss scholarships, government grants, and student loans. If your paper is intended for an audience of high school students, you also would need to discuss the specific costs of attending college so that the readers will have a good idea of how much money they will need. On the other hand, if your paper is intended for an audience of college students, you can assume that the readers already know about college expenses.

Another consideration when you are writing is your audience's attitude toward your topic. How will the reader react to your point of view? The answer to this question will help you select the details that will most effectively address the interests and concerns of the reader. In the paragraph below, for example, the writer is describing to a friend a used car that he hopes to buy.

> The car is a really powerful machine; it can go from zero to sixty miles per hour in fifteen seconds. You should see how it zooms around hairpin turns.

> And it looks great! It's tomato red with wire wheels and black leather seats. Plus it has a stereo that is loud enough to wake up the neighborhood.

In a letter to his parents, however, the writer wisely selects a different set of details to describe the car.

> The car is extremely fuel efficient; it gets up to thirty-five miles per gallon of gasoline. According to *Road and Track* magazine, the car has an excellent repair record and is built to deliver many years of reliable service. Most important, the magazine says that it is one of the safest automobiles on the road.

Instead of discussing speed and appearance, the second paragraph focuses on issues that usually concern parents: economy, reliability, and safety.

When you write for a class assignment, your audience almost always includes your instructor. Although your instructor is intelligent and highly educated, he or she may not have your specialized knowledge about the topic you have chosen. Do not leave out specific information when you write for an instructor because you think "the teacher knows what I mean." Only *you* know what you mean. Since you know more than your instructor does about the topic, you need to supply specific facts and examples to support your point of view. (For more information on using facts and examples, see pages 50–52.)

TRY IT OUT

WOULD EACH OF THE FOLLOWING PASSAGES BE EFFECTIVE IN A MEMO TO YOUR BOSS? EXPLAIN YOUR ANSWERS.

1. I deserve a raise because everyone else in my department has already received one. Also, I have just purchased an expensive house and have to make large mortgage payments.

2. I deserve a raise because I have done a great deal for this company. Things are much better since I started working here. Certainly I should be rewarded for all that I have done.

3. I deserve a raise because my plan to reorganize the office has improved the company's efficiency, thereby lowering its expenses by 22 percent and increasing its profits by 28 percent.

4. I deserve a raise because the company's business is very profitable. We manufacture three of the most popular toys in the world: the Baby Bunting doll, the Space Invaders Warrior, and the Super Shooter Water Gun. Our products are sold by Toys 'R Us, Sears, and Toy City.

II. How Audience Affects Vocabulary. To communicate clearly and effectively when writing, you need to choose the most suitable vocabulary for your audience. For most college writing, you need to use the adult vocabulary that mature, intelligent readers expect. At the same time, you want to avoid filling your sentences with unnecessarily difficult words; instead of sounding intellectual, such writing would seem stiff and pompous. Also, you want to avoid using slang words such as *hassle, gotta,* and *uptight* because they would make your writing sound overly informal and your audience could lose respect for what you have written. (For more information on informal language, see pages 425–28.) Notice in the following sentences how the same statement can be made using three different levels of vocabulary.

Overly Formal: Exceedingly large segments of the populace are expressing their discontent with medical practitioners who seem more interested in amassing financial assets than in providing efficacious care to people with health disorders.

Formal: Many people are complaining about doctors who seem more interested in making money than in providing effective health care.

Informal: A lot of folks are griping about docs who seem more interested in raking in loads of dough than in fixing up dudes who are feeling crummy.

In the overly formal sentence above, the unnecessarily complicated vocabulary makes communication with the reader more difficult. In the informal sentence, the use of slang creates a relaxed writing style that might be appropriate in a letter to a close relative or friend. In most writing situations, you should try to find the middle ground between these two extremes by using clear, direct language to express your ideas.

You also need to define technical terms that your audience may not know. For example, in an article for a computer club newsletter, you might recommend a computer that has a 200-gigabyte hard drive, a modem, a mouse, and a powerful processor that can work quickly with the latest software. If you were writing the same article for the general reading public, you would need to explain several terms: 200-gigabyte hard drive, modem, mouse, processor, and software.

TRY IT OUT

WHO WOULD BE THE MOST SUITABLE AUDIENCE FOR EACH OF THE FOLLOWING PASSAGES? EXPLAIN YOUR ANSWERS.

1. Snead hit a birdie and two eagles to end the day two under par for the course.
2. The cops nabbed the guys who ripped off the ATM at the bank the other night.
3. People who eat a diet with a high fat content have an increased risk of developing atherosclerosis, a buildup of fatty deposits on the inner walls of the arteries. This condition can reduce or cut off the blood flow in arteries serving the major organs of the body.

III. How Audience Affects Tone. The way that you express your ideas on paper helps to establish the tone of your writing. The tone reflects your attitude toward your subject and your audience. If your purpose is to entertain the reader, you might select a light, humorous tone. On the other hand, if you are writing on a serious topic such as drug abuse or poverty, a humorous tone would startle and perhaps even offend the reader. For most of the writing that you do in college, you should use a tone that makes you sound sincere, knowledgeable, and confident of the quality of your ideas.

At the same time, you should show respect for the reader's ideas—even if you strongly disagree with them. The writer of the passage below is so determined to persuade the reader that he unintentionally creates an insulting tone.

> Some people think that it would be a good idea to legalize the use of all drugs. But they do not know what they are talking about. The legalization of drugs would only lead to more problems than we already have.

The tone of this passage would probably anger some readers, making them unwilling to consider the merit of the writer's argument. Notice how the passage below uses a more tactful approach to the same topic.

> Some people think that it would be a good idea to legalize the use of all drugs. At first, this may seem like the best solution to one of society's worst problems. However, studies indicate that the legalization of drugs might lead to more difficulties than we already have.

Here the writer has used a respectful tone that would probably make the reader more receptive to the ideas presented.

TRY IT OUT

WOULD EACH OF THE FOLLOWING PASSAGES BE EFFECTIVE IN AN ARTICLE WRITTEN FOR THE GENERAL READING PUBLIC? EXPLAIN YOUR ANSWERS.

1. Many homeless people are complaining about conditions at the public shelters. These lazy bums have a lot of nerve complaining about anything.
2. Although some of their complaints may be valid, the homeless must keep in mind that the city is currently short of funds to operate other essential services such as trash removal and police protection.
3. Do the homeless people think that taxpayers should foot the bill for them to stay at a Holiday Inn with room service and a swimming pool?

POINTERS FOR IDENTIFYING AN AUDIENCE

The questions below can help you identify the audience for your writing.

Who Will Read My Paper?

1. Do they share any similar characteristics: age, sex, level of education, or economic status?
2. What are their ethnic and cultural backgrounds?
3. What are their occupations, interests, and hobbies?
4. What roles do they play in society? Are they workers? students? parents? voters? military veterans?

How Much Do They Already Know About My Topic?

1. How much new information will I need to provide?
2. Will I need to provide background information on my topic?
3. Will I need to define any terms I use?

What Are Their Attitudes Toward My Topic?

1. Will they already be interested in my topic, or will I need to arouse their interest?
2. Do they already have some opinions about my topic?

(Continued)

(Continued)

3. Will they favor or oppose my point of view on the topic?
4. Will their religious or political beliefs influence their reaction to my topic?

Once you have identified your audience, you can select the most suitable content, vocabulary, and tone for your paper.

If My Audience Is the General Reader . . .

1. **The content** should include any information that the average reader of my local newspaper might not know.
2. **The vocabulary** should be clear and direct so that I sound like a mature, intelligent writer. I should avoid slang, and I should be sure to define all technical terms.
3. **The tone** should make me sound sincere, knowledgeable, and confident.

If My Audience Is a Specific Reader . . .

1. **The content** should include any information that this specific reader might not already know.
2. **The vocabulary** can include technical terms familiar to this audience; unless the terms are unfamiliar, they do not need to be defined.
3. **The tone** may be personal if the reader is a close friend or relative. If my purpose is to amuse, the tone may be light and humorous. For most college writing, the tone should reflect the seriousness of the topic.

EXERCISE 1F: Would each passage below be appropriate for its intended audience? Why or why not?

1. Audience: the general reading public

   After Elvis Presley kicked the bucket in 1977, his record sales went through the roof. Soon a lot of ripoff artists discovered that they could make a bundle by selling any kind of junk that had Presley's kisser on it. This here guy was worth more dead than he was alive!

2. Audience: a U.S. senator

   Life for the Indians on the Navajo reservation in Arizona is terrible. The unemployment rate on the reservation is very high, and many Navajos must live without the basic comforts that most Americans take for granted. Moreover, signs of poverty are everywhere. Thus, it is clear that the federal government must do more to help these people improve their standard of living.

3. Audience: teenagers

About half a million teenagers are using anabolic steroids, even though they are illegal and dangerous. Continued use of steroids can cause jaundice, organ damage, and embolisms in the heart and lungs. Eventually, these drugs can lead to an early and painful death.

4. Audience: your teacher

While federal legislators expound on the necessity to stem the depletion of the ozone layer, gaseous emissions emanating from vehicular traffic and manufacturing facilities perpetuate the contamination of the atmosphere surrounding our nation's major centers wherein the populous resides.

5. Audience: parents

Parents should educate young people about the problems that a pregnant teenager faces. For one thing, a teenage girl with "a bun in the oven" wouldn't be able to run for homecoming queen at her school.

6. Audience: a photography club

The new Olympia Genesis camera does everything automatically. It adjusts the *f*-stop, the shutter speed, and the focus ring so that the picture will look remarkably clear and sharp. All the photographer has to do is select the film with the correct ISO rating for the type of picture that he or she plans to take.

7. Audience: the elderly

Power walking is an excellent form of exercise. To do this type of exercise successfully, try to walk quickly enough to increase your heart rate to 70 percent of its maximum. When you are able to walk a mile in about twelve minutes, start wearing weights around your waist and on your wrists. You will know that you are physically fit when you are able to maintain a fast pace while you are carrying about 15 percent of your body weight.

8. Audience: the readers of your local newspaper

Some organizations are trying to pressure the television networks into reducing the sexual content of their programs. What right do these idiots have to tell me what I can and cannot see and hear? Haven't they heard about the First Amendment to the Constitution?

9. Audience: the President of the United States

Members of Congress should not be permitted to remain in office for more than two terms. Senators serve six-year terms, and Representatives serve two-year terms. These politicians have easy access to the media and enjoy the franking privilege, which allows them to send mail postage-free to the voters they represent. Such benefits give the members of Congress an unfair advantage over the people who run against them in elections. Also, if terms of office were limited, more Americans would have the opportunity to serve their country.

10. Audience: the students in your English class

Deposition Technology, a California company that usually does radar research for the Pentagon, has invented a way to improve microwave popcorn. The company's invention is called a susceptor, which is an extremely thin stainless-steel film. When the film is embedded into the side of a microwave popcorn bag, the steel acts like a built-in hot plate. As the unpopped kernels fall on the susceptor, they get an extra blast of intense heat, guaranteeing that almost all of the corn will pop.

EXERCISE 1G: Your classmate Wilbert ("Willy") Wilkins died yesterday while you were having lunch with him in the school cafeteria. His dying words to you were "Don't eat the pizza!" Although the medical test results are not yet available, experts suspect that the cause of death may be basidiomycetous poisoning. As Willy's closest friend, you are now faced with a number of writing tasks:

1. The town's sheriff has asked you to write a report describing everything that led up to your friend's untimely death.
2. The editor of the town newspaper has asked you to write an obituary that will serve as a tribute to your friend.
3. You want to write a letter of sympathy to Willy's parents in which you express your personal feelings and sense of loss.

4. Angered by your friend's death, you have decided to write an editorial for the school newspaper in which you will demand improvements in the cafeteria service.

5. You want to write a letter to Norbert ("Norby") Nordling to tell him about Willy's death. Norby is an old friend who grew up in the same neighborhood with you and Willy.

The information provided below will help you with your writing tasks. You should feel free to add other details about your dear friend Willy.

WILBERT ("WILLY") WILKINS

Born: July 17, 1979, in Topeka, Kansas, the only child of Wilma and Wendell Wilkins

Died: Yesterday at 12:42 P.M. in the school cafeteria

Education: Graduated with honors from Marble Hill High School, Topeka, Kansas, June 1997

Currently in his junior year at your school; on the dean's list; a member of the baseball team and the school chorus; a volunteer tutor for math students; a geology major

Employment: During high school years, worked part time at Burger King

Currently working as part-time salesperson at Kmart

Military service: Three years in the U.S. Army; served in the war in Iraq; received an honorable discharge

Community service: Taught reading and writing for Literacy Volunteers; raised funds for the Red Cross and the American Cancer Society

Hobbies and interests: Spelunking, photography, numismatics, jazz

Future plans: To become a seismologist; to marry his childhood sweetheart, Winona Wimple

The Topic Sentence

When you write paragraphs and essays, your writing will be clearer and will deliver its message more effectively if you use a topic sentence in each of your paragraphs. Here are a few basic guides for writing a topic sentence.

1. It is generally best to start each paragraph with a topic sentence, which reveals the topic of the paragraph.
2. The function of the topic sentence is to tell what the paragraph will be about. It serves as an introduction to the paragraph because it tells the reader what to expect next in the paragraph.
3. An effective topic sentence usually contains only one main idea. The rest of that paragraph develops that one main idea. Thus, an effective topic sentence makes the main idea stand out clearly so that the paragraph has unity.

Here is an example of a paragraph that starts with a topic sentence and that contains only one main idea.

> Schools should offer a course to help students with the problems of employment. Such a course might begin with a discussion of the job-hunting experience, including how to use classified newspaper advertisements, employment agencies, and contacts with friends and relatives. This might be followed by practice sessions in writing letters of application and in filling out employment application forms. Students would then participate in job interviews staged in the classroom in order to learn the proper technique for answering questions as well as the importance of personal appearance, speech, and manners. After these essential points have been discussed, the course might even deal with the problems of job adjustment, with emphasis on how to adapt to the duties of the job and the role of being under someone's direct supervision. If schools offered such a course, students would be well prepared for the difficult task of finding a job and for the everyday pressures of keeping one.

TRY IT OUT

1. Underline the topic sentence in the paragraph above.
2. Is there more than one main idea in the paragraph?

Here is another example of a paragraph. As you read it, check to see if it starts with a topic sentence and if it contains only one main idea.

A school football game is a good place to make new friends. Everyone who is there has the same interest in mind—to watch the game and to share with others the pleasure of rooting for the home team. This unifying spirit breaks down barriers between strangers. The noisy excitement makes it easy to talk and laugh with someone you have never met before. As you are watching the game, perhaps you prefer the beefy 200-pound tackle who blocks the other team every time, while the enthusiastic fan seated to your left prefers the agile quarterback who passes the ball with bullet-like speed. A disagreement like that just might take a long time to argue—long enough, in fact, to get acquainted.

TRY IT OUT

1. Underline the topic sentence in the paragraph above.
2. Is there more than one main idea in the paragraph?

You will find additional examples of paragraphs that start with a topic sentence and contain only one main idea on pages 50, 52, and 53 in this chapter and on pages 71, 72, 73, 75, 76, and 77 in the next chapter. Read these model paragraphs carefully, with special attention to the topic sentence that starts each.

A good topic sentence always contains words that limit and control what you can discuss in the paragraph. For example, look at the topic sentence that started the sample paragraph on page 40.

Schools should offer a course to help students deal with the problems of employment.

In the paragraph introduced by this sentence, you can discuss only courses that deal with "the problems of employment." You cannot discuss the wide variety of courses that schools offer in science or in the humanities. Each of those topics would need a separate paragraph.

Here are other topic sentences used to start some of the sample paragraphs in this chapter. Notice that each topic sentence contains words that limit and control what can be discussed in the rest of the paragraph.

Topic Sentence	Words That Limit and Control
A school football game is a good place to make new friends.	make new friends
The cockroaches that inhabit many city apartments and homes are parasites that are almost impossible to exterminate completely.	impossible to exterminate completely
Some couples who are determined to reveal their individuality are getting married in unusual ceremonies.	unusual ceremonies

A good topic sentence is not too general or too narrow. A topic sentence that is too general requires much more than a paragraph to develop it. A topic sentence that is too narrow leaves little to be said in the rest of the paragraph. For example, look at these topic sentences and the comments about them:

Topic Sentence	Comments
☒ Managing a large city is a big job.	poor: too general
☒ Garbage is collected in the city on Monday and Thursday.	poor: too narrow
☑ Parking regulations that ban street parking during the rush hour help keep the traffic moving in a large city.	better: not too general or too narrow—just enough to discuss in a paragraph

Unlike an essay title, a topic sentence for a paragraph must be a complete sentence.

☒ The dangers of hitchhiking.

☑ Hitchhiking can be extremely dangerous.

Once you are sure of how a topic sentence operates, you will be ready to write your own topic sentences. Before you begin, consult the list of Pointers for Writing a Topic Sentence on the next page. Then continue to work through the exercises in this chapter.

POINTERS FOR WRITING A TOPIC SENTENCE

Writing is a process. When you write a topic sentence, use the Five-Step Writing Process, which includes prewriting, drafting, revising, editing, and proofreading. (See pages 14–16.)

Prewriting

1. Think before you write. Ask yourself: What topic am I going to write about? What do I want to say about the topic?
2. Explore ideas before you write. Read, talk with friends and family, watch documentary programs on television, look at visuals (photographs, works of art, advertisements, cartoons, posters). Use the prewriting techniques explained on pages 17–22.
3. Plan a topic sentence that is suitable for the purpose of your paragraph. (See pages 23–30 for information on purposes for writing.)

Drafting

1. Write the first draft of your topic sentence.

Revising

1. Read your first draft to see if the topic sentence (a) clearly states what you will be discussing in your paragraph, (b) contains words that limit and control the content of the paragraph, (c) is neither too narrow nor too general, and (d) is a complete sentence. (See pages 104–109 for information on sentence completeness.)
2. Rewrite to get a second draft of your topic sentence, if it is needed.

Editing and Proofreading

1. Edit to check that your grammar, punctuation, and spelling are correct.
2. Proofread to check that you have missed no errors and that your handwriting is legible or typing is neat.

A Special Note: After you have written your paragraph (ways to develop paragraphs are given on pages 50–53 and 71–73), check your topic sentence again. Does it clearly introduce what you discuss in your paragraph? If not, revise your topic sentence, or revise the content of your paragraph.

EXERCISE 1H: Each item in this exercise contains one main idea for a topic sentence and a list of what will be discussed in the paragraph introduced by the topic sentence. You write the topic sentence for the paragraph.

Example: regular exercise
. . . strengthens the heart muscle
. . . improves blood circulation
. . . increases the intake of oxygen

Topic Sentence: Regular exercise is good for people's health.

1. taking care of a large family
. . . cooking meals
. . . cleaning the home
. . . shopping and running errands
. . . providing love and guidance

____

____

2. smoking cigarettes
. . . stained teeth and fingers
. . . bad breath
. . . tobacco odor in clothing

____

____

3. hot weather
. . . dress in lightweight clothing
. . . drink a great deal of liquid
. . . stay out of the sun
. . . avoid great physical effort

____

____

4. automobile security devices
   . . . alarms
   . . . hood locks
   . . . ignition cutoff switches
   . . . removable radios

   ____

   ____

5. finding a job
   . . . go to an employment agency
   . . . read the classified newspaper advertisements
   . . . ask friends and relatives for leads
   . . . send résumés to possible employers

   ____

   ____

EXERCISE 1I: Follow the directions given for each item.

1. a. Jot down three points you might make in a paragraph about personal computers.

      i. ______________________________

      ii. ______________________________

      iii. ______________________________

   b. Could any of your points be included in a paragraph that starts with this topic sentence: "Personal computers are much less expensive than they used to be"?

      i. yes _____ no _____

      ii. yes _____ no _____

      iii. yes _____ no _____

c. Write a topic sentence that could be used for at least one of the points you jotted down about personal computers.

____

____

2. a. Jot down three points you might make in a paragraph about eyeglasses.

i. ____

ii. ____

iii. ____

b. Could any of your points be included in a paragraph that starts with this topic sentence: "Eyeglasses are designed to be fashion accessories"?

i. yes _____ no _____

ii. yes _____ no _____

iii. yes _____ no _____

c. Write a topic sentence that could be used for at least one of the points you jotted down about eyeglasses.

____

____

EXERCISE 1J: In each topic sentence given, underline the words that limit and control what should be discussed in a paragraph that it might introduce.

Example: A blind date can be <u>disastrous.</u>

1. Many television cartoons contain too much violence.
2. For some people, Christmas is a depressing holiday.
3. Convicted criminals sometimes receive very little punishment.
4. A professional athlete's career is usually rather short.
5. The United States is running out of places to dump its garbage.

6. Using an automatic teller machine at a bank can be hazardous.
7. Children raised in foster homes sometimes have emotional problems.
8. Everyone could benefit from learning a foreign language.
9. Drinking too much coffee is bad for a person's health.
10. Day-care centers are very helpful for students with small children.

EXERCISE 1K: Revise each of the following topic sentences so that it is neither too narrow nor too general.

1. Fear affects our lives in many ways.

   ____

   ____

2. Muhammad is the most common name in the world.

   ____

   ____

3. Public transportation is not as good as it should be.

   ____

   ____

4. A police officer has a difficult job.

   ____

   ____

5. An average of seventeen banks are robbed each day in the United States.

   ____

   ____

6. New advances in electronics are improving our quality of life.

   ____

   ____

7. Discrimination is a big problem in our society.

____

____

8. Thomas Edison invented the light bulb in 1879.

____

____

9. Insects are fascinating creatures.

____

____

10. A horse can sleep standing up.

____

____

EXERCISE 1L: Using all of the Pointers for Writing a Topic Sentence, write a good topic sentence for each subject given below. Use your own paper for this assignment.

1. music
2. the post office
3. a state lottery
4. the United States space program
5. dieting
6. doctors
7. magazines
8. parades
9. daydreams
10. thunderstorms

EXERCISE 1M: Essay Analysis Answer these questions about the essay "Rambos of the Road."

1. a. What is the topic sentence of paragraph 5?

____

____

   b. What specific word or words in the topic sentence limit what can be discussed in the paragraph?

____

____

   c. Is there anything in the paragraph that does not belong? __________

2. a. What is the topic sentence of paragraph 7?

____

____

   b. What specific word or words in the topic sentence limit what can be discussed in the paragraph?

____

____

   c. Is there anything in the paragraph that does not belong? __________

3. a. What is the topic sentence of paragraph 11?

____

____

   b. What specific word or words in the topic sentence limit what can be discussed in the paragraph?

____

   c. Is there anything in the paragraph that does not belong? __________

¶ Paragraph Development: Part I

Once you have written your topic sentence, you are ready to write the rest of your paragraph. Paragraph development puts the meat on the bones of your topic sentence. Paragraph development helps you emphasize and drive home your main point.

This chapter introduces you to three methods of paragraph development.

I **Facts**

II **Examples**

III **Incident, Anecdote, or Story**

The next chapter introduces three more methods. Once you are somewhat familiar with these ways to develop a paragraph, you will find it easier to write. As you study and practice these methods, refer to Pointers for Writing a Paragraph on the next page.

I. Facts. Here is an example of a paragraph developed with facts.

The cockroaches that inhabit many city apartments and homes are parasites that are almost impossible to exterminate completely. One hundred seventy million years older than the dinosaur, the cockroach, with its five eyes and six legs, can hide in the dark for weeks without food or water. Whenever a new roach poison is created, some of the insects become immune. And in one year a female can have 35,000 offspring. This, coupled with the fact that there are, at last count, fifty-five kinds of roaches in the United States, makes us hope only to control the pest but probably never to kill the species completely.

HINT: *Facts usually include numbers, statistics, or other things that can be proved.*

TRY IT OUT

1. Underline the topic sentence in the paragraph above.
2. Is there more than one main idea in the paragraph?
3. In your own words, state two of the facts used to develop the paragraph.

POINTERS FOR WRITING A PARAGRAPH

Writing is a process. When you write a paragraph, use the Five-Step Writing Process, which includes prewriting, drafting, revising, editing, and proofreading. (See pages 14–16.)

Prewriting

1. Think before you write. Ask yourself: What subject interests me? What do I want to say about the subject?
2. Explore ideas before you write. Read, talk with friends and family, watch documentary programs on television, look at visuals (photographs, works of art, advertisements, cartoons, posters). Use the prewriting techniques explained on pages 17–22.
3. Begin to organize your material. Plan your topic sentence (for help, see Pointers, page 43), and remember that it limits and controls what you discuss in your paragraph.
4. Select the type of paragraph development that suits your topic sentence and that suits the list of ideas you have drawn up. Paragraphs can be developed in many different ways. This book shows you six of them: facts (page 50); examples (page 52); incident, anecdote, or story (page 53); definition (page 71); comparison and contrast (page 72); S-N-S (statistics, names, and the senses, pages 72–73).

Drafting

5. Write the first draft of your paragraph. As you do, be sure that your paragraph fulfills your purpose for writing: to inform, to persuade, to entertain, or to express yourself. (See pages 23–30.)

Revising

6. Read over your first draft to see what ideas need to be improved. Remember that the key is to *develop*—to go into detail about what you said in your topic sentence. Also keep in mind that the content and tone of your paragraph should be suitable for your audience. (See pages 31–39.)
7. Rewrite to get a second draft and further drafts if they are needed. For help with revising, see pages 79–88.

Editing and Proofreading

8. Edit to check that your grammar, punctuation, and spelling are correct.
9. Proofread to check that you have missed no errors and that your handwriting is legible or typing is neat.

EXERCISE 1N: Choose one of these topic sentences and develop it into a paragraph using facts. Use a separate sheet of paper.

1. Medical care in the United States can be extremely expensive.
2. Working and going to school at the same time is not easy.
3. ______________________ has been my greatest disappointment in life.

II. Examples. Here is an example of a paragraph developed with *examples.*

Some couples who are determined to reveal their individuality are getting married in unusual ceremonies. For example, a couple employed as line workers for the Southwestern Bell Telephone Company exchanged their wedding vows clad in jeans and climbing equipment atop a brightly decorated telephone pole while the justice of the peace shouted instructions from the ground. Elsewhere, a couple dressed in swimsuits were married on the high diving board of a local swimming pool because they felt that swimming was an important part of their lives. Furthermore, one couple was wed at the firehouse where the groom was a fireman because the bride wanted to make their wedding just a little different. Another wedding was held in a 747 jet as it flew over Washington State at an altitude of 10,000 feet. Thus, the wedding ceremony has become another example of how more and more people are showing their individuality today.

TRY IT OUT

1. Underline the topic sentence in the paragraph above.
2. Is there more than one main idea in the paragraph?
3. In your own words, state two of the examples used to develop this paragraph.

EXERCISE 1O: Choose one of these topic sentences and develop it into a paragraph using *examples.* Use a separate sheet of paper.

1. Pets have many ways of communicating with people.
2. Sometimes my relatives really annoy me.
3. At first, college presents many problems of adjustment.

III. Incident, Anecdote, or Story. Here is an example of a paragraph developed with an *incident, anecdote,* or *story.*

Perhaps city residents and wild animals were never meant to go together, even in zoos. Recently a visitor to a large city zoo, ignoring all fences and warning signs, put his arm into the cage of a six-year-old polar bear. Perhaps the man wanted to feed the bear, or touch him, or even tease him. But the bear, basically a citizen of the wilds, almost instantly sprang forward and sank his teeth into the man's hand. As the man screamed for help, and the bear's keeper tried to get the bear under control, the bear sucked in more of the man's arm. Finally, a policeman had to shoot and kill the bear so that the man's arm could be released—which it was. Thus, there was the killing of a polar bear and the wounding of a city citizen, two animals who were meant to be residents of their own worlds, not each other's.

TRY IT OUT

1. Underline the topic sentence in the paragraph above.
2. Is there more than one main idea in this paragraph?
3. In your own words explain why the incident supports the topic sentence.

EXERCISE 1P: Choose one of these topic sentences and develop it into a paragraph using an *incident.* Use a separate sheet of paper.

1. A frightening (sad) experience is hard to forget.
2. Keeping a promise is sometimes difficult to do.
3. Some people have no manners at all.

EXERCISE 1Q: Essay Analysis Answer these questions about the essay "Rambos of the Road."

1. Is paragraph 5 developed with facts, examples, or an incident?

____

2. Is paragraph 7 developed with facts, examples, or an incident?

____

3. Are paragraphs 8, 9, and 10 developed with facts, examples, or an incident?

    ____

4. Is paragraph 11 developed with facts, examples, or an incident?

    ____

EXERCISE 1R: Write an essay on one of the five topics given below. Using the essay outline below, try to use a different type of paragraph development for each of the pressures you select. For help in planning your essay, refer to the Pointers for Writing an Essay below. Use your own paper for this assignment.

The Pressures of Being Married
The Pressures of Being Single
The Pressures of Being a Student
The Pressures of Being an Employee
The Pressures of Being a Pet

I Introduction
II One Pressure (you select)
III Another Pressure (you select)
IV A Third Pressure (you select)
V Conclusion

POINTERS FOR WRITING AN ESSAY

Writing is a process. When you write an essay, use the Five-Step Writing Process, which includes prewriting, drafting, revising, editing, and proofreading. (See pages 14–16.) For more information on writing an essay, see Chapters Seven, Twelve, and Thirteen.

Prewriting

1. Think before you write. Ask yourself: What subject interests me? What do I want to say about the subject? For help with finding a writing topic, see pages 281–85.
2. Explore ideas before you write. Read, talk with friends and family, watch documentary programs on television, look at visuals (photographs, works of art, advertisements, cartoons, posters). Use the prewriting techniques explained on pages 17–22.

(Continued)

(Continued)

3. Plan a thesis statement that presents the main idea of your essay. For help, see pages 286–88.
4. Begin to organize your material. Look over the ideas you have compiled and see what goes together and what is best saved for another essay. Now look over your remaining ideas and divide them into three main idea groups. For help, see pages 289–93.
5. Plan your topic sentences (see Pointers, page 43) to serve as a mini-outline of your essay. Next, plan the content of your paragraphs (see Pointers on page 51, The Introductory Paragraph on pages 303–304, and The Concluding Paragraph on pages 305–306). Try this essay format.

   Introductory Paragraph
   First Main Idea Paragraph
   Second Main Idea Paragraph
   Third Main Idea Paragraph
   Concluding Paragraph

Drafting

6. Write the first draft of your essay. As you do, be sure that your essay fulfills your purpose for writing: to inform, to persuade, or to entertain. (See pages 23–30.)

Revising

7. Read over your first draft. As needed, add new main ideas or better supporting details for your main ideas. Also, as needed, drop ideas that do not fit, and rearrange the material so that it is well organized. As you make these revisions, keep in mind that the content and tone of your essay should be suitable for your audience. (See pages 31–39).
8. Rewrite to get a second draft and further drafts if they are needed. For more help with revising, see pages 79–88 and 311–22.

Editing and Proofreading

9. Edit to check that your grammar, punctuation, and spelling are correct.
10. Proofread to check that you have missed no errors and that your handwriting is legible or typing is neat.

EXERCISE 1S: REFRESHER

ON A SEPARATE SHEET OF PAPER, REWRITE THE FOLLOWING PARAGRAPH. REMOVE ANY MATERIAL THAT IS NOT PART OF THE MAIN IDEA STATED IN THE TOPIC SENTENCE. ADD FACTS, EXAMPLES, OR INCIDENTS TO DEVELOP THE PARAGRAPH MORE FULLY.

Owning an automobile is extremely expensive these days. For example, many new cars cost at least $20,000 to purchase, and even a decent used car can cost several thousand dollars. It is important to buy a used car from a dependable dealer who offers a warranty that will cover the major components of the vehicle for at least a year. Another expense is regular maintenance. Most motorists like to drive a clean car. If they do not have access to a hose, then they will have to rely on the services of a car wash, which can cost as much as $8 a week or over $400 a year. People who are thinking of buying a car should first make sure they can afford all of these expenses.

SPRINGBOARDS TO WRITING

Using your knowledge of the writing process, explained on pages 14–16, write a paragraph or essay related to this chapter's central theme, *the epidemic of auto macho,* which is introduced on pages 4–6.

PREWRITING

To think of topics to write about, look at the advertisement and the cartoon, read the essay, and answer the questions that follow each. If you prefer, select one of the writing springboards below. (All paragraph numbers refer to the essay that starts on page 4.) To develop your ideas, use the prewriting techniques described on pages 17–22.

WRITING A PARAGRAPH *(For help, see the Pointers on page 51.)*

1. I once witnessed an incident of driver rage. (See paragraphs 8–10.)
2. I will never forget my worst day as a driver (or as a passenger in a car).
3. My driving manners are good (bad).
4. I know from personal experience that a car in the hands of a bad driver can be dangerous.
5. Agree or disagree with Martin Gottfried's claim that "in our cars we all become a little crazy." (See paragraph 11.)
6. Why does someone act like a bully? (See paragraph 13.)
7. Rudeness on public transportation is (is not) very common.

WRITING AN ESSAY *(For help, see the Pointers on pages 54–55.)*

8. The Epidemic of Auto Macho (See paragraph 5.)
9. Answer Martin Gottfried's question: "What is it within us that gives birth to such antisocial behavior, and why, all of a sudden, have so many drivers gone around the bend?" (See paragraph 12.)
10. How to Reduce the Epidemic of Auto Macho
11. The Rambo Pattern Can Be Seen in Many Areas of American Life (See paragraph 12.)
12. The Effects of Road Rage
13. What Makes a Safe Driver?
14. Several Types of Drivers Are on America's Roads
15. Is a Car a Luxury or a Necessity?
16. Rudeness Is (Is Not) Becoming a Common Occurrence in American Life
17. Good Manners Are (Are Not) Important in Today's Society
18. I Am (Am Not) a Rude Person
19. Teachers, Administrators, and Staff at My School Are (Are Not) Polite and Helpful to Students

This holiday season, stay away from your relatives.

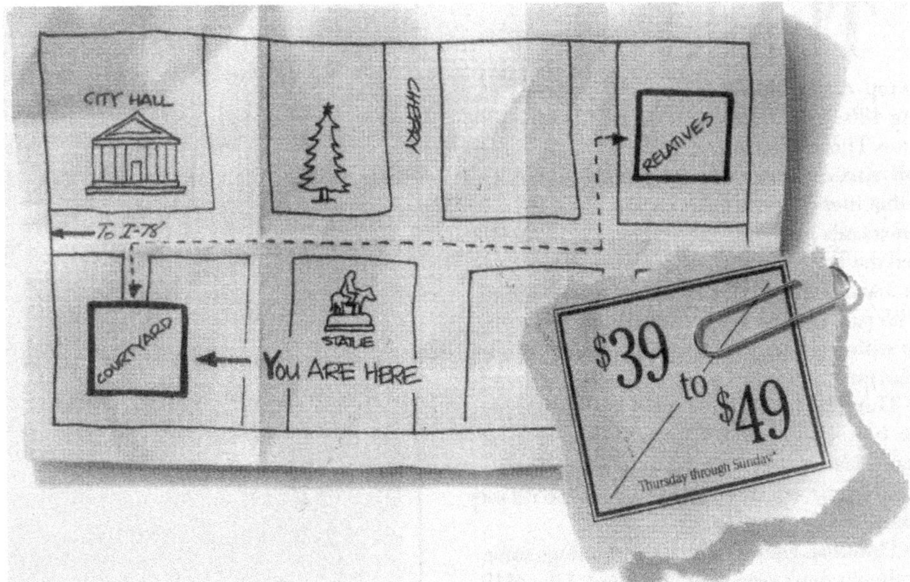

This doesn't mean don't visit them or break fruit cake with them. It just means this year you don't have to spend the night.

Courtyard by Marriott is offering holiday rates of $39 to $49, Thursday through Sunday, through January 10th. Where you'll enjoy your own room, plus a swimming pool, whirlpool, and mini-gym.

Just call your travel agent or 1-800-321-2211 three days in advance for reservations. Because, as much as you love spending time with your relatives, spending the night is another story.

The Hotel Designed by Business Travelers.

* Rooms are limited and some restrictions apply. These rates are not available to groups or in combination with other offers. Rate depends upon location. Special rate for Thursday nights must be in conjunction with Friday night stay. Available at participating locations through 1/10/93. Rate not available 12/31/92. A limited number of blackout dates apply at a few locations.

Chapter 2

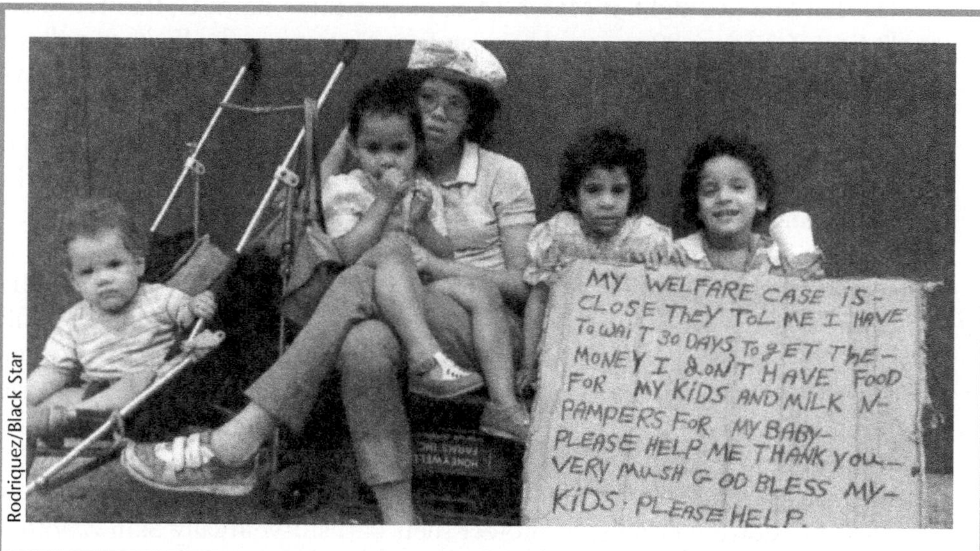

Rodriquez/Black Star

SPRINGBOARDS TO THINKING

For informal, not written, response . . . to stimulate your thinking

1. Look at the headline of the advertisement on the opposite page. What is your first reaction to it? Now read the rest of the advertisement. Would you enjoy spending the night with relatives who live a distance away? Why or why not? Does the idea of being a member of a family give you pleasure? A sense of security? Explain.
2. Can you rely on your family members to help you in time of need? Can you rely on your friends and neighbors? Can they rely on you? Why or why not?
3. Look at the photograph above. What does the sign say? What is your reaction to the photograph?
4. Would you put money in the cup? Why or why not? How else might you help the woman and her children during their thirty-day wait for welfare money? Do you think most people would stop to help the woman? Explain.

Fire, Hope and Charity

Jeanne Marie Laskas

(1) Late on the night of March 14, someone came down Coffee Run Road and lit Sam Z. Yoder's 90-year-old barn on fire. This was in the Kishacoquillas Valley, known as Big Valley, a narrow strip of farmland in central Pennsylvania. Sam Z.—everyone here uses middle initials because there are only three or four last names in Big Valley—is an Amish bishop, 68 years old. The events of that night probably won't ever leave him. His granddaughter woke up first, hearing something crackling. The whole family came charging out. Sam Z. went for the horses. The horses ran into the fire, as horses will do, confused and terrified. Then they turned around and ran right over Sam Z., trampling him. His cows were howling. He struggled to his feet. He had to get to his cows. But his barn was a fireball, and soon it was spitting hot cinders onto the roof of his house.

(2) Meantime, another Amish barn down on Black Mountain Road was torched, and another, and another, and another on Church Lane. It seemed the whole valley was lighting up. Trucks from 24 different fire companies charged into the chaos. Non-Amish neighbors came roaring through the valley in their pickups, alerting farmers to protect their barns. Eventually Sam Z. found himself standing there all beat up, holding a garden hose. He was squirting his house, protecting it from the flames engulfing his barn, listening to the echoes of those cows. When the sun came up on Sunday morning, the fires had destroyed six Amish barns. The corpses of 139 cows and 38 horses lay among the debris. All through the valley the air was thick with a horrible stench.

(3) "And we just don't know why it was done," says Sam Z., standing in the mud where his barn used to be, his hat drooping, his beard reaching clear down to his chest. His is the question that echoes loudest through the valley. The FBI is on the case; special agents in wing tips and blue suits have come out to Sam Z.'s farm with their questions. They go home with few clues and terribly muddy shoes. Sam Z. doesn't have much insight to offer about the culprits. He occupies himself with larger thoughts, which seem to come over him without warning.

"When they did this, it hurt everybody," Sam Z. says, speaking with all the authority of a holy man.

All of the Amish?

"No, I mean it hurt everybody," he says.

All of the people in Big Valley?

"No, I mean, when they did this, it hurt everybody all over the world," he says. "I feel this. I do feel this."

(4) News of the Big Valley barn fires indeed went around the world—partly, perhaps, because the Amish, who moved to this valley in 1791, are always a curiosity and a fascination. These are peace-loving people determined to live a life of simplicity, sheltering themselves from the outside world—no cars, no electricity, no telephones—so as to better focus on the spiritual world. Their lifestyle is a display of innocence, of what the world could be like if life weren't so frantic and hurried. To see these people fall prey to seemingly random acts of violence is to see a brutal victimization, like watching a child get smacked in the face. It demands notice, which explains the donations coming in, and attention from the FBI, CNN, the *Today* show and even Geraldo Rivera. The barn fires of the Kishacoquillas Valley lit something in a lot of people.

(5) Watching an Amish barn-raising is a sight to behold, a gift for the soul. At dawn on March 31 the men start arriving at Sam Z.'s. Just two weeks have passed since the night of the fires, and already Sam M.'s barn on Back Mountain Road is up and so is Sam I.'s over at Plum Bottom. Sam Z. is awed by the turnout. "We feel we're not worth it," he says. It's help from the outside world that has him feeling especially humble.

(6) The Amish divide the world into two. You are either Amish or you are "English." You are either on the inside or the outside. The Amish strive to keep their world from becoming too infected by ours, so they keep away from us. But for this brief moment following the fires, the two worlds have met and the outside is getting a rare peek at the inside.

(7) Sam Z. is still trying to contain in his mind all the money that has come in from places as far away as Hawaii and Germany. The Kishacoquillas Valley National Bank says the Big Valley Barn Fire Relief Fund has grown to $600,000, all of it English money, and contributions are still coming in every day. Sam Z. is thinking of all the livestock and feed that have been donated, all the backhoes and bulldozers that came in and did the cleanup, all the cakes and pies, the great mounds of Kentucky Fried Chicken, the bags upon bags of paper plates and dishwashing detergent donated by the workers of the local Jamesway discount department store. It is hard for Sam Z. to receive all this charity. Ordinarily, the Amish do not accept help from outsiders. They refuse social security checks, and they don't take out insurance policies. To the Amish, worldly things take your mind off what's real: the spiritual world, God's world. And so the Amish have rules to assure that they will not become attached to society.

(8) The 1,500 Amish people living in Big Valley are divided into three sects, each identified by the colors of their horse-drawn buggies: yellow, black or white. Those with yellow tops are the least conservative sect; next come the black toppers; and finally, the most conservative, the white toppers. White toppers do not paint their houses or barns. They do not have indoor plumbing. Black and yellow toppers allow paint and plumbing, and they socialize with one another. White toppers are left pretty much alone down in their end of the valley.

(9) The point behind all the rules is to avoid pride—in yourself, in how you think, in how you look. You must look like everyone else: Men get the same bowl haircuts, do not grow mustaches and are allowed beards only when they come of age. No zippers are allowed on clothes. White toppers are not allowed to show buttons on their jackets—they must use hooks and eyes. Women use straight pins to fasten their clothes. Their hair must not be cut, and heads must be covered. The idea is to avoid becoming stylish or drawing attention to yourself.

(10) Amish behavior is nearly as circumscribed as Amish fashion. Children stop school after the eighth grade. Men do men things and women do women things. You will not see a woman sawing logs at a barn-raising. She will be inside cooking. In the Amish world, human imagination, innovation, intellect and, above all, individuality are intentionally squashed. Outsiders can't help but wonder why anyone would want to live like that.

(11) Already, by eight A.M. on barn-raising day, three walls of Sam Z.'s barn are up. Even Sam Z. thinks that's pretty fast. The cutting of the wood and figuring of the plan have all been done in advance. The wood is green, cut just a week ago up on Jack's Mountain and sawed into lumber at the Plum Bottom mill. The posts and beams have been connected to form the skeletons of walls and the whole thing has been laid out just so on the ground, ready for the barn-raising to happen. When enough people show up, the walls are hoisted, then fitted into the floor in mortice joints. Wooden pegs driven deep will keep it all in place. A school bus arrives with even more workers, so they are sent down to help put up Esle Hostetler's barn near Milroy. Sam Z. has more than 200 men here. They are all gathered in clumps, and while each group has a purpose, it seems no one clump, or individual, is in charge. A community instinct has taken over.

(12) Interestingly, of the six burned barns, all but one belonged to the most conservative Amish, the white toppers. Three belonged to bishops. These facts have a lot of people surmising that whoever did the terrible deed had a purpose in mind. You don't hear many Amish people worrying about who the arsonist was. It is not their way to focus on evil. Still, there are a lot of theories. Almost all the theories come from the English. Perhaps the arsonist was a shunned Amish person, someone who had left the church. Worse, maybe it was someone who is still Amish. But no one wants to entertain the thought that an Amish person could act out so violently, so these theories get whispered, then are dropped.

"I may be wrong, but I think it was some young fellas out on a spree," says Ruth Peachey, who helps her husband, Ivan, run the local branch of the Mennonite Disaster Service.

"I've heard that these barns were burned in order to test the Amish to see if they won't become indignant and arrogant and vengeful," says Lee Kanagy, a Mennonite minister. "It could be. I don't know."

"I think it was more a matter of who was in the firebug urge," says Clair DeLong, a former county farm extension agent.

"I think it was some kind of a cult, and this was their initiation," says a farmer.

"I think the police know who it is, and they won't tell us," says a local dairyman. "We keep giving them our evidence, and then they never tell us what happened with it."

"You just can't sit down over a cup of coffee and tell everyone how your day went in your investigation," says FBI agent Jack Shea.

(13) Just as there is no consensus on the culprits, there is no unanimity on the punishment that should be meted out if an arsonist is caught. "Death penalty," says Blair Auman, an English dairy farmer who would offer this punishment only after a period of torture. "Make him dig them dead burnt animals out with his bare hands. Then let him eat what he dug out." The Amish way, on the other hand, is to forgive, forget and build. They do not press charges. They do not testify in court. An Amish farmer from Black Mountain Road thinks the arsonist should be invited out to watch one of the barn-raisings, then invited inside for a nice Amish dinner—maybe mashed potatoes and roasted chicken, with moon pies for dessert. "That really puts a dig into you," says Auman. "To have these people turn around and invite you in and share food with you, that really cheapens your act, I think."

(14) By noon the superstructure of Sam Z.'s barn is up. Most of the siding is up, and the roof is going on. There has been only one injury. Eli Byler had a hammer come falling down on his head. He was taken to the hospital, and now he is back showing the four stitches he got. "And two shots, one in each arm," he is saying to a group of onlookers. San Z. is handing him a self-addressed stamped envelope to put the bill in when he gets it. Amish health insurance is a lot like Amish barn insurance. Just wait a bit and somebody will come around and take care of it.

(15) By 2:45 children are running down Coffee Run Road with their empty lunch boxes. Home from school, they see that in the spot where there was just wind blowing this morning a barn now stands. Jacob Y. Hostetler is in there sweeping out the sawdust. The children enter timidly and eventually skip in circles, testing the sureness of the new floor. Sam Z. is inside, too, looking up, saying, "Big barn." He seems overwhelmed, unable to say much else. And everybody comments on the pungent smell of the green wood. Pretty soon the first sparrow arrives. It soars among the rafters, checking the place out, as if to wonder, "Where did this barn come from?" It came from God, Sam Z. says, refusing to rejoice in the strength and ingenuity of mankind, refusing to show pride in his new barn. Pride is sinful. Be humble, but be careful. Don't become proud of your humility.

(16) People from the outside world wonder how the Amish can live such secluded rule-bound lives. But such doubters have never seen an Amish barn-raising. You watch all those men dressed alike in their dark clothes and straw hats, all crawling so nimbly over the fresh wood standing against the sky, and you can't help but notice what they look like. They look like ants. It isn't such a bad image. One ant can't do much, but a million ants working together can perform miracles. An Amish barn-raising is a belief system in action: Sacrifice individuality—forget about your self, your clothes, your hair, your creative longings—in favor of the common good.

(17) A visitor from New York City walks up to Sam Z. She has been shaking her head all day in disbelief, watching this barn emerge. "If my house in Brooklyn burned down," she says, "I don't think my neighbors would come around to rebuild it." Sam Z. ponders that piece of information, then says, "We would."

Reading Survey

1. MAIN IDEA

What is the central theme of this essay?

2. MAJOR DETAILS

a. How do the three Amish sects differ from one another?
b. What rules concerning personal appearance do the Amish follow to avoid pride?
c. What theories have been suggested to explain why the barns have been set on fire?

3. INFERENCES

a. Read paragraph 1 again. Why are there only three or four last names in Big Valley?
b. Read paragraph 6 again. Why does the author, Jeanne Marie Laskas, use the word "infected"?

4. OPINIONS

a. Read paragraph 13 again. How do you think the arsonist should be punished? Explain.
b. Read paragraph 16 again. What do you think are some of the advantages and disadvantages of the Amish belief system: "Sacrifice individuality—forget about your self, your clothes, your hair, your creative longings—in favor of the common good"?

Vocabulary Building

Lesson One: The Vocabulary of a Troubled Society

The essay "Fire, Hope and Charity" by Jeanne Marie Laskas includes words that are useful when you are discussing our troubled society.

engulfing (paragraph 2)
debris (2)
stench (2)
prey (4)
random (4)
brutal (4)
circumscribed (10)
shunned (12)
indignant (12)
pungent (15)

In a troubled society, widespread crime is **engulfing**—surrounding and swallowing up—whole neighborhoods.

In a troubled society, city streets are often littered with **debris**—the scattered fragments of things that have been broken or destroyed.

In a troubled society, the **stench**—the disgusting smell—of rotting garbage is everywhere.

In a troubled society, the citizens are easy **prey**—victims to be robbed, attacked, or killed—for the many criminals who roam the streets.

In a troubled society, many people are the victims of **random** violence—violence that is unplanned and has no specific purpose or pattern.

In a troubled society, behavior that is **brutal**—extremely cruel and cold-hearted—is very common.

In a troubled society, many people find that their opportunities for advancement are **circumscribed**—limited or restricted.

In a troubled society, the members of some minority groups are **shunned**—deliberately and consistently avoided—by many of the other citizens.

In a troubled society, some people become **indignant**—filled with anger that is a reaction to unfairness or meanness.

In a troubled society, the air is polluted with odors that are **pungent**—sharp and stinging.

EXERCISE 2A: Using the vocabulary words in this lesson, fill in the blanks.

1. To protect itself from its enemies, a skunk sprays a fluid that has an unpleasantly ________________ odor.
2. After the earthquake, all that was left of our beautiful house was a worthless pile of ________________.
3. The winning numbers in a state lottery are selected at ________________.
4. Spotting an antelope in the distance, the lion moved through the tall grass quietly and then, with a sudden burst of speed, pounced on its ________________.
5. Now that I have become a Democrat, I am ________________ by my Republican relatives.

6. When the tide is low in polluted waters, an awful ______________ often keeps bathers away from the beach.
7. As the elderly woman's arthritis grew worse, her world became increasingly ______________.
8. The flood waters rose quickly, ______________ the entire town as its citizens fled to safety.
9. The ______________ prison guard beat convicts for no reason at all.
10. I became ______________ when I read that women are often paid less than men are for doing the exact same work.

Lesson Two: The Vocabulary of a Healthy Society

The essay "Fire, Hope and Charity" by Jeanne Marie Laskas includes words that are useful when you are discussing a healthy society.

sects (paragraph 8)	**cult** (12)
conservative (8)	**consensus** (13)
innovation (10)	**meted out** (13)
intellect (10)	**ingenuity** (15)
individuality (10)	**humility** (15)

A healthy society guarantees the rights of all religious **sects**—small groups that have broken away from established religious organizations.

A healthy society respects the views of people who are **conservative**—those who want to keep the older, more traditional customs and practices and are against changing them in any way.

A healthy society encourages **innovation**—the introduction of new methods, customs, or devices.

A healthy society places great importance on human **intellect**—the ability to learn, reason, and understand.

A healthy society values **individuality**—all the qualities that make each person different from every other one.

A healthy society permits the existence of a **cult**—a group whose members are extremely devoted either to a person whom they worship or to ideas and beliefs that they consider the only "true way."

A healthy society is governed by citizens who like to reach a **consensus**—a general agreement—concerning future plans for the community.

A healthy society believes that punishment for serious crimes should be **meted out**—distributed or given out—in a fair and evenhanded way.

A healthy society encourages its citizens to make full use of their **ingenuity**—their cleverness and originality.

A healthy society places great value on qualities such as kindness, honesty, and **humility**—a feeling that one is just an average person with abilities and achievements that are ordinary.

EXERCISE 2B: Each of the vocabulary words from this lesson is shown below in italics as the word appeared in context in the essay. Write an explanation of each word within the context of the material given. Use your own paper for this assignment.

1. From paragraph 8: "The 1,500 Amish people living in Big Valley are divided into three *sects*. . . ."
2. From paragraph 8: "Those with yellow tops are the least *conservative* sect. . . ."
3. From paragraph 10: "In the Amish world, human imagination, *innovation, intellect* and, above all, *individuality* are intentionally squashed."
4. From paragraph 12: "I think it was some kind of a *cult*. . . ."
5. From paragraph 13: "Just as there is no *consensus* on the culprits, there is no unanimity on the punishment that should be *meted out* if an arsonist is caught."
6. From paragraph 15: "It came from God, Sam Z. says, refusing to rejoice in the strength and *ingenuity* of mankind. . . ."
7. From paragraph 15: "Don't become proud of your *humility*."

SPELLING

Sound-Alikes

Many of your spelling errors may be caused by a confusion of words that have different spellings but similar pronunciations. Since the confused words sound alike, their pronunciation is no clue to their spelling. Instead you must rely on their meanings if you are to spell them correctly. Below is a list of some of these troublesome Sound-Alikes. They are words that you use frequently in your writing, so be sure to learn to spell them correctly.

1. *capital* (leading city; money)

Albany is the capital of New York.

Pam invested all her capital.

capitol (only the name of a building)
We met on the steps of the Capitol in Washington.

2. *hear* (listen)
We could not hear the radio because of the interference.
here (in this place)
The boys will wait here for their friends.
3. *its* (belongs to it)
The dog could not wag its tail.
it's (it is)
It's the best of all possible worlds.
4. *passed* (went by)
I passed your home on the way to school.
past (a former time)
If we are not careful, the past will catch up with us.
5. *peace* (the absence of war and strife)
The United Nations hopes to bring peace to the world.
piece (a portion)
Have a piece of cake with your coffee.
6. *principal* (most important; chief person; the original amount of a loan)
What is the principal idea of this essay?
Ms. Denn is the school principal.
Sue paid the interest and fifty dollars on the principal.
principle (a basic doctrine or rule)
The many principles of physics are difficult to learn.
7. *then* (at that time)
We went to an early movie, and then we went home.
than (used to compare unequal things)
His speech was much longer than mine.
8. *their* (belonging to them)
It is their privilege to vote against the amendment.
there (at that place)
There is the oldest schoolhouse in America.

they're (they are)

They're the best audience one could hope for.

9. *to* (toward; part of the infinitive)

Phyllis gave her schedule to me.

They like to condemn all his decisions.

too (also; more than enough)

Judy likes Greek tragedy too.

Peter watches too much TV.

two (the number 2)

We consulted two authorities.

10. *weather* (the state of the atmosphere)

The weather was fine for a trip to the lake.

whether (indicates a choice)

Lynn could not decide whether to stay home or go out.

11. *who's* (who is)

Who's against the new French government?

whose (belonging to whom)

Whose children are they?

12. *your* (belonging to you)

It is your decision to make.

you're (you are)

You're the last obstacle to my happiness

A SPECIAL NOTE: Memory tricks are especially helpful for learning these sound-alike words:

Remember that you *hear* with your *ear.*

We waited *here* and not *there.*

The princi*pal* is my *pal* and the chief person in a school.

The princip*le* is a ru*le.*

The capit*o*l has a d*o*me.

The w*ea*ther was cl*ea*r.

He ate a *pie*ce of *pie.*

EXERCISE 2C: Underline the correct word from each set of words in parentheses.

Graffiti, those scribblings and drawings on walls that you have (passed, past) just about every day of (your, you're) life, are one of the oldest methods used by people (to, too, two) communicate. In fact, such wall writings were popular over (to, too, two) thousand years before Christianity; Greek workers (who's, whose) lives were spent building the Great Pyramid at Giza left (their, there, they're) signatures on this Egyptian monument. The ancient Italian city of Pompeii had some of (its, it's) walls marked up with (peaces, pieces) of graffiti (to, too, two). (Their, There, They're) well-preserved clues to the (passed, past) because in 79 A.D. a volcano exploded and (than, then) buried the city under volcanic ash, which protected the graffiti from the (weather, whether) for many hundreds of years.

(Weather, Whether) these wall markings are found in ancient Pompeii or in modern America, they fall into three (principal, principle) categories. The (principal, principle) behind the most common type, identity graffiti, is the graffiti writer's desire to call attention (to, too, two) his or her name in a society in which most people feel lost in the crowd. The example (your, you're) probably most familiar with is "Kilroy was (hear, here)." Another reason for identity graffiti was pointed out by a high school (principal, principle) who found that a teacher (who's, whose) (to, too, two) busy to (hear, here) what students are saying encourages them to scrawl (their, there, they're) names on (their, there, they're) desktops in revenge. The second type of graffiti offers a message or opinion. For example, the thought "(Their, There, They're) will be (peace, piece) in 2010—with or without people" was written on a wall of the (Capital, Capitol) in Washington, D.C. (Their, There, They're) someone also wrote: "Of course I smoke. (Its, It's) safer (than, then) breathing!" The final type of graffiti is decorative and colorful artwork; it can be seen throughout New York City, often called the graffiti (capital, capitol) of the world, where several young people have formed an organization, United Graffiti Artists, to sell (their, there, they're) art. Thus, graffiti are becoming an acceptable form of communication that will likely survive periodic cleanups and paint jobs.

¶ Paragraph Development: Part II

In Chapter One you learned three methods of paragraph development: *facts, examples,* and *incidents.* Here are three other ways of developing a paragraph. These methods are somewhat more complicated because they use a combination of facts, examples, reasons, and incidents. As you study and practice these methods of paragraph development, refer back to Pointers for Writing a Paragraph, page 51.

I Definition

II Comparison and Contrast

III S-N-S (Statistics, Names, and the Senses)

I. Definition. Here is an example of a paragraph developed with a *definition.*

Nowadays, more and more people are enjoying the benefits of organically grown fruits and vegetables. This trend profits from our increased awareness of environmental decay, for no artificial fertilizers or insect sprays are used on the plants. Only natural, organic compounds are used to treat the soil. Some growers even go so far as to raise their crops in a greenhouse with purified, pollution-free air and water. Because of this special care, the produce is often quite expensive; a pound of tomatoes, for example, could cost as much as $5. But compared with ordinary fruits and vegetables, the organically grown varieties are generally larger in size, deeper in color, tastier, and above all, more nourishing. For these reasons, most health food consumers are willing to be called "health food nuts."

TRY IT OUT

1. Underline the topic sentence in the paragraph above.
2. Is there more than one main idea in the paragraph?
3. In your own words state the definition of organically grown fruits and vegetables as given in the paragraph.

EXERCISE 2D: Choose one of these topic sentences and develop it into a paragraph using a definition. Use a separate sheet of paper.

1. Worry can be a very destructive emotion.
2. Being a good friend is not easy.
3. A perfect date would be an unforgettable experience.

II. Comparison and Contrast. Here is an example of a paragraph developed through *comparison and contrast.*

Regular nightly television newscasts differ greatly from newspaper news articles. Although both types of journalism deal with current events, each has to take a different form because of space and time. Television news items are usually brief. Newspaper reports, on the other hand, go into a story in more detail and depth. As much as possible, television news stories try to include a film clip or several photographs, but newspaper articles generally have to depend only on the printed word or perhaps one photograph. Another key difference between television and newspaper news reporting is that the television viewer is locked into the sequence as given, but the newspaper reader can scan and select articles of special interest. Thus, while both television and newspapers deal with the news, the result is two vastly different products.

TRY IT OUT

1. Underline the topic sentence in the paragraph above.
2. Is there more than one main idea in the paragraph?
3. In your own words state three of the comparisons and contrasts used to develop the paragraph.

EXERCISE 2E: Choose one of these topic sentences and develop it into a paragraph using comparison and contrast. Use a separate sheet of paper.

1. It is easy to tell the difference between a bad teacher and a good one.
2. Ten years from now my life will (will not) be very different from what it is like today.
3. It is (is not) more enjoyable to see a movie on a rented videocassette or DVD than at a movie theater.

III. S-N-S (Statistics, Names, and the Senses). Here is an example of a paragraph developed with *S-N-S* (*s*tatistics, *n*ames, and the *s*enses).

Last Saturday night's rock concert brought a new liveliness to the fifty-five-year-old Coliseum Theater. When the show began at 8:30, the stage was completely dark except for a glowing six-foot-high purple and yellow sign announcing the evening's entertainment, the rock group Fire and Ice.

Suddenly, a flash of lightning darted across the stage, quickly followed by a booming explosion of thick white smoke. As the air cleared, the four members of Fire and Ice could be seen, each wearing a silver jumpsuit and red boots. Backed up by an energetic five-piece band, the performers immediately launched into their latest hit, "Forbidden Fruit." Eddie Royal, the lead singer, screamed the song's lyrics as he held a live cobra above his head and pranced about the stage like a playful pony. Urged on by the joyful shrieking of 3,000 young people, the group was able to maintain a hard, driving beat throughout this number as well as fourteen others, many of which were accompanied by such dramatic devices as flames shooting up from the stage and birds flying out of instrument cases. When the concert ended, the audience applauded wildly, satisfied that the ninety minutes of music and spectacle was worth the $50 ticket price.

TRY IT OUT

1. Underline the topic sentence in the paragraph above.
2. Is there more than one main idea in the paragraph?
3. Identify the statistics used in the paragraph. Then identify the names used. Finally, identify the senses used.

EXERCISE 2F: Choose one of these topic sentences and develop it into a paragraph using S-N-S. Use a separate sheet of paper.

1. The school cafeteria should be condemned by the Board of Health.
2. A pet shop is a fascinating place to explore.
3. Watching the players is only a small part of what a fan experiences at a football (soccer, basketball, baseball) game.

EXERCISE 2G: Essay Analysis Answer these questions about the essay "Fire, Hope and Charity."

1. What are the S-N-S details in paragraphs 1 and 2?

____

____

____

2. What is being defined in paragraph 8?

____

____

3. What is being defined in paragraph 10?

____

____

4. What is being contrasted in paragraph 13?

____

____

EXERCISE 2H: Write an essay on one of the six topics given below. Using the essay outline shown below, try to use a different type of paragraph development for each of the qualities you select. For help in planning your essay, refer to the Pointers for Writing an Essay on page 54. Use your own paper for this assignment.

Qualities That Make an Ideal Date
Qualities That Make an Ideal Mate
Qualities That Make an Ideal Parent
Qualities That Make an Ideal Student
Qualities That Make an Ideal Teacher
Qualities That Make an Ideal Friend

I Introduction
II One Quality (you select)
III Another Quality (you select)
IV A Third Quality (you select)
V Conclusion

Ordering of Details in a Paragraph

Now that you know the six basic methods of paragraph development, it will be helpful to plan the details of your chosen method of development. Before haphazardly throwing information into a paragraph, you should decide on a plan for the order and arrangement of your details. The three basic, and most useful, arrangements are:

I Details Arranged by Order of Importance

II Details Arranged by Order of Time

III Details Arranged by Order of Location

The order you select should depend on the topic of the paragraph and the kinds of details that it will be necessary to use. The ordering of details in any of these three ways will improve the clarity and effectiveness of your writing.

I. Details Arranged by Order of Importance. Just as an orchestra begins quietly and builds to the climactic crash of the cymbals, so you may build your paragraph the same way with the least important details first and the most important last. Notice how it is done in this paragraph:

> People often complain about foolish things. Very demanding types will find fault with every little detail, like a speck of grease on a wall or someone being three minutes early or late for an appointment. Other people often feel frustrated by the weather, no matter what it happens to be, or about their health, no matter how minor the illness. Often such lack of judgment is quickly put in its place when a real trauma strikes: loss of a job, serious illness, unexpected death. Now complaining turns to worry or grief, and the petty details picked at previously seem utterly unimportant.

HINT: You may choose to give your most important details first and the least important last, but the opposite order is generally more effective.

EXERCISE 21: Use order of importance to fill in the details for the following topic sentence.

When selecting a college, a person needs to weigh a number of considerations.

1. ______________________________

2. ______________________________

3. ______________________________
4. ______________________________
5. ______________________________
6. ______________________________

EXERCISE 2J: Choose one of these topic sentences and develop it into a paragraph that uses details arranged according to order of importance. Use a separate sheet of paper.

1. Some excuses are better than others.
2. Living alone can be expensive.
3. A person who is popular usually possesses certain qualities.

II. Details Arranged by Order of Time. If you are telling how something is made, how a game is played, or how a system developed, you should use the order of happening, often called *chronological order.* You will be telling the sequence of events in the order of their occurrence. Notice how it is done in this paragraph:

> To study for an examination, first find a quiet room where you will not be disturbed. Be sure that you have good lighting, a comfortable chair, and adequate desk space. After you have gathered together a few pens and pencils, some scrap paper, your class notes, and your books, you are ready to begin studying. Read through your notes completely, so that you can get a total picture of the course and so that you can pick out the major points that need to be studied. Then concentrate on one topic at a time, using a pen and scrap paper to copy important names and dates. Finally, read your textbooks to fill in any gaps in your notes and to reinforce what you have already studied. When you have finished, pray that the test will be easy!

EXERCISE 2K: Use chronological order to fill in the details for the following topic sentence.

If I had only twenty-four hours left on earth, I would not waste a minute.

1. ______________________________
2. ______________________________
3. ______________________________

4. ______________________________

5. ______________________________

EXERCISE 2L: Choose one of these topic sentences and develop it into a paragraph using details arranged according to order of time. Use a separate sheet of paper.

1. It was one of those "I should have stayed in bed" days.
2. ______________ is an easy game to learn.
3. I saw the funniest commercial (strangest music video) on television the other night.

III. Details Arranged by Order of Location. When you describe a place or wish to take your reader from one place to another, you must do it in an orderly fashion so that the reader can picture the scene in his or her mind. You would use order of location to describe such things as a college campus, or your room, or even something as small as a penny. In each instance, you should give the position of one thing in relation to something you have already described. For example:

> A street carnival easily draws people to its festive atmosphere and unusual attractions. With one end of the street left open for people to come and go, the rest of the space is happily jammed with people and booths. On one side of the street a ferris wheel, bordered with flashing multicolored lights, carries delighted customers high up the circle and down. Across the way a spinning rocket fills its riders with thrills and fear. At the far end of the street a merry-go-round attracts the close interest of the younger children. Set between the rides are booths of all descriptions: a wheel of fortune that tests luck; a ball toss game that challenges skill; palm readers who tell fortunes; jars of beans that defy guessing powers; and, of course, food stands that sell ice cream, hot dogs, and other temptations. Though some of the attractions might seem unimportant separately, the carnival atmosphere encourages the enthusiastic participation of everyone who steps into the street.

EXERCISE 2M: Use order of location to fill in the details for the following topic sentence.

______________ is the ugliest (most beautiful) building I have ever seen.

1. ______________________________

2. ______________________________

3. ____

4. ____

5. ____

EXERCISE 2N: Choose one of these topic sentences and develop it into a paragraph using details arranged according to order of location. Use a separate sheet of paper.

1. The ______________ is a great-looking car.
2. The cover of the ______________ music album is a real work of art.
3. My favorite hangout is an unusual (comfortable) looking place.

EXERCISE 2O: Essay Analysis Answer these questions about the essay "Fire, Hope and Charity." Use your own paper for this assignment.

1. a. Are the details in paragraphs 1 and 2 arranged in order of importance, time, or location?

   b. Would another arrangement of the details in paragraphs 1 and 2 have been as effective? Why?

2. a. Are the details in paragraph 8 arranged in order of importance, time, or location?

   b. Would another arrangement of the details in paragraph 8 have been as effective? Why?

3. Paragraph 12 offers several theories about why someone set the six fires. How would you arrange these theories using order of importance? Be prepared to defend the order you select.

¶ Revising a Paragraph

Most people are unable to write well on the first try. Even professional writers often draft several versions of a paragraph before being satisfied with the quality of the work. You, too, should expect to revise your writing many times. During the revision process, you have the chance to add new information, combine some ideas and eliminate others, move sentences around, and change words. The more time that you spend on these activities, the better your final draft is likely to be.

Here are some suggestions that will make the revision process easier and more rewarding.

1. After you complete a first draft, put it aside for at least a day before attempting to revise it. If you can spare only a few hours between drafts, use that time to engage in some activity that will take your mind off your writing. After taking a break, you will be able to look at your writing with more objectivity, making it easier for you to identify the changes that will improve your writing.
2. Ask your classmates, friends, or parents to read your writing and tell you what they did and did not like about it. To make this method work successfully, ask the reader specific questions such as these: Are all of my ideas clear?Do I go off my topic anywhere? Do I repeat myself? Have I given enough examples?
3. If you are writing on a word processor, you are fortunate because a good word-processing program makes it easy for you to add, cut, and move material. If you write your work by hand, double-space and leave wide margins so that you will have enough room to enter any changes.
4. After revising your first draft, copy it neatly or print it out before attempting any additional revisions. If you try to make all of the changes on the same copy, it will probably become a confusing mess that will hamper effective revision and perhaps even lead to unintentional errors in the final draft.
5. When you are in the midst of revising a paragraph, it is very difficult to pay attention to all aspects of your writing at the same time. Therefore, with each draft try to concentrate on a different area of concern. For example, you might use this revision strategy:

   First Draft: Revise content and organization
   Second Draft: Revise style
   Third Draft: Edit for grammar, punctuation, and spelling

Let's see how a student named Michael Riley used this strategy to revise his paragraph on supermarket shopping.

First Draft

Shopping in a supermarket can be a very aggravating experience. When I was at the local A&P recently, you couldn't walk down the cereal aisle because the kid who was restocking the shelves had blocked the aisle with a lot of large cartons. I asked him to move a couple of them so I could pass. He made a nasty remark and went right on doing his work. Just as I entered the store, this woman banged her cart right into my side. She didn't even bother to apologize. Also, I had to wait on a long line at the check out counter because the supermarket didn't have enough cashiers. This shopping trip convinced me that the supermarket environment seems to bring out the worst in some people.

Referring to this textbook's discussion about writing paragraphs, Michael Riley revised his first draft for content and organization.

Revised First Draft

Supermarkets seem to be a breeding gorund for rude
~~Shopping in a supermarket can be a very aggravating~~
behavior.
~~experience~~. ~~When I was at the local A&P recently,~~ Y you

couldn't walk down the cereal aisle because the kid who

was restocking the shelves had blocked the aisle with a

lot of large cartons. I asked him to move a couple of

snapped "Hold your horses!"
them so I could pass. He ~~made a nasty remark~~ and went

local A&P recently
right on doing his work. (Just as I entered the ~~store~~,

this woman banged her cart right into my side. She didn't

even bother to apologize.) Also, I had to wait on a long

These are only a couple of
line at the check out. ~~counter because the supermarket~~ Off the topic

the many experiences that have
~~didn't have enough cashiers. This shopping trip~~ convinced

me that the supermarket environment seems to bring out Not logical

the worst in some people.

I need another incident.

Michael Riley realized that his topic sentence was too broad and unfocused, so he replaced it with one that narrowed the topic to a discussion of rudeness in supermarkets. Next, he eliminated an example that went off the topic and reorganized the two remaining examples using order of time. After making a note to add another incident for support, he revised the closing sentence because he realized that it was not logical to base his conclusion on only one shopping trip. When he was satisfied that his paragraph was well developed and clearly organized, he printed a neat copy of his second draft.

Second Draft

Supermarkets seem to be a breeding ground for rude behavior. Just as I entered the local A&P recently, this woman banged her cart right into my side. She didn't even bother to apologize. You couldn't walk down the cereal aisle because the kid who was restocking the shelves had blocked the aisle with a lot of large cartons. I asked him to move a couple of them so I could pass. He snapped "Hold your horses! and went right on doing his work. These incidents were annoying, but they were nothing compared to what once happened while I was on the express check out line at a Grand Union Supermarket. The cashier pointed out to this guy in front of me that he was well over the ten item limit for that line. Well, he exploded with a steady stream of filthy langage. The manager eventually came over and threw him out of the store. These are only a couple of the many experences that have convinced me that the supermarket environment seems to bring out the worst in some people.

TRY IT OUT

CHOOSE ONE OF THE TOPIC SENTENCES BELOW AND DEVELOP IT INTO A PARAGRAPH. AFTER COMPLETING THE FIRST DRAFT, REVISE IT FOR CONTENT AND ORGANIZATION. FOR ADDITIONAL HELP WITH THE REVISION PROCESS, REFER TO THE POINTERS FOR REVISING A PARAGRAPH ON PAGES 87–88. BE SURE TO MAKE A NEAT COPY OF YOUR SECOND DRAFT. USE YOUR OWN PAPER FOR THIS ASSIGNMENT.

1. My dreams (daydreams) reveal a great deal about the real me.
2. Getting along with parents (a brother or sister) can be difficult (easy).
3. Television talk shows are dealing with some shocking topics these days.

Now Michael Riley is ready to revise his paragraph for style. Below are his revisions and comments to himself.

Revised Second Draft

```
                       For example                                    a
Supermarkets seem to be a breeding ground for rude behavior. ^ Just as I entered the local A&P recently, ~~this~~
                                                            and did not
woman banged her cart right into my side^ ~~She didn't even~~
                    Then          not
bother to apologize.^ You could~~n't~~ walk down the cereal
                 fellow
aisle because the ~~kid~~ who was restocking the shelves had
            way           several                   When
blocked the ~~aisle~~ with ~~a lot of~~ large cartons. ^I asked
                few
him to move a ~~couple~~ of them so I could pass. He snapped
"Hold your horses! and went right on doing his work.
Although                                          minor
^These incidents were annoying, ~~but~~ they were ~~nothing~~
compared to what once happened while I was on the express
```

check out line at a Grand Union Supermarket. ~~The~~ *When* the cashier pointed out to ~~this guy~~ *the man* in front of me that he was well over the ten item limit for that line. ~~Well,~~ he exploded with a steady stream of filthy langage~~.~~ ~~The~~ *that continued until* the manager eventually came over and ~~threw him out of~~ *insisted that he leave* the store. These are only a ~~couple~~ *few* of the many experiences that have convinced me that the supermarket environment seems to bring out the worst in some people.

In this draft, the writer concentrated on his choice of words and sentence structure. To make his paragraph flow more smoothly, he added a few appropriate transitions ("For example" and "Then") and combined sentences using coordination and subordination. To establish a more formal tone, he eliminated the contractions, the slang ("kid" and "guy"), and a few informal phrases ("a lot of" and "a couple of").

TRY IT OUT

REVISE THE SECOND DRAFT OF THE PARAGRAPH YOU WROTE FOR THE TRY IT OUT ON PAGE 83. THIS TIME CONCENTRATE ON STYLE. FOR ADDITIONAL HELP WITH THE REVISION PROCESS, REFER TO THE POINTERS FOR REVISING A PARAGRAPH ON PAGE 87. USE YOUR OWN PAPER FOR THIS ASSIGNMENT.

Now Michael Riley is ready to revise his paragraph for correct grammar, punctuation, and spelling.

Revised Third Draft

Supermarkets seem to be a breeding ground for rude behavior. For example, just as I entered the local A&P recently, a woman banged her cart into my side and did not even bother to apologize. Then ~~you~~ *I* could not walk down the cereal aisle because the fellow who was restocking the shelves had blocked the way with several large cartons. When I asked him to move a few of them so *that* I could pass, ~~H~~*h*e snapped, "Hold your horses!" and went right on doing his work. Although these incidents were annoying, they were minor compared to what once happened while I was on the express checkout line at a Grand Union Supermarket. When the cashier pointed out to the man in front of me that he was well over the ten-item limit for that line, ~~H~~*h*e exploded with a steady stream of filthy ~~langage~~ *language* that continued until the manager eventually came over and insisted that he leave the store. These are only a few of the many ~~experences~~ *experiences* that have convinced me that the supermarket environment seems to bring out the worst in some people.

(Continued)

8. Have you arranged the details in a logical order? (pages 75–77)
9. Have you ended the paragraph with an effective closing sentence?

Revising for Style

1. Have you used necessary transitions? (pages 384–85)
2. Have you used key words to help create unity? (pages 389–92)
3. Have you avoided a series of short sentences by using coordination and/or subordination? (pages 139–40, 144–47 and 152–53)
4. Do you use coordination correctly? (pages 139–40)
5. Do you use subordination correctly? (pages 144–47)
6. Have you avoided informal language if it is not suitable for your purpose and audience? (pages 425–28)
7. Have you avoided unnecessarily repeating the same words?

Editing for Grammar, Punctuation, and Spelling

1. Have you eliminated sentence fragments? (pages 104–109)
2. Have you eliminated run-ons and comma splices? (pages 114–17)
3. Do the verbs agree with their subjects? (pages 181–84)
4. Have you used *-ed* verb endings wherever necessary? (pages 199–204)
5. Have you used pronouns correctly? (pages 238–45, 249–50, and 255–59)
6. Have you used parallelism correctly? (pages 446–49)
7. Have you eliminated misplaced modifiers? (pages 452–54)
8. Have you eliminated dangling modifiers? (pages 457–58)
9. Have you used commas correctly? (pages 341–47)
10. Have you used apostrophes correctly? (pages 337–38)
11. Have you used the other marks of punctuation correctly? (pages 354–56 and 409–10)
12. Is your usage correct? (pages 412–18)
13. Have you used the *-s* ending on plural nouns when they are needed? (pages 375–79)
14. Have you used capital letters when they are needed? (pages 171–73)
15. Have you corrected any misspelled words?

EXERCISE 2P: First, revise the paragraph below for content and organization. Be sure to make a neat copy of the second draft. Then revise the second draft for style. Finally, edit the revised paragraph for grammar, punctuation, and spelling. For help with this assignment, refer to the Pointers for Revising a Paragraph on pages 87–88. Use your own paper for this assignment.

First Draft

Going out on a date can be expensive these days. Two tickets to a movie, together with a tub of popcorn and a couple of sodas, will cost quite a bit. The sad part is that most movies shown today aren't really worth the price of admission. But most other forms of entertainment are even more expensive. If you decide to go out to eat before the movie, dinner for two at any decent restaurant will cost a lot of money. And if you want to do something after the movie, the bill for the evening could really go through the roof. That's why for some couples a date often consists of sharing a pizza while watching TV.

EXERCISE 2Q: REFRESHER

On a separate sheet of paper, rewrite the following paragraph. Remove any material that is not part of the main idea stated in the topic sentence. Add facts, examples, incidents, definitions, comparisons and contrasts, or S-N-S to develop the paragraph more fully.

People can take many steps to reduce the stress produced by their hurried lifestyles. For example, physical exercise such as jogging, swimming, or playing tennis is an excellent method for relieving muscle tension and using up nervous energy. Such exercise also strengthens the heart, improves blood circulation, and helps with weight control. Another way to reduce stress is by doing deep-breathing exercises a few times each day; slowly inhaling and exhaling helps the body relax as the mind rids itself of troublesome thoughts. People who use these methods often experience a feeling of well-being that improves the overall quality of their lives.

SPRINGBOARDS TO WRITING

Using your knowledge of the writing process, explained on pages 14–16, write a paragraph or essay related to this chapter's central theme, *the Amish lifestyle*, which is introduced on page 60.

PREWRITING

To think of topics to write about, look at the advertisement and the photograph, read the essay, and answer the questions that follow each. If you prefer, select one of the writing springboards below. (All paragraph numbers refer to the essay that starts on page 60.) To develop your ideas, use the prewriting techniques described on pages 17–22.

WRITING A PARAGRAPH *(For help, see the Pointers on page 51.)*

1. Agree or disagree with the Amish philosophy: "worldly things take your mind off what's real: the spiritual world, God's world." (See paragraph 7.)
2. Agree or disagree with the Amish opinion that men should do "men things" and women should do "women things." (See paragraph 10.)
3. Read paragraph 13. Agree or disagree with the Amish philosophy of forgive and forget.
4. Agree or disagree with the Amish belief that "pride is sinful." (See paragraph 15.)
5. My neighbors would (would not) help me in time of need. (See paragraph 17.)

WRITING AN ESSAY *(For help, see the Pointers on pages 54–55.)*

6. I Would (Would Not) Like to Be a Member of an Amish Community
7. What I Admire About the Amish Lifestyle
8. Agree or disagree with the Amish belief system: "Sacrifice individuality—forget about your self, your clothes, your hair, your creative longings—in favor of the common good." (See paragraph 16.)
9. Things I Could Live Without
10. My Personal Rules of Behavior
11. Most Americans Are (Are Not) Too Materialistic
12. The Ideal Lifestyle for Me
13. Agree or disagree with this statement by John Burroughs: "For anything worth having one must pay the price; and the price is always work, patience, love, self-sacrifice."
14. The Major Qualities of a Good Person
15. All Young People Should (Should Not) Be Required to Give a Year of Community Service
16. The Government Should (Should Not) Provide a Welfare System to Help the Poor (See paragraph 7.)

How can the opinion of so few outweigh the rights of so many?

Most Americans want Big Government off their backs and out of their private lives. But a group of extremists isn't getting the message. These self-appointed "lifestyle police" believe they know what's best for all of us and they're pushing to control many aspects of our daily lives. If they succeed, we lose our basic right to free choice.

Today, the "lifestyle police" are targeting smokers. But who's next? If 50 million smokers can lose their rights, anyone can.

If you care and want to do something about it, please call us. **1-800-224-3322.**

Defending smokers' rights protects everyone's.

Chapter 3

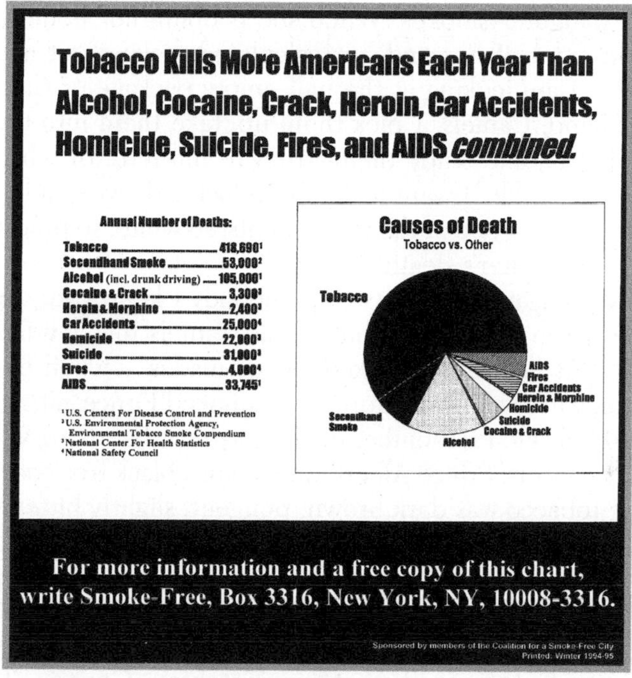

Tobacco Kills More Americans Each Year Than Alcohol, Cocaine, Crack, Heroin, Car Accidents, Homicide, Suicide, Fires, and AIDS *combined*.
Annual Number of Deaths:
Tobacco .... 418,690[1]
Secondhand Smoke .... 53,000[2]
Alcohol (incl. drunk driving) .... 105,000[1]
Cocaine & Crack .... 3,300[3]
Heroin & Morphine .... 2,400[3]
Car Accidents .... 25,000[4]
Homicide .... 22,000[3]
Suicide .... 31,000[3]
Fires .... 4,000[4]
AIDS .... 33,745[1]
[1] U.S. Centers For Disease Control and Prevention
[2] U.S. Environmental Protection Agency, Environmental Tobacco Smoke Compendium
[3] National Center For Health Statistics
[4] National Safety Council
Causes of Death
Tobacco vs. Other
Tobacco
AIDS
Fires
Car Accidents
Heroin & Morphine
Homicide
Suicide
Cocaine & Crack
Alcohol
Secondhand Smoke
For more information and a free copy of this chart, write Smoke-Free, Box 3316, New York, NY, 10008-3316.
Sponsored by members of the Coalition for a Smoke-Free City
Printed: Winter 1994-95

SPRINGBOARDS TO THINKING

For informal, not written, response . . . to stimulate your thinking

1. Read the advertisement on the opposite page. Are certain groups of people acting like "life-style police" who are trying to take away some of our basic rights? In recent years, have smokers lost some of their rights? Explain.
2. Do you agree with the ban on smoking in schools, theaters, airplanes, and other public places? Why or why not?
3. Do you think that "defending smokers' rights protects everyone's" rights? Explain.
4. Read the advertisement above. Are you surprised by the information it provides? Why or why not? Do you think this information would persuade someone not to start smoking? Do you think this information would persuade a smoker to quit the habit? Why or why not?

My Daughter Smokes

Alice Walker

(1) My daughter smokes. While she is doing her homework, her feet on the bench in front of her and her calculator clicking out answers to her algebra problems, I am looking at the half-empty package of Camels tossed carelessly close at hand. Camels. I pick them up, take them into the kitchen, where the light is better, and study them—they're filtered, for which I am grateful. My heart feels terrible. I want to weep. In fact, I do weep a little, standing there by the stove holding one of the instruments, so white, so precisely rolled, that could cause my daughter's death. When she smoked Marlboros and Players I hardened myself against feeling so bad; nobody I knew ever smoked these brands.

(2) She doesn't know this, but it was Camels that my father, her grandfather, smoked. But before he smoked "ready-mades"—when he was very young and very poor, with eyes like lanterns—he smoked Prince Albert tobacco in cigarettes he rolled himself. I remember the bright-red tobacco tin, with a picture of Queen Victoria's consort, Prince Albert, dressed in a black frock coat and carrying a cane.

(3) The tobacco was dark brown, pungent, slightly bitter. I tasted it more than once as a child, and the discarded tins could be used for a number of things: to keep buttons and shoelaces in, to store seeds, and best of all, to hold worms for the rare times my father took us fishing.

(4) By the late forties and early fifties no one rolled his own anymore (and few women smoked) in my hometown, Eatonton, Georgia. The tobacco industry, coupled with Hollywood movies in which both hero and heroine smoked like chimneys, won over completely people like my father, who were hopelessly addicted to cigarettes. He never looked as dapper as Prince Albert, though; he continued to look like a poor, overweight, overworked colored man with too large a family; black, with a very white cigarette stuck in his mouth.

(5) I do not remember when he started to cough. Perhaps it was unnoticeable at first. A little hacking in the morning as he lit his first cigarette upon getting out of bed. By the time I was my daughter's age, his breath was a wheeze, embarrassing to hear; he could not climb stairs without resting every third or fourth step. It was not unusual for him to cough for an hour.

(6) It is hard to believe there was a time when people did not understand that cigarette smoking is an addiction. I wondered aloud once to my sister—who is perennially trying to quit—whether our father realized this. I wondered how she, a smoker since high school, viewed her own habit.

(7) It was our father who gave her her first cigarette, one day when she had taken water to him in the fields.

"I always wondered why he did that," she said, puzzled, and with some bitterness.

"What did he say?" I asked.

"That he didn't want me to go to anyone else for them," she said, "which never really crossed my mind."

So he was aware it was addictive, I thought, though as annoyed as she that he assumed she would be interested.

(8) I began smoking in eleventh grade, also the year I drank numerous bottles of terrible sweet, very cheap wine. My friends and I, all boys for this venture, bought our supplies from a man who ran a segregated bar and liquor store on the outskirts of town. Over the entrance there was a large sign that said COLORED. We were not permitted to drink there, only to buy. I smoked Kools, because my sister did. By then I thought her toxic darkened lips and gums glamorous. However, my body simply would not tolerate smoke. After six months I had a chronic sore throat. I gave up smoking, gladly. Because it was a ritual with my buddies—Murl, Leon, and "Dog" Farley—I continued to drink wine.

(9) My father died from "the poor man's friend," pneumonia, one hard winter when his bronchitis and emphysema had left him low. I doubt he had much lung left at all, after coughing for so many years. He had so little breath that, during his last years, he was always leaning on something. I remember once, at a family reunion, when my daughter was two, that my father picked her up for a minute—long enough for me to photograph them—but the effort was obvious. Near the end of his life, and largely because he had no more lungs, he quit smoking. He gained a couple of pounds, but by then he was so emaciated no one noticed.

(10) When I travel to Third World countries I see many people like my father and daughter. There are large billboards directed at them both: the tough, "take-charge," or dapper older man, the glamorous, "worldly" young woman, both puffing away. In these poor countries, as in American ghettos and on reservations, money that should be spent for food goes instead to the tobacco companies; over time, people starve themselves of both food and air, effectively weakening and addicting their children, eventually eradicating themselves. I read in the newspaper and in my gardening magazine that cigarette butts are so toxic that if a baby swallowed one, it is likely to die, and that the boiled water from a bunch of them makes an effective insecticide.

(11) My daughter would like to quit, she says. We both know the statistics are against her; most people who try to quit smoking do not succeed.*

(12) There is a deep hurt that I feel as a mother. Some days it is a feeling of futility. I remember how carefully I ate when I was pregnant, how patiently I taught my daughter how to cross a street safely. For what, I sometimes wonder;

*Three months after reading this essay my daughter stopped smoking.

so that she can wheeze through most of her life feeling half her strength, and then die of self-poisoning, as her grandfather did?

(13) But, finally, one must feel empathy for the tobacco plant itself. For thousands of years, it has been venerated by Native Americans as a sacred medicine. They have used it extensively—its juice, its leaves, its roots, its (holy) smoke—to heal wounds and cure diseases, and in ceremonies of prayer and peace. And though the plant as most of us know it has been poisoned by chemicals and denatured by intensive mono-cropping and is therefore hardly the plant it was, still, to some modern Indians it remains a plant of positive power. I learned this when my Native American friends, Bill Wahpepah and his family, visited with me for a few days and the first thing he did was sow a few tobacco seeds in my garden.

(14) Perhaps we can liberate tobacco from those who have captured and abused it, enslaving the plant on large plantations, keeping it from freedom and its kin, and forcing it to enslave the world. Its true nature suppressed, no wonder it has become deadly. Maybe by sowing a few seeds of tobacco in our gardens and treating the plant with the reverence it deserves, we can redeem tobacco's soul and restore its self-respect.

(15) Besides, how grim, if one is a smoker, to realize one is smoking a slave.

(16) There is a slogan from a battered women's shelter that I especially like: "Peace on earth begins at home." I believe everything does. I think of a slogan for people trying to stop smoking: "Every home a smoke-free zone." Smoking is a form of self-battering that also batters those who must sit by, occasionally cajole or complain, and helplessly watch. I realize now that as a child I sat by, through the years, and literally watched my father kill himself: surely one such victory in my family, for the rich white men who own the tobacco companies, is enough.

Reading Survey

1. MAIN IDEA

What is the central theme of this essay?

2. MAJOR DETAILS

a. What happened to the author's father during the many years that he smoked cigarettes?
b. What information about cigarettes did the author discover in her newspaper and gardening magazine?
c. Whom does the author blame for the harm that cigarettes do? Why?

3. INFERENCES

a. Read paragraphs 6 and 7 again. Why is the sister "puzzled" and "bitter" about her father giving her her first cigarette?
b. Read paragraphs 14 and 15 again. Why does the author think the idea of smoking a slave is especially awful?

4. OPINIONS

a. Read paragraph 10 again. How important do you think advertising is in persuading people to start smoking?
b. Read paragraph 16 again. Do you agree with the author's statement, "Smoking is a form of self-battering that also batters those who must sit by, occasionally cajole or complain, and helplessly watch"? Why?

VOCABULARY BUILDING

Lesson One: The Vocabulary of Cigarette Addiction, Part I

The essay "My Daughter Smokes" by Alice Walker includes words that are useful when you are discussing cigarette smoking.

addicted (paragraph 4) . . .
 addiction (6)
a wheeze (5) . . . **wheeze** (12)
toxic (8)
chronic (8)
ritual (8)
emphysema (9)
emaciated (9)
enslaving (14) . . . **enslave** (14)
reverence (14)
restore (14)

People who smoke cigarettes are usually well aware that they are **addicted**—that they have a very strong physical need, often for a harmful drug. The drug in tobacco that causes **addiction**—strong physical need—is nicotine.

People who smoke cigarettes for many years often begin to **wheeze**—to breathe with difficulty, making a whistling sound. When every breath is no more than **a wheeze,** a person cannot get enough oxygen to maintain good health.

People who smoke cigarettes inhale the **toxic**—poisonous—chemicals in smoke.

People who smoke cigarettes often develop a **chronic** cough, one that occurs often and lasts for months or years.

People who smoke cigarettes often make their first cigarette of the day a **ritual** or ceremony, an act repeated the same way time after time.

discarded (paragraph 3)
segregated (8)
tolerate (8)
eradicating (10)
futility (12)
empathy (13)
liberate (14)
suppressed (14)
redeem (14)
cajole (16)

People who do not smoke cigarettes often complain when they see empty cigarette packs and cigarette butts that have been **discarded**—thrown away—in elevators and public hallways.

People who do not smoke cigarettes often want smokers **segregated** in restaurants—formally separated from the rest of the group.

People who do not smoke cigarettes often do not **tolerate**—allow or permit—any smoking in their presence.

People who do not smoke may be in favor of **eradicating**—totally eliminating or wiping out—smoking in all public places because it is unhealthy for smokers and nonsmokers alike.

People who do not smoke may feel a great sense of **futility**—disappointment over useless or wasted effort—when they see teenagers taking up smoking, even when they know the risks.

People who do not smoke may have little **empathy**—understanding for another person's feelings—for smokers who say they try but just cannot quit.

People who do not smoke may not understand why smokers do not quit and **liberate** or free themselves from the risk of lung cancer, emphysema, and heart disease.

People who do not smoke may have once **suppressed**—used control to keep down or hold back—any desire to smoke.

People who do not smoke often think smokers can **redeem** themselves—deliver themselves from wrongdoing—by quitting smoking to prevent a horrible illness.

People who do not smoke may try to **cajole** smokers into quitting—persuade them by pleading, using flattery, or making false promises.

EXERCISE 3B: Match each sentence with a vocabulary word from this lesson.

1. I try to understand the feelings of other people. 1. ____________________
2. The clothes were out of style, so I threw them away. 2. ____________________
3. Because I need my job, I used control to hold back my desire to tell off my boss. 3. ____________________

4. Even if you hit your thumb with a hammer, the most Grandma will allow is an "Oh, golly-gee." 4. ______________________

5. Helen refused to go out with me even though I pleaded with her, told her how beautiful she is, and promised to buy her an expensive bracelet. 5. ______________________

6. I stood in line for hours to get tickets for the Rolling Stones concert, and then the person in front of me got the last seats. What a feeling of disappointment and wasted effort. 6. ______________________

7. The United Nations achieved the goal of wiping out smallpox worldwide. 7. ______________________

8. If you raise tropical fish, you know that you must keep male betas separated from other fish. 8. ______________________

9. You don't have to be a slave to a bad habit; you can set yourself free. 9. ______________________

10. I've lied and cheated; what must I do to get back my good name? 10. ______________________

SPELLING

Spelling Rule—Changing Y *to* I

Many of the words in the essay can be learned easily with the help of this one simple spelling rule.

Words ending in *y* preceded by a consonant change *y* to *i* before suffixes—*except* when the suffix begins with *i.*

TRY IT OUT

ADD THE SUFFIXES INDICATED TO THE FOLLOWING WORDS.

	-ed	*-ing*	*-(e)s*
hurry	__________	__________	__________
obey	__________	__________	__________
reply	__________	__________	__________

Here are some examples.

story + *es* = stor*ies*
destroy + *ed* = destroy*ed*
family + *es* = famil*ies*

apply + *ing* = appl*ying*
classify + ed = classif*ied*
lovely + est = lovel*iest*

TRY IT OUT

APPLY THE *Y* TO *I* RULE TO THE FOLLOWING WORDS.

mystery + e(s) = __________
funny + est = __________
annoy + ing = __________

noisy + ly = __________
bury + al = __________
try + ed = __________

A SPECIAL NOTE: Here are four words that you see frequently which are exceptions to the above rule.

lay + ed = laid
say + ed = said

pay + ed = paid
day + ly = daily

EXERCISE 3C: Apply the *y* to *i* rule to these new words.

1. boundary + (e)s = __________
2. luxury + ous = __________
3. destroy + (e)s = __________
4. pretty + er = __________
5. wordy + ness = __________
6. classify + ed = __________
7. duty + ful = __________
8. carry + ing = __________
9. industry + al = __________
10. qualify + cation = __________
11. beauty + fy = __________
12. happy + ly = __________
13. theory + (e)s = __________
14. accompany + ment = __________
15. rely + ance = __________
16. pray + ed = __________
17. lively + hood = __________
18. category + (e)s = __________
19. apply + ing = __________
20. envy + able = __________
21. busy + est = __________
22. necessary + ly = __________
23. turkey + (e)s = __________
24. vary + ation = __________
25. say + ed = __________
26. marry + age = __________
27. enjoy + able = __________
28. empty + ness = __________
29. hurry + ing = __________
30. display + ed = __________

 The Sentence Fragment

A group of words set off as a sentence must be complete. This is a simple requirement and an easy one to test, but the writing of sentence fragments is a common error for the beginning writer. To avoid writing sentence fragments, you must learn when sentences are complete.

Three-Step Test of Sentence Completeness

I Find the Conjugated Verb

II Find the Subject

III Look to See If the Subject and Verb Are Introduced by a Danger Word. (See list on page 107.) If this is so, the sentence is not a complete thought

I. Find the Conjugated Verb. A *verb* expresses action, existence, or occurrence. A word is usually a verb if it can be put into the past tense.

Today I *want.*	Yesterday I *wanted.*
Today I *am.*	Yesterday I *was.*
Today I *have.*	Yesterday I *had.*
Today I *give.*	Yesterday I *gave.*

A verb in a sentence must be complete and conjugated. A conjugated verb has the correct word ending to match the subject. For example, notice in the example below that an *-s* ending has been added to the present tense verb when the subject is *he, she,* or *it.*

I talk	he talk*s*	we talk
you talk	she talk*s*	they talk
	it talk*s*	

Notice that there are two ways a verb is not conjugated.

When a Verb Is Not Conjugated

a. A verb is not conjugated if it has an *-ing* ending without a helping verb.

Fragment	*Corrected*
☒ Jim studying data processing	☑ Jim *is* studying data processing.
	OR
	☑ Jim *was* studying data processing.

b. A verb is not conjugated if it is an infinitive (*to* run, *to* go, *to* do).

Fragment	*Corrected*
☒ Jim to program a computer	☑ Jim *is* to program a computer.
	OR
	☑ Jim program*s* a computer.

Each sentence must have a complete conjugated verb. The verb in one sentence cannot be thought of as part of the next sentence; the verb *must actually appear* in the sentence.

☒ Marie has many varied interests. Such as art, psychology, and politics.

The first statement is a complete sentence; the second is a fragment because it has no verb.

TRY IT OUT

DRAW TWO LINES UNDER THE VERBS IN THE FOLLOWING WORD GROUPS. THEN CORRECT ANY FRAGMENTS SO THAT THEY ARE COMPLETE SENTENCES.

1. The shiny red Corvette with black leather seats, a four-speaker stereo radio, and an expensive alarm system.
2. The lifeguard trying to save a 300-pound man from drowning in this bathtub.
3. Tapeworms can grow over 100 feet long.

II. Find the Subject. The *subject* is the noun or pronoun unit about which something is said. To find the subject of a sentence, first find the complete conjugated verb. Then simply ask: *Who* or *what* is doing the action?

☑ The boy threw the ball.

The verb is *threw. Who* or *what* threw? The *boy* threw. Therefore, *boy* is the subject of the sentence.

In a command, the subject is usually not given but it is implied as *you.*

☑ Run for your life!

☑ Close the window before it rains!

Who should run? *You.* Who should close the window? *You.* Therefore, *you* is the subject of these and most commands.

A word group may sometimes be the subject of a sentence.

☑ Going to a movie is great fun.

☑ Whoever can pass the test will be given an A as a grade.

To find the subject, you just find the verb and ask the same question: *Who* or *what* is great fun? *Going to a movie. Who* or *what* will be given an A as a grade? *Whoever can pass the test.* Therefore, a word group is the subject of each sentence.

You may sometimes forget to include the subject of a sentence because you have just used it in the preceding sentence and it seems to be the subject of the fragment. However, you must always remember that the subject *must* be included in each sentence (with the exception of a command).

☒ The athlete felt nervous as she ran across the mat. Did a forward somersault and then finished with a back flip.

The first statement is a complete sentence; the second is a fragment because it has no subject. *Who* did a forward somersault and a back flip? The fragment does not tell us.

To correct this error:

Connect the fragment to the preceding sentence.

Examples: The athlete felt nervous as she ran across the mat, did a forward somersault, and then finished with a back flip.

OR

Put a subject into the fragment.

She did a forward somersault and then finished with a back flip.

TRY IT OUT

DRAW TWO LINES UNDER THE VERBS AND ONE LINE UNDER THE SUBJECTS IN THE FOLLOWING WORD GROUPS. IF A SUBJECT IS MISSING, PUT ONE IN TO CHANGE THE FRAGMENT INTO A COMPLETE SENTENCE.

1. The actor slid helplessly across the wet stage.
2. Flew into the orchestra pit and then fell headfirst into the kettledrum.

III. Look to See If the Subject and Verb are Introduced by a Danger Word. If the conjugated verb and its subject are introduced by a Danger Word, you do not have a complete sentence; it does not express a complete thought. It is a cliff-hanger, because it begins a statement but does not finish it.

Example: If you come home . . . [*what?*]

Commonly Used Danger Words

after	unless	who
although (though)	how	whom
as (as if)	when	which
because	where	that
before	while	whoever
if	until	whomever
once	so that	what
since	whether	whatever

Most of the Danger Words are readily noticed because they come before the expression they affect.

☒ Because he is a very ambitious person

☒ After the waiter calculated the bill

☒ Although a family budget is important

The introductory Danger Word leaves each of these a fragment without a complete thought. What happened because he is such an ambitious person? What happened after the waiter calculated the bill? What happened although a family budget is important? The Danger Words suggest that the answers to these questions must be included in the sentence.

In the box on the previous page, the Danger Words that are listed in the right-hand column (especially *who, which,* and *that*) frequently appear between the subject and verb.

☒ A person who is very competitive

☒ The movie which won many awards

☒ The trash that clutters our streets

None of these sentence fragments tells the reader what happened. What will a person who is very competitive do? What about the movie? What about the trash? The thought is not complete.

A Special Note: Do not avoid the Danger Words completely. When used correctly, they are excellent tools for writing complex sentences. This use will be fully illustrated in the next chapter.

To correct the fragment caused by a Danger Word:

Attach the fragment to the previous sentence or to the one that follows, whichever is most closely connected in thought to the fragment.	*Examples:* Tom is looking for a better job because he is a very ambitious person. After the waiter calculated the bill, he presented it to the customer.
OR	
Complete the fragment with the necessary words.	A person who is very competitive usually enjoys sports.

A PROOFREADING SUGGESTION: You may find it easier to spot a fragment in your writing if you read your paragraphs from the last sentence to the first sentence. In this way, you disconnect the fragment from the surrounding sentences, which are usually closely linked to the fragment in thought and which, therefore, might blend when you read them.

TRY IT OUT

DRAW TWO LINES UNDER THE VERBS, DRAW ONE LINE UNDER THE SUBJECTS, AND CIRCLE ANY *DANGER WORDS* IN THE FOLLOWING WORD GROUPS. CORRECT THE FRAGMENTS SO THAT THEY ARE COMPLETE SENTENCES.

1. Some farmers wear earplugs when feeding their pigs.
2. Because pigs can make more noise than a chainsaw.
3. A noise that can permanently damage a person's hearing.

EXERCISE 3D: Rewrite any fragments so that they are complete sentences. Some of the word groups may already be complete; if the word group is complete, put a period at the end and write nothing else.

1. To make enough money to pay for college

   ____

2. Although soccer is very popular in Europe and South America

   ____

3. Sylvester Stallone, one of the wealthiest actors in the world

   ____

4. A disease that strikes people of all ages

   ____

5. Whoever watches six hours of television a day

   ____

6. An article about the dangers of motorcycle racing

____

7. A cow has four stomachs

____

8. Because the cost of living is so high these days

____

9. Students who listen to MP3 players in class

____

10. Training a parrot to recite "The Pledge of Allegiance"

____

11. If you want to have an exciting date

____

12. An award as the world's worst singer

____

13. What my parents never taught me

____

14. After getting dizzy on the Lightning Loops roller coaster

____

15. Amazed by her ability to lift 600 pounds

____

16. Whenever I need money, my friends disappear

____

17. Driving a car on the sidewalk at a hundred miles per hour

____

18. Before I jumped from the burning building

____

19. The President's proposal to raise income taxes

____

20. A job working with children at a neighborhood day-care center

____

EXERCISE 3E: Each of the following paragraphs contains one fragment. Underline each fragment. Then rewrite it as a complete sentence. Use the space provided.

1. Mrs. Bernard Scheinberg of Austria had sixty-nine children. Including four sets of quadruplets, seven sets of triplets, and sixteen pairs of twins. After Mrs. Scheinberg died at the age of 56, her husband remarried. During his remaining years, he fathered an additional eighteen children by his second wife.

____

____

2. According to information from the Bureau of Justice Statistics, a branch of the United States Justice Department. It is dangerous to be a teenager in this country. Indeed, teenagers are more than twice as likely as adults to be raped, robbed, assaulted, or murdered. In one recent year, for example, more than 60 of every 1,000 teens were victims of violent crime, compared with 27 of every 1,000 adults.

____

____

3. Mrs. Sarah Winchester of San Jose, California, was afraid that she would die as soon as her house was finished. So she had workers adding on to her mansion continuously for nearly thirty-eight years. By the time she died at the age of 83, it had already become the world's largest private dwelling. A seven-story house covering six acres and containing 160 rooms, 2,000 doors, 10,000 windows, 9 kitchens, and miles of secret passageways.

____

____

4. Catherine I of Russia had an affair with her servant William. When her husband, Czar Peter the Great, learned of the affair, he had William's head cut off. And then had it bottled in preservatives and placed on a dresser in Catherine's bedroom. Catherine was never unfaithful again.

____

____

5. An electric eel can produce a shock of over 600 volts. More than enough power to kill a full-grown human. The eel uses this power as radar to find live food. Then it electrocutes its victim before eating it.

____

____

6. How to become financially secure for the rest of your life. First, go to college to get a good education. Then, find a job with a company that offers many opportunities for advancement. Finally, if the first two steps do not prove successful, buy a lottery ticket and pray that you win a fortune.

____

____

7. In 1901 King C. Gillette decided to start a safety razor company. Because he was poor, he got twenty of his friends to invest in his venture. Each of the people paid $250 for 500 shares of the new company. An investment which would now be worth about $50 million.

____

____

8. The Mormon Family History Library in Salt Lake City, Utah, helps people of all races and religions to trace their roots. This unusual facility has so far gathered information about 2 billion of the world's inhabitants. Almost a third of all those who have ever lived on the earth since the beginning of written records in the 1500's. The library's information is also available through approximately 800 Family History Centers located around the country.

____

____

9. After the Mayflower delivered the Pilgrims to the New World in 1620. The ship was then used to bring slaves from Africa. On later trips she carried rice and other types of food. Eventually, the Mayflower was converted into a barn that still stands in Buckingham, England.

____

____

10. Erich von Kardoff, a seventeenth-century German knight, fought three deadly duels. Each time simply because his opponents had spelled his name with only one *f*. He killed the first two offenders and was himself killed in the third duel. Perhaps he just should have changed his name.

____

____

11. The builders of the Egyptian pyramids apparently had an almost superhuman ability. They were able to lift five-ton blocks of stone hundreds of feet into the air without electrical machinery. The workers were also able to fit together over 2 million of these huge blocks to form a perfect pyramid shape. An amazing accomplishment when one considers that the pyramids were built over 4,000 years ago with only the simplest tools.

____

____

12. The healthiest period of a human being's life is between the ages of 5 and 15. The years of a person's greatest natural protection against diseases. The protection continues well into a person's twenties. From the thirties onward, however, the quality of the body's overall health decreases.

____

____

 Comma Splices and Run-On Sentences

Like sentence fragments, the comma splice and the run-on sentence are serious errors which can be eliminated with the help of the Three-Step Test of Sentence Completeness (see page 104). Let's use the test on the following sentences.

✔ Tony is immoral. He steals hubcaps for a living.

Both of these sentences are complete because each has a subject and verb not introduced by a Danger Word. Now let's examine the same sentences which have undergone one seemingly minor change.

☒ Tony is immoral, he steals hubcaps for a living.

We still have the same complete sentences, but they have now been joined by a comma. Because two complete sentences cannot be joined by just a comma, the above illustration is an error. It is called a *comma splice.*

Notice how the next set of sentences makes the same mistake.

☒ The U.S. Post Office Department provides reliable service, however, sometimes a letter is not delivered for weeks, months, or even years.

There are two separate subjects and two separate verbs. Thus, we have two distinct sentences that should not be joined with a comma, as the corrected sentences below indicate.

✔ The U.S. Post Office Department provides reliable service. However, sometimes a letter is not delivered for weeks, months, or even years.

Now use the test of sentence completeness to examine the following:

☒ Because Karen was very competitive, she entered a pie-eating contest, then she had to spend a week in the hospital.

Although the first possible subject and verb are canceled out by the Danger Word *because,* we are still left with two subject–verb sets. Again, we have two sentences that have been joined together with a comma and need to be separated.

> ✔ Because Karen was very competitive, she entered a pie-eating contest. Then she had to spend a week in the hospital.

Now compare the previous error to the one made in the next sentences.

> ☒ Sex education must certainly be a thought-provoking subject it is easy to form a discussion group for such a topic.

Here we also have two separate subject–verb sets in what should be two sentences. But unlike the comma splice, these sentences have been joined together without even a comma. This is called a *run-on sentence.*

> ✔ Sex education must certainly be a thought-provoking subject. It is easy to form a discussion group for such a topic.

Now the sentences are written correctly. You should note that the run-on is considered a more serious error than the comma splice because it implies that the writer does not sense a pause between two distinct thoughts.

When you proofread your writing for mistakes, pay particular attention to certain words and thought relationships that can lead to comma splices and run-ons. The Pointers chart on this and the following page illustrates some of the most common types of these errors.

POINTERS FOR AVOIDING COMMA SPLICES AND RUN-ONS

1. Words and expressions such as *therefore, however, then, furthermore, for example,* and *thus* (see page 385 for a complete list) help your writing to flow more smoothly. But do *not* use these words to join two complete sentences.

Many people are lonely however, few know how to make friends.

☒ Many people are lonely, however, few know how to make friends.

✔ Many people are lonely. However, few know how to make friends.

(Continued)

(Continued)

2. The words *I, you, he, she, we, they,* and *it* refer to someone or something already mentioned. But do *not* use these words to join two complete sentences.	☒ Bicycles are enjoyable to ride they give people a feeling of great freedom. ☒ Bicycles are enjoyable to ride, they give people a feeling of great freedom. ✔ Bicycles are enjoyable to ride. They give people a feeling of great freedom.
3. A sentence sometimes explains or adds to a point made in a previous sentence. Although the two sentences are closely linked in thought, they must be punctuated as two separate sentences.	☒ There are many varieties of tomato beefsteak and plum are two popular ones. ☒ There are many varieties of tomato, beefsteak and plum are two popular ones. ✔ There are many varieties of tomato. Beefsteak and plum are two popular ones.

There are several ways to correct the comma splice and run-on sentence. The method you choose will depend on the content of your sentences. To correct your error you might use one of these methods.

End the first sentence with a period and begin a new sentence with a capital letter.	*Examples:* The U.S. Post Office Department provides reliable service. However, sometimes a letter is not delivered for weeks, months, or even years.
OR	
Place a semicolon between two sentences if they are closely related in idea. Do not begin the second sentence with a capital letter.	Because Karen was very competitive, she entered a pie-eating contest; then she had to spend a week in the hospital.
OR	
If the two sentences are of equal importance, join them with one of these seven conjunctions: *and, or, nor, but, for, so, yet.* Notice that the conjunction is preceded by a comma.	Tony is immoral, for he steals hubcaps for a living.

TRY IT OUT

DRAW TWO LINES UNDER THE VERBS, DRAW ONE LINE UNDER THE SUBJECTS, AND CIRCLE ANY DANGER WORDS IN THE FOLLOWING WORD GROUPS. THEN CORRECT THE COMMA SPLICES AND RUN-ON SENTENCES.

1. Before the yo-yo was ever used as a toy, it was a weapon in the Philippine Islands it weighed four pounds and had a twenty-foot cord.

2. George Washington was not the first President of the United States the first President was John Hanson, who was elected by the Continental Congress to serve for one year.

3. The cormorant bird weighs between six and eight pounds, however, it usually eats about fifteen pounds of food a day.

EXERCISE 3F: Identify the comma splices and run-ons and revise them in the spaces provided. Some of the sentences may be correct as they are; if they are correct, write *correct.*

1. When astronauts first shaved in space, their weightless whiskers floated up to the ceiling, as a result, a special razor had to be developed to suck in the whiskers like a vacuum cleaner.

 ____

 ____

2. Teabags used to be made of silk now they are made of paper.

 ____

 ____

3. Pigs are smart animals they can be taught to sit up and roll over.

 ____

 ____

4. New Zealand was the first country in the world to give women the right to vote Switzerland, on the other hand, did not allow women to vote in national elections until 1971.

 ____

 ____

5. If you could travel at the speed of light, you could reach the sun in only eight minutes, isn't that fascinating?

 ____

 ____

6. Lakewood, Australia, is a town on wheels located in the heart of the lumber and gold mining area, it has its homes, shops, a post office, and a police station mounted on railroad cars.

 ____

 ____

7. The North Pole has only one sunrise and one sunset each year the sun rises on March 21 and sets on September 21.

8. A person's feet can expand as much as 5 percent during an average day, therefore, it is best to shop for shoes in the afternoon or evening.

9. My Uncle Joe had no luck he made payments on a cemetery plot for ten years then he fell off a ship and was lost at sea.

10. If all the blood vessels in a person's body were straightened out and placed end to end, they would stretch for a distance of about 100,000 miles, which is long enough to go around the equator four times.

11. When the Australian toad frog is threatened by a snake, it does not hop away to safety instead it puffs itself up and floats away like a toy balloon.

12. Florida is not the southernmost state in the United States Hawaii is farther south.

13. During a fierce battle in World War II, Ernest Young of Pasadena, Texas, was shot in the chest he coughed up the bullet twenty-eight years later.

14. If hot water is suddenly poured into a glass, the glass is more likely to break if it is thick than if it is thin, that is why test tubes are made of thin glass.

____

____

15. Butchers get veal and beef from the same type of cattle veal comes from calves less than three months old beef comes from older animals.

____

____

16. A fish can produce a huge number of offspring, for example, a seven-pound cod can lay 7 million eggs at one time.

____

____

17. Please close your eyes I want to surprise you.

____

____

18. New batteries should be stored in a refrigerator, otherwise, they will begin to lose their freshness quickly.

____

____

19. When an airliner is flying at 40,000 feet, the temperature inside the cabin is 72 degrees, the outside temperature is between 80 and 100 degrees below zero.

____

____

20. The king cobra has venom so deadly that one drop could kill 150 people, nevertheless, W. E. Haast of Miami, Florida, has managed to survive sixty-eight cobra bites.

____

____

EXERCISE 3G: Follow the directions for each item. Be sure to use whatever punctuation is required. If necessary, refer back to page 117 for help.

1. Write a statement about fireworks, using two complete sentences joined by one of the seven connectors: *and, but, for, nor, or, so, yet.*

   ____

   ____

2. Write two complete sentences about your most important possession. Begin the second sentence with the word *it.*

   ____

   ____

3. Using an amusement park as your subject, write two complete sentences that can be joined by a semicolon.

   ____

   ____

4. Write two complete sentences about divorce, beginning the second sentence with the word *therefore.*

   ____

   ____

5. Write a statement about cable television, using two complete sentences joined by one of the seven connectors: *and, but, for, nor, or, so, yet.*

   ____

   ____

6. Write two complete sentences describing your plans for the future. Begin the second sentence with the word *then.*

   ____

   ____

7. Using jealousy as your subject, write two complete sentences that can be joined by a semicolon.

   ____

   ____

8. Write two complete sentences about the food served at your favorite restaurant. Begin the second sentence with the expression *for example.*

____

____

9. Write two complete sentences about a person you admire, beginning the second sentence with the word *he* or *she.*

____

____

10. Write two complete sentences about your writing ability, beginning the second sentence with the word *however.*

____

____

EXERCISE 3H: REFRESHER

1. CORRECT THE FRAGMENTS, COMMA SPLICES, AND RUN-ONS IN THE PARAGRAPHS BELOW.
2. ANSWER THE ADDITIONAL QUESTIONS THAT FOLLOW THE PARAGRAPHS.

Drinking on campus is a much more serious problem than most students realize. In fact, 10 to 15 percent of college students are alcoholics. These students may take alcohol for granted. Because they have seen their parents drink it regularly at home. When the students get to college, drinking seems to be accepted there too, beer companies may even advertise in the campus newspaper. Being away from home and in a new environment can be difficult. As a result, some students start drinking to cover feelings of loneliness then at a college party, they may drink to feel accepted and at ease in a new social situation. Later, they may begin drinking more heavily to escape the pressure of writing term papers and studying for exams, however, because of the alcohol abuse, the students get poor grades. To escape the feeling of failure, they drink even more. Until eventually what seemed like a harmless habit has become a dangerous addiction.

Students who abuse alcohol do not realize the risks they are taking. Research studies indicate that one in five students does not practice safe sex when drinking, which he or she would probably do if sober. At least 90 percent of all college rapes occur when the victim or the assailant has been drinking, in addition, more than 30 percent of all fatal drunk-driving accidents are caused by drivers under the age of 25. From time to time, tragic alcohol-related accidents also happen on campus. For example, a drunk student at a wild party falling from a second-floor window and being paralyzed, or a fraternity pledge chugging a whole bottle of bourbon, falling into a coma, and dying. Indeed, alcohol abuse on campus is a serious problem that will not go away until students begin to treat alcohol like what it is. A dangerous drug that happens to be legal.

ADDITIONAL QUESTIONS

1. What is the topic sentence of each paragraph?

   a. Paragraph 1: ______________________

   ____

   b. Paragraph 2: ______________________

   ____

2. Is there more than one main idea in each paragraph?

   a. Paragraph 1: ______________________

   ____

   b. Paragraph 2: ______________________

   ____

3. What order is used to develop the first paragraph?

   ____

SPRINGBOARDS TO WRITING

Using your knowledge of the writing process, explained on pages 14–16, write a paragraph or essay related to this chapter's central theme, *smoking as an addiction,* which is introduced on pages 94–96.

PREWRITING

To think of topics to write about, look at the advertisements, read the essay, and answer the questions that follow each. If you prefer, select one of the writing springboards below. (All paragraph numbers refer to the essay that starts on page 94.) To develop your ideas, use the prewriting techniques described on pages 17–22.

WRITING A PARAGRAPH *(For help, see the Pointers on page 51.)*

1. Do you agree with Alice Walker's statement that "most people who try to quit smoking do not succeed"? (See paragraph 11.)
2. Do parents who smoke get their children addicted by setting a bad example?
3. Cigarette smoking should (should not) be banned from movies and T.V.
4. Do you agree with Alice Walker that cigarette companies target poor people? (See paragraph 10.)
5. The federal government should (should not) greatly increase the tax on cigarettes to discourage people from smoking.
6. I remember the first time I ever smoked a cigarette.

WRITING AN ESSAY *(For help, see the Pointers on pages 54–55.)*

7. Why Do People Smoke Cigarettes?
8. My Plan to Get People to Stop Smoking
9. Smoking Cigarettes Does (Does Not) Have Some Good Effects
10. Why I Can't Quit Smoking
11. It's a Free Country and I'll Smoke If I Want To
12. Cigarette Smoking Should (Should Not) Be Banned in All Public Places
13. Agree or disagree: Cigarette advertising should be banned and tobacco companies should be required to pay for antismoking advertising.
14. Cigarettes Should (Should Not) Be Made Illegal
15. Alcoholic Beverages Should (Should Not) Be Made Illegal (For a start, see the Refresher on page 123.)
16. The Sale of Marijuana Should (Should Not) Be Legalized
17. The Major Reasons Why People Take Illegal Drugs
18. Agree or disagree with this statement by W. Somerset Maugham: "The unfortunate thing about this world is that the good habits are much easier to give up than the bad ones."

STAN MACK'S TRUE TALES

Evaluating His Values

MY PARENTS SAY IT'S TIME I CAME HOME. BUT I JUST MET LISA IN CLASS AND HAD MY FIRST DATE EVER.

COLLEGE OF BUSINESS ADMINIS-TRATION

AS LISA AND I CAME OUT OF THE MOVIE, A CAB PULLED UP. THE DRIVER WAS A FRIEND FROM MY COUNTRY.

I KNEW IF HE SAW ME, HE'D TELL MY ROOM-MATES WHO'D TELL MY PARENTS WHO'D HAVE A HEART ATTACK.

I DUCKED AWAY. LISA SAID, "WHAT'S UP?" I SAID, "IN MY CULTURE YOU DON'T DATE TILL YOU'RE GETTING MARRIED."

IN FRONT OF THE MUSEUM, I COULDN'T HELP IT, WE KISSED! THEN I APOLOGIZED 30 TIMES.

I SAID, "THAT WAS MY FIRST KISS— WAS IT YOURS?" THEN I FELT STUPID BECAUSE SHE WAS BORN HERE.

I WENT TO THE MOSQUE AND PRAYED FOR MY LOST VALUES... AS I REALIZED IT WOULD HAPPEN AGAIN.

MY PARENTS SAY, "IF YOU STAY IN AMERICA, YOU'LL BECOME DIVORCED, A SINGLE PARENT, AND YOU'LL SEND US TO A NURSING HOME."

B·B·Q CHEESESTEAK BURGERS FRIES

BUT I'M THINKING OF ASSIMILATING AND CHANGING MY MAJOR FROM BUSINESS TO FILM.

SLURP

e-mail: stanmack@aol.com

Chapter 4

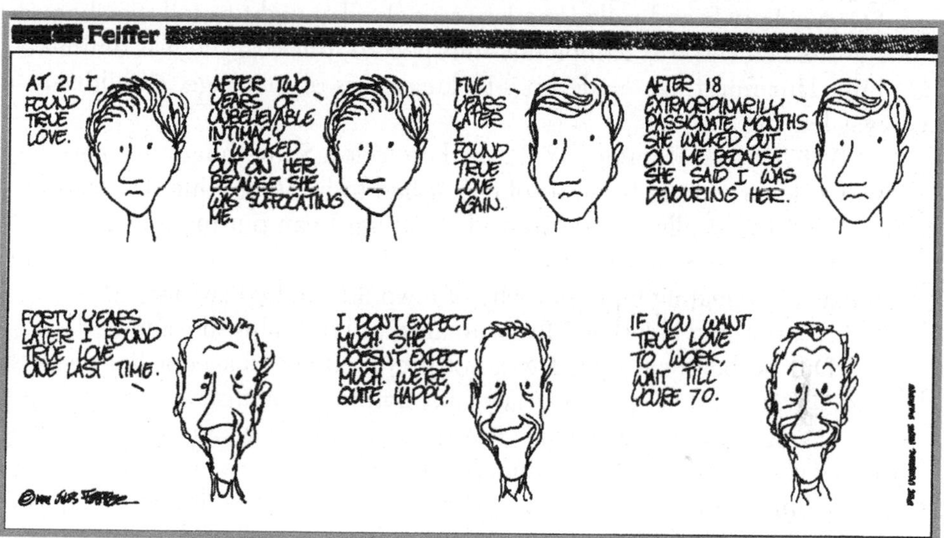

SPRINGBOARDS TO THINKING

For informal, not written, response . . . to stimulate your thinking

1. Read the cartoon on the opposite page. Do you think that people from other countries have better values than Americans? Explain your point of view.
2. If the boy stays in America, do you think that he will probably become divorced? . . . that he will probably become a single parent? . . . that he will probably send his parents to a nursing home? Why or why not?
3. What is the underlying message of the cartoon at the top of the page?
4. Do you think that most married Americans expect too much from their husbands or wives? Explain your point of view.
5. Why do you think the divorce rate is so high in the United States?

Pursuit of Happiness

Dympna Ugwu-Oju

(1) My best friend called me late on Saturday-night to tell me she was leaving her husband. It was completely unexpected, but yes, she was definitely leaving him. Her mind was made up—16 long years of marriage, 4 children—and she was leaving.

"Why? What Happened?" I asked on reflex. Something must have happened; why else would she be so resolute? It had to be something devastating.

"Nothing, really," she answered, "nothing I can put my finger on."

"Is he having an affair? Is he involved with someone else?" He didn't strike me as the cheating type, but why else would she be leaving?

"No, nothing like that." I was amazed at how calm she sounded.

"Did he beat you up?" I was not prepared yet to accept her dismissive attitude. Women don't end marriages for nothing. She just wasn't leveling.

"It's nothing in particular." She spoke haltingly, weighing every word. "All I know is that I've been very unhappy lately."

"Uhm, I'm listening," I nudged her, waiting for the litanies of abuse, of deprivation. But she said no more. "I just thought you should hear it from me," she added as we said our goodbyes.

(2) I waited two days and called her back. I knew I had to tread very lightly. "Just tell me one thing and I'll leave you alone: Are *you* having an affair?" That wasn't the question I wanted to ask, but it popped out.

"No! Are you crazy? How could you even ask me that?" She laughed out loud. Then sensing my need to come to terms with her news, she said she'd call me back after her husband was asleep.

(3) As I waited, I pondered the inquisition our friends would put me through. My friend and I and both our husbands, like a majority of our friends, are Nigerians. While we've lived in the United States for most of our adulthood and for all intents and purposes live like Americans, we identify closely with our traditional Ibo culture. An Ibo woman is born (educated if she is lucky), marries, procreates (a definite must, male children preferably) and dies when her time comes, God rest her soul. Women of our generation, educated and all, are expected to live through our husbands and children as our mothers and grandmothers did before us.

(4) An Ibo woman has very little personal identity, even if she lives in the United States and has success in her career. Our culture takes very little pride in a woman's accomplishment. At an Ibo gathering a woman is more likely to be asked whose wife or mother she is before she is asked her name or what she does for a living. If the woman is accomplished but unmarried, people will say, "But where is she going with all that success?" Ibos cling to the adage that a woman is worth nothing unless she's married and has children.

(5) I am as guilty as any other Ibo woman living in the United States in perpetuating this. Professionally, I am more successful than the majority of Ibo men I've met in this country, yet when we gather for a party, usually to celebrate a marriage or birth, I join the women in the kitchen to prepare food and serve the men. I remember to curtsy just so before the older men, looking away to avoid meeting their eyes. I glow with pride when other men tease my husband about his "good wife." I often lead the women in the Ibo wedding song: "It is as it should be; give her the keys to her kitchen." At birth ceremonies, I start the chant: "Without a child, what would a woman be?" It is a song my mother sang and one which every Ibo woman knows like her own name.

(6) I know the rules and the consequences of breaking them. Our culture is unforgiving of a stubborn woman. She always gets the maximum punishment—ostracism. "She thinks she's smart; let's see if she can marry herself" is how mistreatment of a noncompliant woman is justified.

(7) To the surprise of my American friends. I've never had difficulty separating my Ibo self from my professional and everyday American life. At work, I'm as assertive as any American-born female. I raise my voice as loud as necessary to be heard in meetings. At conferences where I present papers on "Women from the Third World," I make serious arguments about the need for international intervention in countries where women are deprived of all rights, where women are subjected to clitorectomies, where baby girls are killed to make room for boys. Yet as easily as I switch from speaking English to Ibo, I am content to slide into the role of the submissive and obedient wife. I never confuse my two selves.

(8) Hundreds of thousands of women from the third world and other traditional societies share my experience. We straddle two cultures, cultures that are often in opposition. Mainstream America, the culture we embrace in our professional lives, dictates that we be assertive and independent—like men. Our traditional culture, dictated by religion and years of socialization, demands that we be docile and content in our roles as mothers and wives—careers or not.

(9) But, suddenly, my best friend, steeped in the Ibo culture as much as I am, tells me she's leaving her husband—not for any offenses he's committed but because she is unhappy. I think of the question my mother and her mother would ask: "What on earth does she want?" She has everything any woman (Ibo woman, that is) would want: a professional husband (from a good family back

In a traditional culture, women go along in **perpetuating**—continuing forever—the belief that they must serve men to avoid being punished.

In a traditional culture, women who do not follow the rules face **ostracism**—the state of being cut off from family and friends, having no spoken or personal contact.

In a traditional culture, women may be **subjected to**—forced to experience—cruel treatment by their husbands because they have no legal rights.

In a traditional culture, women must be **submissive** to their husbands in that they must surrender themselves to their husbands' control.

In a traditional culture, women must be **obedient** in that they must do what they are told to do.

In a traditional culture, women must do whatever their husbands **dictate** or order them to do.

In a traditional culture, women are encouraged to be **docile**—easily managed and willing to do as told.

EXERCISE 4A: Match each sentence with a vocabulary word from this lesson.

1. The sergeant told the new recruits that they must surrender themselves to his control.	1. ____________
2. My wedding will be based on customs that have been handed down for generations.	2. ____________
3. After my dog attacked the letter carrier, I trained her to do what she is told.	3. ____________
4. The idea that he might not graduate on time overpowered his thoughts and feelings.	4. ____________
5. Because she cheated on the exam, her classmates cut off all spoken and personal contact with her.	5. ____________
6. My sick grandmother is easily managed and willing to do as she's told.	6. ____________
7. When I go on a diet, I am forbidden to have fattening foods.	7. ____________

8. He can't order me to stay home while he goes out with his friends. 8. ____________________

9. Although people may complain about some aspects of democracy, most of us are in favor of continuing it forever. 9. ____________________

10. The witness was forced to experience long hours of questioning by the lawyer. 10. ____________________

11. When the power company turned off the electricity, it was a great loss. 11. ____________________

Lesson Two: ***The Vocabulary of Women in Mainstream America***

The essay "Pursuit of Happiness" by Dympna Ugwu-Oju includes words that are useful when you are discussing women in mainstream America.

mainstream (paragraph 8)
resolute (1)
litanies (1)
pondered (3)
accomplished (4)
noncompliant (6)
justified (6)
assertive (7)
opposition (8)
fulfillment (10)

Women in **mainstream** America follow the customs and beliefs that are widely accepted by society.

Women in mainstream America are **resolute**—absolutely firm and determined—that they have the same rights that men have.

Women in mainstream America can recite **litanies**—long lists that are repeated over and over—of unequal treatment such as not receiving the same salaries and promotions that men receive.

Women in mainstream America have **pondered**—thought long and carefully—about how to get full equality.

Women in mainstream America who are as **accomplished** or skilled as men in a job expect equal pay.

Women in mainstream America are **noncompliant**—unwilling to give in to others' wishes—in their desire for full equality.

Women in mainstream America who have jobs feel **justified** or right in expecting their husbands to share the family work.

Women in mainstream America are **assertive**—forceful and confident in stating their opinions—expecting that others recognize their rights, no matter how long it takes.

Women in mainstream America face many different kinds of **opposition**—attempts to work forcefully against them—the goals that many women want to achieve.

Women in mainstream America find great **fulfillment**—sense of personal accomplishment—in the progress they have made toward equal rights with men.

EXERCISE 4B: For each word in italics, circle the definition closest in meaning.

1. If an action is *justified,* it is
   a. popular.
   b. right.
   c. easy to do.
   d. important.
2. If you *pondered* a decision, you
   a. delayed making it.
   b. talked to a friend about it.
   c. thought about it long and carefully.
   d. changed your mind about it several times.
3. A sense of *fulfillment* is
   a. a feeling of being too full after eating.
   b. a feeling of extreme confidence.
   c. a feeling of having too many responsibilities.
   d. a feeling of personal accomplishment.
4. If you are *resolute,* you are
   a. tired and discouraged.
   b. firm and determined.
   c. eager to please others.
   d. calm and relaxed.
5. If you face *opposition,* you face
   a. others trying to keep you from achieving your goals.
   b. going into debt.
   c. losing your eyesight.
   d. someone trying to sell you something you do not want.

6. If you are *accomplished* at something, you are
   a. able to do it with either your left or your right hand.
   b. one of very few people who can do it.
   c. skilled at doing it.
   d. very clumsy at doing it.
7. People who are *assertive*
   a. try to make other people happy.
   b. travel around the country giving speeches.
   c. state their opinions forcefully.
   d. are always willing to help others.
8. *Litanies* are
   a. portable beds used to carry sick people.
   b. long lists that are repeated over and over again.
   c. price lists at discount department stores.
   d. a new kind of scorecard used by professional sports teams.
9. If you are part of *mainstream* America, you are
   a. following the widely accepted beliefs.
   b. living near a large body of water.
   c. in the middle of a disagreement between powerful forces.
   d. part of the movement to clean up our environment.
10. Someone who is *noncompliant* is
    a. unprepared for a serious emergency.
    b. unable to keep a secret or promise.
    c. unable to break a bad habit that bothers others.
    d. unwilling to give in to others' wishes.

SPELLING

Proofreading

When a friend or teacher points out a misspelled word in your writing, do you sometimes insist, "But I know how to spell that word"? As we search for errors in our writing, we all tend to overlook the easy words and concentrate on the difficult ones. This leads to the painful experience of losing credit on a paper because of careless spelling errors. Thus, one of the most important skills that a writer can learn is to proofread.

When you first learned to read, your eyes concentrated on each word and each letter within that word. But as your reading speed increased, you began to scan the sentences, paying attention only to certain key words. This is a fine technique for reading—but not for *proofreading*. To proofread your writing with success, you must slow down your reading speed in order to take in the individual letters of each word. It has been found that the most effective way to do this is to place a ruler or sheet of paper under the line you are proofreading. Your eyes are now forced to move more slowly because they cannot automatically run on to the next line.

With the sheet of paper or ruler placed under the line, begin to examine each word, allowing the tip of your pen or pencil to rest on each syllable as you read it. If necessary, pronounce each word aloud. Most important, as you proofread do not exceed your vision span; that is, do not exceed the number of letters you are able to identify clearly with a single glance. To determine your vision span, look at the top of the following triangle and then look down, reading the letters on each line *without moving your eyes.* When you can no longer identify all the letters on a line with a single glance, you have reached your limit and have determined your vision span.

e
e n
e n h
e n h s
e n h s v
e n h s v k
e n h s v k b
e n h s v k b t
e n h s v k b t m
e n h s v k b t m l
e n h s v k b t m l o

Most people are able to identify about six letters without moving their eyes. Whatever your span, do not try to exceed it when you are proofreading your writing. Now read the triangle of words given below. When you reach a group of letters that exceeds your vision span, you should divide them into smaller units that you can check more accurately.

I
a m
s a d
w h e n
b o o k s
r e v e a l
v a r i o u s
p e r s o n a l
h a r d s h i p s
c o n c e r n i n g
i l l u s t r i o u s
g o v e r n m e n t a l
a c q u a i n t a n c e s

These few simple proofreading techniques can probably help you eliminate about half of your spelling errors. Just remember to place a sheet of paper or a ruler under the line of writing, to use a pen or pencil to mark off the syllables, and not to exceed your vision span.

Although this discussion has been limited to proofreading for spelling errors, the methods given are also useful for finding errors in grammar and punctuation. Again, it is a matter of reading slowly and with enough concentration to pick out your errors.

EXERCISE 4C: Proofreading Using the proofreading techniques given in this chapter, proofread the following paragraph for spelling errors. Make the needed corrections in the space directly above the misspelled words. If necessary, check your spelling against the list of Spelling Demons in Appendix III.

Studies indicate that arguments about financal matters are often a major factor in a couple's desicion to get a divorce. The studies also emphasise that these money problems influnce the marrages of people from all age groups and economic levels of society. For example, a teenage couple may not be perpared to handel the responsibity of spending money wisely. As a result, they could fail to antisipate the need for funds to deal with a posible emergency. Then when such a special ocassion arises, the financal pressures can *lead to arguments that realy destroy the marrage. Such arguments can also devide a wealthy couple. In one instance, a famous comedian who earned $5 million a year from television apearences planed to file for divorce because of his wife's rediculus spending habits. Durning the course of just one year, she spent $500,000 entirly on her wardrobe. Perhaps disasterous marrages such as these can be avoided if couples have honest discusions about how to handel money.*

Coordination

When two ideas are mentioned in a sentence, it is good to show their relationship to one another. One way to show relationship of ideas is to put them together using *coordination.* When you coordinate ideas, be sure that both ideas are related and of *equal importance.*

How to Employ Coordination

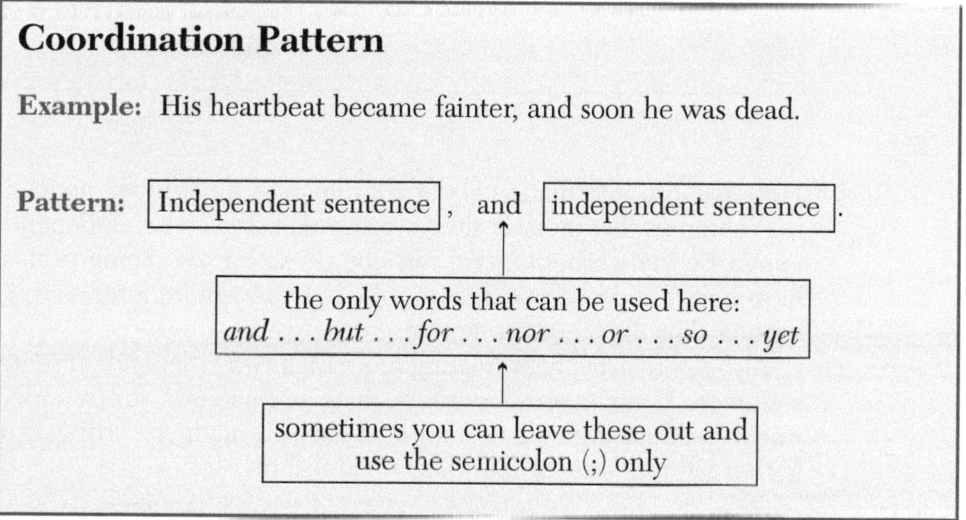

Coordination Pattern
Example: His heartbeat became fainter, and soon he was dead.
Pattern: Independent sentence , and independent sentence .
the only words that can be used here:
and . . . but . . . for . . . nor . . . or . . . so . . . yet
sometimes you can leave these out and use the semicolon (;) only

More examples:

She had prayed he would live, *but* she knew he would die.

She wept very hard, *for* now she was alone.

She would never forget his face, *nor* would she forget his warm eyes.

There was no one else in her life, *so* she missed him very much.

She knew she had to start getting over her sense of loss, *yet* she thought of him constantly.

Even months later she would listen for his heavy breathing, *or* she would expect to hear his frisky bark.

It was time to buy a new puppy; everyone told her that she must.

TRY IT OUT

Practice correct coordination. Does (a) or (b) coordinate better?

1. The weather was very cold, ____.
   a. but the sun shone brilliantly.
   b. but the lake froze.

2. Either we stop spending more than we can earn, ______.
   a. or we will have extra cash next month.
   b. or we will soon be bankrupt.

3. The captain gave the order to abandon ship, _____.
   a. for there were not enough lifeboats aboard.
   b. for the steamship was hopelessly ablaze.

Here is more information about coordination. First of all, notice in the preceding examples that there is always a comma between two independent sentences joined by the word *and, but, for, nor, or, so,* or *yet.* Some professional writers have begun to leave out this comma, but you will be safer as you practice your writing skills if you continue to use it.

Also, try to avoid coordinating more than two independent sentences into one sentence. If you overuse words such as *and* and *but,* for example, your writing might become difficult to read because you might be stringing your ideas together without attention to their relationships.

TRY IT OUT

Write the following with correct coordination.

1. A sentence about gossip. ______________________________

   ____

2. A sentence about boxing. ______________________________

   ____

3. A sentence about charity. ______________________________

   ____

EXERCISE 4D: Does (a) or (b) coordinate better?

1. Most television comedy shows are silly and boring, _____.
   a. but very few people watch them.
   b. but millions of people watch them.
2. Computer programming is a good occupation, _____.
   a. for many high-paying jobs are available.
   b. for it requires a great deal of training.
3. The President of the United States is paid $200,000 a year, _____.
   a. and he is given free use of the White House.
   b. and he has a very hard job.
4. Professional baseball players demand higher salaries, _____.
   a. or they will try to win more games this season.
   b. or they will go on strike.
5. The rock star mumbled all of the song lyrics, _____.
   a. yet they were hard to hear.
   b. yet they were easy to hear.
6. Most fast foods are not very nutritious, _____.
   a. nor are they inexpensive.
   b. nor are they available twenty-four hours a day.
7. The volcano exploded violently, _____.
   a. and the June weather was unusually cold.
   b. and the sky filled with a thick cloud of gray ash.
8. The sun can cause skin cancer, _____.
   a. yet some people sunbathe for hours at a time.
   b. yet many people use sunscreening lotions.
9. Anyone who owns an original Picasso painting is lucky, _____.
   a. for it could be worth a fortune.
   b. for Picasso painted for over seventy-five years.
10. Most Americans want cars that offer good gas mileage, _____.
    a. so automatic seat belts are available on all models.
    b. so four-cylinder models are selling well.

EXERCISE 4E: For each item, write an independent sentence that coordinates well with the sentence given. Remember that both parts must be related and of equal importance.

1. The spectators in the courtroom were becoming noisy, so ______________

____

2. Before you ride on a motorcycle without wearing your helmet, ______________

____

____

3. As long as people watch television for five or six hours a day, ______________

____

____

4. ______________________________, the school has started a new student-security system against muggers.

5. ______________________________, the Senate could not assemble enough votes to pass the anti-pollution regulations.

6. ______________________________, many childhood diseases such as measles and mumps can be avoided.

7. ______________________________, the presence of a nuclear power plant is frightening to many people.

8. Unless the rock concert is well organized, ______________________

____

9. Whether you like it or not, ______________________________

____

10. Because everyone was welcome at the garage sale, ______________________

____

____

EXERCISE 4I: Fill in a dependent section after the independent sentences given. Notice that a comma is not used.

1. An automobile can be a dangerous weapon ______________________

____

2. A few troublemakers can ruin a class ______________________

____

3. The train conductor stepped on the emergency brake ________________

____

4. Blind people can learn to live independently ____________________

____

____

5. People who wait on customers must have patience and good manners ____

____

____

EXERCISE 4J: On a separate sheet of paper, write a sentence using subordination for each topic below. Put the subordination section before the independent section, and use a comma to separate the parts.

1. cell phones
2. child abuse
3. income taxes
4. a horror film
5. being famous
6. a tourist attraction
7. Madonna
8. wrestling
9. "The Star-Spangled Banner"
10. Halloween

EXERCISE 4K: Here are sentences that use coordination. A few are better in this form, but most should be changed to subordination. Decide which ones would benefit from a change to subordination and rewrite them accordingly.

1. A chilling rain was falling, but hundreds of people turned out for the marathon race.

____

____

2. The painters had finished their job, and they asked the landlord for immediate payment.

____

____

3. The newspaper-delivery girl saved part of her weekly earnings, so she was finally able to buy the ten-speed bicycle she wanted.

____

____

4. Douglas likes to rebuild old cars, for he can sell them at a profit.

____

____

5. Dogs often make lively pets, yet many people prefer cats or birds because they demand much less attention than dogs do.

____

____

6. The surgeon operated with unusual speed, for the patient's vital signs were weak.

____

____

7. You keep practicing your ping-pong skills, and you will have a good chance to make the town's team.

____

____

8. This is what we can do: Either we apologize for our bad manners, or we will never be invited to their home again.

____

____

9. The presidential candidate was unable to gather enough support, so he decided to withdraw from the primary election.

____

____

10. The deaf student did not complain about his handicap, nor did he give up when he faced a new challenge.

____

____

EXERCISE 4L: Essay Analysis In the essay "Pursuit of Happiness," find examples of subordinate sentences that start with dependent sections. Give the first and last word of the entire sentence.

	First Word	. . .	*Last Word*
1. paragraph 3:	__________	. . .	__________
2. paragraph 3:	__________	. . .	__________
3. paragraph 4:	__________	. . .	__________
4. paragraph 12:	__________	. . .	__________

 A Special Case of Subordination

Subordination that starts with *who* or *which* often works best in the middle of the sentence.

Subordination Pattern 3

Example: Juan, who is worried about pollution, plans to be an ecologist.

Special Case Pattern: Independent, who ~~~~~~~~, sentence .

More examples: The *S.S. Norway*, which is docked at Pier 67, is crippled by a dock workers' strike.

Julia, who has an analytical mind, thinks carefully before she acts.

TRY IT OUT

FILL IN AN APPROPRIATE SUBORDINATION SECTION.

1. Martin Luther King, Jr., who ______________________________ was born on January 15, 1929.
2. Maine, which ______________________________ is the only state whose name contains just one syllable.

Here is more information about subordination. Use *who* to refer to a person, and use *which* to refer to a thing or place.

Note that in the pattern above, commas surround the subordinate section. This is because the subordination *adds information about a specific subject.* In the examples above, Juan is a specific man, the S.S. *Norway* is a specific ship, and Julia is a specific woman. Therefore, the information given in the subordination is *added information* not basic for identification, and you need to *add commas. When the information is needed* for basic identification, however, *no commas* are used to surround the subordinate section.

Subordination Pattern 4

Example: The man who is worried about pollution plans to be an ecologist.

Pattern: Independent who ~~~~~~~ sentence .

More examples: The ship that is docked at Pier 67 is crippled by a dockworkers strike.

The woman who has an analytical mind thinks carefully before she acts.

TRY IT OUT

FILL IN AN APPROPRIATE SUBORDINATE SECTION. ARE COMMAS NEEDED?

1. The child who ______________________________ probably started the fight.
2. The blizzard that ______________________________ finally blew out to sea.

EXERCISE 4M: Fill in an appropriate subordinate section. Surround the section with commas when necessary.

1. The old factory building that ______________________________ was destroyed by fire.
2. The young guitarist who ______________________________ agreed to perform for his classmates.
3. San Francisco, which ______________________________ is a city of great beauty.
4. The woman who ______________________________ dove into the water and saved the child's life.
5. The French language, which ______________________________ is spoken in Haiti.
6. John F. Kennedy, who ______________________________ was in constant pain from a back injury.

7. Houseplants that ______________________________ will stay healthy.

8. Anyone who ______________________________ can pass the examination.

9. The island of Cuba, which ______________________________ is located ninety miles south of Key West, Florida.

10. Arnold Schwarzenegger, who ______________________________ is paid about $20 million for each film he makes.

EXERCISE 4N: Combine these sentences using the words of coordination and subordination given in parentheses. Be sure to insert commas where needed. First, look at the examples given. Use your own paper if you need more space.

Examples:

A. Franklin was once the name of one of the United States.
Today it is a part of the state of Tennessee.
(but)
Franklin was once the name of one of the United States, but today it is a part of the state of Tennessee.

B. Beethoven believed that cold temperatures would stimulate his brain.
He often poured ice water over his head before sitting down to compose music.
(because)
Because Beethoven believed that cold temperatures would stimulate his brain, he often poured ice water over his head before sitting down to compose music.

C. Casanova spent his older years working as a librarian.
Casanova was considered the greatest lover and adventurer of his time.
(who)
Casanova, who was considered the greatest lover and adventurer of his time, spent his older years working as a librarian.

1. It takes seventeen muscles to smile.
It takes forty-three muscles to frown.
(but)

____

____

2. The expression “blind as a bat” is not scientific.
   Bats have eyes and can see.
   (for)

   ___

   ___

3. Large elephants eat over a hundred pounds of food each day.
   It is no wonder that these animals often weigh more than five tons.
   (because)

   ___

   ___

4. Howard Carter discovered King Tut’s tomb in Egypt.
   He quickly became known as a great archaeologist.
   (after)

   ___

   ___

5. The Atlanta airport in Georgia is the largest airport in the world.
   Chicago’s airport is the busiest.
   (while)

   ___

   ___

6. A junk has a flat bottom and two four-cornered sails.
   A junk is a Chinese sailboat made of wood.
   (which)

   ___

   ___

7. The earth travels through space at 66,000 miles per hour.
   You cannot feel the motion.
   It is so smooth.
   (but, because)

   ___

   ___

8. George Washington's wife had four children from a previous marriage.
George Washington had no children of his own.
There are no direct descendants of the first President of the United States.
(although, so)

____

____

____

9. Pericles was self-conscious about his pointed head.
Pericles was a leader in ancient Greece.
Pericles would pose for portraits only when wearing a helmet.
(who, so)

____

____

____

10. James Madison was the shortest President of the United States.
James Madison was five feet, four inches tall.
Abraham Lincoln was the tallest President.
Abraham Lincoln measured six feet, four inches.
(who, and, who)

____

____

____

11. River sand, not desert sand, must be used for building purposes.
Saudi Arabia must import sand from Scotland for use in construction.
Saudi Arabia contains one of the largest deserts in the world.
(because, which)

____

____

____

12. Nero did not fiddle while Rome burned.
The fiddle had not yet been invented.

Nero was in Antium, fifty miles away.
(because, and)

---

13. A poor swimmer goes into the Dead Sea.
He or she need not fear drowning.
The water is 25 percent salt, making it impossible to sink.
(if, because)

---

14. There is a street in New York City called Madison Avenue.
The building known as Madison Square Garden is on Eighth Avenue.
Madison Square Garden is a sports arena and convention center.
Madison Square Garden is not square.
Madison Square Garden does not contain a garden.
(although, which, and, and)

---

15. Many people thought that the idea was crazy.
Pirates believed that piercing the ears and wearing an earring improved their eyesight.
Today, a growing number of people no longer think this idea is so foolish.
According to acupuncture theory, putting a needle in the "auricular point" in the earlobe helps the eyes.
(although, but, because)

EXERCISE 4O: Combine these sentences using words of coordination and subordination. Be sure to insert commas where needed.

1. The planet Mercury is closest to the sun.
   The planet Pluto is farthest.

   ____

   ____

2. Strains occur in the muscles.
   Sprains occur in the ligaments.

   ____

   ____

3. Wolfgang Mozart was a great composer.
   No one knows where he is buried.

   ____

   ____

4. A starfish is cut into pieces.
   Each piece will grow a whole starfish.

   ____

   ____

5. Commercial jets are considered one of the safest forms of travel.
   Many people are afraid to fly.

   ____

   ____

6. A blackthorn tree always bursts into bloom on the coldest day of winter.
   The tree grows in the city of Bra, Italy.

   ____

   ____

7. Sweating helps people cool off.
   Dogs cool off by panting hard with their tongues hanging out.

   ____

   ____

8. Jean Causeur worked as a butcher for 101 years until he was 121.
   He died at the age of 131.

   ____

   ____

9. One invention that has changed little over the years is the parking meter.
   It was designed by Carl Magee from Oklahoma City in 1935.

   ____

   ____

10. It was not until 1941 that scientists established that no two sets of fingerprints are alike.
    Fingerprints were not accepted as evidence in court until after that time.

    ____

    ____

11. A tropical cyclone that gets its start in the Caribbean or West Indies is called a hurricane.
    The exact same type of storm system is called a typhoon when it originates in the West Pacific Ocean or the South China Sea.

    ____

    ____

12. There is a Chinese symbol.
    It means "good."
    It is formed by combining the symbol for *woman* with the symbol for *child*.

    ____

    ____

13. A crab is captured by its leg.
    It can escape by letting its leg fall off.
    Then it is able to grow a new leg to replace the lost one.

    ____

    ____

14. The Braille reading system for the blind was named after Louis Braille.
Louis Braille was blinded at the age of 3.
Louis Braille invented his reading method when he was in his twenties.

____

____

15. Russian aircraft bombed Finland on November 30, 1939.
The first bomb hit the Russian Embassy building.
The first bomb was dropped on the capital city of Helsinki.

____

____

EXERCISE 4P: REFRESHER

1. FIND AND CORRECT ANY FRAGMENTS, COMMA SPLICES, AND RUN-ONS.
2. REWORK THE SENTENCES SO THAT THERE ARE AT LEAST THREE EXAMPLES OF SUBORDINATION AND ONE OF COORDINATION.

A judge in Traverse City, Michigan, has made an unusual decision in a divorce case. When Allen Church and his former wife, Cheryl, appeared before Judge Charles M. Forster. They each asked for custody of their three teenage sons. Court testimony showed that both of the Churches were good parents. Judge Forster granted them joint custody of the boys. A joint custody decision usually means that the children live with one parent for six months of the year and then with the other parent for the rest of the year. An arrangement that often prevents youngsters from gaining the sense of security that is brought about by a stable home environment. To help prevent this problem, Judge Forster ruled that the three boys would continue to occupy the family home while the parents would take monthly turns living with them. At first, the Churches were shocked by the judge's decision, however the arrangement has worked out well so far. At the end of every month, one parent moves out of the house then the other one moves in. Each of them has a second home nearby for use during the "off months." Allen and Cheryl Church no longer live in the house on a full-time basis they share all of the bills for its upkeep. As strange as this whole custody arrangement may seem, it does guarantee that the children will see both of their parents frequently. Without being pulled away from old friends, familiar school surroundings, and a permanent home setting.

SPRINGBOARDS TO WRITING

Using your knowledge of the writing process, explained on pages 14–16, write a paragraph or essay related to this chapter's central theme, *the search for happiness,* which is introduced on pages 128–30.

PREWRITING

To think of topics to write about, look at the cartoons, read the essay, and answer the questions that follow each. If you prefer, select one of the writing springboards below. (All paragraph numbers refer to the essay that starts on page 128.) To develop your ideas, use the prewriting techniques described on pages 17–22.

WRITING A PARAGRAPH *(For help, see the Pointers on page 51.)*

1. Agree or disagree with the Ibo belief that women should live through their husbands and children. (See paragraphs 3–5.)
2. Agree or disagree with the Ibo saying: "Without a child, what would a woman be?" (See paragraph 5.)
3. The author's friend did (did not) do the right thing in leaving.
4. Agree or disagree: Our laws should make it harder to get married than to get divorced.
5. Should marriage licenses have an expiration date, just as other licenses do?
6. ____________________ is a cultural celebration that has great meaning in my family.

WRITING AN ESSAY *(For help, see the Pointers on pages 54–55.)*

7. Why Get Married?
8. What Makes a Good Marriage?
9. What I Learned About Marriage from Observing My Parents' Marriage
10. Should People Live Together Before They Get Married?
11. Why Do People Get Divorced?
12. Children Are (Are Not) the Biggest Losers in a Divorce
13. Single Parenting Is Very Difficult
14. Why I Would (Would Not) Marry Someone from Another Cultural Background
15. It Is (Is Not) Possible for a Married Woman to Have a Successful Career Without Neglecting Her Family

16. Women Are (Are Not) Treated Like Second-Class Citizens in the United States
17. It Is (Is Not) Difficult for Immigrants to Preserve Their Culture in the United States
18. Americans Do (Do Not) Place Too Much Emphasis on Being Happy
19. What I Need to Be Happy
20. What Is a "Best Friend"?
21. My Friends Do (Do Not) Live Up to My Expectations of Them
22. The American Concept of Womanhood Is (Is Not) "Personal Satisfaction, No Matter the Cost" (See paragraph 14.)
23. Agree or disagree with Allan K. Chalmers' statement about happiness: "The grand essentials of happiness are: something to do, something to love, and something to hope for."
24. American Culture Is Similar to (Different from) the Culture of ____________ (Fill the blank space with the name of another country.)

THE MAN ON THE LEFT IS 75 TIMES MORE LIKELY TO BE STOPPED BY THE POLICE WHILE DRIVING THAN THE MAN ON THE RIGHT.

It happens every day on America's highways. Police stop drivers based on their skin color rather than for the way they are driving. For example, in Florida 80% of those stopped and searched were black and Hispanic, while they constituted only 5% of all drivers. These humiliating and illegal searches are violations of the Constitution and must be fought. Help us defend your rights. Support the ACLU.

american civil liberties union

125 Broad Street, 18th Floor, NY, NY 10004 www.aclu.org

Chapter 5

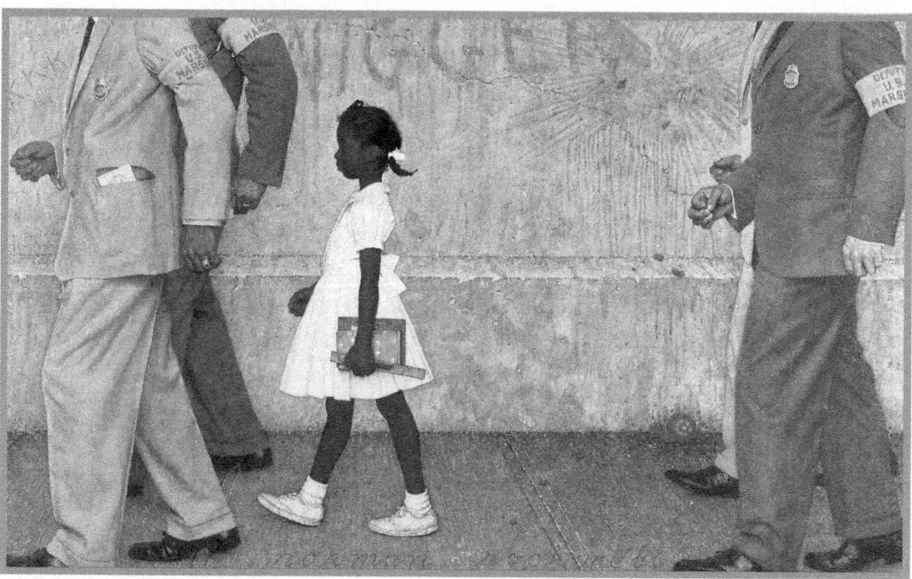

SPRINGBOARDS TO THINKING

For informal, not written, response . . . to stimulate your thinking

1. *The Problem We All Live With,* the painting reproduced above, is by American artist Norman Rockwell. It depicts six-year-old Ruby Bridges and four U.S. Deputy Marshals, who are escorting her to an all-white New Orleans elementary school in 1960. What details does the artist use to indicate the racial attitudes of the time?
2. Why did the artist paint the little girl in a white dress? What is she holding and what do these things tell you about her? Why did the artist choose not to show the heads of the marshals?
3. Have public schools become fully integrated in the years since Ruby was escorted to school? Explain. Do students from different racial backgrounds mingle or do they remain separate? Explain.
4. Why does the advertisement on the opposite page include photographs of Dr. Martin Luther King, Jr. and Charles Manson, a cult leader responsible for at least nine murders? What is the main message of the advertisement?
5. Have you ever witnessed any incidents of racial discrimination? If so, describe them.

The "Black Table" Is Still There

Lawrence Otis Graham

(1) During a recent visit to my old junior high school in Westchester County, I came upon something that I never expected to see again, something that was a source of fear and dread for three hours each school morning of my early adolescence: the all-black lunch table in the cafeteria of my predominantly white suburban junior high school.

(2) As I look back on 27 years of often being the first and only black person integrating such activities and institutions as the college newspaper, the high school tennis team, summer music camps, our all-white suburban neighborhood, my eating club at Princeton or my private social club at Harvard Law School, the one scenario that puzzled me the most then and now is the all-black lunch table.

(3) Why was it there? Why did the black kids separate themselves? What did the table say about the integration that was supposedly going on in hotel rooms and gym classes? What did it say about the black kids? The white kids? What did it say about me when I refused to sit there, day after day, for three years?

(4) Each afternoon, at 12:03 P.M., after the fourth period ended, I found myself among 600 12-, 13-, and 14-year-olds who marched into the brightly-lit cafeteria and dashed for a seat at one of the 27 blue formica lunch tables. No matter who I walked in with—usually a white friend—no matter what mood I was in, there was one thing that was certain: I would not sit at the black table. I would never consider sitting at the black table. What was wrong with me? What was I afraid of?

(5) I would like to think that my decision was a heroic one, made in order to express my solidarity with the theories of integration that my community was espousing. But I was just 12 at the time, and there was nothing heroic in my actions. I avoided the black table for a very simple reason: I was afraid that by sitting at the black table I'd lose all my white friends. I thought that by sitting there I'd be making a racist, anti-white statement. Is that what the all-black table means? Is it a rejection of white people? I no longer think so.

(6) At the time, I was angry that there was a black lunch table. I believed that the black kids were the reason why other kids didn't mix more. I was ready to believe that their self-segregation was the cause of white bigotry. Ironically, I even believed this after my best friend (who was white) told me I probably

shouldn't come to his bar mitzvah because I'd be the only black and people would feel uncomfortable. I even believed this after my Saturday afternoon visit, at age 10, to a private country club pool prompted incensed white parents to pull their kids from the pool in terror. In the face of this blatantly racist (anti-black) behavior, I still somehow managed to blame only the black kids for being the barrier to integration in my school and my little world. What was I thinking?

(7) I realize now how wrong I was. During that same time, there were at least two tables of athletes, an Italian table, a Jewish girls' table, a Jewish boys' table (where I usually sat), a table for kids who were into heavy metal music and smoking pot, a table of middle class Irish kids. Weren't these tables just as segregationist as the black table? At the time, no one thought so. At the time, no one even acknowledged the segregated nature of these other tables.

(8) Maybe it's the color difference that makes all-black tables or all-black groups attract the scrutiny and wrath of so many people. It scares and angers people; it exasperates. It did those things to me, and I'm black.

(9) As an integrating black person, I know that my decision *not* to join the black lunch table attracted its own kind of scrutiny and wrath from my classmates. At the same time that I heard angry words like "Oreo" and "white boy" being hurled at me from the black table, I was also dodging impatient questions from white classmates: "Why do all those black kids sit together?" or "Why don't you ever sit with the other blacks?"

(10) The black lunch table, like those other segregated tables, is a comment on the superficial inroads that integration has made in society. Perhaps I should be happy that even this is a long way from where we started. Yet, I can't get over the fact that the 27th table in my junior high school cafeteria is still known as the "black table"—14 years after my adolescence.

Reading Survey

1. MAIN IDEA

What is the central theme of this essay?

2. MAJOR DETAILS

a. Why didn't the author ever sit at the "black table"?

b. What racist incidents did the author experience while he was in junior high school?

c. When the author was in junior high school, whom did he blame for the existence of the "black table"? Whom does he now blame?

3. INFERENCES

a. Read paragraph 1 again. Why didn't the author expect to see the "black table" during a recent visit to his old junior high school?
b. Read paragraph 6 again. Why did the author believe that the students at the "black table" were responsible for the bigotry?

4. OPINIONS

a. Read paragraph 7 again. Answer the author's question: "Weren't these tables just as segregationist as the black table?"
b. Read paragraph 9 again. Should the author have sat with the other black students? Why or why not?

VOCABULARY BUILDING

Lesson One: ***The Vocabulary of Racism, Part I***

The essay "The 'Black Table' Is Still There" by Lawrence Otis Graham includes words that are useful when you are discussing racism.

racist (paragraph 5)
dread (1)
suburban (1)
integrating (2)
institutions (2)
scenario (2)
solidarity (5)
espousing (5)
segregation (6)
bigotry (6)

People with **racist** attitudes believe that their race is superior to the others.

People with racist attitudes may be filled with **dread**—great fear or uneasiness—at the idea of meeting someone of a different race.

People with racist attitudes may prefer to live in all-white **suburban**—outside the city—neighborhoods.

People with racist attitudes think that **integrating** public places—opening public places to people of all races—is a bad idea.

People with racist attitudes often prefer to have separate **institutions**—organizations—for people of different races.

People with racist attitudes may imagine a negative **scenario**—series of events—if someone of a different race moves into their neighborhood.

People with racist attitudes may seek **solidarity**—a unity based on common interests or values—with other racists.

People with racist attitudes may even be **espousing**—supporting as a cause—hatred and violence toward those who are different.

People with racist attitudes usually believe in **segregation**—separation of the races.

People with racist attitudes sometimes have frightening ways of displaying their **bigotry**—hatred of other races and a total disrespect for other people's beliefs and opinions.

EXERCISE 5A: For each word in italics, circle the definition that is closest in meaning.

1. The workers declared their *solidarity*.
   a. friendship
   b. unity
   c. intention to strike
   d. refusal to bargain
2. A feeling of *dread* swept over her.
   a. illness
   b. hatred
   c. fear
   d. happiness
3. I cannot accept *bigotry*.
   a. cheating
   b. dishonesty
   c. prejudice
   d. favoritism
4. We need to improve our *institutions*.
   a. prisons
   b. hospitals
   c. schools
   d. organizations
5. What is the most likely *scenario*?
   a. series of events
   b. plan
   c. outcome
   d. cause
6. We work in a *suburban* area.
   a. run-down
   b. near the city
   c. wealthy
   d. all-white
7. We are slowly *integrating* our workplace.
   a. improving the conditions of

b. computerizing the activities of
c. opening up to other races
d. connecting to other businesses

8. The actor was criticized for making a *racist* comment.
 a. showing respect for all races
 b. showing fear of other races
 c. feeling sorry for other races
 d. feeling superior to other races

9. The mayor's plan was based on *segregation.*
 a. separation of the races
 b. improvement of the races
 c. hatred of some races
 d. love of all races

10. What were they *espousing*?
 a. teaching
 b. protesting
 c. supporting
 d. investigating

Lesson Two: The Vocabulary of Racism, Part II

The essay "The 'Black Table' Is Still There" by Lawrence Otis Graham includes more words that are useful when you are discussing racism.

rejection (paragraph 5)
prompted (6)
incensed (6)
blatantly (6)
barrier (6)
scrutiny (8)
wrath (8)
exasperates (8)
superficial (10)
inroads (10)

Victims of racism often face **rejection**—the refusal of other people to accept them—when dealing with people of another race.
Victims of racism may sometimes be **prompted**—moved to action—to correct the problem.
Victims of racism are frequently **incensed**—made very angry—by the way they are treated.
Victims of racism may be treated in **blatantly**—obviously—unfair ways.
Victims of racism must overcome one **barrier**—something that stands in the way—after another.

Victims of racism often find themselves under **scrutiny**—close, careful examination or study.
Victims of racism may react with **wrath**—strong, forceful anger.
Victims of racism say that the unfairness they face **exasperates** them—makes them feel angry or irritated.
Victims of racism may think their progress has been **superficial**—lacking in depth and thoroughness.
Victims of racism complain that they have made few **inroads**—advances beyond the original limits—into all-white neighborhoods and workplaces.

EXERCISE 5B: Using the vocabulary words in the lesson, fill in the blanks. Use each word only once.

1. The father was _______________ by his son's disrespectful remark.
2. The lawyer's refusal to obey the law was _______________ illegal.
3. The airport security guard kept the strange man under constant _______________.
4. The traffic delay _______________ the employee to call the office to say she would be late.
5. After hours of sifting through the rubble, residents of the trailer park finally began to make _______________ into the wreckage left by the tornado.
6. Standing in line for hours to register for my courses _______________ me.
7. Most actors face a great deal of _______________ before they are eventually offered a role.
8. The preacher threatened sinners with the _______________ of God.
9. Because the student did not have time to research his topic thoroughly, his term paper was _______________.
10. After the workers finished filling all the potholes, the police officer removed the _______________ so that traffic on the road could flow smoothly again.

SPELLING

Capitalization

The misuse of capital letters is as serious an error as a misspelled word. Unfortunately, some careless writers do not realize this and ignore the rules of capitalization. As you read the material that follows, you will begin to realize that a key word to remembering capitalization is *specific.* If you keep this word in mind, you should have less trouble applying these simple and easy-to-understand rules when you write.

1. CAPITALIZE:

the name of a specific person	*Martin Luther King, Jr.* *Elizabeth Taylor*
a title that precedes the name	*President Lincoln* *Admiral Dewey*
a title that replaces the name	the *Pope* the *Secretary of State*
the name of a group of people	*Hispanics* *Indian*
the name of an organization or a department of the government	the *Knights of Columbus* *Republicans* *Congress* the *Coca-Cola Company*
the pronoun I	Slowly *I* turned the key in the lock.

2. CAPITALIZE:

the name of a specific place	*New York* *Great Britain*
the name of a specific region	the *South* the *Northeast*
the name of a specific street	*Fifth Avenue* *Elm Street*
the name of a specific building	the *Empire State Building* *Independence Hall*
the names of the planets and stars with the exception of earth, sun, and moon	*Mars* *Venus* the *Milky Way*

3. CAPITALIZE:

the names of languages	*French* *Spanish*
the name of a specific school course	*Physics 14A* *Geometry 26D*
the names of publications	the *New York Times* *People* magazine

the name of a specific school or college	*Van Buren High School* *Yale University*
brand names	*Heinz Ketchup* *Ford Mustang*

4. CAPITALIZE:

the days of the week and the months of the year	*Monday* *September*
the names of specific holidays	*Christmas* *New Year's Day*
the names of historical events and periods	*World War II* the *Renaissance*

5. CAPITALIZE:

all words denoting a specific deity	*God* *Allah* *Buddha*
all words referring to God	It is said that *God* created us in *His* image.
all names of religions and religious writings	*Christianity* the *Bible*, the *Koran* *Zen Buddhism*

6. CAPITALIZE:

the first word of a sentence and the first word of a direct quotation	*The* actor exclaimed, "*Do* not touch me!"
the first and last words and all important words in the title of a book, play, short story, essay, or poem	*Death of a Salesman* *The Catcher in the Rye*
the first word and all nouns in the salutation of a letter	*Dear Mr. Lyons:* *My* dear *Sir:*
the first word of the close of a letter	*Sincerely* yours,

EXERCISE 5C: Capitalize whichever words need to be capitalized.

1160 blackpine drive
santa fe, new mexico 87501
march 12, 2003

mr. albert finnegan
editor-in-chief
newsguide magazine
wedgewood office building
chicago, illinois 60657

dear mr. finnegan:

i have just finished reading your article "the wasted college education," in which you state, "a college education is totally unnecessary for the american housewife, who usually deals with nothing more complicated than the price of kleenex tissues or kraft cheese." as an american housewife—and as a graduate of the university of alabama—i strongly disagree with your argument.

i must admit that when we discussed the american revolutionary war in professor young's history 101 class, i never realized that someday that discussion would help me explain to my children the significance of the independence day celebration. similarly, the knowledge i gained from my astronomy class recently helped me answer my children's questions about the space ship that has explored jupiter and saturn. during our trip to the south of france last summer, the ability i acquired in college to speak french proved to be invaluable on many occasions. as a member of the american indian assistance organization, i am frequently called upon to use my college-learned skills as a public speaker to help raise funds for the needy native americans in the southwest. thus, i am a living example of the bible's message that each person must strive to fulfill the potential that god, in his infinite wisdom, gave to us all.

sincerely yours,

mrs. gail grayson

The -*s* Verb Ending

This section will introduce you to the basic principles of subject-verb agreement:

I The Subject-Verb Agreement Pattern

II Special Cases

III *To Be, To Have, To Do*

As you already know from the discussion of sentence fragments, every complete sentence must have a subject and a verb, which can be either singular or plural in form. Logically, a singular verb should be used with a singular subject and a plural verb with a plural subject.

A politician needs campaign funds.

Students need time to study.

George and Helen need a new car.

I. The Subject-Verb Agreement Pattern. As you can see from the examples above, verb agreement centers on one letter: the *s*. Below is a quick way to check that you have used the *s* correctly. In the chart, the *s* can take only one of the two roads available to it; therefore, if you use the *s* on the top road, you cannot use it on the bottom road.

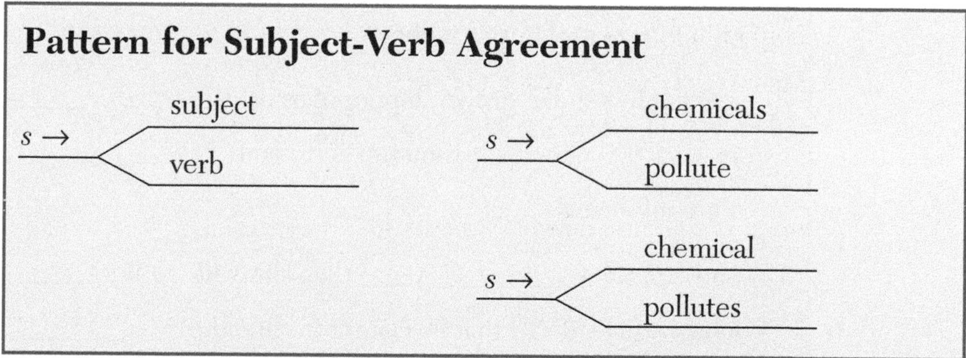

TRY IT OUT

USING THE CORRECT PRESENT TENSE FORMS OF THE VERBS GIVEN IN PARENTHESES, FILL IN THE BLANK SPACES PROVIDED.

1. Hair (to grow) ______________ faster in the summer than in the winter.
2. English judges and lawyers (to wear) ______________ white wigs in court.
3. The average American (to see) ______________ and (to hear) ______________ about 560 advertisements a day.

II. Special Cases. The chart on the preceding page will not help you when you use a pronoun *(I, you, he, she, it, we, they)* for a subject or when you use plural words that do not end in *s (children, people).* Similarly, this chart will not help you when the verb follows one of these words: *shall, will, would, could, should, might, must, can.* Verbs following these words do not end with *s* whether the subject ends with *s* or not.

TRY IT OUT

USING THE CORRECT PRESENT TENSE FORMS OF THE VERBS GIVEN IN PARENTHESES, FILL IN THE BLANK SPACES PROVIDED.

1. Most children (to require) ______________ from eight to nine hours of sleep each night, but most elderly people (to need) ______________ only four to six hours a night.
2. Although a fully grown hippopotamus (to weigh) ______________ about 8,000 pounds, it sometimes (to run) ______________ faster than a human being.
3. She (to say) ______________ that she will (to bet) ______________ her brother a dollar that he cannot (to breathe) ______________ and (to swallow) ______________ at the same time; only a small baby can (to do) ______________ that.

III. *To Be, To Have, To Do.* Some writers have trouble with the present tense forms of the verbs *to be, to have,* and *to do* because these verbs change their spellings to agree with different subjects. These verbs are used much more frequently than any others in the English language, so it is important to study them carefully.

to be		*to have*		*to do*	
I	am	I	have	I	do
you	are	you	have	you	do
he	is	he	has	he	does
she	is	she	has	she	does
it	is	it	has	it	does
we	are	we	have	we	do
they	are	they	have	they	do

TRY IT OUT

USING THE CORRECT PRESENT TENSE FORMS OF THE VERBS GIVEN IN PARENTHESES, FILL IN THE BLANK SPACES PROVIDED.

1. Although Utah (to be) _______________ 400 miles from the nearest ocean, the state bird (to be) _______________ a seagull.
2. Snakes (to have) _______________ no vocal cords, yet they (to do) _______________ produce a frightening hissing sound.
3. Why (to do) _______________ a woman's heart usually beat faster than a man's?
4. Most pencils (to be) _______________ made of cedar wood.
5. The University of Calcutta in India (to have) _______________ 175,000 students.

EXERCISE 5D: Using the subject and verb given for each item below, write two complete sentences, one with a singular subject and one with a plural subject. Be sure to keep the verb in the present tense and to use the *s* wherever necessary. Use your own paper for this assignment.

Example:

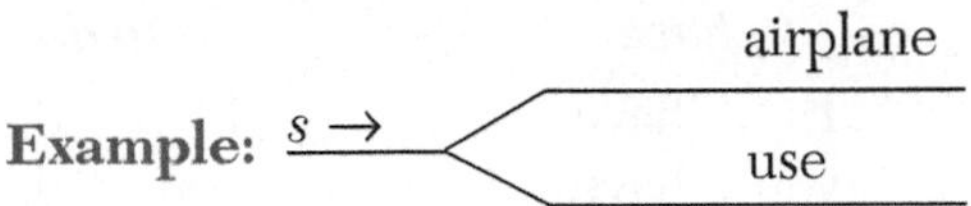

An airplane uses a great deal of fuel.
Airplanes use a great deal of fuel.

1. *s* → rock singer / make

2. *s* → restaurant / serve

3. *s* → credit card / help

4. *s* → politician / try

5. *s* → house / cost

6. *s* → college / should provide

7. *s* → airline pilot / travel

8. *s* → woman / work

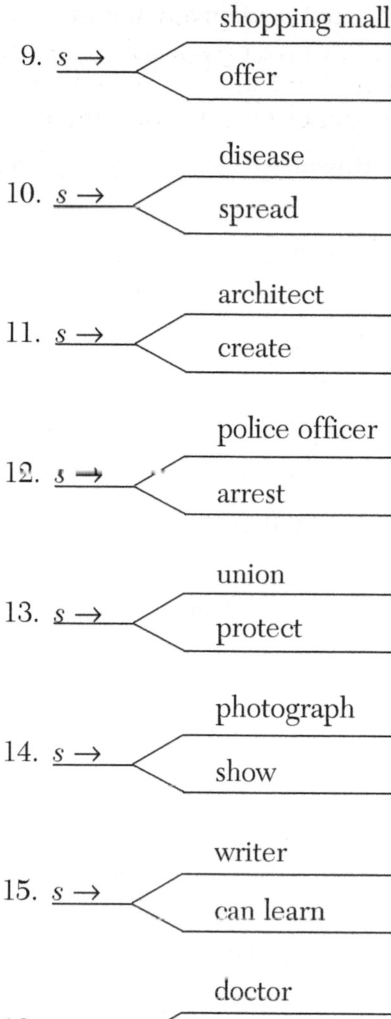

EXERCISE 5E: Using the verb given in front of each sentence, fill in the correct form of the verb in the blank space provided. Keep all the verbs in the present tense.

1. *to be:* Over 2,800 different languages ________________ spoken on earth.
2. *to grow:* The flowering hop vine ________________ a foot a day.
3. *to contain:* A twelve-ounce can of Pepsi Cola ________________ ten teaspoons of sugar.

4. *to do:* Buttermilk _______________ not contain any butter.
5. *to live:* Queen termites may _______________ for fifty years.
6. *to have:* Chow dogs _______________ black tongues.
7. *to carry:* The subway in Moscow, Russia, _______________ 6.5 million passengers each day.
8. *to be:* Ninety percent of Alaska's land _______________ owned by the United States government.
9. *to continue:* A person's nose and ears _______________ to grow throughout his or her lifetime.
10. *to give:* One oyster _______________ birth to 500 million young each year.
11. *to drown:* A whale will _______________ if kept underwater too long.
12. *to do:* Grasshoppers _______________ $30 million worth of damage to crops every year.
13. *to have:* A human tooth _______________ at least fifty miles of canals inside it.
14. *to become:* Each day over 100 people _______________ millionaires in the United States.
15. *to contain:* A person's feet _______________ one-fourth of the 206 bones in the human body.
16. *to blow:* In Commonwealth Bay, Antarctica, the wind sometimes _______________ at up to 200 miles per hour.
17. *to fly:* A deer botfly can _______________ faster than a jet plane.
18. *to speak:* Did you know that more than 15 percent of the people in Louisiana _______________ French as their first language?
19. *to weigh:* The feathers of a pigeon _______________ more than its bones.
20. *to occur:* Each year more than 50,000 earthquakes _______________ somewhere on earth.

Agreement of Subject and Verb

If you have mastered the use of the *-s* ending for the present tense forms of verbs, you are now ready for these additional pointers about subject-verb agreement.

I (a). Words That Separate the Subject and Verb. Words that come between a subject and its verb do not count as part of the subject. The verb, therefore, agrees with the subject, not with the words between.

The train with the beach crowds leaves at noon.

The men in the office work long hours.

I (b). Expressions That Separate the Subject and Verb. Expressions introduced by such words as *together with, in addition to, including, except,* and *as well as* do not count as part of the subject. The verb agrees only with the subject.

Professor Tobin, as well as his students, was surprised.

The President, together with his cabinet members, has left for vacation.

TRY IT OUT

IN THE FOLLOWING SENTENCES UNDERLINE THE CORRECT VERB FORM.

1. One of the streams in this state (is, are) stocked with game fish every year.
2. The host of the party, along with his guests, (was, were) trying to name ten parts of the human body that are spelled with only three letters.
3. The producer of the television situation comedies (has, have) decided to rerun the best ones during the summer.

II (a). ***Either . . . Or, Neither . . . Nor, Not Only . . . But Also.*** When subjects are joined by *either . . . or, neither . . . nor*, or *not only . . . but also*, the verb agrees with the subject closer to it.

Neither Joe nor his sisters like to study.

Either the captains or the umpire calls time out.

II (b). **Compound Subjects.** Subjects joined by *and* are usually plural and take a plural verb. However, when *each* or *every* precedes singular subjects joined by *and*, a singular verb should be used.

Mike and Sally exercise every day.

Every man and woman has the need to accomplish something.

TRY IT OUT

IN THE FOLLOWING SENTENCES UNDERLINE THE CORRECT VERB FORM.

1. Neither the instructor nor her students (was, were) satisfied with the new schedule of classes.
2. Either pushups or weight lifting (is, are) an excellent way to build body muscle.
3. Each baker and pastry maker in the dessert contest (hope, hopes) to win first prize.

III (a). The Introductory *There, Here, Where.* In sentences beginning with *there is, there are, here is, here are, where is*, or *where are,* be especially careful to look ahead and find the subject. *Here, there,* and *where* are never subjects.

There are now four television networks.

Here is the most powerful computer in the world.

III (b). The Introductory *It.* The introductory *it* is always followed by a singular verb.

It is the most appropriate gift possible.

It is the citizens who will make the nation strong.

III (c). Titles and Names. The title of a written work, or the name of a business or company, even when plural in form and ending in *-s,* takes a singular verb.

The Grapes of Wrath is one of Steinbeck's best works.

Lever Brothers produces many household products.

TRY IT OUT

IN THE FOLLOWING SENTENCES UNDERLINE THE CORRECT VERB FORM.

1. It (is, are) the politician's good looks that appeal to television viewers.
2. General Motors (is, are) the largest automobile maker in the United States.
3. Where (is, are) the firefighters going with that box of marshmallows?

IV (a). Indefinite Pronouns. When used as subjects, *each, every, everyone, everybody, anybody, anyone, nobody, someone, somebody, something, everything, either, neither,* and *nothing* regularly take singular verbs.

Everyone is fascinated with space exploration.

Each of us lives a rather complex existence.

IV (b). *None, Some, Any, All.* *None, some, any,* and *all* may be either singular or plural. Decide which is correct from the context of the sentence.

None are so appreciative as those who have little.

None is so appreciative as he who has little.

IV (c). Collective Subjects. *Class, number, family, group,* and all other collective subjects take a singular verb when the subject is regarded as a unit. A plural verb is used when the subject refers to the individuals of a group.

The whole family is going on the trip.

The family have gone their separate ways.

TRY IT OUT

IN THE FOLLOWING SENTENCES UNDERLINE THE CORRECT VERB FORM.

1. The Flatt family (own, owns) one of the busiest gas stations in town.
2. Neither of the hikers (want, wants) to walk in the rain.
3. None (is, are) so fortunate as the person who has good health.

V (a). Amounts. Words stating an amount (time, money, weight, etc.) are usually singular and take a singular verb.

Two weeks is the usual vacation.

Six ounces of cough syrup is what I ordered.

V (b). Unusual Singular Subjects. Subjects that are plural in form but singular in meaning usually take singular verbs. These include *economics, civics, genetics, mathematics, physics, news, measles, mumps,* and *ethics.*

Economics is my favorite subject.

Measles is a common childhood disease.

V (c). Special Plural Subjects. The words *trousers, jeans, scissors, eyeglasses, thanks, riches,* and *means* usually take a plural verb.

The scissors are on the table.

The millionaire's riches are to be given to charity.

TRY IT OUT

IN THE FOLLOWING SENTENCES UNDERLINE THE CORRECT VERB FORM.

1. Physics (is, are) a requirement for engineering students.
2. One hundred sixty-five pounds (is, are) a normal weight for a man who is five feet, eleven inches tall.
3. For students who have trouble seeing the chalkboard clearly, eyeglasses (is, are) a necessity.

EXERCISE 5F: Using the verb given in front of each sentence, fill in the correct form of the verb in the blank space provided. Keep all the verbs in the present tense.

1. *to want:* Every swimmer and diver on the team ______________ to please the demanding coach.
2. *to know:* Neither the injured victim nor the two witnesses ______________ the license plate number of the hit-and-run car.
3. *to have:* The president, along with her advisers, ______________ decided to resign.
4. *to come:* From many countries of the world ______________ immigrants to the shores of America.
5. *to be:* There ______________ sand dunes in France as high as 350 feet.
6. *to build:* General Dynamics ______________ nuclear submarines.
7. *to cause:* Both sun and wind ______________ dryness of the skin.
8. *to be:* Alexander Dumas' *The Three Musketeers* ______________ a classic novel that has been made into a movie many times.
9. *to help:* Economics ______________ people understand the reasoning behind financial decisions made by industry and government.
10. *to be:* "Three hundred and fifty dollars ______________ too much to pay for that broken-down heap you call a car!" the man exclaimed.
11. *to add:* Either many jelly beans or a large slice of chocolate layer cake ______________ hundreds of calories to a person's diet.
12. *to have:* The governor's staff ______________ parked their cars in a no-parking zone.

13. *to spend:* Most rice-growing farmers who live in Southeast Asia ______________ their entire lives without ever seeing a doctor.
14. *to remember:* Each of us usually ______________ something special about a first date.
15. *to be:* It is estimated that there ______________ as many insects in one square mile of fertile land as there are people on this planet.
16. *to study:* In preparing for their final examinations, some people ______________ harder than others do.
17. *to provide:* A 128-cubic-foot woodpile, known as a cord, ______________ the same amount of energy as 140 gallons of oil.
18. *to persuade:* "Neither your sweet kisses nor your promise of wealth ______________ me to marry you," he sighed.
19. *to supply:* A fresh carrot, as well as most other fresh vegetables, ______________ many essentials of good nutrition.
20. *to be:* It ______________ in the hands and feet where you will find more than half the total number of bones in the human body.

EXERCISE 5G: Rewrite each of the sentences given, making sure that the verb agrees with the new subject given.

Examples: Joe never *leaves* the office before six.
The men never *leave* the office before six.

1. Banks loan money both to people and to businesses.

   A bank ______________________________

   ____

2. At least two of the hostages were safe.

   At least ______________________________

   ____

3. Snow and sleet create dangerous driving conditions.

   Snow ______________________________

   ____

4. Either chili or tacos are being served at the Mexican festival.

   Either tacos or chili ______________________________

   ____

5. National Guardsmen are being called in to patrol the disaster area.

   The National Guard ______________________________

   ____

6. Both of the typewriters need repair.

   One of the typewriters ______________________________

   ____

7. Your loyalty is very comforting.

   Your good wishes ______________________________

   ____

8. Is a wild gorilla a peaceful or bad-tempered animal?

   ______ wild gorillas peaceful or bad-tempered animals?

   ____

9. Your taste buds, as well as your nose, tell you what the "taste" of food is.

   Your nose, as well as your taste buds, ______________________________

   ____

10. Newspapers that are filled with gossip about movie and television stars are very popular nowadays.

    A newspaper ______________________________

    ____

11. Almost all hot dogs contain unhealthy fats and preservatives.

    Almost every hot dog ______________________________

    ____

12. Included in the examination were two trick questions.

    ______________________________ a trick question.

    ____

13. Neither exercise nor good eating habits guarantee a long life.

    Neither good eating habits nor exercise ______________________________

    ____

14. Those are the pandas that make the Memphis zoo a popular attraction.

    It ______________________________

    ____

15. "Silent Night, Holy Night" is a famous Christmas carol.

    "Jingle Bells" ______________________________

    ____

16. Those two pilots practice every day to qualify for flight duty in the U.S. Air Force.

    The entire squadron of pilots ______________________________

    ____

17. Hard work, together with talent and luck, makes a successful professional athlete.

    Talent and luck, together with hard work, ______________________________

    ____

18. There are many families left homeless by the flood.

    ______ a family left homeless by the flood.

    ____

19. Both of my former business partners were honest.

    Neither of my former business partners ______________________________

    ____

20. The screws in the bridge supports have to be removed.

    The rust on the bridge supports ______________________________

    ____

Irregular Verbs

To avoid serious verb problems in your writing, you need to know the basic uses of irregular verbs:

I The Past Tense

II The Past Participle

III The Verb *To Be*

I. The Past Tense. Most verbs are considered "regular verbs." These verbs use the *-ed* ending to form the past tense. However, some verbs are irregular. They usually change their spellings to form the past tense.

Regular Verbs: The driving instructor *smiled* nervously as his student *turned* the steering wheel sharply and the car *swerved* in front of an oncoming truck.

Irregular Verbs: Colonel Sanders, who *became* a millionaire when he *sold* his Kentucky Fried Chicken business, *gave* most of his money to charity.

TRY IT OUT

USING THE VERBS GIVEN IN PARENTHESES, FILL IN THE CORRECT PAST TENSE FORMS IN THE BLANK SPACES PROVIDED. CONSULT THE LIST OF IRREGULAR VERBS ON PAGES 191–94. BE CAREFUL TO SPELL THE VERB CORRECTLY.

1. The United States government (to pay) _______________ Russia $7.2 million for Alaska; thus, the forty-ninth state (to cost) _______________ less than 2 cents an acre.
2. The American Indians (to teach) _______________ the settlers how to grow corn, and the settlers (to steal) _______________ their lands in return.
3. When the Wright Brothers (to make) _______________ their first airplane flight, very few people (to know) _______________ about it.

II. The Past Participle. The past participle is a frequently used verb form. This is the verb form that can be combined with forms of *to be* or *to have* to create many different verb tenses. The forms of *to be* include *am, is, are, was, were, be, being*, and *been.* The forms of *to have* are *have, has, had, having.* To form the past participle, regular verbs use the *-ed,* and irregular verbs usually change their spellings. (For a list of the past participles of irregular verbs, see pages 191–94.)

Regular Verbs: The government's student loan program *is being investigated* because many college students *have failed* to repay the tuition money that they *borrowed.*

Irregular Verbs: Pistachio nuts *are grown* in Turkey, Lebanon, and Afghanistan.

The United States *has begun* a trade program with China.

Shakespeare *had written* 38 plays before he died in 1616.

TRY IT OUT

USING THE VERBS GIVEN IN PARENTHESES, SELECT EITHER THE PAST TENSE FORM OR THE PAST PARTICIPLE FORM, WHICHEVER IS CORRECT. THEN FILL IN THAT FORM IN THE BLANK SPACES PROVIDED. CONSULT THE LIST OF IRREGULAR VERBS ON PAGES 191–94.

1. "The Star-Spangled Banner" was (to choose) _______________ to be the national anthem in 1931.
2. Ronald Reagan had (to make) _______________ many Hollywood movies before he (to go) _______________ into politics and eventually (to become) _______________ President.
3. Some Americans have (to forget) _______________ the true meaning of Thanksgiving.

III. The Verb *To Be*. Like the other irregular verbs, the verb *to be* does not use the *-ed* ending to form the past tense and the past participle. Instead, the spellings change.

THE VERB *TO BE*

past tense		*past participle*
I	was	been
you	were	
he	was	
she	was	
it	was	
we	were	
they	were	

Examples: John Hanson *was* really the first President of the United States, but his powers of office *were* limited.

Tennis *has been* popular for hundreds of years.

TRY IT OUT

FILL IN THE BLANK SPACES BELOW WITH THE CORRECT FORMS OF THE VERB TO BE.

1. Although Amerigo Vespucci _______________ not the first European to visit the New World, the North and South American continents _______________ named in his honor.
2. Only 700 people _______________ lucky enough to survive the sinking of the Titanic.
3. James Garfield had _______________ President of the United States for only 199 days when he _______________ assassinated.

Commonly Used Irregular Verbs

Verb	*Past*	*Past Participle*
arise	arose	arisen
awake	awoke *or* awaked	awaked *or* awoken
be (is, am, are)	was, were	been
bear	bore	borne *or* born
beat	beat	beaten

Verb	*Past*	*Past Participle*
become	became	become
begin	began	begun
bend	bent	bent
bet	bet	bet
bid (offer)	bid	bid
bid (command)	bade	bidden
bind	bound	bound
bite	bit	bitten *or* bit
blow	blew	blown
break	broke	broken
bring	brought	brought
build	built	built
burst	burst	burst
buy	bought	bought
cast	cast	cast
catch	caught	caught
choose	chose	chosen
cling	clung	clung
come	came	come
cost	cost	cost
creep	crept	crept
cut	cut	cut
deal	dealt	dealt
dig	dug	dug
dive	dived *or* dove	dived
do	did	done
draw	drew	drawn
drink	drank	drunk
drive	drove	driven
eat	ate	eaten
fall	fell	fallen
feed	fed	fed
feel	felt	felt
fight	fought	fought
find	found	found
flee	fled	fled
fling	flung	flung
fly	flew	flown
forbid	forbade *or* forbad	forbidden
forget	forgot	forgotten *or* forgot
forgive	forgave	forgiven
forsake	forsook	forsaken
freeze	froze	frozen
get	got	got *or* gotten

Verb	*Past*	*Past Participle*
give	gave	given
go	went	gone
grow	grew	grown
hang (suspend)	hung	hung
*hang (execute)	hanged	hanged
have	had	had
hear	heard	heard
hide	hid	hidden
hit	hit	hit
hold	held	held
hurt	hurt	hurt
keep	kept	kept
know	knew	known
lay	laid	laid
lead	led	led
leave	left	left
lend	lent	lent
let	let	let
lie	lay	lain
light	lighted *or* lit	lighted *or* lit
lose	lost	lost
make	made	made
mean	meant	meant
meet	met	met
pay	paid	paid
prove	proved	proved *or* proven
quit	quit	quit
**raise	raised	raised
read	read	read
rid	rid	rid
ride	rode	ridden
ring	rang	rung
rise	rose	risen
run	ran	run
say	said	said
see	saw	seen
seek	sought	sought
sell	sold	sold
send	sent	sent
set	set	set
shake	shook	shaken

*Not an irregular form. Shown here to emphasize contrast with other use of the same word.
**Not an irregular form. Shown here to emphasize contrast with the word *rise*.

Verb	*Past*	*Past Participle*
shine (glow)	shone	shone
*shine (polish)	shined	shined
shoot	shot	shot
show	showed	shown *or* showed
shrink	shrank	shrunk
sing	sang	sung
sink	sank	sunk
sit	sat	sat
slay	slew	slain
sleep	slept	slept
sling	slung	slung
speak	spoke	spoken
spend	spent	spent
spin	spun	spun
spring	sprang *or* sprung	sprung
stand	stood	stood
steal	stole	stolen
sting	stung	stung
stink	stank *or* stunk	stunk
stride	strode	stridden
strike	struck	struck
strive	strove	striven
swear	swore	sworn
sweep	swept	swept
swim	swam	swum
swing	swung	swung
take	took	taken
teach	taught	taught
tear	tore	torn
tell	told	told
think	thought	thought
throw	threw	thrown
understand	understood	understood
wake	woke *or* waked	waked *or* woken
wear	wore	worn
win	won	won
wring	wrung	wrung
write	wrote	written

*Not an irregular form. Shown here to emphasize contrast with other use of the same word.

EXERCISE 5H: Using the verbs given in parentheses, fill in the correct past tense or past participle forms in the blank spaces provided. Consult the list of irregular verbs on pages 191–94.

1. Elbert Hubbard (to write) _______________ a book called *Essay on Silence* that consisted of 200 blank pages.
2. Twenty years after he composed "Take Me Out to the Ball Game," Albert von Tilzer (to see) _______________ his first baseball game.
3. One million people are (to bite) _______________ by animals each year in the United States.
4. Until recently, most working women (to be) _______________ earning less money than men (to be) _______________ for the same work.
5. The letters I.O.U. (to do) _______________ not originally mean "I owe you" but rather "I owe unto you."
6. In 1968, when a tidal wave (to sweep) _______________ a Hawaiian man's home out to sea, he used a plank of wood from the house as a surfboard and (to ride) _______________ a fifty-foot wave back to shore.
7. Because hundreds of thousands of bald eagles have been (to shoot) _______________ by hunters, America's national bird is now an endangered species.
8. Last year more Americans were (to hurt) _______________ in falls in their homes than in any other type of accident except automobile crashes.
9. After a honeybee has (to sting) _______________ someone, it dies.
10. In Arizona recently the police checked the backgrounds of 100 hitchhikers and (to find) _______________ that 84 (to have) _______________ criminal records and 12 (to be) _______________ runaways.
11. Queen Elizabeth I of England, who was born in 1533, (to be) _______________ the daughter of Henry the Eighth and the ill-fated Anne Boleyn.
12. The homes of the natives of the Bissagos Islands are (to build) _______________ around large trees so that the branches can serve as the roofs.

13. While he (to be) _______________ President of the United States, Theodore Roosevelt always (to find) _______________ time to read two or three books a day.
14. Because their voices are so sweet, the singing frogs of Japan often are (to keep) _______________ in cages in people's homes.
15. Columbus (to send) _______________ a report of his landing in the New World to the king and queen of Spain, but it (to get) _______________ lost and (to take) _______________ 359 years to arrive.
16. Some people never have (to have) _______________ a headache, but everyone has (to have) _______________ a cold at one time or another.
17. Henry Aaron has (to hit) _______________ more home runs than Babe Ruth (to do) _______________.
18. If you had (to understand) _______________ sign language, you would have (to know) _______________ that his hands were saying, "I am happy to meet you."
19. Before he died, Albert Einstein had (to tell) _______________ his family not to mark his grave in any way, and they (to go) _______________ along with his wishes.
20. Most people have always (to be) _______________ fascinated by unusual facts and information.

EXERCISE 5I: Rewrite each of the following sentences so that all of the actions take place in the past.

Example: The windows *shake* when the jets *fly* overhead. (present)
The windows *shook* when the jets *flew* overhead. (past)

1. The garbage begins to smell when it sits in the sun all day.

____

2. The newborn babies sleep after they eat.

____

3. The diamond shines when you hold it up to the light.

4. On March 21 and September 21, the sun rises and sets exactly twelve hours apart.

5. I am happy that you are happy that Santa Claus is coming to town.

6. The doctor cuts his finger, bleeds a little, and then feels faint.

7. The highway patrol officer catches many speeders when she drives an unmarked car.

8. The artist draws pictures of people who feed pigeons in the park.

9. Maybe she is lucky: Because of the air pollution, she has sinus problems, but because of her stuffed nose, she does not smell the pollution.

10. Each semester the teacher brings a rubber chicken to class in his briefcase, and he flings it onto his desk when it is time to surprise his students.

EXERCISE 5J: Write at least ten sentences using the subjects in column A, the verbs in column B, and the past participle forms of the verbs listed in column C. Try to use each verb in column B several times, but use each verb in column C only once. Use a separate sheet of paper.

Example:

A	B	C
The popcorn eating contest	has	given

everyone a stomachache.

A	*B*	*C*
Madonna	has	to fall
the federal government	have	to make
a pickpocket	had	to write
the Siamese cat		to take
Robin Williams		to choose
the cost of living		to give
my high school		to sing
the mayor		to rise
soap operas		to speak
Oprah Winfrey		to steal
pizza parlors		to begin
newspaper reporters		to hide
my best friend		to get
helicopters		to swear
the witness		to see
a tornado		to go
DVD players		to fly

The -*ed* Verb Ending

The -*ed* verb ending has many uses in the English language. Most people tend not to pronounce the ending clearly in everyday speech because the -*ed* frequently comes at the end of an unstressed syllable or is immediately followed by a word that starts with a *t* or *d* sound. For example, read the following sentence aloud.

When Jamaal finished doing his homework, he was supposed to walk the dog, but he listened to the music on his iPod instead.

Did you pronounce all three -*ed* endings clearly? If you didn't, you might forget to add the -*ed* when you need it in your writing. To help avoid this problem, listen carefully for the endings of words when you speak, and review these major guidelines for using the -*ed:*

- **I The Past Tense**
- **II Verbs That Follow *To Have***
- **III Verbs That Follow *To Be***
- **IV Adjectives with -*ed* Endings**
- **V Verbs That Do Not Take -*ed* Endings**

I. The Past Tense. The -*ed* ending is used to indicate the past tense of regular verbs. (The past tense forms of irregular verbs are discussed on pages 189–94.) Notice in the following sentences that all of the actions started and ended in the past.

As the crowds *cheered,* the marathon runner *stumbled* across the finish line and *collapsed* into her husband's arms.

The residents *decided* to leave the area before the volcano *exploded* again.

TRY IT OUT

ADD *-ED* ENDINGS WHEREVER NECESSARY IN THE FOLLOWING SENTENCES. USE A SEPARATE SHEET OF PAPER IF NEEDED.

1. During yesterday's press conference, the President announce his latest plans, explain his recent actions, and answer the reporters' questions.
2. After Alexander Graham Bell file a patent for the telephone in 1875, over 600 people sue him for stealing their ideas.
3. When the ancient Egyptians construct the pyramids, they use millions of limestone blocks that weigh as much as 30 tons apiece.

II. Verbs That Follow *To Have*. The *-ed* ending is added to regular verbs that follow a form of the verb *to have*. Because the verbs follow *to have*, they are in their past participle *-ed* forms. (The past participle forms of irregular verbs are discussed on pages 189–94.)

Pattern for Verbs That Follow *To Have*

$$\text{subject} + \begin{bmatrix}\text{has}\\ \text{have}\\ \text{had}\end{bmatrix} + \text{verb} + \text{-ed}$$

The rain + *has* + stopp*ed*.

Notice in the following sentences how this verb pattern changes the time when the action takes place.

Frank *worked* at McDonald's.	(*He doesn't anymore.*)
Frank *has worked* at McDonald's for two years.	(*He worked there in the past and he still does.*)
Frank *had worked* at McDonald's until he joined the Army.	(*He left his job before he joined the Army.*)

TRY IT OUT

ADD -*ED* ENDINGS WHEREVER NECESSARY IN THE FOLLOWING SENTENCES. USE A SEPARATE SHEET OF PAPER IF NEEDED.

1. Carol has study for her math test every day this past week.
2. Abraham Lincoln had dream of his death a short time before John Wilkes Booth kill him.
3. Over the last several years, gasoline prices have soar.

III (a). Verbs That Follow *To Be.* The *-ed* ending is added to regular verbs that follow a form of the verb *to be*. Because the verbs follow *to be,* they are in their past participle *-ed* forms. (The past participle forms of irregular verbs are discussed on pages 189–94.)

Pattern for Verbs That Follow *To Be*

subject + [is / am / are / was / were] + verb + -ed

The class + *was* + cancel*ed.*

In most English sentences, the subject is doing the action of the verb. In this verb pattern, the action of the verb is being done to the subject.

Da Vinci painted the Mona Lisa.	(*The subject,* Da Vinci, *is doing the action.*)
The Mona Lisa was painted by Da Vinci.	(*The subject,* the Mona Lisa, *is receiving the action.*)
We elect senators for six-year terms.	(*The subject,* we, *is doing the action.*)
Senators are elected by us for six-year terms.	(*The subject,* senators, *is receiving the action.*)

III (b). In the "to be" pattern above, helping verbs such as *has, have, had, will, would, could,* and *should* may be combined with *be, being,* or *been* to create many different verb tenses.

V (d). The *-ed* ending is *not* added to a verb that follows *can, could, should, would, may, might, must, shall,* or *will.*

Charles Atlas *could pull* a 145,000-pound railroad car down a track.
We *must save* the whale population of the earth.

Notice in the following sentences that the *-ed* ending is added when a form of the verb *to be* or *to have* is also included.

You *should have laughed* at the boss's joke.
Over 2 million American couples *will be married* this year.

TRY IT OUT

MAKE ANY NECESSARY CORRECTIONS IN THE VERBS IN THE FOLLOWING SENTENCES. YOU MAY HAVE TO REMOVE *-ED* ENDINGS OR CHANGE THE SPELLING OF THE VERBS. USE A SEPARATE SHEET OF PAPER IF NEEDED.

1. An ant can lifted fifty times its own weight.
2. My wife still has not forgived me because last week I buyed a new car that costed too much.
3. The driving instructor did explained everything clearly, but I failed the test anyway.
4. If you wanted to listened to loud rock music until three o'clock this morning, you should have used earphones.

A SPECIAL NOTE: The spelling of a regular verb sometimes changes slightly when *-ed* is added. (1) This happens sometimes when a verb ends with a *y.* See page 102 for more information. (2) This happens when the final consonant of some verbs has to be doubled. See page 472 for more information.

EXERCISE 5K: Rewrite each of the following sentences so that all of the actions take place in the past.

Example: After we *move* the rug out of the way, we *dance* all night. (present)
After we *moved* the rug out of the way, we *danced* all night. (past)

1. Charles diets constantly, but he gains weight anyway.

____

____

2. Many students who need money to pay for school expenses apply for financial aid.

____

____

3. A cigarette pack that coughs when anyone touches it seems like a good idea.

____

____

4. As the Voyager space capsule passes through the Milky Way, it explores the planets and sends pictures back to earth.

____

____

5. Eighty thousand people see the Super Bowl game live while 50 million others stay home and watch it on television.

____

____

6. The unemployment rate drops during the Christmas season because many stores hire additional workers.

____

____

7. Some community groups complain when a theater that shows pornographic films opens in their neighborhood.

____

____

8. Few people believe the advertisement that offers a real diamond for just $5.

____

____

9. The Sony Corporation is developing a 3D television set.

   A 3D television set ______________________________

   ____

10. By the end of this decade, drug companies will manufacture a birth control pill for men.

   By the end of this decade, a birth control pill for men ______________________________

   ____

EXERCISE 5N: For each item, first use the past participle form of a verb listed below to complete the sentence marked "a." Then place the same past participle verb in front of the subject provided in "b" and complete the new sentence by adding whatever words you think are reasonable.

Example: The jeans are *faded*.
The *faded* jeans cost $40.

to fade	to scratch	to haunt
to satisfy	to crack	to desert
to spoil	to spill	to damage
to marry	to whip	to frighten
to divorce	to broil	to qualify
to trap	to bake	to starve

1. a. The house looks ______________________________.

   b. The ______________ house ______________________________.

2. a. The student felt ______________________________.

   b. The ______________ student ______________________________.

3. a. The cream was ______________________________.

   b. The ______________ cream ______________________________.

4. a. The teacher seems ______________________________.

   b. The ______________ teacher ______________________________.

5. a. The lion became ______________________________.

   b. The ______________ lion ______________________________.

6. a. The old woman appears ______________________________.
   b. The ______________ old woman ______________________.
7. a. The couple got ______________________________.
   b. The ______________ couple ______________________.
8. a. The lobsters were ______________________________.
   b. The ______________ lobsters ______________________.
9. a. The mirror is ______________________________.
   b. The ______________ mirror ______________________.
   a. The child acts ______________________________.
   b. The ______________ child ______________________.

EXERCISE 50: Add the *-ed* ending wherever it is needed in the following sentences. Use a separate sheet of paper, if needed.

1. Most people are surprise to learn that ants are equip with five different noses; each one is design to accomplish a different task.
2. Four out of five divorce people get marry again within two or three years.
3. Robert Earl Hughes, who weigh 1,067 pounds when he die in 1958, was bury in a piano case.
4. The first candy on a stick was call a lollipop because its inventor was impress with a famous racehorse of the time, Lolly Pop.
5. The island of Nauru, which is locate in the Central Pacific Ocean, is compose mainly of bird droppings. This phosphate-rich land has provide Nauruans with tremendous wealth and has allow them to build a 51-story skyscraper in Melbourne, Australia.
6. As the narcotics agents search the ship yesterday, they use specially train dogs that bark loudly when they smell the hidden drugs.
7. The Dutch artist Van Gogh became so depress that he was commit to an insane asylum, where he continue to paint. After he kill himself fourteen months later, his brother discover many valuable paintings pile up in the attics and basements where Van Gogh had live during his ten-year career as an artist.
8. The first motel open in California in 1925. Its owners had create the word "motel" by using a shorten form of "motor hotel."

9. George Washington had suffer from malaria, smallpox, pleurisy, and dysentery, all before he reach 30 years of age.
10. Scientists are interest in a new liquid that was invent by a Dr. Willard of Rapid City, South Dakota. Burns that have been treat with this "Willard Water" have heal quickly, and gardens that have been water with it have produce gigantic vegetables.
11. After James Monroe, Alexander Hamilton, and other powerful politicians had decide in 1786 that the United States need a king, they invite Prince Henry of Prussia to take the position. However, before the Prince reply to the offer, the Americans had change their minds and had decide to elect a president instead.
12. The American Medical Association has warn that people with heart disease should limit their intake of such foods as scramble eggs, French fry potatoes, chop meat, and ice tea.
13. When Napoleon rule France, he straighten out the confuse system of French law, modernize tax collection, improve education, and led over half a million men into battle. Yet he was terrify of cats.
14. At Brookside Gardens in Wheaton, Maryland, disable visitors are delight to discover that all of the flowers and bushes are describe on Braille signs for the blind and that the beds are plant waist-high so that they can be touch by those confine to wheelchairs.
15. Florence Nightingale, who establish professional nursing, own a pet owl and carry it in her pocket whenever she travel.
16. A few years ago the government try to create featherless chickens that would not have to be pluck before they are market. But the experiment fail because the naked birds start to catch colds.
17. A team of California researchers has discover that in addition to humans, pigs and hippos are capable of getting sunburn.
18. Albert Einstein, the great scientist who develop the theory of relativity, was ask to become the president of Israel. Although he felt honor by the offer, he turn it down.
19. On June 25, 1876, General Custer and his arm forces attack Chief Sitting Bull's village because the Indians refuse to give up their lands. Neither Custer nor any of his men survive the battle.
20. You may be amaze to find out that yesterday, Americans consume about 500 million cups of coffee and smoke about 1.6 billion cigarettes.

Verb Tense Consistency

As you write, you will sometimes find it necessary to move from one verb tense to another to show a change in time.

Example: A pear tree that *was planted* in Danvers, Massachusetts, in 1630 still *bears* fruit today.

In the example above, the sentence starts in the past tense and then moves to the present tense; this shift in tenses is appropriate to convey the meaning of the sentence. To avoid confusing verb tense shifts in your writing, review these important guidelines about verb tense consistency:

I **Confusing Verb Tense Shifts**

II **Confusing Verb Tense Shifts in a Story**

III ***Can/Will*** **and** ***Could/Would***

I. Confusing Verb Tense Shifts. If you move from one verb tense to another when this shift in tenses is not appropriate, you will confuse the reader. For example, notice the inconsistent use of verb tenses in the example below.

Confusing: After I *spent* several hours working at my computer, I *start* to get a headache.

To be consistent, both verbs must be either in the present tense or the past tense.

Clear: After I *spend* several hours working at my computer, I *start* to get a headache.

OR

Clear: After I *spent* several hours working at my computer, I *started* to get a headache.

TRY IT OUT

FIND AND CORRECT ANY ERRORS IN VERB TENSE CONSISTENCY IN THE SENTENCES BELOW.

1. The underwear worn by nineteenth-century Japanese warriors is made of iron.
2. When most people stop smoking, they started to eat more and gained some weight.
3. King Perseus, who ruled the ancient kingdom of Macedonia, was executed by the Romans; they kill him by keeping him awake until he dies of exhaustion.

II. Confusing Verb Tense Shifts in a Story. When you are telling a story or incident that has already happened, be sure that you keep all the verbs in the past tense. Otherwise, the reader will be confused.

Confusing: A German woman *woke* her husband three times during the night to ask for help with a crossword puzzle she *was working* on. When she *wakes* him up a fourth time, he *strangles* her to death. The court later *found* him not guilty on the grounds of temporary insanity.

In the example above, notice how the incident begins in the past tense, shifts to the present tense, and then shifts back to the past tense. To be consistent, the entire incident must be in the past tense.

Clear: A German woman *woke* her husband three times during the night to ask for help with a crossword puzzle she *was working* on. When she *woke* him up a fourth time, he *strangled* her to death. The court later *found* him not guilty on the grounds of temporary insanity.

TRY IT OUT

FIND AND CORRECT ANY ERRORS IN VERB TENSE CONSISTENCY IN THE FOLLOWING STORY.

In February 1891, a British sailor named James Bartley fell off a whaling ship and was swallowed by a wounded sperm whale. Several hours later, the whale is captured. When it is cut open, Bartley is discovered—still alive—in the gigantic stomach. After a three-week bout of insanity, Bartley recovers and tells about his incredible adventure. He says it was easy to breathe inside the whale, but the heat and humidity were terrible. Bartley suffered no lasting injury, although his hair and skin are permanently bleached white.

III. *Can/Will* and *Could/Would.* The verbs *can* and *will* are used for the present tense. The verbs *could* and *would* are used for the past tense.

Confusing: When Jason *gets* a bank loan, he *could* buy a new car.

Clear: When Jason *gets* a bank loan, he *can* buy a new car.

OR

When Jason *got* a bank loan, he *could* buy a new car.

Confusing: Whenever I *play* the piano, my neighbors *would* start complaining.

Clear: Whenever I *play* the piano, my neighbors *will* start complaining.

OR

Whenever I *played* the piano, my neighbors *would* start complaining.

TRY IT OUT

FIND AND CORRECT ANY ERRORS IN VERB TENSE CONSISTENCY IN THE FOLLOWING SENTENCES.

1. An entertainer named John W. Horton made his living by eating whatever was placed before him; in fact, he can eat large quantities of eggshells, newspapers, or glass without getting sick.
2. Before my math teacher gives the class a test next week, she would review all the important material.
3. Panasonic is now manufacturing a television set that is just $4\frac{1}{2}$ inches deep and could hang on a wall like a picture.

EXERCISE 5P: Find and correct any errors in verb tense consistency in the following sentences.

1. In 1906, Alphonse Constantini invented motor-driven roller skates that can travel 40 miles an hour.
2. During the American Revolution, a German officer named Baron von Steuben trained the colonial soldiers to march, maneuver, and fight even though he knows no English.
3. After Emperor Yang Kuang of China emptied the country's treasury to pay for his fancy lifestyle, he orders all the citizens to pay ten years of taxes in advance. Soon after he issues this order, he is assassinated.
4. Mother's Day was started by a woman named Anna Jarvis of Grafton, West Virginia. In 1907 Mrs. Jarvis began a campaign for the nationwide celebration of motherhood. At first no one pays attention to her, but gradually churches and local town organizations begin inviting her to speak at their

meetings. Soon her idea catches on throughout the country, and on May 9, 1914, President Woodrow Wilson made the holiday official.

5. Until about a hundred years ago, the custom of "sin-eating" was widespread in England. When someone died, the official village sin-eater was notified. He goes to the house of the dead person, sits on a stool near the door, and eats a large meal. When he is finished, he will rise and announce that he had just traded souls with the deceased.

6. Do you know why we shiver when we get cold? The body produced heat through muscular activity. When we get cold, we automatically shivered to stir up the muscles and get warm from the friction this causes.

7. Before the first voyage of Columbus, Queen Isabella of Spain had offered a lifetime pension equivalent to $60 a year to the first man to sight land. As it later turned out, a sailor named Rodrigo is the first person to sight land in the New World. However, when it comes time to collect the pension, Columbus himself claims the prize.

8. At the age of 30, Cézanne was the most thoroughly rejected painter in Paris, for no one seemed to like his highly original artwork. To keep up his confidence, he buys a parrot that can be trained to talk. While the artist paints all day in his studio, the parrot will keep repeating, "Cézanne is a great artist! Cézanne is a great artist!" The parrot was apparently smarter than the critics.

9. On June 6, 1896, George Harbo and Frank Samuelson rowed out of New York harbor in a boat that was only eighteen feet long and had no sail to catch the wind. They took along five pairs of oars, sixty gallons of water, and a stock

of canned food. The two men put in eighteen hours a day at the oars so that they can keep to their schedule of crossing fifty-four miles of ocean each day. On August 1, fifty-six days after leaving New York, Harbo and Samuelson row into a quiet coastal area of England. Although no cheering crowds greet them, they had completed one of the most daring voyages ever undertaken.

10. In September 1803, Joseph Samuels of Sydney, Australia, was accused of stealing a bag of coins and killing a policeman in the process. Although he protests his innocence, he is convicted of the crimes and sentenced to be hanged. On the day of the execution, the marshals try three times to carry out the sentence. On the first try, the hangman's knot becomes undone, and Samuels drops to the ground. On the second try, the rope unravels. On the third try, the rope breaks completely. Samuels was returned to jail and then released. A few years later, the police discovered that another man had committed the crimes.

EXERCISE 5Q: Find and correct any errors in verb tense consistency in the following paragraphs.

Thomas Alva Edison overcame great odds to become one of our best known inventors. Edison was born into a very poor family in 1847. When he went to school, the teacher tells him that he is too stupid to learn, and he drops out after only three months. By age 12, he has a full-time job selling newspapers and candy on railroad trains. One day a few railroad workers playfully lift Edison by his ears onto a train. He already suffered some deafness from having had scarlet fever as a child, and this prank worsens his condition. But being poor, uneducated, and partly deaf does not stop him. While working on the railroad, he will spend every spare moment doing experiments and educating himself. Unfortunately, he eventually loses his job after one of his experiments sets a train on fire. During his twenties, Edison finally began to make money from his inventions, and at age 30, he won national fame when he introduced the first phonograph.

Although Edison patented over 1,000 inventions during his lifetime, he is probably most famous for inventing the electric light bulb. When Edison first became interested in working on this invention, he asked some bankers to sell shares of stock to finance the research. When no one buys the stock, Edison tells the newspapers that he has already invented the electric light. His lie works because people rushed to pay a total of $50,000 for shares in this exciting invention. During the next year, Edison worked twenty hours a day with five assistants, but he was confronted with the same problem that other inventors had experienced. Seventy years before, an English inventor had developed the concept of passing an electric current through something called a filament that would then light up. However, no one can find a filament that will not burn up in the process. In October 1879, Edison finally realizes how to overcome this problem. He takes his filament to a glassblower, who encloses it in a glass bulb. Then Edison removes all the oxygen from the bulb and sends an electric current through the filament. The filament glowed and did not burn up because nothing can burn without oxygen. Edison and his assistants stayed up for forty hours straight to watch their electric light.

Today we take the electric light for granted. But the next time you flick on a light switch, think of Thomas Alva Edison and how his hard work and determination change the world. If it weren't for Edison, you might be reading this book by candlelight or a kerosene lamp.

EXERCISE 5R: REFRESHER

1. **FIND AND CORRECT ANY IRREGULAR VERB ERRORS.**
2. **FIND AND CORRECT ANY SENTENCE FRAGMENTS.**

A two-year study recently conducted by the United States Civil Rights Commission reveals that Asian immigrants have increasingly became targets of hatred and violence in many parts of the nation. In California, for example, graffiti "artists" have scrawled words of hate throughout Asian neighborhoods, and in Massachusetts several Cambodian refugees have been assaulted. A group of Laotians fleed from Philadelphia. After arsonists burned their homes to the ground. Even worse, in New York a Vietnamese boy was recently beat to death with a baseball bat. According to the Commission study, much of this racial hatred stems from jealousy. As many Asians have build up successful businesses. Some people have began to spread lies to explain the Asians' economic gains. The most popular rumor is that either an Asian religious group or the United States government has gave the immigrants the money they needed to go into business. The study finded that when these groups first settled in the United States. They seen that hard work could lead to financial success. Encouraged by this opportunity, many Asians have took low-level jobs, have worked very long hours. And have went to school to learn English as well as a variety of useful skills. Then after much hard work and sacrifice, they have pooled their resources to purchase businesses that enable them to earn a decent living. Unfortunately, their dreams of a peaceful, economically secure existence are sometimes shattered. By the violence and hatred that can result from racial prejudice.

SPRINGBOARDS TO WRITING

Using your knowledge of the writing process, explained on pages 14–16, write a paragraph or essay related to this chapter's central theme, *racism*, which is introduced on pages 166–67.

PREWRITING

To think of topics to write about, look at the advertisement and the painting, read the essay, and answer the questions that follow each. If you prefer, select one of the writing springboards below. (All paragraph numbers refer to the essay that starts on page 166.) To develop your ideas, use the prewriting techniques described on pages 17–22.

WRITING A PARAGRAPH *(For help, see the Pointers on page 51.)*

1. Lawrence Otis Graham was (was not) wrong for refusing to sit at the "black table."
2. Read paragraph 7 and then answer the author's question: "Weren't these tables just as segregationist as the black table?"
3. I will never forget the time when I was a victim of discrimination (or when I witnessed an act of discrimination).
4. Forced busing to achieve school integration is (is not) a good idea.
5. Quotas should (should not) be used to increase the number of minority students in medical and law schools.

WRITING AN ESSAY *(For help, see the Pointers on pages 54–55.)*

6. Agree or disagree with the author that integration has made only "superficial inroads" in society. (See paragraph 10.)
7. The Major Kinds of Self-Segregation in American Society (See paragraph 7.)
8. Racism Is (Is Not) Common in My High School (on My College Campus)
9. Why Some People Are Prejudiced (For a start, see the Refresher.)
10. My Plan to Help Achieve Racial Equality
11. Why Interracial Marriage Can (Cannot) Work
12. Job Quotas Should (Should Not) Be Used to Give Minorities Better Job Opportunities

13. Are Minorities Portrayed Accurately on Television?
14. Are Minorities Treated Fairly by the American System of Justice?
15. The Case for (Against) Bilingual Education
16. Racial (Religious) Stereotypes Are (Are Not) Accurate
17. Discrimination Against Foreigners (Teenagers, Women, Extremely Overweight People, Gays) Is Widespread in the United States
18. How Minorities Have Enriched American Culture

Chapter 6

Nick Kelsh

SPRINGBOARDS TO THINKING

For informal, not written, response . . . to stimulate your thinking

1. Look at the photograph of the Barbie Dolls. Do these dolls have the body shape of the average woman? Explain.
2. More than a billion Barbie Dolls have been sold since they were introduced in 1959. Has playing with Barbie Dolls given little girls an unrealistic picture of what they should look like when they become adults? Explain.
3. Look at the photograph of a modern beauty salon. Describe all that you see. What do you think is the main message of the photograph? Do you agree or disagree with that message? Explain.
4. Notice the person sitting at the far left in the photograph. Are you surprised to see a man using the services of a beauty salon? Why or why not?
5. Do you think that most men are as concerned with their physical appearance as many women are? Explain.

The Ugly Truth About Beauty

Dave Barry

(1) If you're a man, at some point a woman will ask you how she looks.

"How do I look?" she'll ask.

You must be careful how you answer this question. The best technique is to form an honest yet sensitive opinion, then collapse on the floor with some kind of fatal seizure. Trust me, this is the easiest way out. Because you will never come up with the right answer.

(2) The problem is that women generally do not think of their looks in the same way that men do. Most men form an opinion of how they look in seventh grade, and they stick to it for the rest of their lives. Some men form the opinion that they are irresistible stud muffins, and they do not change this opinion even when their faces sag and their noses bloat to the size of eggplants and their eyebrows grow together to form what appears to be a giant forehead-dwelling tropical caterpillar.

(3) Most men, I believe, think of themselves as average-looking. Men will think this even if their faces cause heart failure in cattle at a range of 300 yards. Being average does not bother them; average is fine, for men. This is why men never ask anybody how they look. Their primary form of beauty care is to shave themselves, which is essentially the same form of beauty care that they give to their lawns. If, at the end of his four-minute daily beauty regimen, a man has managed to wipe most of the shaving cream out of his hair and is not bleeding too badly, he feels that he has done all he can, so he stops thinking about his appearance and devotes his mind to more critical issues, such as the Super Bowl.

(4) Women do not look at themselves this way. If I had to express, in three words, what I believe most women think about their appearance, those words would be: "not good enough." No matter how attractive a woman may appear to be to others, when she looks at herself in the mirror, she thinks: woof. She thinks that at any moment a municipal animal-control officer is going to throw a net over her and haul her off to the shelter.

(5) Why do women have such low self-esteem? There are many complex psychological and societal reasons, by which I mean Barbie. Girls grow up playing with a doll proportioned such that, if it were a human, it would be seven feet tall and weigh 81 pounds, of which 53 pounds would be bosoms. This is a difficult appearance standard to live up to, especially when you contrast it with the

standard set for little boys by their dolls . . . excuse me, by their action figures. Most of the action figures that my son played with when he was little were hideous-looking. For example, he was very fond of an action figure (part of the He-Man series) called "Buzz-Off," who was part human, part flying insect. Buzz-Off was not a looker. But he was extremely self-confident. You could not imagine Buzz-Off saying to the other action figures: "Do you think these wings make my hips look big?"

(6) But women grow up thinking they need to look like Barbie, which for most women is impossible, although there is a multibillion-dollar beauty industry devoted to convincing women that they must try. I once saw an Oprah show wherein supermodel Cindy Crawford dispensed makeup tips to the studio audience. Cindy had all these middle-aged women applying beauty products to their faces; she stressed how important it was to apply them in a certain way, using the tips of their fingers. All the women dutifully did this, even though it was obvious to any sane observer that, no matter how carefully they applied these products, they would never look remotely like Cindy Crawford, who is some kind of genetic mutation.

(7) I'm not saying that men are superior. I'm just saying that you're not going to get a group of middle-aged men to sit in a room and apply cosmetics to themselves under the instruction of Brad Pitt, in hopes of looking more like him. Men would realize that this task was pointless and demeaning. They would find some way to bolster their self-esteem that did not require looking like Brad Pitt. They would say to Brad: "Oh YEAH? Well what do you know about LAWN CARE, pretty boy?"

(8) Of course, many women will argue that the reason they become obsessed with trying to look like Cindy Crawford is that men, being as shallow as a drop of spit, WANT women to look that way. To which I have two responses:

1. Hey, just because WE'RE idiots, that does not mean YOU have to be; and
2. Men don't even notice 97 percent of the beauty efforts you make anyway.

Take fingernails. The average woman spends 5,000 hours per year worrying about her fingernails; I have never once, in more than 40 years of listening to men talk about women, heard a man say, "She has a nice set of fingernails!" Many men would not even notice if a woman had upward of four hands.

(9) Anyway, to get back to my original point: If you're a man, and a woman asks you how she looks, you're in big trouble. Obviously, you can't say she looks bad. But you also can't say that she looks great, because she'll think you're lying, because she has spent countless hours, with the help of the multibillion-dollar beauty industry, obsessing about the differences between herself and Cindy Crawford. Also, she suspects that you're not qualified to judge anybody's appearance. This is because you have shaving cream in your hair.

Reading Survey

1. MAIN IDEA

What is the central theme of this essay?

2. MAJOR DETAILS

a. According to the author, how do most men think they look? How do most women think they look?
b. According to the author, why do most women have low self-esteem?
c. What does the author say to women who blame their obsession with beauty on the need to satisfy men's expectations?

3. INFERENCES

a. Read paragraph 5 again. Why does the author apologize for calling little boy's toys "dolls" instead of "action figures"?
b. Read paragraph 7 again. Why would men find this task demeaning?

4. OPINIONS

a. Read paragraphs 3 and 4 again. Do you agree with the author that "women generally do not think of their looks in the same way that men do"? Explain your point of view.
b. Read paragraph 5 again. Do you agree with the author that Barbie dolls and He-Man action figures have influenced the ways in which men and women view their personal appearance? Explain your point of view.

Vocabulary Building

Lesson One: The Vocabulary of Self-Image, Part I

The essay "The Ugly Truth About Beauty" by Dave Barry includes words that are useful when you are discussing a person's self-image.

irresistible (paragraph 2)
bloat (2)
regimen (3)
devote (3)
critical (3)
self-esteem (5)
hideous (5)
self-confident (5)
demeaning (7)
to bolster (7)

People who have a good self-image may think they are **irresistible**—extremely attractive and hard to resist.

People who have a good self-image may think they are good-looking even if parts of their bodies **bloat**—become large and swollen.

People who have a good self-image may follow a simple **regimen**—a step-by-step plan for maintenance or improvement—in caring for their appearance.
People who have a good self-image may **devote** themselves—spend their time and energy entirely on a particular activity—to more important things than their looks.
People who have a good self-image may not think that their appearance is **critical**—extremely important or necessary—to their success in life.
People who have a good self-image usually have a high level of **self-esteem**—respect for themselves.
People who have a good self-image probably do not worry that they will look **hideous**—ugly and disgusting.
People who have a good self-image are usually **self-confident**—sure of themselves.
People who have a good self-image tend to think that trying to look like a supermodel is **demeaning**—causing a loss of pride, self-respect, and status.
People who have a good self-image usually find ways **to bolster**—to support or boost—their confidence in themselves.

EXERCISE 6A: Match each classified ad with a vocabulary word from the lesson. Use each word only once.

PROFESSIONAL SERVICES

LOSE WEIGHT NOW! Our proven five-step plan can help you shed pounds fast. Call the Digby Diet Center today to improve your looks one step at a time.

1. ______________________

BANISH UNWANTED HAIR! Are you tired of plucking those ugly-looking hairs from your eyebrows? Get rid of the disgusting things! Call Electra's Electrolysis now!

2. ______________________

TUMMY TROUBLE? When you eat certain foods, does your stomach become large and swollen? Try Gas-Away and feel good again!

3. ______________________

HE CAN'T TAKE HIS EYES OFF YOU since you went to Professional Models School. Want to become extremely attractive and hard to resist? Call Ima N. Ifull.

4. ______________________

HELP WANTED

DO YOU BELIEVE IN YOURSELF? Self-starter needed to open a new sales office and build a business from the ground up. Call Eager Beaver Headhunters.

5. ______________________________

KEY PERSON needed to manage busy emergency room. This is an extremely important position, on call 24 hours a day. Send résumé to Human Resources Director, Central City Hospital.

6. ______________________________

IS YOUR JOB BRINGING YOU DOWN? Getting coffee when you should be getting ahead? Escape your lowly status and regain your self-respect! Call Ima Climber at A1 Employment.

7. ______________________________

DEDICATE YOURSELF to a worthwhile goal! Make a five-year commitment to City Mission, a volunteer group serving the homeless.

8. ______________________________

BOOST YOUR SPIRITS with Higher Horizons, a workshop that will raise your confidence and help you get the job you always wanted. Call Ike N. DuWunders.

9. ______________________________

YOU'RE TOPS! You know you're good at what you do. You know you can do even better. Call Excel Employment; we'll treat you with the respect you deserve.

10. ______________________________

Lesson Two: The Vocabulary of Self-Image, Part II

Here are more words from the essay "The Ugly Truth About Beauty" by Dave Barry that are useful when you are discussing a person's self-image. The list includes two additional words that are often used when discussing self-image.

proportioned (paragraph 5)
dispensed (6)
dutifully (6)
observer (6)
remotely (6)
genetic mutation (6)
obsessed (8)
shallow (8)
inferior
self-conscious

People who have a poor self-image may think that their bodies are not well **proportioned**—balanced in size and shape.

People who have a poor self-image may think that good looks can be **dispensed**—given out in portions—from a medicine bottle.

People who have a poor self-image tend to follow beauty tips **dutifully**—as if they are required to do so.

People who have a poor self-image usually are not good **observers**—people who pay careful attention to what they see—of their own appearance.

People who have a poor self-image may have a mental picture of themselves that is not even **remotely**—slightly or distantly—related to real life.

People who have a poor self-image may admire supermodels who appear to be **genetic mutations**—individuals who look different from other people because of a change in their genes before birth.

People who have a poor self-image are often **obsessed** with—overly concerned with or troubled by—their appearance.

People who have a poor self-image may have a **shallow**—not very deep—idea of what beauty is.

People who have a poor self-image may think they are **inferior**—second-rate and not as good as others.

People who have a poor self-image are often **self-conscious**—overly aware of their own appearance or behavior.

EXERCISE 6B: Match each classified ad with a vocabulary word from the lesson. Use each word only once.

PROFESSIONAL SERVICES

DO YOU FEEL SECOND-RATE? I can help you overcome your poor opinion of yourself. Call Dr. S. Freud at 447–2859.

1. ______________________

HIPS TOO WIDE? LEGS TOO SHORT? Our designers can hide those shortcomings. Call The Perfect Torso for clothes that make your body look well balanced.

2. ______________________

ARE YOU A FEATHERWEIGHT? Try Weight-On, the great new pill that builds strong bodies fast. It's safe; this medical miracle will be given to you in exactly the right portions. Call us at Body-in-a-Bottle.

3. ______________________

WISH YOU COULD CHANGE YOUR APPEARANCE OVERNIGHT? No, this isn't science fiction. Call Dr. Gene N. Jineering for a whole new you!

4. ______________________

UNCOMFORTABLE IN SOCIAL SITUATIONS? If you are overly aware of the way you look, group therapy can help you. Join Shy People Anonymous and stop worrying about your appearance.

5. ______________________

IS YOUR BEAUTY SKIN DEEP? Discover your inner beauty at Still Waters Spiritual Center. Call Notveri Deep for an in-depth interview.

6. ______________________

MIRROR, MIRROR ON THE WALL! Does the image in your head match the one in the mirror? If not, you need help. Call The Looking Glass and learn to pay careful attention to what you see.

7. ______________________

HELP WANTED

CAN'T STOP THINKING ABOUT WORK? We want to employ you! Call us 24/7/365 at Overdoers, Inc.

8. ______________________

ARE YOU A LOYAL SOLDIER? You've served your boss faithfully for years, doing everything your job description requires. Let us promote you! Call The Service.

9. ______________________

NOT EVEN SLIGHTLY INTERESTED IN YOUR JOB? Only a slim chance of getting promoted? Then it's time for a change! Major company seeks foreign sales person. Stay distantly connected via e-mail. Call Far-Flung Enterprises International.

10. ______________________________

SPELLING

Commonly Confused Words

You may sometimes misspell a word because you confuse it with another word that is similar in appearance. Unlike the Sound-Alikes given in Chapter Two, the sets of words listed below are not pronounced alike, but there is a close resemblance in their spelling; often the difference is just a letter or two. Because they are commonly used words, you should try to learn them.

I. A/An/And. *A* and *an* are two forms of the same word; both *a* and *an* mean "one."

a. *An* is used before a word beginning with a vowel sound (*a, e, i, o, u*).

an *a*thlete   an *o*nion   an *u*mbrella

A is used before a word beginning with a consonant sound (all letters other than the vowels).

a *h*orse   a *n*urse   a *w*indow

TRY IT OUT

FILL IN EACH BLANK WITH *A* OR *AN*.

________ class   ________ teacher   ________ snake

________ orange   ________ insect   ________ answer

b. *An* is used before a word beginning with a silent *h*.

an *h*our an *h*onorable discharge

A is used before a word beginning with a vowel when that vowel sounds like a consonant. Note in the examples below that both the vowel *u* and the *Eu* vowel combination sound like the consonant *y*.

a *u*niform a *Eu*ropean a *u*nit

TRY IT OUT

FILL IN EACH BLANK WITH *A* OR *AN*.

_______ union _______ hour _______ university

_______ honor _______ U-turn _______ honest answer

c. *And* joins two words or ideas together. *And* means "plus" or "in addition to."

Smith *and* Johnson are the most common last names in America.
The largest planet in our solar system is Jupiter, *and* the smallest is Pluto.

TRY IT OUT

FILL IN EACH BLANK WITH *A, AN,* OR *AND.*

1. _______ cat's tail contains three times as many muscles as _______ human hand _______ wrist do.

2. _______ elephant eats as much as five hundred pounds of food _______ day _______ sleeps only two or three hours _______ night.

II. Other Commonly Confused Words

a. *accept* (to receive)

I would be happy to accept the dinner invitation.

except (excluding)

Everyone except Joe passed the English test.

b. *advice* (a recommendation)

My mother gave me good advice concerning my future plans.

advise (to give a recommendation)

I advised Jack to see a doctor.

c. *affect* (to change or influence)

The bad weather will affect my plans for the day.

effect (to cause; the result)

The doctor is working to effect a cure.

Alcohol has a strange effect on many people.

d. *breath* (an exhalation)

I could smell liquor on his breath.

breathe (to inhale and exhale)

It is unhealthy to breathe polluted air.

e. *choose* (to select—present tense)

Because I am lazy, I always choose the easiest courses.

chose (to select—past tense)

Ann chose a Buick as her next car.

f. *clothes* (garments)

Lou changed his clothes before going out for dinner.

cloths (pieces of fabric)

We have a drawer full of dusting cloths.

g. *costume* (a suit or dress)

Helen wore a gypsy costume to the masquerade ball.

custom (the usual course of action)

It is a custom to tip a waiter.

h. *desert* (to leave or abandon; a dry, wasted region)

Do not desert those in need.

The Sahara Desert is in North-Central Africa.

dessert (the last course of a meal)

Strawberry shortcake is my favorite dessert.

i. *later* (coming after)

Mike promised to do his homework later.

latter (the second of two things)

The millionaire has both a Rolls-Royce and a Jaguar XKE; the latter is a very expensive sports car.

j. *loose* (not tight)

The car has a loose wire.

lose (to misplace)

I had better tighten this button before I lose it.

loss (the fact of being misplaced)

Phyllis was upset about the loss of her watch.

k. *moral* (an ethical issue)

There is a moral to be learned from many children's fables.

morale (mental state)

The soldiers' morale was improved by the visiting entertainers.

l. *quiet* (silent)

You must be quiet in a library.

quite (completely)

She was quite tired after the long trip.

A Special Note: Memory tricks may help you to distinguish between these often confused words.

Remember that *ex*cept means *ex*clude.

The expression "cause and effect" will help you link *effect* with "to cause."

Strawberry *s*hortcake is a de*ss*ert.

Three vowels in a row are very q*uie*t.

EXERCISE 6C: Fill in each blank with *a, an,* or *and.*

1. _______ English medical journal claims that _______ overweight child who does not slim down by age 7 will probably stay fat for _______ lifetime.

2. While it is growing, _______ banana consumes oxygen, gives off carbon dioxide, _______ creates its own heat.

3. _______ old Biblical saying insists that it is more difficult for _______ rich person to enter into the kingdom of heaven than it is for _______ camel to pass through the eye of _______ needle.

4. _______ ant is equipped with five different noses, each designed to accomplish _______ specific task.

5. _______ average seven-inch pencil is capable of drawing _______ line thirty-five miles long.

6. Felix Mendelssohn, the famous German composer _______ musician, had already written _______ opera, _______ overture, _______ several symphonies by the time he was 17.

7. _______ United Nations study says that Hungary has the highest recorded suicide rate _______ Mexico has the lowest.

8. _______ angry Los Angeles librarian took away _______ man's library card because the fellow had _______ unusual habit of using _______ strip of raw bacon as _______ bookmark.

9. _______ Japanese inventor has created _______ vending machine that freshly cooks _______ serves _______ plate of spaghetti with meat sauce in twenty-seven seconds.

10. According to _______ recent study of color preferences, _______ intellectual person usually prefers blue _______ _______ athletic person usually prefers red.

11. _______ Georgia law makes it illegal to slap _______ friend on the back, _______ _______ Florida law makes it illegal to break more than three dishes _______ day.

12. The little metal or plastic tip on the end of _______ shoelace is called _______ aglet.

13. _______ ostrich can run twice as fast as _______ human being can.

14. _______ thirsty camel can drink twenty-five gallons of water in half _______ hour.

15. In New Hampshire it is legal for _______ 14-year-old boy _______ _______ 13-year-old girl to get married.

EXERCISE 6D: Underline the correct word from each set of words in parentheses.

In certain parts of the world, it is the (costume, custom) to (accept, except) treatment from "doctors" who have had no medical training whatsoever but are apparently (quiet, quite) successful at giving medical (advice, advise) and performing a mysterious form of surgery. Perhaps the most famous of these healers was an uneducated Brazilian named Arigo, who in the (later, latter) years of his life (adviced, advised) more than 2 million people, some of whom came from as far away as Tokyo and the Sahara (Desert, Dessert). When a team of fourteen American scientists (choose, chose) to investigate his work, they traveled to his clinic in a (deserted, desserted) region of Brazil, where they watched what occurred between each of 1,000 patients and Arigo. In about one minute's time, the (later, latter) would complete his examination and give an accurate diagnosis and the appropriate prescription to (affect, effect) a cure. To perform an operation, he wore his (loose, lose, loss) native (costume, custom) instead of the surgical (clothes, cloths) usually seen in hospitals. In one instance, he decided to (choose, chose) a pocket knife as his surgical tool and, as his patient took a deep (breath, breathe), Arigo inserted the dirty blade into the patient's arm and cut out an egg-shaped tumor. (Accept, Except) for a slight (loose, lose, loss) of blood, the surgery had no bad (affect, effect) on the patient's health.

Arigo's methods may have spread to the Philippine Islands and (affected, effected) a group of men who use their bare hands to perform operations and yet rarely (loose, lose, loss) a patient. In a typical operation, a woman complaining of a constant pain in her stomach lay down on a table while the surgeon dipped some cotton (clothes, cloths) in a bowl of water and then rubbed her abdomen with them. Soon a watery liquid that looked like blood began to gurgle up between the surgeon's fingers as they started to poke around inside the woman's belly. The patient continued to (breath, breathe) normally and remained (quiet, quite) throughout her ordeal; indeed, her (moral, morale) was very good. After removing a large round lump from her belly, the surgeon wiped her abdomen clean with a towel, leaving no wound whatsoever. The woman then got off the table, walked home, and managed to eat an entire dinner from soup to (desert, dessert). Although some American scientists are impressed by these apparently miraculous medical procedures, the (moral, morale) issue cannot be overlooked: Should individuals who have no medical training be permitted to practice medicine?

Pronoun Choice

A pronoun takes the place of a noun, a word that indicates a person, place, or thing. For example:

In 1972, Michael Gallen established a new world's record for eating bananas; *he* consumed sixty-three of *them* in just ten minutes.

In the sentence above, *he* takes the place of *Michael Gallen,* and *them* takes the place of *bananas.* If the nouns were used instead of the pronouns, the sentence would become very wordy.

Pronouns have different forms—or cases—depending on how they function in a sentence. For example:

Arnold Bly was able to write the entire Lord's Prayer on a single grain of rice. *He* demonstrated *his* remarkable lettering ability at the 1939 World's Fair in New York.

Notice that *He* and *his* both refer back to *Arnold Bly.* Yet the two pronouns differ in form. Some major forms of pronouns are

I Subject Pronouns

II Object Pronouns

III Possessive Pronouns

IV Pronouns Ending in *-self* or *-selves*

I (a). Subject Pronouns

The Subject Pronouns

Singular	*Plural*
I	we
you (one person)	you (more than one person)
he	they
she	
it	

These pronouns are the subjects of verbs. A subject explains who or what is doing the action of the verb.

She can whistle "The Star-Spangled Banner."
In less than one hour *they* spent $3,000 on clothing.

Who or what can whistle? *She* can. Who or what spent? *They* spent. Therefore, *she* and *they* are subject pronouns.

I (b). Subject pronouns are also used after a form of the verb *to be: am, is, are, was, were, be, been.*

My father thought it was *I* who dented the car.
It is *she* who runs the entire company.

I (c). A subject pronoun is used even when it is joined with other subjects in a sentence.

Joan and *I* fell into the quicksand.

If you are tempted to write "Joan and *me*" in the sentence above, check yourself by reading only the pronoun with the rest of the sentence. The correct pronoun will sound right.

Wrong: *Me* fell into the quicksand.

Right: *I* fell into the quicksand.

Also, notice that the pronoun *I* always follows the other subjects in a sentence. Thus, you would write "Joan and *I*," not "*I* and Joan."

TRY IT OUT

UNDERLINE THE CORRECT PRONOUN FROM EACH SET OF WORDS GIVEN IN PARENTHESES.

1. It was (them, they) who covered the sidewalk with graffiti.
2. (He, Him) and (I, me) work part time at the local Burger King.
3. When are you and (her, she) finally going to get married?

II (a). Object Pronouns

The Object Pronouns

Singular	*Plural*
me	us
you (one person)	you (more than one person)
him	them
her	
it	

These pronouns may be the objects of verbs. An object explains who or what is receiving the action of the verb. To find an object, simply ask *whom* or *what* after the verb.

Denise slapped *him* in the face.
The banker hid *them* under the mattress.

Denise slapped whom? She slapped *him. Him* is the object pronoun. The banker hid what? He hid *them. Them* is the object pronoun.

II (b). Object pronouns are also used after prepositions, such as *at, between, by, for, from, in, inside, into, near, next to, of, on, onto, over, through, under, with,* and *without.*

The ground began to move *under him.*
The flying saucer landed right *next to me.*

II (c). An object pronoun is used even when it is joined with other objects in a sentence.

The roller coaster ride made my wife and *me* sick.

If you are tempted to write "my wife and *I*" in the sentence above, check yourself by reading only the pronoun with the rest of the sentence. The correct pronoun will sound right.

Wrong: The roller coaster ride made ***I*** sick.

Right: The roller coaster ride made *me* sick.

TRY IT OUT

UNDERLINE THE CORRECT PRONOUN FROM EACH SET OF WORDS GIVEN IN PARENTHESES.

1. The police arrested Bob and (her, she) for using stolen credit cards.
2. I could not keep up with (he, him) and the other marathon runners.
3. After picking up the tip, the waiter gave Susan and (I, me) a dirty look.

III (a). Possessive Pronouns

The Possessive Pronouns

Singular	*Plural*
my, mine	our, ours
your, yours	your, yours
his	their, theirs
her, hers	
its	

Possessive pronouns show ownership or possession.

A hummingbird flaps *its* wings over 4,000 times a minute.
Your car is beautiful; *theirs* is a nightmare on wheels.

Notice that the possessive pronouns do not use apostrophes. Be careful not to confuse these pronouns with contractions such as *it's* (it is), *you're* (you are), or *they're* (they are). (For more information on contractions, see pages 337–38.)

III (b). Possessive pronouns are used before an *-ing* verb that is used as a noun.

The audience was put to sleep by *his singing.*
My *passing* this course could mean the difference between summer school and a summer job.

What put the audience to sleep? *His singing.* Because *singing* functions as a noun in this sentence, a possessive pronoun precedes it. What could mean the difference between summer school and a summer job? *My passing* this course. Because *passing* functions as a noun here, a possessive pronoun precedes it.

TRY IT OUT

UNDERLINE THE CORRECT PRONOUN FROM EACH SET OF WORDS GIVEN IN PARENTHESES.

1. If (its, it's) very hungry, a camel will eat (its, it's) owner's tent.
2. My husband complains about (me, my) watching football games on television every Sunday afternoon.
3. (Your, You're) going to be late for (your, you're) own graduation.

IV (a). Pronouns Ending in -*Self* or -*Selves*

The -*Self* & -*Selves* Pronouns

Singular	*Plural*
myself	ourselves
yourself	yourselves
himself	themselves
herself	
itself	

These pronouns are used to indicate an action that affects the one who performs it.

I cut *myself* while shaving this morning.
The children got *themselves* into trouble with the police.

IV (b). These pronouns are also used for emphasis.

The chef *himself* could not eat the meal.
We do not understand punk rock music *ourselves*.

When you write these pronouns, be careful to form them correctly. There are no words such as *hisself, ourself, theirself, themself,* and *theirselves.*

IV (c). None of these pronouns can be used as the subject of a sentence.

Barbara and ~~myself~~ I refused to eat the chocolate-covered ants.

TRY IT OUT

UNDERLINE THE CORRECT PRONOUN FROM EACH SET OF WORDS GIVEN IN PARENTHESES.

1. Jack always laughs whenever he looks at (himself, hisself) in a mirror.
2. The doctor and (I, me, myself) argued about his ridiculously high fees.
3. Nurses have to pay for their uniforms (theirselves, themself, themselves).

You probably use most pronouns correctly without having to think about rules of grammar, but following are a few types of sentence structure that may cause you trouble.

Comparisons. When making a comparison, be careful to select the correct pronoun to follow *than* or *as.* Some comparisons need subject pronouns to follow *than* or *as.*

You are lazier *than I.*
That old woman can run as fast *as he.*

Comparisons like these are shortened forms of longer ones. To check that the pronoun is correct, add the missing word or words to the comparison.

You are lazier than *I am.*
That old woman can run as fast as *he can run.*

With these comparisons completed, the pronoun *I* is clearly the subject of the verb *am,* and the pronoun *he* is clearly the subject of the verbs *can run.*

Some comparisons need object pronouns to follow *than* or *as.*

Our English teacher praises you more often *than her.*
Calculus confuses me as much *as them.*

When these shortened comparisons are completed, the pronouns *her* and *them* are clearly objects of verbs.

Our English teacher praises you more often than *he praises her.*
Calculus confuses me as much as *it confuses them.*

Be careful to use the correct type of pronoun in a comparison; the type of pronoun that is placed after *than* or *as* can change the meaning of a sentence.

Dad loves my sister more than *I.* (more than I love her)
Dad loves my sister more than *me.* (more than he loves me)

To make sure that the reader does not misunderstand the meaning, it is always a good idea to write the complete comparison; avoid shortened comparisons.

TRY IT OUT

UNDERLINE THE CORRECT PRONOUN FROM EACH SET OF WORDS GIVEN IN PARENTHESES.

1. Lisa is smarter than (I, me), but I have more money than (her, she).
2. The boss gave you a bigger raise than (her, she).
3. The other bowlers on the team are not as good as (us, we).

Who/Whom, Whoever/Whomever. *Who* and *whoever* are subject pronouns.

The jury convicted the thief *who* had robbed the supermarket.
Whoever made dinner needs cooking lessons.

In the first example above, *who* is the subject of the verbs *had robbed.* In the second example, *whoever* is the subject of the verb *made.*

Who or *whoever* may follow a preposition if the pronoun is the subject of a verb.

The college should give a scholarship to *whoever* needs one.

Although *whoever* follows the preposition *to,* the pronoun is not the object of the preposition; *whoever* is the subject of the verb *needs.*

Whom and *whomever* are object pronouns.

To *whom* are you addressing that insult?
Tom always bores *whomever* he dates.

In the first example above, *whom* is the object of the preposition *to.* In the second example, *whomever* is the object of the verb *dates.*

TRY IT OUT

UNDERLINE THE CORRECT PRONOUN FOR EACH SET OF WORDS GIVEN IN PARENTHESES.

1. (Who, Whom) dropped that chocolate cream pie on the rug?
2. Some mothers are prepared to dislike (whoever, whomever) their sons marry.
3. With (who, whom) are you having dinner tonight?
4. The cereal company will give a free baseball to (whoever, whomever) sends in 500 box tops.

We/Us. The pronouns *we* and *us* are sometimes followed by a noun that identifies who *we* or *us* is.

We drivers need lower automobile insurance rates.
The television networks have been treating *us viewers* like idiots.

To determine the correct pronoun, simply read the sentence without the noun.

We need lower automobile insurance rates.
The television networks have been treating *us* like idiots.

TRY IT OUT

UNDERLINE THE CORRECT PRONOUN FROM EACH SET OF WORDS GIVEN IN PARENTHESES.

1. Mr. Higgins gave (us, we) students just five days to do a ten-page essay.
2. (Us, We) consumers are protected by many federal laws.

EXERCISE 6E: Underline the correct pronoun from each set of words given in parentheses.

1. Although (her, she) and her business partner are having financial problems, she is one of the few factory owners (who, whom) (us, we) workers can really trust when the time comes to negotiate a new contract.
2. Just between you and (I, me), (I, me) don't think that our gym teacher is as intelligent as (us, we).
3. (Its, It's) amazing that a giant clam may weigh up to 500 pounds, and (its, it's) shell may measure up to four feet across.
4. The other witness and (I, me, myself) thought it was (her, she) (who, whom) committed the crime.
5. (Me, My) father is not happy about (me, my) joining the Army because he (himself, hisself) was a Navy man.
6. Oscar invites you and (I, me) for dinner more often than (them, they); (them, they) are lucky, for Oscar is a terrible cook.
7. (Their, They're) offering a reward to (whoever, whomever) finds (their, they're) pet tarantula.
8. (Us, We) men had better get (ourself, ourselves) into shape if we hope to look better than (he, him).
9. Stella and (I, me, myself) are tired of being treated so poorly; indeed, (your, you're) treating (your, you're) cat better than (us, we).
10. Firefighters frequently put (theirselves, themself, themselves) in danger to help (whoever, whomever) they find in a burning building. I certainly do not have as much courage as (them, they).
11. (He, Him, His) playing the stereo at 3 A.M. got (us, we) neighbors so angry that we woke his wife and (he, him) at 6 A.M. to complain.
12. (He, Him) and Shirley are the people to (who, whom) you should turn for advice.
13. Our driving instructor must dislike you as much as (I, me); after all, (he, him) threw (us, we) both out of the car.
14. Al, (who, whom) has a newer car than (I, me), has more trouble with his car than (I, me) do with mine.
15. (Their, Them, They) constant complaining got (us, we) waiters so annoyed that no one will wait on (them, they) anymore.

EXERCISE 6F: Correct any pronoun errors in the paragraphs below. Use your own paper, if needed.

Us softhearted people can easily get ourself into a great deal of trouble. For example, last Saturday me and my friend Jack went into a local supermarket to get refreshments for a party. As we were walking down an aisle, we noticed an old man and woman whom seemed to be following us. Indeed, each time Jack and myself turned down another aisle we would hear people close behind us, and when we turned around it would be them again, staring at my friend and I. Finally, I could not take any more of them spying on us, so I turned and asked harshly, "Who are you staring at?" Immediately, the old couple started to tremble and they're eyes filled with tears. Upset by them crying, I quickly apologized.

"We're sorry," the old woman responded. "Its just that you remind we old people of our son. Your a little taller than him, but otherwise you look exactly like him."

"Big deal!" I shot back.

With more tears in her eyes, the woman explained, "Our son got hisself killed recently in a car accident."

My eyes lowered in shame as the old man spoke for the first time. "We would be very grateful if when we leave the store, you would wave goodbye to my wife and I and say, 'Bye, Mom and Dad!'"

His request sounded ridiculous, but I agreed anyway. Then Jack and myself went off looking for the rest of the party food. When we later got on the checkout line, we noticed that the couple were already at the counter chatting with the cashier. As the cashier finished packing they're groceries, the couple turned around and yelled, "Bye, son!" Feeling stupid, I waved and yelled back, "Goodbye, Mom and Dad!" With that, they smiled to theirselves and left the store. A few minutes later me and Jack finally reached the cashier. As she finished putting our groceries into a bag, she said, "That will be $83.40." Shocked, us fellows blurted out, "What?" After all, how could a six-pack of beer and some peanuts and pretzels cost that much?

Looking directly at me, the cashier explained, "You're parents said that your paying for everything."

"My parents!" I burst out. "I don't even know whom those people are."

EXERCISE 6G: For each of the words and phrases given below, write a complete sentence that uses the word or phrase correctly. Use your own paper for this assignment.

Example: her and her sister
The truck almost hit *her and her sister.*

1. we students
2. us Americans
3. himself
4. themselves
5. me and him
6. she and her boyfriend
7. my winning the state lottery
8. their laughing at my appearance
9. who
10. whom
11. its
12. it's
13. the coach and us
14. they and their families
15. better than me
16. longer than she
17. as rich as they
18. as much as us
19. your
20. you're

Pronoun Agreement

A pronoun must agree in number with the word or words for which it stands. If a pronoun stands for a singular word, the pronoun should be singular; if the pronoun stands for a plural word, the pronoun should be plural.

Mike said that he would fulfill his plans.

The astronauts left their space capsule to walk in space.

These examples are easy enough to understand. But there are some common problems in agreement of pronouns and the words for which they stand. These problems are like those discussed in the earlier section on the agreement of subject and verb. On the following pages you will find the most important pronoun agreement rules.

I (a) Indefinite Pronouns

I (b) Collective Nouns

II (a) Compound Nouns

II (b) *Either . . . or* and *Neither . . . nor*

I (a). Indefinite Pronouns. Use a singular pronoun to refer to indefinite pronouns such as *somebody, someone, something, everybody, everyone, everything, nobody, no one, nothing, anybody, anyone, one, either, neither,* and *each.* In addition, use a singular pronoun to refer to *person, man,* and *woman.*

According to widely accepted traditional usage, the pronouns *he, him, his,* and *himself* are used to refer to these words. However, according to newer usage, the combinations *he or she, him or her, his or her,* or *himself or herself* are used. Because of the word *or,* these combinations are singular, not plural.

Everyone can learn to benefit from his mistakes. (traditional usage)

Everyone can learn to benefit from his or her mistakes. (newer usage)

A person should practice what he preaches. (traditional usage)

A person should practice what he or she preaches. (newer usage)

For good style, try to avoid more than one combination in a sentence. You might try to restructure your sentence. One way is to change to a plural subject, if possible.

Cluttered:	When a person practices what he or she preaches, he or she tends to be somewhat cautious in giving advice.
Clear:	When people practice what they preach, they tend to be somewhat cautious in giving advice.

I (b). Collective Nouns. Collective nouns such as *group, team, class,* and *family* take a singular pronoun when the noun refers to the group as a whole and a plural pronoun when the noun refers to the individual members of the group.

The team is practicing for its biggest game.

The team are going their separate ways after this game.

TRY IT OUT

INSERT THE CORRECT PRONOUN IN THE SPACES PROVIDED.

1. The oil company paid for television commercials that would improve ______________ public image.
2. Someone parked ______________ car on the sidewalk.
3. The rock band surprised ______________ audience by playing "The Beer Barrel Polka."

II (a). Compound Nouns. Use a plural pronoun when you are referring to two or more words joined by *and.* However, when *each* or *every* precedes singular words joined by *and,* a singular pronoun should be used to stand for these words.

Lynn and David are transforming their basement into a playroom.

Every girl and young woman needs to choose a career for herself.

II (b). *Either . . . or* and *Neither . . . nor*. When two words are joined by *either . . . or* or *neither . . . nor,* the pronoun should agree with the word that is closer.

Either Dan or Ted will read his article.

Neither the general nor his officers have revealed their secret.

TRY IT OUT

INSERT THE CORRECT PRONOUNS IN THE SPACES PROVIDED.

1. Neither the professor nor her students were able to find ______________ classroom.
2. A lion and a tiger like ______________ meat very rare.
3. Every waiter and busboy needs comfortable shoes, or ______________ feet will hurt at the end of ______________ work shift.
4. Either the tenants or the landlord will be given a chance to present ______________ complaints about poor garbage-pickup service provided by the city.

EXERCISE 6H: Underline the correct pronoun from each set of words given in parentheses.

John and Janet were getting disgusted with (his or her, their) apartment. Neither Mr. Hand, the superintendent, nor (his, their) helpers were doing (his, their) jobs properly. As a result, everyone in the building was complaining because (he or she, they) did not have enough heat in (his or her, their) apartment. Because many of the burned-out lights had not been replaced in the lobby, one of the tenants, Ms. Foot, tripped in the dark and hurt (her, their) back. The filthy hallways were enough to make every person in the building sick to (his or her, their) stomach. To make matters worse, people could not get anything repaired in (his or her, their) apartments. Each of the tenants complained, but the landlord, Mr. Head, paid no attention to (him or her, them). Therefore, the unhappy residents of the building formed (his or her, their) own tenants' association to pressure the landlord. It was clear that either the tenants or the landlord would have (his, their) way. On several occasions, the association presented (its, their) demands, but the landlord ignored (it, them). At this point, John and Janet decided to move, but first (he or she, they) had one small matter to take care of. To get even with (his or her, their) landlord, (he or she, they) placed a newspaper advertisement which read: "Wanted: 2000 live cockroaches. We are willing to pay top dollar for (it, them). Call 789-7767." The first person to call was a Ms. Finger, who said that (she, they) wanted to know why John and Janet needed 2,000 live cockroaches. John happily explained, "Our lease requires us to leave the apartment exactly as we found (it, them), and that's just what we intend to do!"

EXERCISE 6I: Rewrite the following sentences, making sure to correct any errors in verb and pronoun agreement.

1. Because the group of shopowners were pleased with their profits, they decided to sponsor a Little League team this year.

   ____

   ____

2. Doctors tell us that fifty pounds are too much for a person to lose in only three months if they want to remain healthy.

   ____

   ____

3. The Navy, as well as the other U.S. armed services, are eager to attract well-qualified recruits to their ranks.

   ____

   ____

4. Either of the two applicants have their own good reasons for wanting a job taming lions for the circus.

   ____

   ____

5. Every person who tries to take advantage of poor people should be condemned for their actions.

6. Neither the gorillas nor the zookeeper want to have their picture taken with the visiting politician.

7. Because automobile sales has been poor, General Motors have closed several of their factories.

8. Here stand the astronaut who traveled to the moon and reported their adventures in an exciting interview on television.

9. Everyone were frozen with fear when they saw the flying saucers landing in the parking lot.

10. The scissors you lent me was so dull that I could not cut butter with it.

11. The Teamsters are a large union of people who drive trucks to earn its living.

12. The student government were grateful that the faculty were willing to give their support to the idea of weekend classes for students who work.

____

____

13. Each of the people who sign a lease to share an apartment should realize that they are responsible for all of the rent, not just a part of it.

____

____

14. *Roots*, known for their extremely detailed history of a black family, were written by Alex Haley.

____

____

15. Either prune juice or sauerkraut are sometimes used for their special powers.

____

____

16. A reptile, unlike most creatures, have two lower jawbones that hinge to allow them to swallow food larger than their body.

____

____

17. None are so foolish as he who always believes others.

____

____

18. The government's list of vocational training programs are valuable because they provide information about career possibilities.

____

____

Pronoun Reference and Consistency

A pronoun should always refer clearly to a noun that has already been used, so that a reader will understand immediately which noun the pronoun is replacing. For example:

In Petersburg, West Virginia, a farmer was planting horseradish when *he* found a shiny, greasy stone. Fifteen years later *he* discovered that *it* was a 32-carat diamond.

In the sentences above, the pronoun *he* clearly refers to the farmer and the pronoun *it* clearly refers to the stone.

If the relationship between a pronoun and its noun is not completely clear, your writing will not be easily understood. To avoid this problem, review these important guidelines about pronoun reference and consistency:

I (a) Unclear Reference

I (b) Possessives

II *This, That, Which*

III (a) Unstated Nouns

III (b) *It* and *They*

IV (a) Careless Pronoun Shifts

IV (b) *Person* and *People*

IV (c) Careless Pronoun Shifts in a Paragraph

V Unnecessary Pronouns

I (a). Unclear Reference. A pronoun usually refers to the closest noun that has just been mentioned. If a pronoun can possibly refer to more than one noun that has been mentioned, the reader will be confused.

Confusing: Whenever John plays tennis with Jimmy, *he* always wins.

Who always wins? John or Jimmy? The reader cannot be sure because the pronoun *he* could refer to either person. To avoid such a problem, either repeat the correct noun or restructure the entire sentence.

Clear: Whenever John plays tennis with Jimmy, John always wins.

OR

John always wins whenever he plays tennis with Jimmy.

I (b). Possessives. A pronoun cannot refer to a noun in its possessive form.

Confusing: During the President's press conference, *he* announced a tax increase.

The pronoun *he* cannot refer to *President's,* which is a possessive form. The best way to correct this problem is to restructure the sentence.

Clear: The President announced a tax increase during his press conference.

TRY IT OUT

REVISE THESE SENTENCES TO CLARIFY THE PRONOUN REFERENCES. USE YOUR OWN PAPER IF NEEDED.

1. A log fell right on my foot just as I was about to chop it in half.
2. Because many of Joan Crawford's movies are still shown on television, she will not be forgotten.
3. Snails are eaten by many people even though they are slimy creatures that live in the garden.

II. *This, That, Which.* The pronouns *this, that,* and *which* can be used in place of either a noun or a specific idea that has already been stated. If the pronoun seems to refer to more than one noun or idea, the reader will be confused.

Confusing: My new Pontiac Trans Am was stolen last week, but my insurance company may pay me almost its full value. I was very upset about *that.*

What was I really upset about? That my Pontiac Trans Am was stolen last week? Or that my insurance company may pay me almost its full value? The reader cannot be sure because the pronoun *that* could refer to either idea. To avoid such a problem, either add a noun or restructure the sentences.

Clear: My new Pontiac Trans Am was stolen last week, but my insurance company may pay me almost its full value. I was very upset about *the theft.*

OR

I was very upset that my new Pontiac Trans Am was stolen last week, but my insurance company may pay me almost its full value.

The unclear use of the pronoun *which* can make a sentence unintentionally funny.

Confusing: Kathy gave herself a permanent the night before her wedding *which* made all of her hair fall out.

Did the wedding make all of her hair fall out? Or was the hair loss caused by the permanent?

Clear: The night before her wedding, Kathy gave herself a permanent which made all of her hair fall out.

TRY IT OUT

REVISE THESE SENTENCES TO CLARIFY THE PRONOUN REFERENCES. USE YOUR OWN PAPER IF NEEDED.

1. After Senator Simmons was arrested for drunk driving, he entered an alcohol rehabilitation program. This may hurt his chances for reelection.
2. The city was completely paralyzed by just a few inches of snow. That got many of the citizens angry.
3. Hal stopped using narcotics after he overdosed on heroin which made all of his friends happy.

III (a). Unstated Nouns. A pronoun cannot refer to a noun that has been suggested but never actually stated.

Confusing: My mother is a lawyer, but I am not interested in *it.*

The reader will probably guess that *it* refers to the law, but this noun has not been stated. To correct this problem, replace the unclear pronoun.

Clear: My mother is a lawyer, but I am not interested in the law.

OR

My mother is a lawyer, but I am not interested in becoming one.

III (b). ***It* and *They*.** The pronouns *it* and *they* can be used only when the noun has already been clearly stated.

Confusing: On television last night, *they* said the heat wave will continue for another week.

Who is *they*? To clarify the sentence, supply the missing noun.

Clear: On television last night, the weather forecaster said the heat wave will continue for another week.

TRY IT OUT

REVISE THESE SENTENCES TO CLARIFY THE PRONOUN REFERENCES. USE YOUR OWN PAPER IF NEEDED.

1. Mark got married a few months ago, but it lasted only six days.
2. In Washington, D.C., they just voted to increase defense spending.
3. In most classrooms it says, "No Smoking."

IV (a). **Careless Pronoun Shifts.** Pronouns have to be consistent with the nouns they refer to. For example, a sentence about criminals as its subject would consistently use the pronouns *they, them,* or *their* to refer to criminals. If the sentence suddenly shifted to a different pronoun, the reader would be confused.

Confusing: When criminals were convicted for stealing in ancient China, *you* would be punished by having *your* nose sliced off.

Notice in the example above that the subject shifts from criminals to the pronouns *you* and *your,* which do not refer to criminals.

Clear: When criminals were convicted for stealing in ancient China, *they* would be punished by having *their* noses sliced off.

The tendency to shift to the pronouns *you* and *your* is a common one. To avoid this problem, use *you* and *your* only when referring specifically to the reader.

IV (b). ***Person* and *People*.** A sentence with *person* as its subject should consistently use *he* (or *he or she*) to refer to *person*. (See page 249 for more information on the use of *he or she* instead of *he*.) A sentence with *people* as its subject should consistently use *they* to refer to *people*. If a sentence with *person* or *people* as its subject suddenly shifts to the wrong pronoun, the reader becomes confused.

Confusing: When a *person* is learning to cook, *they* make many mistakes at first.

Can *they* refer to *a person*? No. Use *he* (or *he or she*).

Clear: When a *person* is learning to cook, *he or she* makes many mistakes at first.

Similarly, the pronoun used with *people* should not shift incorrectly.

Confusing: Whenever I hear about *people* who work long hours, I wonder how *he or she* can manage to have time for relaxation.

Can *he or she* refer to *people*? No. Use *they*.

Clear: Whenever I hear about *people* who work long hours, I wonder how *they* can manage to have time for relaxation.

IV (c). **Careless Pronoun Shifts in a Paragraph.** Some careless pronoun shifts may occur as a writer goes from one sentence to the next in a paragraph.

Confusing: *Muggers* do not care whom *they* hurt. *He* can use a knife or a gun without even thinking about the victim. *They* are determined to get what *they* want.

In the example above, the writer lost sight of the pronoun *they* in the first sentence and shifted to *he* in the second sentence. In the third sentence the writer wandered back to the correct pronoun.

Clear: *Muggers* do not care whom *they* hurt. *They* can use a knife or a gun without even thinking about the victim. *They* are determined to get what *they* want.

TRY IT OUT

CORRECT ANY ERRORS IN PRONOUN CONSISTENCY IN THE SENTENCES BELOW. USE YOUR OWN PAPER IF NEEDED.

1. From where I was standing, you could see Mount Rushmore very clearly.
2. As a person gets older, their nose continues to grow larger.
3. Some people like to eat raw hamburger meat, but he or she runs the risk of getting sick from bacteria in the meat.
4. I will never forget my first airplane trip. The flight was so bumpy that you could not eat your meal without spilling it all over yourself.

V. **Unnecessary Pronouns.** A noun and its pronoun should not be used immediately following one another.

Wordy: Susan B. Anthony *she* worked for women's rights.

Clear: Susan B. Anthony worked for women's rights.

Wordy: In the newspaper, *it* gives the winning lottery numbers.

Clear: The newspaper gives the winning lottery numbers.

If you use unnecessary pronouns, your sentences will be cluttered and confusing.

TRY IT OUT

ELIMINATE ANY UNNECESSARY PRONOUNS IN THE SENTENCES BELOW. USE YOUR OWN PAPER IF NEEDED.

1. In the Pentagon they have 25,000 telephones.
2. Marie Curie, who discovered radium, she won two Nobel Prizes.

EXERCISE 6J: In the following sentences correct any unclear pronoun references and errors in pronoun consistency. Also, eliminate any unnecessary pronouns. Use your own paper for this assignment.

1. When a person has "aviophobia," you suffer from a fear of flying.

2. To make one pound of butter, they use twenty-one quarts of milk.

3. Grasshoppers are used as food by some people; in fact, they are three times as nutritious as beefsteak.

4. Prison riots have been occurring more frequently because they are complaining that their poor living conditions are a violation of basic human rights.

5. People who jog should do muscle-stretching exercises before they start running so that you can prevent injuries as much as possible.

6. The Rivoli Theater may be torn down after Bruce Springsteen's concert. That should not be allowed to happen.

7. If a person started counting twenty-four hours a day at birth, they would not get to a trillion for 31,688 years.

8. In the newspaper it said that about 57 million Americans become victims of crime every year.

9. Many women need to eat a diet that is rich in iron; otherwise, you can easily become anemic.

10. An octopus can gather up as many as twenty-five crabs at one time in its eight arms. Then it eats them one by one.

11. An insect's skeleton grows outside its body.

12. Ralph Cambridge, the oldest bridegroom in history, he was 105 years old when he married a 70-year-old woman in South Africa in 1971.

13. Mark Spitz won seven gold medals for swimming in the Olympics at Munich, Germany, which really amazed everyone.

14. Child abuse has become such a widespread problem that several states are passing stricter laws to protect them.

15. When people use toothpicks or talk with toothpicks in their mouths, he or she is in danger because more people choke to death on toothpicks than on anything else.
16. They used to make gum from chicle, the milky juice of a tropical evergreen tree. Now they frequently make gum from plastics.
17. Back in the 1960's Americans took the nation's energy supply for granted. After all, you could buy a gallon of gasoline for just 29 cents.
18. According to a book of unusual facts, the oil used by jewelers to lubricate clocks and watches it costs about $3,000 a gallon.
19. Many people are donating money to help feed the millions of people who are starving throughout the world. This sounds like a good idea.
20. In ancient China and parts of India, they ate mice on special occasions.
21. The women's liberation movement has helped many of them to gain equal employment opportunities.
22. The members of a Philadelphia family have been written about in several well-known medical journals because they have no fingerprints.
23. Our coach told everyone that I had failed my gym class. That really got me upset.
24. They show advertisements in many movie theaters these days.
25. People are the only animals that can cry. He has tear ducts that respond to emotions or pain. Also, he is the only animal that will kill for pleasure.

EXERCISE 6K: Correct any unclear pronoun references and eliminate any unnecessary pronouns in the following paragraphs. Use your own paper for this assignment.

Martha she enjoyed working as a waitress at Joe's Diner because he treated her well. But she hated to wait on a regular customer named Mrs. Swope. Mrs. Swope she was a bad-tempered old woman who had a well-earned reputation as a complainer. Thus, she was not surprised on one particular day that the old woman started complaining as soon as she sat down at her table. "This water glass is dirty," she insisted as she pointed a finger across the table. Although it was sparkling clean, she got her another one. Then while ordering her meal, she demanded to have strips of bacon instead of fried onions with her broiled liver. When she pointed out that it clearly stated, "No substitutions allowed," the old woman she started to complain loudly enough to disturb the other diners. To quiet her, she quickly agreed to get them for her. Next, she brought her a bowl of steaming soup, which Mrs. Swope insisted was cold. Throughout all of this, she kept reminding herself that they had told her to be courteous at all times. So she hid her anger and did everything she could to please her.

But later in the meal, she shrieked, "Waitress!" and banged her hand forcefully on the table. At that moment, Martha realized that she could not take any more of this. "Waitress," Mrs. Swope repeated, glancing down at her plate with a look of disgust, "this baked potato is bad." Determined to stay calm, she smiled politely as she carefully lifted the potato from the customer's plate. Shaking a finger at it, Martha said angrily in a voice everyone could hear, "Bad potato! Bad, bad potato!" Then she replaced it on her plate and added, "Madam, if it gives you any more trouble, tell me right away and I shall punish it at once!" She remained silent for the rest of her meal and never again uttered a complaint in Joe's Diner.

EXERCISE 6L: Find and correct any errors in pronoun consistency in the following paragraphs. Some pronoun changes may also require verb ending changes in order to maintain correct subject-verb agreement. Use your own paper for this assignment.

The Amish people, who live in their own farming communities in Pennsylvania and twenty other states, cling to the lifestyle of America's pioneer days. The Amish grow their own food, make their own clothes, and refuse most of the conveniences brought by technology. They live this way because of their religion. Guided by a strict interpretation of the Bible, the Amish are against anything not mentioned or accepted by the Bible. Thus, you cannot use electricity, telephones, automobiles, or most store-bought items. You travel by horse and buggy, heat your homes with wood- or coal-burning stoves, and create light with kerosene lamps. Moreover, your children go to a one-room Amish school for just eight years and then go to work in the fields or the home.

Amish children learn early in life that their highly structured world demands strict discipline and set rules for men and women. When an Amish boy reaches sixteen, he is given an open "courting buggy" and horse. With this buggy, you can attend hymn-singing sessions which are held for the young Amish on Sunday afternoons. These social events give you the opportunity to become acquainted with the single girls in your area. After meeting the right one, you must court her politely until you announce your desire to marry, usually when you are in your early twenties. The wedding, always held after the harvest in the fall, draws friends and relatives from several states. After they are married, the couple spend a month or two visiting relatives all over the country. During this honeymoon trip, you receive many wedding gifts, all of which are practical items needed by a farm family.

When you return home, you live with the husband's parents and become hard-working members of the household. Indeed, the young couple's workday, with the exception of Sunday, starts before sunrise and lasts until sundown. The husband tends the crops, fields, and livestock without the help of tractors and the other modern farm equipment that is banned by the Amish. Meanwhile, the wife takes care of the house and does cooking and canning. In your spare time, you also make new clothing or wash and mend the old clothing. Eventually, you will have several children to care for as well, since the Amish generally have large families. Although such work forms the backbone of Amish life, the couple do have some leisure-time activities. In the evenings and on Sundays, you can socialize at barn-raisings, quilting bees, auctions, and songfests. But you cannot go to a movie or relax in front of a television set, for such activities are not permitted.

To an outsider, this life may seem difficult because there are few conveniences and no luxuries in the Amish world. But to the Amish, their way of life is quite peaceful and happy.

EXERCISE 6M: REFRESHER

ANSWERS MAY VARY SOMEWHAT.

1. FIND AND CORRECT ANY ERRORS IN VERB AGREEMENT.
2. FIND AND CORRECT ANY ERRORS IN PRONOUN AGREEMENT, VAGUE PRONOUN REFERENCE, OR PRONOUN CONSISTENCY.

Several recent research studies indicates that a man's physical appearance can greatly influence the way in which he is treated by society. This begins in childhood; according to the research, a good-looking boy usually receive less punishment than an unattractive boy receive for making the same mistake. In a high school or college English class, an essay written by a good-looking young man is frequently graded higher by fellow students than is the same essay written by an unattractive male classmate. In the business world, personnel directors often prefers to hire a handsome man to work as a salesman or counselor because it involves a great deal of personal contact. On the job, a handsome man is generally seen as being capable and deserving of promotion. If you are tall, you have an additional advantage, for society places more confidence in a tall man than they do in a short one. In fact, a six-foot-tall man typically earns $4,200 a year more than a five-foot-tall man do in a similar job. If a tall man decides to run for President, their chances of winning is overwhelming if their opponent is even the slightest bit shorter than they are. Indeed, the taller of the two major party candidates have won all but one presidential election since 1900. Obviously, then, a tall, good-looking man has an easier time achieving success in American society.

SPRINGBOARDS TO WRITING

Using your knowledge of the writing process, explained on pages 14–16, write a paragraph or essay related to this chapter's central theme, *personal appearance*, which is introduced on pages 222–25.

PREWRITING

To think of topics to write about, look at the photographs, read the essay, and answer the questions that follow each. If you prefer, select one of the writing springboards below. (All paragraph numbers refer to the essay that starts on page 224.) To develop your ideas, use the prewriting techniques described on pages 17–22.

WRITING A PARAGRAPH *(For help, see the Pointers on page 51.)*

1. Agree or disagree with Dave Barry's statement: "Most men, I believe, think of themselves as average-looking." (See paragraph 3.)
2. Agree or disagree with the author's statement about men: "Being average does not bother them; average is fine, for men." (See paragraph 3.)
3. Agree or disagree with the author's claim that most women think their appearance is "not good enough." (See paragraph 4.)
4. Agree or disagree with the author's claim that many women have low self-esteem because they played with Barbie dolls. (See paragraph 5.)
5. Agree or disagree with the author's claim that "men don't even notice 97 percent of the beauty efforts" that women make. (See paragraph 8.)
6. Describe a time when you were treated either very badly or very well because of your personal appearance.

WRITING AN ESSAY *(For help, see the Pointers on pages 54–55).*

7. Agree or disagree with Dave Barry's statement that "women generally do not think of their looks in the same way that men do." (See paragraph 2.)
8. Why Do Some Women Have Low Self-Esteem? (See paragraph 5.)
9. How to Increase Self-Esteem
10. Is Beauty an Important Asset in Today's Society?
11. My Idea of Beauty
12. The Advantages (Disadvantages) of Being Physically Attractive
13. Why Good Looks Matter More to Women Than to Men
14. Society Does (Does Not) Place Too Much Emphasis on Physical Appearance
15. Agree or disagree with James Matthew Barrie's statement about beauty: "'If you have it, you don't need to have anything else, and if you don't have it, it doesn't much matter what else you have."
16. Often, Women Tend to Behave Differently from Men
17. Men Are (Are Not) Superior to Women
18. Women Are (Are Not) Superior to Men

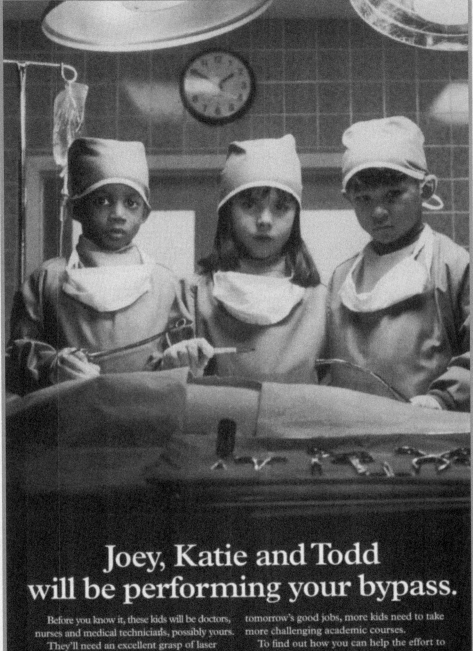

Joey, Katie and Todd will be performing your bypass.

Before you know it, these kids will be doctors, nurses and medical technicians, possibly yours.

They'll need an excellent grasp of laser technology, advanced computing and molecular genetics. Unfortunately, very few American children are being prepared to master such sophisticated subjects.

If we want children who can handle tomorrow's good jobs, more kids need to take more challenging academic courses.

To find out how you can help the effort to raise standards in America's schools, please call 1-800-96-PROMISE. If we make changes now, we can prevent a lot of pain later on.

Chapter 7

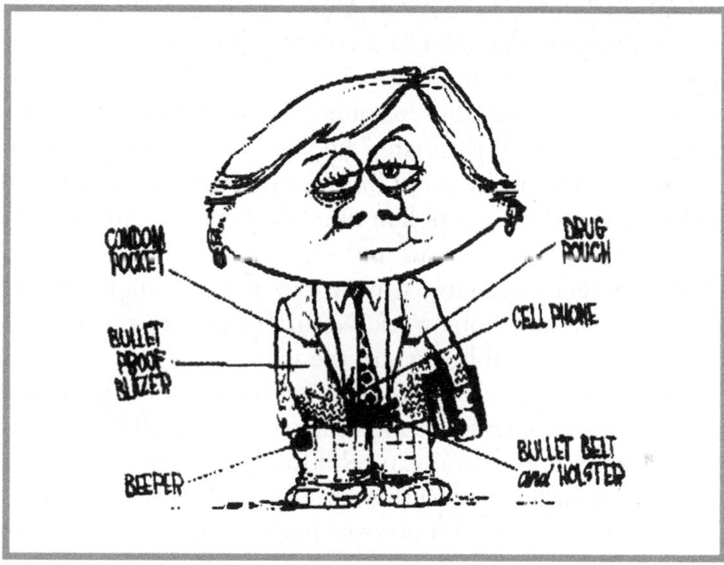

SCHOOL UNIFORMS

SPRINGBOARDS TO THINKING

For informal, not written, response . . . to stimulate your thinking

1. Read the advertisement on the opposite page. Do you agree that very few American children are being prepared to master such sophisticated subjects as laser technology, advanced computing, and molecular genetics? Explain.
2. Do you think it is necessary to take more challenging academic courses to get a good job? Why or why not? Have you taken any challenging academic courses? Why or why not?
3. What do you think should be done to raise standards in American schools?
4. What is the underlying message of the cartoon above? Would you add any other items to this school uniform? If so, which ones?
5. Are some students doing poorly in school because they are preoccupied with drug use, sex, violence, and electronic communication? Explain.

Teenagers in Dreamland

Robert J. Samuelson

(1) Meet Carlos. He's a senior at American High School in Fremont, California. He's also a central character in a recent public television documentary on U.S. education. Carlos is a big fellow with a crew cut and a friendly manner. We see him driving his pickup truck, strolling with a girlfriend and playing in a football game. "I don't want to graduate," he says at one point. "It's fun. I like it."

(2) If you want to worry about our economic future, worry about Carlos and all those like him. It is the problem of adolescence in America. Our teenagers live in a dreamland. It's a curious and disorienting mixture of adult freedoms and childlike expectations. Hey, why work? Average high school students do less than an hour of daily homework. Naturally, they're not acquiring the skills they will need for their well-being and the nation's.

(3) Don't mistake me: I'm not blaming today's teenagers. They are simply the latest heirs of an adolescent subculture—we have all been part of it—that's been evolving for decades. American children are becoming more and more independent at an earlier and earlier age. By 17, two-fifths of Americans have their own car or truck. About 60 percent have their own telephones and televisions. Adult authority wanes, and teen-age power rises. It's precisely this development that has crippled our schools.

(4) Consider the research of sociologist James Coleman of the University of Chicago. He found that students from similar economic and social backgrounds consistently do better at Catholic high schools than at public high schools. The immediate explanation is simple: students at Catholic schools take more rigorous courses in math, English and history, and they do nearly 50 percent more homework. But why do Catholic schools make these demands when public schools don't?

(5) The difference, Coleman concluded, lies with parents. "Parents [of public school students] do not exercise as much authority over their high-school-aged students as they once did," he recently told a conference at the Manhattan Institute. Since the 1960s, public schools have become less demanding—to discipline, required course work and homework—because they can't enforce stiffer demands. By contrast, parents of parochial school students impose more control. "The schools therefore [are] able to operate under a different set of ground rules," Coleman said.

(6) There are obviously many good public schools and hard-working students. But the basic trends are well-established and have been altered only slightly by

recent "reforms." Change comes slowly, because stricter academic standards collide with adolescent reality. In the TV documentary, Tony—a pal of Carlos—is asked why he doesn't take tougher math courses to prepare him as a computer technician, which is what he wants to be. "It's my senior year," he says, "and I think I'm going to relax."

(7) Adolescent autonomy continues to increase. "Teens have changed so dramatically in the past decade that more advertisers . . . are targeting 'adults' as 15-plus or 13-plus rather than the typical 18-plus," notes Teenage Research Unlimited, a market research firm. It estimates that the average 16-to-17-year-old has nearly $60 a week in spending money from jobs and allowances. By junior year, more than 40 percent of high school students have jobs.

(8) These demanding school-time jobs are held predominantly by middle-class students. Popular wisdom asserts that early work promotes responsibility, but the actual effect may be harmful. In a powerful book (*When Teenagers Work*), psychologists Ellen Greenberger of the University of California (Irvine) and Laurence Steinberg of Temple University show that jobs hurt academic performance and do not provide needed family income. Rather, they simply establish teenagers as independent consumers better able to satisfy their own wants. Jobs often encourage drug use.

(9) Our style of adolescence reflects prosperity and our values. We can afford it. In the nineteenth century, children worked to ensure family survival; the same is true today in many developing countries. Our culture stresses freedom, individuality and choice. Everyone has "rights." Authority is to be questioned. Self-expression is encouraged. These attitudes take root early. My 4-year-old daughter recently announced her philosophy of life: "I should be able to do anything I want to do."

(10) Parental guilt also plays a role. The American premise is that the young ought to be able to enjoy their youth. Schools shouldn't spoil it, as if an hour and a half of daily homework (well above the average) would mean misery for teenagers. Finally, more divorce and more families with two wage-earners mean that teenagers are increasingly left to themselves. They often assume some family responsibilities—shopping or caring for younger children. Many teenagers feel harried and confused, because the conflicts among all these roles (student, worker, child and adult) are overwhelming.

(11) Americans, young and old, delude themselves about the results of these changes. A recent study of 13-year-olds in six countries placed Americans last in mathematics and Koreans first. But when students were asked whether they were "good at mathematics," 68 percent of the Americans said yes (the highest) compared with only 23 percent of the Koreans (the lowest).

(12) This was no quirk. Psychologist Harold Stevenson of the University of Michigan, who has studied American and Asian students for years, finds the same relationship. Americans score lower in achievement but, along with their parents, are more satisfied with their performance. "If children believe they are already dong well—and their parents agree with them—what is the purpose of studying harder?" he writes.

(13) Good question. No one should be surprised that U.S. businesses complain about workers with poor skills, or that a high school diploma no longer guarantees a well-paying job. More school spending or new educational "theories" won't magically give students knowledge or skills. It takes work. Our style of adolescence is something of a national curse. Americans are growing up faster, but they may not be growing up better.

Reading Survey

1. MAIN IDEA

What is the central theme of this essay?

2. MAJOR DETAILS

a. When sociologist James Coleman compared students at Catholic high schools with those at public high schools, what did he find?
b. How has parental guilt contributed to the problem of poor academic performance?
c. What were the findings in the study of 13-year-olds in six countries?

3. INFERENCES

a. Read paragraph 2 again. What "childlike expectations" do some teenagers have?
b. Read paragraph 8 again. Why might jobs encourage drug use?

4. OPINIONS

a. Read paragraph 8 again. Do you agree that holding a job hurts academic performance? Explain your point of view.
b. Read paragraph 13 again. Do you agree that "Americans are growing up faster, but they may not be growing up better"? Explain your point of view.

Vocabulary Building

Lesson One: ***The Vocabulary of Today's Adolescent Subculture, Part I***

The essay "Teenagers in Dreamland" by Robert J. Samuelson includes words that are useful when you are discussing today's adolescent subculture.

adolescent subculture (paragraph 3)
central (1)
evolving (3)
wanes (3)
rigorous (4)
impose (5)
reforms (6)
autonomy (7)
ensure (9)
premise (10)

Teenagers are members of an **adolescent subculture,** a group within our society that has a common set of beliefs and behavior patterns.

In today's adolescent subculture, many teenagers think their **central**—main or most important—goal in life is to enjoy their youth.

In today's adolescent subculture, many teenagers are following beliefs and behavior patterns that have been **evolving**—developing gradually—for many years.

In today's adolescent subculture, many teenagers find that their interest in school **wanes**—lessens or shrinks—in favor of a job that provides spending money.

In today's adolescent subculture, many teenagers complain if their homework is too **rigorous**—strict or demanding.

In today's adolescent subculture, many teenagers try to **impose**—or force—their will on their parents.

In today's adolescent subculture, many teenagers are shocked when parents reduce their freedom by introducing **reforms**—improvements or changes to correct problems.

In today's adolescent subculture, many teenagers have a great deal of **autonomy** or personal freedom.

In today's adolescent subculture, many teenagers think possessions such as cellular telephones, cars, and designer clothes are all they need to **ensure** or guarantee a good life.

In today's adolescent subculture, many teenagers accept growing up fast and on their own as a basic **premise** of life—a statement or idea that is accepted as true.

EXERCISE 7A: Match each sentence with a vocabulary word from this lesson.

1. If students can't agree on dormitory rules, the dean will set rules and force everyone to obey. 1. ____________________

2. If he isn't winning a game, his interest in playing lessens. 2. ____________________

3. The supervisor gives her co-workers a great deal of personal freedom. 3. ____________

4. If you want to be healthy, you must exercise; this is an idea most people accept as true. 4. ____________

5. The store is losing money, but the manager is making changes to correct the problems. 5. ____________

6. The training program for nurses is strict and demanding. 6. ____________

7. Don't worry about the details; try to remember the most important idea. 7. ____________

8. I think we made our reservations early enough to get good seats, but I cannot guarantee it. 8. ____________

9. In the United States, certain beliefs and behavior patterns set teenagers apart from the rest of society. 9. ____________

10. Over the years, the artist's style has been developing gradually. 10. ____________

Lesson Two: The Vocabulary of Today's Adolescent Subculture, Part II

Here are more words from the essay "Teenagers in Dreamland" by Robert J. Samuelson that are useful when you are discussing today's adolescent subculture.

disorienting (paragraph 2)	**promotes** (8)
altered (6)	**academic** (8)
collide (6)	**prosperity** (9)
predominantly (8)	**harried** (10)
asserts (8)	**delude** (11)

In today's adolescent subculture, many teenagers fill the roles of children, students, workers, and adults all at once, a situation which is very **disorienting** or confusing.

In today's adolescent subculture, many teenagers see their lives greatly **altered** or changed after their parents divorce.

In today's adolescent subculture, many teenagers find that childlike expectations and adult freedoms **collide**—crash into each other.

In today's adolescent subculture, many teenagers work **predominantly**—mainly or chiefly—to buy things they want rather than to help support their families.

In today's adolescent subculture, many teenagers **assert**—state positively and forcefully—their right to stay out as late as they want.

In today's adolescent subculture, many teenagers claim that work **promotes**—contributes to the growth of—responsibility.

In today's adolescent subculture, many teenagers are capable of doing much better **academic** work—work having to do with school and learning.

In today's adolescent subculture, many teenagers can find good jobs because this is a time of great **prosperity**—economic success and wealth—in the United States.

In today's adolescent subculture, many teenagers find that meeting the responsibilities of school and work leaves them feeling **harried**—worried, annoyed, and under attack.

In today's adolescent subculture, many teenagers **delude**—fool or trick—themselves into thinking that having fun is more important than preparing for their future.

EXERCISE 7B: For each word in italics below, circle the definition closest in meaning.

1. Something that is *academic* has to do with
   a. investment decisions.
   b. school and learning.
   c. a newspaper or magazine.
   d. health care decisions.

2. If television *promotes* violence, it
   a. encourages people to speak out against violence.
   b. shows people how to prevent violence.
   c. contributes to the growth of violence.
   d. urges people to avoid violence at all costs.

3. A prisoner who *asserts* his or her innocence
   a. states it positively and forcefully.
   b. states it over and over.
   c. states it emotionally and tearfully.
   d. states it in public.

4. If two cars *collide,* they
   a. barely escape an accident.
   b. stop suddenly.
   c. run off the road.
   d. crash into each other.

5. If you *delude* someone, you
   a. ignore that person.
   b. defend that person.
   c. insult that person.
   d. trick that person.

6. If a room is *predominantly* blue, it is
   a. partly blue.
   b. completely blue.
   c. mostly blue.
   d. mostly another color.

7. If you wish for *prosperity,* you wish for
   a. success and wealth.
   b. good physical health.
   c. great happiness and joy.
   d. good luck and a long life.

8. If something is *disorienting,* it is
   a. frightening.
   b. confusing.
   c. difficult.
   d. dangerous.

9. If your plans are *altered,* they are
   a. changed.
   b. cancelled.
   c. difficult to carry out.
   d. easy to carry out.

10. If you are *harried,* you feel
    a. unloved and unlovable.
    b. worried and annoyed.
    c. excited and eager.
    d. tired and let down.

Spelling

Spelling Rule—IE *and* EI

Many of the words in Robert Samuelson's essay can be learned easily with the help of this simple spelling rule.

Use *i* before *e*

Except after *c*,

Or when sounded like *a*

As in *neighbor* or *weigh*.

TRY IT OUT

FILL IN *IE* OR *EI* IN EACH OF THE FOLLOWING WORDS.

ch____f	bel____ve	rec____ve
w____gh	perc____ve	interv____w

Here are some examples.

f*ie*ld	dec*ei*ve	fr*ei*ght
b*ei*ge	ach*ie*ve	c*ei*ling
conc*ei*ve	v*ei*l	y*ie*ld
w*ei*ght	th*ie*f	rec*ei*pt

TRY IT OUT

FILL IN *IE* OR *EI* IN EACH OF THE FOLLOWING WORDS.

p____ce	conc____ted	br____f
n____ghbor	rel____f	____ghty

A SPECIAL NOTE: *Here are some common words that are exceptions to the above rule.*

*ei*ther for*ei*gn w*ei*rd s*ei*ze l*ei*sure n*ei*ther

EXERCISE 7C: Insert *ie* or *ei* in each of the following words.

1. f____rce
2. dec____ve
3. misch____f
4. for____gn
5. sh____ld
6. p____r
7. chow m____n
8. rec____pt
9. fr____nd
10. pat____nt
11. gr____f
12. ____ther
13. p____ce
14. r____ndeer
15. n____ce
16. l____sure
17. c____ling
18. rev____w
19. fr____ght
20. ach____ve
21. pr____st
22. hyg____ne
23. sl____gh
24. v____n
25. rel____ve
26. s____ge
27. conc____vable
28. handkerch____f
29. r____gn
30. gr____vance

 From Paragraph Principles to Essay Writing

Frequently you will be required to write on topics that cannot be discussed fully in just a single paragraph. In these instances, you need to write a series of paragraphs that form an essay. An essay always contains an introduction, main body paragraphs, and a conclusion. Often college essays contain three main body paragraphs. However, when you write on a complicated topic, your essay may include four or more main body paragraphs.

As you examine the essay form on the next page, you are likely to notice that an essay has the same structure as a paragraph, except that an essay discusses a topic in more depth and uses additional specific examples.

The Paragraph	Purpose	The Essay
the topic sentence	to state, limit, and control the main idea	the thesis statement
development with use of facts; examples; incident; definition; comparison and contrast; or statistics, names, and the senses	to develop the main idea with specific points	the main body paragraphs (there should be at least three of them)
in certain cases: the concluding sentence	to conclude by coming back to the general main idea	the concluding paragraph

Before you start drafting an essay, you can benefit from planning the foundation on which it will be built. The three steps to help you plan are

Finding a Writing Topic

Drafting a Thesis Statement

Forming Main Body Ideas

THE ESSAY FORM

Essay Title

The introduction usually begins with a device to capture the reader's interest. (See pages 303–304.) The introduction usually ends with a thesis statement that presents the main idea of the essay. (See pages 286–88.)

Main body paragraph I usually begins with a topic sentence that presents the main idea of the paragraph. (See pages 40–43.) That main idea is then developed with specific information such as facts, examples, and incidents. (See pages 50–53 and 71–73.)

Main body paragraph II usually begins with a topic sentence that presents the main idea of the paragraph. That main idea is then developed with specific information such as facts, examples, and incidents.

Main body paragraph III usually begins with a topic sentence that presents the main idea of the paragraph. That main idea is then developed with specific information such as facts, examples, and incidents.

The conclusion reemphasizes the topic of the essay and gives the essay a feeling of completeness. (See pages 305–306.)

 Finding a Writing Topic

Some instructors give a specific writing assignment, while others allow students to select their own topic. When you are given the opportunity to choose your own topic, try to pick one that really interests you. If you enjoy what you are writing about, you probably will put in the time and effort needed to develop an essay that explores the subject with enthusiasm and originality. If you have trouble coming up with an interesting writing topic, you might use one of the following methods to stimulate your thinking.

I Ask Yourself Questions.

II Use the Prewriting Techniques.

III Use a Textbook Index.

IV Narrow a Broad Topic.

I. Ask Yourself Questions. Your mind is like a powerful computer that has stored up a lifetime of memories covering a wide range of personal experiences with your family, your friends, your teachers, and your co-workers. Over the years, these experiences have helped you develop your own view of the world and your place in it. Packed away in your mind are some fascinating ideas and opinions that could be explored in an essay. To help yourself rediscover them, try using these questions.

1. What subject have I read or heard about in school or seen on television that I find especially interesting?
2. What topics have I discussed with my friends and relatives recently?
3. What ideas, opinions, or experiences make me angry or happy?
4. What subject am I curious to learn more about?
5. What things would I like to change about my life? About my town or city? About my state or country?

After you have used these questions to find a subject that interests you, be sure that it is not too broad for an essay. For help with narrowing down a broad topic, see pages 284–85.

TRY IT OUT

USE THE QUESTIONS LISTED ABOVE TO DISCOVER SEVERAL INTERESTING WRITING TOPICS.

II. Use the Prewriting Techniques. The prewriting techniques described on pages 17–22 of Chapter One can also help you to find a suitable writing topic. Writing nonstop, for example, stimulates your thinking, allowing some long-forgotten ideas and feelings to tumble out onto the page. In addition, if you are keeping a journal, you will find it an excellent sourcebook when you are searching for an appealing writing topic. Here is a journal entry that one student used as the springboard for an essay assignment.

> My parents are coming over in a little while, so I have to get my place cleaned up fast. If they saw what a mess I'm living in, they'd have a fit. I hate cleaning. I hate it, hate it, hate it! The dusting and vacuuming aren't that bad. But cleaning the kitchen and the bathroom is the pits. When I moved out on my own, I didn't realize how hard life was gonna be. Sometimes I wonder if I made a mistake.
>
> Jason Ruiz
> Student

When Jason looked back through his journal, he realized that he had much more to say about the topic discussed in this particular entry, and so he decided to write an essay about the problems of living alone.

TRY IT OUT

USE ONE OF THE PREWRITING TECHNIQUES DESCRIBED IN CHAPTER ONE TO DISCOVER AN INTERESTING WRITING TOPIC. FOR HELP WITH NARROWING DOWN A BROAD TOPIC, SEE PAGES 284–85.

III. Use a Textbook Index. In some classes, your instructor may permit you to write an essay on any topic related to the course work. Sometimes you might recall a challenging idea that was mentioned during a class discussion. Perhaps you can examine this idea in more detail on paper. When you are unable to think of a suitable topic, try searching through the index of a textbook for the course. The index is an excellent source for writing topics because it is a detailed alphabetical list of all the subjects covered in the book. As you look through the index, you are bound to spot a number of topics that spark your interest. Notice, for example, some of the intriguing topics that are included in a portion of the index for the textbook *Psychology* by Charles G. Morris.

"Shy child," 354
Significance, statistical, 674
Similarity, interpersonal attraction and, 631, 659
Simple cells, 117
Simple phobias, 555
Situational approach to leadership, 684
Situationist personality theories, 489–90, 507

This small section of the index lists many subjects that can be narrowed down into topics that might be appropriate for a psychology paper:

Subject	*Topic*
"shy child"	The Major Causes of Shyness How to Overcome Shyness How Shyness Affects a Person's Life
sleep	The Benefits of Sleep Why Some People Have Trouble Sleeping Why Do People Dream? How the Lack of Sleep Affects People
smell	How the Sense of Smell Influences Human Behavior The Function of Smell in the Lives of Animals
smoking	The Psychological Needs Fulfilled by Smoking How to Overcome the Need to Smoke Why People Should Not Smoke How Society Discriminates Against People Who Smoke
stress	The Major Causes of Stress Ways to Live with Stress How Stress Affects a Person's Life

TRY IT OUT

HERE IS ANOTHER PORTION OF THE INDEX FOR THE TEXTBOOK *PSYCHOLOGY* BY CHARLES G. MORRIS. USE THIS MATERIAL TO CREATE AS MANY ESSAY TOPICS AS POSSIBLE. FOR HELP WITH NARROWING DOWN THESE SUBJECTS, SEE PAGES 284–85. USE YOUR OWN PAPER FOR THIS ASSIGNMENT.

Divorce, 408
  adolescents coping with, 401
  extreme stress from, 533
Domestic violence, 19
Dominant genes, 68
Door-in-the-face effect, 647–48
Dopamine, 42, 577
Double approach/avoidance conflict, 519, 520
Double-blind procedure, 163
Doubt and shame, autonomy vs., 482
Dreams, 150–57, 180–81
  functions of, 151–52
  needs for, 154–55
  remembering, 242–43
Drive, 429–30, 466. *See also* Motivation
Drive reduction theory, 429–30, 466
Drug abuse, organizations for treating, 604
Drugs:
  birth defects and father's use of, 381
  consciousness-altering, 161–79, 181–82
    depressants, 163–70, 177, 181–82
    hallucinogens, 174–76, 177, 182
    hearing under anesthesia, 179
    marijuana, 44, 176–78, 182
    stimulants, 170–74, 177, 182
  synapses and, 43–45, 75
Drug therapies, 609–11, 620
Dual-career families, 374, 410
Dynamic therapy, 593

IV. Narrow a Broad Topic. After you have found an interesting topic to write on, you need to be sure that it is appropriate for an essay. Some topics are suitable for a book but too broad for an essay; other topics are suitable for a paragraph but too limiting for an essay. For example, suppose that you wish to write a five-paragraph essay on the general topic of *alcoholism.*

Good Topic: Some Causes of Alcoholism

Too Broad: Alcoholism Is a Serious Problem

Too Limiting: Alcohol Is a Clear Liquid

Before you can be sure that a topic is good for an essay, it is best to think ahead to *each of the three main points* that you will discuss in *each of the three paragraphs of the main body of the essay.* Try to think of three sensible, interesting main ideas, each of which can be stated in a good topic sentence and which can be developed with one of the six methods presented in Chapters One and Two. If you cannot, the chances are that the topic you have chosen is not suitable.

As you think ahead to the three main points that you plan to make, write them down. Looking at the three main points you have listed will make more visibly clear whether or not a topic is suitable for a five-paragraph essay. Compare the plan for each of the following topics, and notice the judgment made for each plan.

	A Some Causes of Alcoholism	B Alcoholism Is a Serious Problem	C Alcohol Is a Clear Liquid
Introduction	introduce the three main ideas that follow	←	←
Main Body (three main ideas)	I. curiosity II. peer group influence III. feelings of loneliness	I. crime II. deaths III. rehabilitation programs	I. what it looks like II. why it is clear III. how to identify it
Conclusion	summarize the three main ideas	←	←

Judgments:

A is fine; not too broad or too limiting.

B is too broad; each development would be shallow and general.

C is too limiting; the main points are similar and repetitious.

TRY IT OUT

WHICH TOPIC IS MOST SUITABLE FOR A FIVE-PARAGRAPH ESSAY?

1. a. Dieting
   b. A Sensible Way to Lose Weight
   c. Pies Are Very Fattening
2. a. Marriage
   b. Recent Changes in Marriage Styles
   c. Marriage Through the Ages
3. a. How to Take Proper Care of House Plants
   b. How to Water House Plants
   c. The Different Types of House Plants

Drafting a Thesis Statement

A thesis statement is the sentence that presents the main idea of the essay. It expresses your point of view about your topic. The thesis statement often comes at the end of the introductory paragraph. In that position, it tells the reader what to expect, and it helps you, the writer, to limit and control what you will discuss in the essay.

To create an effective thesis statement, you might start by asking yourself: What do I want to say about my topic? For example, after rereading one of his journal entries, the student Jason Ruiz decided to write an essay about living alone. (See Ruiz's journal entry on page 282.) He first asked himself what he wanted to say about living alone. Then he used his response to form this thesis statement:

Living alone can be very difficult.

After gathering information and writing a first draft of his essay, Jason found that he needed to revise his thesis statement to make it more specific:

Living alone can be very difficult because a person must deal not only with loneliness but also with many financial and household responsibilities.

As you develop your essay, you may also decide to go back and revise your thesis statement at least once. When you do, be sure to keep the following guidelines in mind:

I Take a Position on a Topic.

II Write a Thesis Statement That Is Not Too Broad or Too Narrow.

III Use Specific Language.

I. Take a Position on a Topic. A thesis statement is a complete sentence that takes a position on a topic. That position reflects the writer's attitude or opinion concerning the topic. Notice how only the third thesis statement below meets this guideline.

Thesis Statement	*Comment*
☒ The major problems of a teenage marriage.	not a complete sentence
☒ About 75 percent of all teenage marriages in the United States end in divorce.	takes no position on the topic
☑ When teenagers marry, they face three serious problems that threaten their happiness.	complete sentence; takes a position on the topic

TRY IT OUT

REWRITE ANY SENTENCES BELOW THAT WOULD NOT BE EFFECTIVE THESIS STATEMENTS FOR A FIVE-PARAGRAPH ESSAY.

1. Fast-food restaurants usually pay most of their workers the minimum wage.
2. The joys of listening to rock music.
3. Prizefighting is a dangerous sport that should be banned in the United States.
4. Many Americans graduate from high school without learning how to speak a foreign language.
5. How to stay in good physical condition.

II. Write a Thesis Statement That Is Not Too Broad or Too Narrow. An effective thesis statement is neither too broad nor too narrow. It is broad enough for the main idea to be developed with specific information in an essay containing the number of paragraphs your instructor requires. At the same time, the thesis statement cannot be so broad that a book could be written on the topic. After you have written your thesis statement, ask yourself: What information will I need to provide to develop the main idea? The answer to this question will help you to decide whether your thesis statement is narrow enough for an essay. Only the third thesis statement below could be developed adequately in an essay.

Thesis Statement	*Comment*
☒ Watching television affects our lives in many ways.	too general for an essay
☒ The average American youngster spends between four and six hours a day watching television.	too narrow for an essay
✔ Soap operas are popular because they entertain, inform, and help to fulfill the viewer's emotional needs.	neither too broad nor too narrow—just enough to discuss in an essay

TRY IT OUT

REWRITE ANY SENTENCES BELOW THAT WOULD NOT BE EFFECTIVE THESIS STATEMENTS FOR A FIVE-PARAGRAPH ESSAY.

1. Smoking cigarettes can stain the teeth and fingers.
2. Coin collecting can be a challenging, educational, and profitable hobby.
3. Charities provide valuable services to the community.

III. Use Specific Language. An effective thesis statement uses specific language so that the reader has a clear idea of what is discussed in the body of the essay. Vague words such as *good, bad, nice, great, interesting,* and *things* are avoided. To guide the reader even more, the thesis statement may mention the main points covered in the essay. In the following thesis statements, notice how the same topic can be made more specific.

Thesis Statement	*Comment*
☒ New York City is a nice place to visit.	too vague
✔ New York City offers visitors a wide variety of cultural attractions to keep them busy.	more specific
✔ New York City offers visitors a wide variety of museums, concerts, and live theater to keep them busy.	even more specific—mentions the main points covered in the essay

TRY IT OUT

REWRITE ANY SENTENCES BELOW THAT WOULD NOT BE EFFECTIVE THESIS STATEMENTS FOR A FIVE-PARAGRAPH ESSAY.

1. Many of today's horror films depend too much on special effects, sex scenes, and bloody violence.
2. College students have to deal with many things.
3. It is a good idea for older people to have pets.

 Forming Main Body Ideas

Forming three main body ideas before you begin to write can help you in several important ways. First, your main body ideas help you see if your topic is either too broad or too narrow for an essay. In addition, they are useful when you evaluate and revise your thesis statement to make it more specific. Finally, they guide you as you select and organize the information that will form the body of your essay.

At times, several good main body ideas may come to mind as soon as you choose a topic. At other times, however, you might not think of these ideas easily. To help you in those instances, here are three methods that can make it easier for you to develop three effective main body ideas.

I Use the Prewriting Techniques.

II Use the Focus of the Topic.

III Use the Main Body Idea Patterns.

I. Use the Prewriting Techniques. The prewriting techniques of brainstorming and making a subject map can stimulate your mind to come up with main body ideas that support your topic. (For more on these techniques, see pages 17–22.) In brainstorming, for example, you first jot down whatever words, phrases, or sentences occur to you as you think about your topic. Then you group together the items in your list that seem related to one another. As you do this, your main body ideas will become apparent.

Here is the list that Jason Ruiz brainstormed for his topic, the problems of living alone. (See Ruiz's journal entry on page 282.)

rent
big phone bills
cleaning all the time
Mom nagging me to come home
cooking
electricity
lonely
food shopping and errands
cable TV
just barely making it
laundry
alone when sick
alone when upset
vacuuming
dusting
scrubbing kitchen & bathroom
buying furniture & appliances
hate being alone
no one to tell the good stuff to
spooky sounds in the night

After Jason finished his brainstormed list, he wanted to see whether he had enough ideas for three separate main body paragraphs. He tried to group the items that belonged together, and he ignored items that did not. He ended up with these three separate lists.

I
rent
big phone bills
electricity
cable TV
buying furniture & appliances

II
cleaning all the time
vacuuming
dusting
scrubbing kitchen & bathroom
cooking
laundry
food shopping & errands

III
lonely
alone when sick
alone when upset
no one to tell the good stuff to
spooky sounds in the night

The lists helped Jason discover the points he would make in the body paragraphs of his essay on living alone.

I. expensive
II. no one to share household responsibilities with
III. lonely at times

Jason then used each of these main body ideas as the topic for focused freewriting. (For more on this technique, see pages 19–20.) This activity generated additional specific information to support the three points. With this information in mind, Jason was now ready to start writing his essay. But first he decided to rewrite his thesis statement to include his three main body ideas:

Living alone can be very difficult because a person must deal not only with loneliness but also with many financial and household responsibilities.

TRY IT OUT

USE EITHER BRAINSTORMING OR MAPPING TO DEVELOP THREE MAIN BODY IDEAS FOR THE TOPIC *HOW TO IMPROVE HIGH SCHOOL EDUCATION*. USE YOUR OWN PAPER FOR THIS ASSIGNMENT.

II. Use the Focus of the Topic. An essay topic often contains a key word that can serve as the focus for the essay. The focus word tells what the content of the essay should emphasize. Using the focus word to stimulate your thinking can help you to form effective main body ideas for your topic. Notice in each of the following examples how the focus word provides a clear direction for the body paragraphs of the essay.

Topic: The Major Causes of Teenage Crime
Focus: causes
Main Body Ideas: I. poverty
II. boredom
III. lack of supervision

Topic: The Effects of Air Pollution
Focus: effects
Main Body Ideas: I. health problems
II. destruction of nature
III. economic loss

Topic: The Pressures of Being a Single Parent
Focus: pressures
Main Body Ideas: I. working
II. taking care of the child
III. taking care of the home

Topic: The Problems of Growing Old
Focus: problems
Main Body Ideas: I. illness
II. loneliness
III. crime

Topic: The Advantages (Disadvantages) of Using Credit Cards
Focus: advantages or disadvantages
Main Body Ideas: I. useful for unexpected purchases
II. helpful in an emergency
III. safer than cash

Some types of essays have a focus that is not actually stated as part of the topic. For example, essays that *argue an opinion* try to persuade the reader to agree with the writer's point of view on an issue. To do this effectively, the essay needs to focus on reasons that support the opinion. (For more information on arguing an opinion, see pages 597–607.) Notice in the example at the top of the next page that the three main body ideas are reasons that support the writer's point of view.

Topic: Sports Superstars Are Worth the Enormous Salaries They Receive
Focus: reasons
Main Body Ideas:
I. They train for many years.
II. They increase attendance at sporting events.
III. Their careers are relatively short.

Essays that *construct a definition* break a subject into parts that can be clearly understood. These parts may be characteristics or qualities. (For more information on constructing a definition, see pages 581–89.) For example, in an essay describing the perfect teacher, the three main body ideas would present the important qualities or characteristics that might be used to define the person.

Topic: The Perfect Teacher
Focus: qualities or characteristics
Main Body Ideas:
I. Explains the subject matter clearly.
II. Has a good sense of humor.
III. Understands students' problems.

Essays that *explain a process* often give step-by-step directions that teach the reader how to do something. (For more information on explaining a process, see pages 516–24.) For example, in an essay that explains how to prepare for a job interview, the main body ideas would focus on the steps of the process.

Topic: How to Prepare for a Job Interview
Focus: steps
Main Body Ideas:
I. Prepare your credentials.
II. Gather information about the company.
III. Dress appropriately.

TRY IT OUT

FOR EACH ESSAY TOPIC GIVEN BELOW, USE THE FOCUS TO HELP YOU THINK OF THREE EFFECTIVE MAIN BODY IDEAS.

1. The Case For (Against) the Death Penalty
2. What Makes a Good Parent?
3. The Advantages (Disadvantages) of Going to College

III. Use the Main Body Idea Patterns. Often you might not have difficulty thinking of two main body ideas to support your topic, but thinking up the third point can become troublesome. If you run out of ideas, look through the main body idea patterns below. These patterns—which you should feel free to adapt, rearrange, or change—might help you find three main points of value for your own essay.

Main Body Idea Patterns

I. past
II. present
III. future

I. personal
II. family
III. social group

I. the individual
II. the community (or nation)
III. the nation (or world)

I. childhood
II. adulthood
III. old age

I. personality
II. character
III. ability

I. science
II. business
III. the arts

I. political
II. economic
III. social (or substitute for any: religious)

I. home
II. business (or school)
III. leisure time

I. physical
II. psychological
III. spiritual

I. students
II. workers
III. government officials (or bosses)

Here are some examples of how to use these patterns.

Women Are Superior to Men
I. personality
II. character
III. ability

Some Effects of War
I. political
II. economic
III. social

New Uses of the Computer
I. science
II. business
III. the arts

What Makes People Feel Secure?
I. childhood
II. adulthood
III. old age

TRY IT OUT

FOR EACH ESSAY TOPIC GIVEN BELOW, THINK OF THREE MAIN BODY IDEAS THAT COULD BE USED TO DEVELOP THE TOPIC. IF YOU NEED HELP, REFER TO THE MAIN BODY IDEA PATTERNS ON PAGE 293.

1. A Person's Definition of Success Often Changes
2. Using Shortcuts Can Cause Problems
3. The Advantages of Having a Sense of Humor

EXERCISE 7D: Each item in this exercise presents an essay topic and the three points that might be used to develop the body paragraphs. After reading the topic and the main body ideas, write an effective thesis statement for the essay.

1. Topic: Why Many Americans Eat an Unhealthy Diet

   Thesis statement: ______________________________

   ____

   Main Body Ideas: I. lack time to eat properly
   II. are influenced by advertising
   III. have poor eating habits

2. Topic: How Divorce Affects Children

   Thesis statement: ______________________________

   ____

   Main Body Ideas: I. lowered standard of living
   II. lack of adequate supervision
   III. emotional turmoil

3. Topic: The Case Against Legalized Gambling Casinos

   Thesis statement: ______________________________

   ____

   ____

   Main Body Ideas: I. encourage people to become addicted to gambling
   II. attract the criminal underworld
   III. increase crime in the community

4. Topic: The Rewards of Doing Community Service

   Thesis statement: ______________________________

   ____

   Main Body Ideas: I. helps improve the community
   II. helps the volunteers learn new skills
   III. improves the volunteers' sense of values

5. Topic: The Major Problems in Our Nation's Prisons

   Thesis statement: ______________________________

   ____

   ____

   Main Body Ideas: I. overcrowding
   II. lack of adequate health care
   III. lack of adequate job training

EXERCISE 7E: Rewrite any sentences that would not be effective thesis statements for a five-paragraph essay.

1. About 35 million Americans do not have any form of medical insurance.

   ____

   ____

   ____

2. This essay is about sex education in the public schools.

   ____

   ____

3. The benefits of working for a year before going to college.

   ____

   ____

4. The Honda Accord is a great car.

   ____

   ____

5. The weather affects our lives in many ways.

____

____

6. Arguments about money, friends, and household responsibilities can strain the relationship between parents and their children.

____

____

7. Most shopping malls offer the convenience of free parking.

____

____

8. The President's proposal to raise taxes is a bad idea.

____

____

9. Advertising has a definite influence on our society.

____

____

10. Physicians are not entitled to the large fees that they charge.

____

____

EXERCISE 7F: For each essay topic given, think of three main ideas which you might use to develop the topic.

1. What Causes Injuries at Rock Concerts?

   I. ______________________________________

   II. ______________________________________

   III. ______________________________________

2. What Makes a Good Friend?

   I. ______________________

   II. ______________________

   III. ______________________

3. Why Get Married?

   I. ______________________

   II. ______________________

   III. ______________________

4. The Problems of Using Public Transportation

   I. ______________________

   II. ______________________

   III. ______________________

5. The Major Effects of Shyness

   I. ______________________

   II. ______________________

   III. ______________________

6. How Drug Addicts Affect Our Society

   I. ______________________

   II. ______________________

   III. ______________________

7. Can an Individual Express Himself/Herself Fully in America?

   I. ______________________

   II. ______________________

   III. ______________________

8. Are Big Families a Good Idea?

   I. ______________________________

   II. ______________________________

   III. ______________________________

9. How Has Women's Liberation Affected Our Lives?

   A. ______________________________

   B. ______________________________

   C. ______________________________

10. The Advantages (Disadvantages) of Being a Famous Entertainer

   A. ______________________________

   B. ______________________________

   C. ______________________________

EXERCISE 7G: For each of the general topic areas given, create a suitable topic for a five-paragraph essay. Next, think of three main ideas that could be used to develop the essay. Finally, write a thesis statement that clearly states the main idea of the essay.

1. General subject: crime

   Suitable topic for a five-paragraph essay: ______________________________

   ____

   Thesis statement: ______________________________

   ____

   Main Body I: ______________________________

   Main Body II: ______________________________

   Main Body III: ______________________________

2. General subject: movies

   Suitable topic for a five-paragraph essay: ______________________________

   ____

   Thesis statement: ____

   ____

   Main Body I: ____

   Main Body II: ____

   Main Body III: ____

3. General subject: sports

   Suitable topic for a five-paragraph essay: ______________________________

   ____

   Thesis statement: ____

   ____

   Main Body I: ____

   Main Body II: ____

   Main Body III:

4. General subject: education

   Suitable topic for a five-paragraph essay: ______________________________

   ____

   Thesis statement: ____

   ____

   Main Body I: ____

   Main Body II: ____

   Main Body III: ____

5. General subject: work

   Suitable topic for a five-paragraph essay: ________________________

   ____

   Thesis statement: ________________________________

   ____

   Main Body I: ____________________________________

   Main Body II: ___________________________________

   Main Body III: __________________________________

6. General subject: health

   Suitable topic for a five-paragraph essay: ________________________

   ____

   Thesis statement: ________________________________

   ____

   Main Body I: ____________________________________

   Main Body II: ___________________________________

   Main Body III: __________________________________

7. General subject: transportation

   Suitable topic for a five-paragraph essay: ________________________

   ____

   Thesis statement: ________________________________

   ____

   Main Body I: ____________________________________

   Main Body II: ___________________________________

   Main Body III: __________________________________

8. General subject: love

   Suitable topic for a five-paragraph essay: ______________________________

   ____

   Thesis statement: ____

   ____

   Main Body I: ____

   Main Body II: ____

   Main Body III: ____

9. General subject: food

   Suitable topic for a five-paragraph essay: ______________________________

   ____

   Thesis statement: ____

   ____

   Main Body I: ____

   Main Body II: ____

   Main Body III: ____

10. General subject: computers

    Suitable topic for a five-paragraph essay: ______________________________

    ____

    Thesis statement: ____

    ____

    Main Body I: ____

    Main Body II: ____

    Main Body III: ____

EXERCISE 7H: Essay Analysis Although the essays in this book are each more than five paragraphs long, the authors have followed the pattern of introduction, main body, and conclusion. Answer these questions about the main body paragraphs of the following two essays.

1. In "Teenagers in Dreamland," which appears at the beginning of Chapter Seven, the main body is organized to present four major points. For each set of paragraphs listed below, give the major point presented. Select four from the list of six choices.

paragraphs 3–6	____	a. how to improve the public school system
paragraphs 7–9	____	b. how American students compare to Asian students
paragraph 10	____	c. why the public school system is crippled
paragraphs 11–12	____	d. how new laws contribute to the problem
		e. how parental guilt contributes to the problem
		f. how jobs contribute to the problem

2. In "Money and Freedom," which appears at the beginning of Chapter Eleven, the main body is organized to present four major points. For each set of paragraphs listed below, give the major point presented. Select four from the list of six choices.

paragraphs 2–4	____	a. Marshall's life after quitting his job
paragraph 5	____	b. why Marshall regrets his decision to quit his job
paragraphs 6–7	____	c. Marshall's success as a stockbroker
paragraph 8	____	d. how Marshall decided on his career goal in college
		e. Marshall's expensive lifestyle as a successful stockbroker
		f. how Marshall's first months at Shearson were a nightmare

The Introductory Paragraph

It is important to write an introductory paragraph that will convince the reader that the essay is worth reading. To be completely effective, this opening paragraph must accomplish two things: it must *capture the reader's interest,* and it must *state the topic of the essay in a thesis statement.* Any one of several devices may be used to create interest in the essay.

I Emphasize the Importance of the Topic.

II Ask a Provocative Question.

III Use an Appropriate Quotation.

IV State the Divisions of the Topic.

V Use a Stimulating Incident or Anecdote.

Naturally, the method that you choose will depend on the nature of the topic and on your own preferences. Any one of these devices can help make the reader receptive to an essay. After each device is explained below, there is an example of an appropriate introduction that could be used for an essay titled "The Case Against Experimenting with Drugs."

I. Emphasize the Importance of the Topic. The writer may impress the reader by explaining the current interest in the topic or by indicating that the subject may influence our lives. For example:

> Every day the newspapers and television and radio news programs are flooded with stories about the tragic results of drug addiction. Indeed, in the past year over 2,000 people died from drug abuse in the United States alone. About 200 of these victims were teenagers who were probably just satisfying their natural curiosity or were searching for a few thrills—and got more than they bargained for. Their deaths provide the most dramatic evidence that experimenting with drugs can be physically, psychologically, and socially destructive.

II. Ask a Provocative Question. The reader's interest can be stimulated by the writer's asking a question that does not have an easy answer. The essay that follows should then be concerned with finding a possible answer. For example:

> Should people be encouraged to try new things? "Of course!" one may likely answer. But what if heroin or crack is new to someone? Why is it all right to taste new foods and to visit new places, but not to try out drugs? It is precisely this problem that is confusing young people who have been encouraged by their parents to experience all that life has to offer. To end this

confusion, society must convince young people that experimenting with drugs can totally destroy their lives.

III. Use an Appropriate Quotation. A quotation is an easy and effective device to use—if it is used sparingly. The daily newspapers are a good source of quotations suitable for current topics. If the subject is of a more general nature, the book *Bartlett's Familiar Quotations,* which you can find in the reference section of the library, may provide appropriate material. For example:

> "Heroin is a death trip. I really enjoyed it. But once you get the habit, you're in trouble. One good friend is in the hospital with an $80 a day habit. Another is almost dead from hepatitis. Two others I know, one a girl, died from overdoses. Every time you stick that needle in your arm you're playing with your life." This statement was made by a 19-year-old boy who, like many of his friends, had tried drugs out of curiosity and soon discovered that he could destroy his physical and mental health as well as his relationships with others.

IV. State the Divisions of the Topic. A brief idea of the plan of the essay, if stated in an effective manner, can hint at the interesting points which you intend to cover. For example:

> Many young people who have been using drugs for a short time are still filled with the excitement of trying something that is new and somewhat mysterious to them. But few of these drug users realize that their physical well-being may be permanently ruined, that their mental capacity may be destroyed to the point of insanity, and that their ability to maintain a normal social life may be lost. Surely, the initial thrill of experimenting with drugs is not worth the many types of agony that can follow.

V. Use a Stimulating Incident or Anecdote. The use of an interesting incident or anecdote can act as a teaser to lure the reader into the remainder of the essay. Be sure that the device is appropriate for the subject and focus of what is to follow. For example:

> Happy to be released after serving a six-month sentence for prostitution, Florence hurried toward the drug pusher who was waiting for her in the lobby of the jail building. According to a prearranged plan, she gave him $20 in exchange for a needle filled with heroin. Because she was desperate for a fix, Florence then rushed into a nearby telephone booth, where she quickly injected the needle through her clothes and into her hip. When she later tried to leave the building, she was arrested by a plainclothes officer who had viewed the entire incident. This woman is just one of thousands who have wasted their lives with shoplifting and prostitution in order to finance their own physical and mental destruction. They, better than most people, know the horrifying results of experimenting with drugs.

The Concluding Paragraph

Because no reader likes to be jarred by an abrupt ending, a concluding paragraph should be used to give the essay a feeling of completeness. An effective conclusion *reemphasizes the topic of the essay,* leaving the reader with a strong impression of what has been said. Any one of the following methods may be used.

I Make a Plea for Change.

II Draw the Necessary Conclusions from What Has Been Said.

III Summarize the Major Points of the Essay.

When choosing a method for ending an essay, remember that the conclusion should flow naturally out of the body of the paper; it should not appear to be tacked on. After each method is explained below, there is an example of a conclusion that could be used for an essay titled "The Case Against Experimenting with Drugs."

I. Make a Plea for Change. A conclusion may make a plea for a change of attitude or for specific action. The following paragraph does both.

> The parents, the schools, and the government must make a combined effort to educate young people about the dangers of drug abuse. Moreover, the whole society must change its attitude concerning such over-the-counter preparations as sleeping pills, diet pills, and tranquilizers. The careless use of these drugs creates an atmosphere that invites the use of illegal narcotics. When we realize our full responsibility for dealing with this problem, drug addiction may begin to disappear as a national menace.

II. Draw the Necessary Conclusions from What Has Been Said. Drawing on the facts given in the essay, you may use the concluding paragraph to form judgments about the topic. For example:

> Thus it can be seen that the strong warnings about drug abuse heard on radio and television and seen in newspapers and magazines are not an exaggeration. The evidence is overwhelming and only one overriding conclusion can be drawn: drugs are deadly, and experimenting with them can lead people and, in fact, our entire society to the point of extinction.

III. Summarize the Major Points of the Essay. A restatement of the major points—using new words—will help the readers remember what they have read. A summary is usually most effective in a long essay; it would seem repetitious at the end of a short essay. For example:

Narcotics, then, can affect the user in a variety of ways, most of which are frightening and dangerous. When someone tries an illicit drug, he or she may experience immediate effects such as severe hallucinations, serious mental changes, and a loss of appetite. Taken over a long period of time, drugs may cause hepatitis, a complete mental breakdown—or even death from an overdose. If people can be made to truly understand these effects, the seductive appeal of drugs will disappear and thousands of useful lives will be saved from the terrifying results of narcotics addiction.

A Special Note: Aside from the methods given here, certain devices presented in the section on introductory paragraphs can be useful in concluding paragraphs—for example, the quotation, the question, and the incident or anecdote.

Common Errors to Avoid in Introductions and Conclusions

1. Never use expressions such as these: "Now I will tell you about . . .," "I would like to discuss . . .," or "In my paper I will explain . . . ." Such expressions make the structure of your essay too obvious.
2. Avoid absolute statements such as "This proves that . . ." or "If we take this action, the problem will be solved." To be as accurate as possible, you need to qualify these statements: "This seems to prove that . . ." or "If we take this action, we will be helping to solve the problem."
3. Avoid using clichés and overworked quotations. An essay on marriage would not benefit from a reminder that love and marriage go together like a horse and carriage. "To err is human, to forgive divine" has long since lost its freshness and would add nothing to an essay.
4. Never apologize for what you are going to write or for what you have written. If you begin your essay with "I don't know very much about this subject," you will immediately lose the reader's interest. In addition, if you end with "Of course there are many other opinions about this subject, and I certainly do not know everything," you will destroy the impact of your essay. If you really do feel unsure of your opinions, change your topic to something that you can be more certain about.
5. The introduction and conclusion should not seem tacked on; make sure that they are an integral part of the whole essay. The introduction should state the topic of the *entire* essay, and the conclusion should relate to the general topic rather than one specific point.
6. The length of the introduction and conclusion should not be out of proportion to the length of the whole essay. An introduction or conclusion of 200 words would certainly be too long for a theme of 500 words. However, a long paper may require a 200-word introduction or conclusion.

EXERCISE 71: Referring to the list of common errors to avoid, evaluate the effectiveness of the following sets of introductions and conclusions. Make any corrections that you think will improve these introductions and conclusions. Some of them may have to be completely rewritten.

1. The following introduction and conclusion are from a 500-word expository essay.

The Pressures of a College Student

Introduction

There are many pressures that a college student must face.

Conclusion

Perhaps the greatest pressure college students feel is the need to fulfill course requirements. A full-time student may have to spend at least three or four hours a night doing homework assignments and going over class notes. During any one semester, a student may also have to prepare three or four research papers, each of which requires several visits to the library and many days of organizing the information and writing and typing the final copy. In the midst of all this work, the student may spend an evening studying for a quiz and certainly several evenings studying for a major examination. Thus, it is not surprising that many students complain about not having enough free time.

2. The following introduction and conclusion are from a 500-word expository essay.

The Case Against Food Additives

Introduction

Would you drink a glass filled with glycerol ester of wood rosin, potassium sorbate, and sodium silico aluminate? Although the idea of drinking these substances seems horrifying, these manufactured chemicals and a large number of others have been added to many of the foods you eat every day. As I will show in my essay, food additives can cause cancer and other deadly illnesses.

Conclusion

I must admit that my knowledge of the subject is somewhat limited and that the effects of food additives on the human body must be investigated further. But on the basis of the evidence given, I believe that people should stop buying foods that contain unnatural chemicals.

3. The following introduction and conclusion are from a 500-word expository essay.

Today's Consumers Are Being Cheated

Introduction

I had never realized how underhanded and sneaky some businesses could be until I recently purchased a clock radio. I arrived at a local appliance store at 9:15 A.M. on the first day of the sale to buy a clock radio that had been advertised for $10 less than its usual price. This clock radio had lighted digital numbers, a snooze alarm, and an imitation walnut case. After the fast-talking salesman informed me that the item I wanted was already sold out, he showed me another clock radio that was $15 more than the one I had come to buy. Although this was more than I wanted to spend, I bought this clock radio anyway because it was similar to the one I had originally wanted and I had gone to great trouble to get to the store in the first place. I had had to hire a babysitter and borrow my neighbor's car because mine was being repaired. As I was driving home, it suddenly occurred to me that if the less expensive clock radios had all been sold in just fifteen minutes, then the store had probably had very few of them and had advertised the sale to attract customers who would then be shown the more expensive clock radio. This incident made me start thinking about all the ways that consumers are being cheated today.

Conclusion

Therefore, in an effort to reduce the number of instances of overpricing, false advertising, and the misrepresentation of merchandise by salespeople, the federal, state, and local governments must pass and strictly enforce stronger consumer protection laws and must also begin a large-scale consumer education program. In addition, consumers themselves must be on guard against being cheated when they shop. Although these actions will certainly not bring about a complete end to the problem, they will help to protect the public still further against the dishonest practices of greedy businessmen.

4. The following introduction and conclusion are from a 500-word expository essay.

The Need for Physical Exercise

Introduction

Physical exercise has become a popular pastime for many millions of Americans. More people than ever are going to health spas, public gymnasiums, and exercise classes offered by local schools and colleges. In addition, sales of bicycles, chinning bars, weights, and other exercise equipment have risen sharply in recent years. Indeed, even the federal government encourages physical exercise through the President's Council on Physical Fitness.

Conclusion

Therefore, you should participate in a daily program of active, lively exercise. In this way, you will prevent a deadly disease from striking and you will undoubtedly lengthen your life.

5. The following introduction and conclusion are from a 500-word expository essay.

The Need for Patriotism

Introduction

Because the United States faces so many serious problems such as poverty, unemployment, and the energy crisis, now more than ever the people must renew their patriotism in order to preserve American democracy. As Abraham Lincoln reminded us, "Democracy is the government of the people, by the people, for the people." Thus, we must give three cheers for the red, white, and blue to uphold the land of the free and the home of the brave.

Conclusion

As I have proved in my essay, if the people would become more patriotic, our way of life would improve and American democracy would be strengthened.

EXERCISE 7J: Look back at the essay topics and plans you created for Exercise 7G. On a separate sheet of paper, write an appropriate introduction and conclusion for each essay.

EXERCISE 7K: Essay Analysis Answer each set of questions given below.

1. Look back at the essay "The 'Black Table' Is Still There," which appears at the beginning of Chapter Five.

   a. What device does the author use as the basis for his three-paragraph introduction?

   ____

b. With what words in the introduction does the author state the topic of the essay?

____

2. Look back at the essay "Teenagers in Dreamland," which appears at the beginning of this chapter.

   a. What two devices does the author use as the basis for his two-paragraph introduction?

   ____

   b. With what words in the introduction does the author state the topic of the essay?

   ____

   ____

3. What method is used to develop the introduction of each of the following essays?

   a. "Rambos of the Road" (Chapter One): ______________

   b. "Fire, Hope and Charity" (Chapter Two): ______________

   c. "Pursuit of Happiness" (Chapter Four): ______________

4. What method is used to develop the conclusion of each of the following essays?

   a. "Rambos of the Road" (Chapter One): ______________

   b. "Pursuit of Happiness" (Chapter Four): ______________

   c. "The 'Black Table' Is Still There" (Chapter Five): ______________

   d. "Teenagers in Dreamland" (Chapter Seven): ______________

   e. "The Shadow of a Stranger" (Chapter Twelve): ______________

   f. "The Ways We Lie" (Chapter Thirteen): ______________

   ____

Revising an Essay

After completing the first draft of an essay, you are ready to begin the revision process. You will want to add new information, combine some ideas and eliminate others, move around sentences and paragraphs, and change words. As you work at improving your essay, use scissors and transparent tape to rearrange sections of the draft into a more logical order. In addition, follow the suggestions for revising a paragraph (pages 79–88), which will also help you to achieve a successful essay. In particular, try to do a series of drafts, each time concentrating on a different area of concern. For example, you might use this revision strategy:

First Draft:	Revise content and organization
Second Draft:	Revise style
Third Draft:	Edit for grammar, punctuation, and spelling

Let's see how a student named Phyllis Costa used this strategy to revise her essay on the major problems of owning a car.

First Draft

The Major Problems of Owning a Car

For most Americans, a car is no longer a luxury but a major necessity that adds convenience and freedom to their hectic lives. However, many new drivers don't realize that with the pleasures of car ownership comes a lot of problems.

One common problem today is theft. Every day hundreds of parked cars are stolen. No matter where you live, your car is not safe. If thieves don't steal the whole car, they take parts of it. In just a couple of minutes, someone can remove lots of different parts of a car without getting caught. My father's car was stolen last year. Three hours later it was found completely stripped, it was left sitting naked on some concrete blocks in a dark alleyway. It was really a pathetic sight. Unlike most people in my neighborhood, my father hadn't bothered to have an alarm installed in his car. Now he's sorry that he didn't do anything to protect his precious Cutlass Supreme.

When your car breaks down, it can really be very annoying and maybe even dangerous. If the driver is lucky, they may have only a minor problem with the car that will make them late for an appointment. But some breakdowns can be life-threatening. Recently, my cousin Larry was seriously injured when his car got a blowout and rolled over into a ditch at the side of the road. Larry probably would have been killed if he hadn't been wearing his seat belt. All 50 states should have laws requiring everyone to wear seat belts because they do save many lives. It certainly helped to save Larry's life.

Last summer a family of four was stranded in the Mojave Desert after their cars water pump broke. They were found several hours later, they were suffering from dehidration caused by the intense desert heat.

Another problem is car expenses, which can really add up to a small fortune. Most new automobiles cost so much these days that the loan payments could drag on for as long as five years. Then, of course, the car needs gas to run, this will be about $15 for each tankful. Routine servicing and minor repairs could add as much as $500 to the huge bill in car expenses every year.

Car insurance is a major problem too. It seems that every year the rates keep going up. People under 25 years of age are especially hard hit. Most of my friends have their insurance under their parents names so they don't have to pay such high rates. Otherwise, they wouldn't be able to afford the payments.

To prevent this problem, people who are thinking of buying an automobile should make sure that they can afford all of the expenses. If you can, then owning a car can be a pleasurable experience.

Referring to this textbook's discussions about writing paragraphs and essays, Phyllis Costa revised her first draft for content and organization.

Revised First Draft

The quote I heard on TV would help here

The Major Problems of Owning a Car

For most Americans, a car is no longer a luxury but a major necessity that adds convenience and freedom to their hectic lives. However, many new drivers don't realize that with the pleasures of car ownership comes a lot of problems.

One common problem today is theft. *According to the FBI, a car is stolen somewhere in this country about every 33 seconds.* ~~Every day hundreds of parked cars are stolen. No matter where you live, your car is not safe.~~ If thieves don't steal the whole car, they take parts of it. In just a couple of minutes, someone can *pull off the hubcaps, yank the radio out of the dashboard, and remove the spare tire from the trunk.* ~~remove lots of different parts of a car without getting caught.~~ My father's car was stolen last year. Three hours later it was found completely stripped, *sitting without wheels on concrete blocks, the car looked as if hungry piranha fish had picked it clean right down to its blue metal shell.* ~~it was left sitting naked on some concrete blocks in a dark alleyway. It was really a pathetic sight.~~ Unlike most *car owners* ~~people~~ in my neighborhood, my father *or other antitheft device*

hadn't bothered to have an alarm ^ installed in his car. Now he's sorry that he didn't do anything to protect his precious Cutlass Supreme.

Move this ¶ after expenses ¶

When your car breaks down, it can really be very annoying and maybe even dangerous. If the driver is lucky,
they may have to deal with nothing more significant than a flat tire
~~they may have only a minor problem with the car that~~
or a dead battery on a cold winter morning.
~~will make them late for an appointment.~~ But some breakdowns can be life-threatening. Recently, my cousin Larry

speeding

was seriously injured when his ^ car got a blowout and rolled over into a ditch at the side of the road. Larry probably would have been killed if he hadn't been wearing his seat belt. ~~All 50 states should have laws requiring everyone to wear seat belts because they do save many lives. It certainly helped to save Larry's life.~~

I'm off the topic

Last summer a family of four was stranded in the Mojave Desert after their cars water pump broke. They were found several hours later, they were suffering from dehidration caused by the intense desert heat.

Move this before Larry's accident

Another problem is car expenses, which can really add

at least $10,000

up to a small fortune. Most new automobiles cost ~~so much~~

so monthly *may be close to $300*

these days ~~that the~~ ^ loan payments ~~could drag on~~ for as long as five years. Then, of course, the car needs gas to run, this will be about $15 for each tankful. Routine servicing and minor repairs could add as much as $500 to the *total yearly bill of more than $8,000 in car expenses.* ~~huge bill in car expenses every year.~~

(move before gas)

Car insurance is a major problem too. It seems ~~that~~ *car insurance can cost $3,000 or more for* ~~every year the rates keep going up.~~ People under 25 years of age are ~~especially hard hit. Most of my friends have their insurance under their parents names so they don't have to pay such high rates. Otherwise, they wouldn't be able to afford the payments.~~ *(I'm repeating myself)*

To prevent this problem, people who are thinking of buying an automobile should make sure that they can afford all of the expenses. If you can, then owning a car can be a pleasurable experience. *(I need to tie in thefts & breakdowns here)*

Phyllis Costa decided that her introduction was unlikely to capture the reader's interest, so she made a note to start the paragraph with an appropriate quotation she had heard recently on television. Next, she added several specific facts and examples to the body paragraphs and eliminated some material that went off the topic. Realizing that her paragraph on insurance merely repeated the same point over and over, she cut most of the sentences and integrated what remained into the paragraph on car expenses. In the paragraph on breakdowns, she used order of time to reorganize the two incidents. Then she moved this paragraph to the end of the main body because this paragraph dealt with the most serious of the problems discussed in the essay. Finally, she made a note to rewrite her conclusion so that it would relate to all three of the main body ideas.

When she was satisfied that her essay was well developed and clearly organized, she printed a neat copy of her second draft.

TRY IT OUT

CHOOSE ONE OF THE TOPICS BELOW AND DEVELOP IT INTO AN ESSAY. AFTER COMPLETING THE FIRST DRAFT, REVISE IT FOR CONTENT AND ORGANIZATION. FOR ADDITIONAL HELP WITH THE REVISION PROCESS, REFER TO THE POINTERS FOR REVISING AN ESSAY ON PAGES 321–22. BE SURE TO MAKE A NEAT COPY OF YOUR SECOND DRAFT. USE YOUR OWN PAPER FOR THIS ASSIGNMENT.

1. The Advantages (Disadvantages) of Living Alone
2. What Makes a Good (Bad) Parent?
3. Why I Would (Would Not) Like to Be a Famous Entertainer
4. My Neighborhood Is (Is Not) Becoming Unlivable
5. How the United States Could Be Improved

After finishing her second draft, the writer revised it for style. To connect the three body paragraphs, she used linking sentences to open the paragraphs on expenses and breakdowns. Then to make each paragraph flow more smoothly, she added appropriate transitions ("In addition," "For example," and "Thus") and combined sentences using coordination and subordination. She also established a more formal tone by eliminating the contractions and a few informal phrases ("a lot of" and "a couple of").

In her third draft, Phyllis Costa edited her essay for correct grammar, punctuation, and spelling. Finally satisfied that this essay represented her best work, she made a neat copy of her last draft.

Final Draft

The Major Problems of Owning a Car

On The Tonight Show recently, Jay Leno said, "In the United States, every person is entitled to life, liberty, and a car in which to pursue happiness." This comment is not only humorous but it also contains an element of truth, for most Americans now think of a car as a major necessity that adds convenience and freedom to their hectic lives. However, many new drivers do not realize that with the pleasures of car ownership come a number of problems.

One common problem today is theft. According to the FBI, a car is stolen somewhere in this country about every thirty-three seconds. If thieves do not steal the whole car, they take parts of it. In just a few minutes, someone can pull off the hubcaps, yank the radio out of the dashboard, and remove the spare tire from the trunk. Only three hours after my father's car was stolen last year, it was found completely stripped; sitting without wheels on concrete blocks, the car looked as if hungry piranha fish had picked it clean right down to its blue metal shell. Unlike most car owners in my neighborhood, my father had not bothered to have an alarm or other antitheft device installed in his car. Now he is sorry that he did not do anything to protect his precious Cutlass Supreme.

As disturbing as theft can be, an even bigger problem is trying to pay for all of the car expenses. Because most new automobiles cost at least $10,000 these days, the monthly loan payments may be close to $300 for as long as five years. Another large expense is insurance, which can cost $3,000 or more for a driver under 25 years of age. Then, of course, the car needs gas to run; this will come to about $15 for each tankful. In addition, routine servicing and minor repairs could add as much as $500 for a total yearly bill of more than $8,000 in car expenses.

Although these expenses can be a major burden, the worst problem of owning a car may occur when it breaks down. If the driver is lucky, he or she may have to deal with nothing more significant than a flat tire or a dead battery on a cold winter morning. But some breakdowns can be life-threatening. Last summer, for example, a family of four were stranded in a lonely area of the Mojave Desert after their car's water pump broke. When they were found several hours later, they were suffering from dehydration caused by the intense desert heat. More recently, my cousin Larry was seriously injured when his speeding car got a blowout and rolled over into a ditch at the side of the road. Larry probably would have been killed if he had not been wearing his seat belt.

Car ownership, then, brings with it both good times and difficulties. Thus, people who are thinking of buying an automobile should first make sure that they can afford the expense. If they decide to go ahead with the purchase, they should install antitheft devices and keep the vehicle in good repair. Although an occasional problem may still occur, these steps will help make owning a car a pleasurable experience.

TRY IT OUT

REVISE THE SECOND DRAFT OF THE ESSAY YOU WROTE FOR THE TRY IT OUT ON PAGE 317. FIRST, CONCENTRATE ON STYLE. THEN EDIT THE ESSAY FOR GRAMMAR, PUNCTUATION, AND SPELLING. FOR ADDITIONAL HELP WITH THE REVISION PROCESS, REFER TO THE POINTERS FOR REVISING AN ESSAY ON PAGES 321–22. BE SURE TO PRINT A NEAT COPY OF YOUR FINAL DRAFT. USE YOUR OWN PAPER FOR THIS ASSIGNMENT.

POINTERS FOR REVISING AN ESSAY

The questions given in this chart will help you evaluate the strengths and weaknesses in your essays. A "no" answer to any question may indicate a specific aspect of your writing that needs attention. Use the page numbers in parentheses to find material in this book that will explain the writing skills included in this chart.

Revising for Content and Organization

1. Is the topic of the essay suitable for an essay rather than for a book or a single paragraph? (pages 284–85)
2. Does your essay have an appropriate title?
3. Does your thesis statement clearly communicate the topic and purpose of the essay? (pages 23–27 and 286–88)
4. Does your essay begin with an effective introduction? (pages 303–304)
5. Is the essay topic supported by suitable main body paragraph ideas? (pages 289–93)
6. Does each main body paragraph contain a topic sentence with a clearly stated main idea? (pages 40–43)
7. Is the main idea in each topic sentence narrow enough to be developed fully in a single paragraph? (pages 40–43)
8. Is each paragraph fully developed with specific information? (pages 50–53 and 71–73)
9. Does this information fulfill your audience's needs? (pages 31–36)
10. Have you based your opinions on facts and specific evidence rather than on personal judgments and emotional reactions? (pages 597–600)
11. Have you cut out any material that goes off the topic? (pages 40–42)
12. Have you cut out material that repeats a point already made?
13. Are the details within each paragraph arranged in logical order? (pages 75–77)
14. Are the main body paragraphs presented in logical order? (pages 518–19)
15. Does your essay end with an effective conclusion? (pages 305–306)

(Continued)

(Continued)

Revising for Style

1. Have you used necessary transitions? (pages 384–85)
2. Have you used key words to help create unity? (pages 389–92)
3. Have you used linking sentences to show the relationships between paragraphs? (pages 390–92)
4. Have you avoided a series of short sentences by using coordination and/or subordination? (pages 139–40, 144–47, and 152–53)
5. Do you use coordination correctly? (pages 139–40)
6. Do you use subordination correctly? (pages 144–47)
7. Have you avoided informal language if it is not suitable for your purpose and audience? (pages 425–28)
8. Have you avoided unnecessarily repeating the same words?

Editing for Grammar, Punctuation, and Spelling

1. Have you eliminated sentence fragments? (pages 104–109)
2. Have you eliminated run-ons and comma splices? (pages 114–17)
3. Do the verbs agree with their subjects? (pages 181–84)
4. Have you used *-ed* verb endings wherever necessary? (pages 199–204)
5. Have you used pronouns correctly? (pages 238–45, 249–50, and 255–59)
6. Have you used parallelism correctly? (pages 446–49)
7. Have you eliminated misplaced modifiers? (pages 452–54)
8. Have you eliminated dangling modifiers? (pages 457–58)
9. Have you used commas correctly? (pages 341–47)
10. Have you used apostrophes correctly? (pages 337–38)
11. Have you used the other marks of punctuation correctly? (pages 354–56 and 409–10)
12. Is your usage correct? (pages 412–18)
13. Have you used the *-s* ending on plural nouns when needed? (pages 375–79)
14. Have you used capital letters when needed? (pages 171–73)
15. Have you corrected any misspelled words?

EXERCISE 7L: First, revise the essay below for content and organization. Be sure to print a neat copy of the second draft. Then revise the second draft for style. Finally, edit the revised essay for grammar, punctuation, and spelling. For help with this assignment, refer to the Pointers for Revising an Essay on pages 321–22. Use your own paper for this assignment.

First Draft

Why Shopping Malls Are So Popular

Over the last couple of decades, the shopping habits of many Americans have changed. Instead of going to stores in their own neighborhoods, people would rather drive several miles to a shopping mall. In the following paragraphs, I will discuss why these malls have become so popular.

The main reason is that they contain a wide variety of stores. Most malls have some large department stores as well as a lot of smaller shops that sell just about anything you could want. If you don't find what you need in one store, you only have to walk a short distance to find it in another. Then when you get hungry, you can choose from many different restaurants and types of food.

People also prefer to shop in malls because they are climate controlled. On a cold, snowy day, malls are warm and dry. On a hot, humid day, they are refreshingly cool. No matter what the weather is like outside, people can shop in a comfortable atmosphere.

In addition, malls usually have a pleasant environment that people enjoy. In the center of each walkway, they have lots of plants and pretty fountains. Surrounding the plants are wooden benches where you can sit and rest your tired feet and listen to the music playing softly in the background. Throughout the day, maintenance workers pick up litter so that the walkways are always clean.

Another reason why malls are popular is that they have a lot of free parking. If you try to park by your neighborhood stores, it can be a real pain in the neck. But malls are always surrounded by huge lots that hold thousands of cars.

So now you can see why shopping malls are so popular.

EXERCISE 7M: REFRESHER

1. Find and correct any irregular verb errors.
2. Find and correct any sentence fragments.

More and more colleges have begun offering guarantees with their diplomas. A practice that comes from the business world. When you buy a new car or a new washing machine. You get a guarantee that it will work. Similarly, some colleges think they should guarantee the education they offer. One of these schools is Rockland Community College in New Jersey. Students who have went to Rockland and have not finded jobs in six months can return to school, and it will cost them nothing. Also, employers who seen Rockland graduates with poor skills can send them back for extra courses. In Texas, seventy community colleges have took back students for nine free credits. If employers decided that the students needed more skills. St. John Fisher College in Rochester, New York, even offers students $5,000 cash if they don't got a job in six months.

Some educators strongly oppose such guarantees for education. First, they say a guarantee makes sense only for technical subjects. After all, a college can promise that its lab technician graduates can do blood tests. But cannot promise that students can apply what they have learned in history or sociology classes. Therefore, a guarantee is just a gimmick to compete for students. Second, guaranteeing a college education like a toaster or a new roof lessens the importance of education. Finally, say the critics, these colleges have gave employers the right to set educational standards. However, educators who have chose to use guarantees believe in them. At Henry Ford Community College in Michigan, for example, only one student has been sended back by an employer in nine years. College officials say this shows that the school done a good job for the community. At a time when many people are critical of education. Perhaps these guarantees will inspire confidence in both students and employers.

SPRINGBOARDS TO WRITING

Using your knowledge of the writing process, explained on pages 14–16, write a paragraph or essay related to this chapter's central theme, *today's adolescent subculture*, which is introduced on pages 268–72.

PREWRITING

To think of topics to write about, look at the advertisement and cartoon, read the essay, and answer the questions that follow each. If you prefer, select one of the writing springboards below. (All paragraph numbers refer to the essay that starts on page 270.) To develop your ideas, use the prewriting techniques described on pages 17–22.

WRITING A PARAGRAPH *(For help, see the Pointers on page 51.)*

1. Agree or disagree. Most teenagers are forced to grow up too fast because their parents do not have time for them.
2. It is (is not) a good idea to be independent at an early age. (See paragraph 3.)
3. High schools should (should not) be stricter and give more homework.
4. Agree or disagree: Teenagers grow up so fast today that they have nothing to look forward to as adults.
5. Agree or disagree: "Jobs often encourage drug use." (See paragraph 8.)
6. Should public schools have a dress code?
7. Physical punishment should (should not) be allowed in public schools.

WRITING AN ESSAY *(For help, see the Pointers on pages 54–55.)*

8. Many Teenagers Are (Are Not) Living in a Dreamland (See paragraph 2.)
9. Agree or disagree: "Americans are growing up faster, but they may not be growing up better." (See paragraph 13.)
10. Most Teenagers Are (Are Not) Too Interested in Material Possessions
11. The Many Roles I Fill in Life (See paragraph 10.)
12. Most Parents Are (Are Not) Doing a Good Job of Raising Their Children (See paragraph 10.)
13. The Benefits of Having a Job
14. What Is Good (Bad) About Today's Schools?
15. How Our High Schools Could Be Improved

16. Why Students Drop Out of School
17. All High School Students Should (Should Not) Have to Pass Competency Tests to Graduate
18. Should Colleges Offer a Guarantee to All Graduates? (For a start, see the *Refresher* on page 325.)
19. How College Is Different from High School
20. A College Education Should (Should Not) Be Available to Everyone
21. Agree or disagree with this statement made by Harold Howe II, a former U.S. Commissioner of Education: "Teenagers go to college to be with their boyfriends or girlfriends; they go because they can't think of anything else to do; they go because their parents want them to and sometimes because their parents don't want them to; they go to find themselves, or to find a husband, or to get away from home, and sometimes even to find out about the world in which they live."
22. Is a College Education Necessary to Succeed in Life?
23. High School and College Work/Study Programs Are (Are Not) a Good Idea
24. College Is (Is Not) What I Expected It to Be
25. What School Does Not Teach About Life

Twenty-five years after *Roe v. Wade*, Planned Parenthood® gives new meaning to "choice."

Planned Parenthood, as our name suggests, has always looked to the future.

25 years after the Supreme Court's decision affirming a woman's right to choose whether or not to have a child, we reflect on the profound meaning of reproductive choice, the work yet to be done to assure real choices for all, and the responsibility born of our freedom to choose.

The responsibility to fulfill the vision of making every child a wanted child and every pregnancy intentional. The responsibility to respect and support women's choices about child-bearing or abortion. The responsibility to keep these decisions moral and medical — not political.

A generation after *Roe v. Wade*, America has far to go to realize these noble goals. A few examples:

▶ Legislative assaults and anti-choice violence have taken away access to abortion and family planning for many, especially the vulnerable, the poor, the young, and the geographically isolated.

▶ Early medical abortion has been kept from American women.

▶ Despite all the talk about reducing the need for abortion, many health insurance plans don't cover family planning — women's most common health care need — and most fail to cover the full range of birth control options.

▶ Emergency contraception is not widely available, even though it could prevent half of all abortions.

▶ Nearly 60% of teens say they don't have enough information about birth control and 45% don't know where to get it.

Clearly, the freedom to choose whether or when to have a child is fundamental. The *right* to choose abortion must never be taken for granted. But it is not enough.

Full access to family planning and all reproductive health care, fair insurance coverage, emergency contraception, responsible sex education, early medical and surgical abortion methods, and the development of new, more reliable birth control options can give people the genuine chance to make reproductive choices freely and responsibly.

We think it's time to fulfill the promise made a generation ago. And make life better for the generations to come.

You can help by mailing the coupon below. Thank you.

YES! I want to support Planned Parenthood's ***Responsible Choices*** campaign promoting genuine reproductive choices for all Americans. [ ] I want free information about the ***Responsible Choices*** campaign.
[ ] I'm enclosing my tax-deductible contribution to Planned Parenthood's activities and programs:
__$15 __$25 __$50 __$75 __$100 __$500 or $___.

Name

Address

City State Zip

Telephone

Planned Parenthood®
Federation of America

810 Seventh Ave., N.Y., N.Y. 10019-5882
www.plannedparenthood.org

Public Media Center

Planned Parenthood. Responsible Choices.

Chapter 8

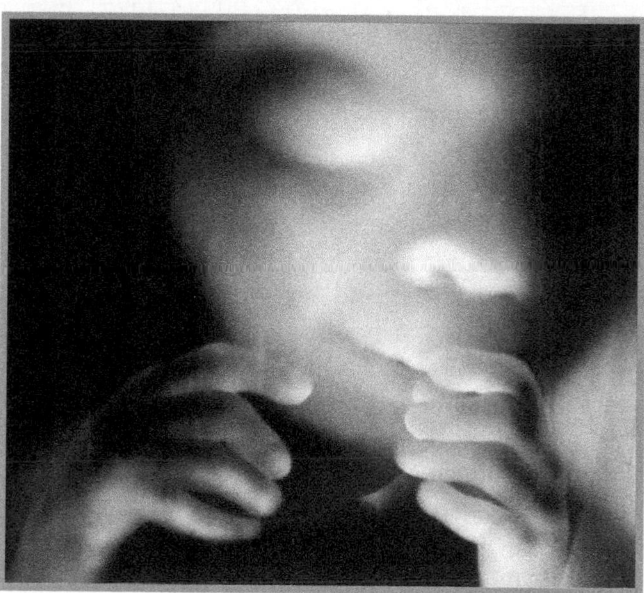

SPRINGBOARDS TO THINKING

For informal, not written, response . . . to stimulate your thinking

1. Read the advertisement on the opposite page. Do you agree with Planned Parenthood's position that every child should be "a wanted child and every pregnancy intentional"? Explain your point of view.
2. Do you agree with Planned Parenthood that people should have full access to family planning? Fair insurance coverage? Emergency contraception? Responsible sex education? Early medical and surgical abortion methods? More reliable birth control options? Explain your point of view on each of these issues.
3. The photograph at the top of this page shows a human fetus in the womb at $4\frac{1}{2}$ months. Does this photograph influence your feelings about abortion? Why or why not?
4. One of the debates surrounding abortion concerns the question of exactly when life begins. Does it begin at the moment of conception? Or does it begin when the embryo becomes a fetus at the beginning of the third month? Or does life begin when a baby is born? Explain your point of view.

Abortion Is Too Complex to Feel All One Way About

Anna Quindlen

(1) It was always the look on their faces that told me first. I was the freshman dormitory counselor and they were the freshmen at a women's college where everyone was smart. One of them could come into my room, a golden girl, a valedictorian, an 800 verbal score on the SAT's, and her eyes would be empty, seeing only a busted future, the devastation of her life as she knew it. She had failed biology, messed up the math; she was pregnant.

(2) That was when I became pro-choice.

(3) It was the look in his eyes that I will always remember, too. They were as black as the bottom of a well, and in them for a few minutes I thought I saw myself the way I had always wished to be—clear, simple, elemental, at peace. My child looked at me and I looked back at him in the delivery room, and I realized that out of a sea of infinite possibilities it had come down to this: a specific person born on the hottest day of the year, conceived on a Christmas Eve, made by his father and me miraculously from scratch.

(4) Once I believed that there was a little blob of formless protoplasm in there and a gynecologist went after it with a surgical instrument, and that was that. Then I got pregnant myself—eagerly, intentionally, by the right man, at the right time—and I began to doubt. My abdomen still flat, my stomach roiling with morning sickness, I felt not that I had protoplasm inside but instead a complete human being in miniature to whom I could talk, sing, make promises. Neither of these views was accurate; instead, I think, the reality is something in the middle. And there is where I find myself now, in the middle, hating the idea of abortions, hating the idea of having them outlawed.

(5) For I know it is the right thing in some times and places. I remember sitting in a shabby clinic far uptown with one of those freshmen, only three months after the Supreme Court had made what we were doing possible, and watching with wonder as the lovely first love she had had with a nice boy unraveled over the space of an hour as they waited for her to be called, degenerated into sniping and silences. I remember a year or two later seeing them pass on campus and not even acknowledge one another because their conjoining had caused them so much pain, and I shuddered to think of them married, with a small psyche in their unready and unwilling hands.

(6) I've met 14-year-olds who were pregnant and said they could not have abortions because of their religion, and I see in their eyes the shadows of 22-year-

olds I've talked to who lost their kids to foster care because they hit them or used drugs or simply had no money for food and shelter. I read not long ago about a teenager who said she meant to have an abortion but she spent the money on clothes instead; now she has a baby who turns out to be a lot more trouble than a toy. The people who hand out those execrable little pictures of dismembered fetuses at abortion clinics seem to forget the extraordinary pain children may endure after they are born when they are unwanted, even hated or simply tolerated.

(7) I believe that in a contest between the living and the almost living, the latter must, if necessary, give way to the will of the former. That is what the fetus is to me, the almost living. Yet these questions began to plague me—and, I've discovered, a good many other women—after I became pregnant. But they became even more acute after I had my second child, mainly because he is so different from his brother. On two random nights 18 months apart the same two people managed to conceive, and on one occasion the tumult within turned itself into a curly-haired brunet with merry black eyes who walked and talked late and loved the whole world, and on another it became a blond with hazel Asian eyes and a pug nose who tried to conquer the world almost as soon as he entered it.

(8) If we were to have an abortion next time for some reason or another, which infinite possibility becomes, not a reality, but a nullity? The girl with the blue eyes? The improbable redhead? The natural athlete? The thinker? My husband, ever at the heart of the matter, put it another way. Knowing that he is finding two children somewhat more overwhelming than he expected, I asked if he would want me to have an abortion if I accidentally became pregnant again right away. "And waste a perfectly good human being?" he said.

(9) Coming to this quandary has been difficult for me. In fact, I believe the issue of abortion is difficult for all thoughtful people. I don't know anyone who has had an abortion who has not been haunted by it. If there is one thing I find intolerable about most of the so-called right-to-lifers, it is that they try to portray abortion rights as something that feminists thought up on a slow Saturday over a light lunch. That is nonsense. I also know that some people who support abortion rights are most comfortable with a monolithic position because it seems the strongest front against the smug and sometimes violent opposition.

(10) But I don't feel all one way about abortion anymore, and I don't think it serves a just cause to pretend that many of us do. For years I believed that a woman's right to choose was absolute, but now I wonder. Do I, with a stable home and marriage and sufficient stamina and money, have the right to choose abortion because a pregnancy is inconvenient right now? Legally I do have that right; legally I want always to have that right. It is the morality of exercising it under those circumstances that makes me wonder.

(11) Technology has foiled us. The second trimester has become a time of resurrection; a fetus at six months can be one woman's late abortion, another's premature, viable child. Photographers now have film of embryos the size of a grape, oddly human, flexing their fingers, sucking their thumbs. Women have amniocentesis to find out whether they are carrying a child with birth defects that they may choose to abort. Before the procedure, they must have a sonogram, one of those fuzzy black-and-white photos like a love song heard through static on the radio, which shows someone is in there.

(12) I have taped on my VCR a public-television program in which somehow, inexplicably, a film is shown of a fetus in utero scratching its face, seemingly putting up a tiny hand to shield itself from the camera's eye. It would make a potent weapon in the arsenal of the antiabortionists. I grow sentimental about it as it floats in the salt water, part fish, part human being. It is almost living, but not quite. It has almost turned my heart around, but not quite turned my head.

Reading Survey

1. MAIN IDEA

What is the central theme of this essay?

2. MAJOR DETAILS

a. What experiences influenced Anna Quindlen's decision to become pro-choice?
b. What experiences caused the author to question her position on abortion?
c. Why does technology make it more difficult to come to terms with abortion?

3. INFERENCES

a. Read paragraph 9 again. What does the author mean when she says that right-to-lifers have tried "to portray abortion rights as something that feminists thought up on a slow Saturday over a light lunch"?
b. Read paragraph 12 again. What does the author mean by the last sentence, "It has almost turned my heart around, but not quite turned my head"?

4. OPINIONS

a. If you were a freshman dormitory counselor, what advice would you give to a pregnant student? Why?
b. In paragraph 10, Anna Quindlen wonders: "Do I, with a stable home and marriage and sufficient stamina and money, have the right to choose abortion because a pregnancy is inconvenient right now?" What advice would you give to the author? Explain your point of view.

Vocabulary Building

Lesson One: ***The Vocabulary of the Pro-Choice Movement***

The essay "Abortion Is Too Complex to Feel All One Way About" by Anna Quindlen includes words that are useful when you are discussing the pro-choice movement.

pro-choice (paragraph 2)
elemental (3)
gynecologist (4)
fetuses (6)
endure (6)
random (7)
intolerable (9)
stamina (10)
potent (12)
arsenal (12)

Members of the **pro-choice** movement believe that a pregnant woman should have the right to obtain a legal abortion.

Members of the pro-choice movement believe that having complete control over their own bodies is an **elemental**—most basic and simple—right.

Members of the pro-choice movement want to protect a pregnant woman's right to have an abortion performed by a **gynecologist,** a licensed medical doctor who specializes in women's health and especially the reproductive system.

Members of the pro-choice movement think of **fetuses**—unborn babies from three months to birth—as the stage before human life.

Members of the pro-choice movement think many unwanted children who are brought into the world **endure**—put up with or suffer—neglect and abuse.

Members of the pro-choice movement think having a child should be carefully planned, not a decision made at **random**—by chance or unplanned.

Members of the pro-choice movement think outlawing a woman's right to an abortion is **intolerable**—not to be allowed or stood for.

Members of the pro-choice movement draw a great deal of **stamina**—staying power—from their strong belief in individual rights.

Members of the pro-choice movement think their most **potent**—powerful or effective—weapon is sex education.

Members of the pro-choice movement believe another important weapon in their **arsenal**—store of weapons—is family planning.

EXERCISE 8A: Match each sentence with a vocabulary word from this lesson.

1. Mountain climbing requires a great deal of physical and mental staying power. 1. ________________

2. Equal treatment under the law is one of our most simple and basic rights. 2. ____________

3. The soldiers had a large store of weapons. 3. ____________

4. Growing up poor meant we had to put up with many hardships. 4. ____________

5. Killing civilians in war is not to be allowed. 5. ____________

6. Vinegar is a good kitchen cleaner; it is not only all-natural but also powerful and effective. 6. ____________

7. I always pick my lottery numbers by chance. 7. ____________

8. He believes it is a woman's right to obtain a legal abortion. 8. ____________

9. Unborn babies are called *embryos* until they reach three months of development, and then a new term is used. 9. ____________

10. In medical school, she specialized in women's health and reproduction. 10. ____________

Lesson Two: The Vocabulary of the Right-to-Life Movement

The essay "Abortion Is Too Complex to Feel All One Way About" by Anna Quindlen includes words that are useful when you are discussing the right-to-life movement.

right-to-lifers (paragraph 9)
degenerated (5)
execrable (6)
to plague (7)
acute (7)
quandary (9)
monolithic (9)
foiled (11)
viable (11)
embryos (11)

Members of the right-to-life movement, also called **right-to-lifers,** believe that abortions should be made illegal.

Members of the right-to-life movement think that American society has **degenerated**—fallen to a lower moral level—since abortion has become legal.

Members of the right-to-life movement think that abortion is **execrable**—horrible, as bad and wrong as can be imagined.
Members of the right-to-life movement think that the psychological effects of having an abortion will continue **to plague**—cause great mental suffering to—a woman for her entire life.
Members of the right-to-life movement think that most people do not understand the **acute**—sharp and severe—emotional pain of abortion.
Members of the right-to-life movement often provide counseling for pregnant women who are in a **quandary**—a state of confusion—about whether or not to have their babies.
Members of the right-to-life movement believe that life begins at the moment of conception; they see this position as **monolithic**—firm and uniform.
Members of the right-to-life movement are working to have abortion on demand **foiled**—prevented or blocked.
Members of the right-to-life movement point out that modern medical advances make many more fetuses **viable**—capable of maintaining life.
Members of the right-to-life movement think **embryos**—unborn babies from conception through two months of development—are innocent lives and must be protected.

EXERCISE 8B: For each word in italics, circle the definition closest in meaning.

1. A *viable* fetus is
   a. unlikely to develop normally.
   b. capable of maintaining life.
   c. developing too rapidly.
   d. a test-tube baby.
2. If you are in a *quandary*, you are in
   a. a serious legal situation.
   b. a serious argument with someone.
   c. a state of confusion.
   d. a deep hole in the earth where marble is found.
3. *Right-to-lifers* are
   a. against war.
   b. against suicide.
   c. for abortion.
   d. against abortion.

4. If your plans are *foiled,* they are
   a. blocked.
   b. unrealistic.
   c. challenged.
   d. unchanged.

5. *Embryos* are
   a. unborn babies older than two months.
   b. unborn babies through two months.
   c. infants who are born prematurely.
   d. infants who are born with physical problems.

6. If a problem is *acute,* it is
   a. severe.
   b. silly.
   c. easily solved.
   d. annoying.

7. If an action is *execrable,* it is
   a. carefully planned.
   b. surprising.
   c. horrible.
   d. highly effective.

8. If a meeting *degenerated,* it
   a. was often interrupted.
   b. fell to a lower moral level.
   c. was run democratically.
   d. led to many people being fired.

9. A *monolithic* point of view is
   a. supported by research.
   b. serious and believable.
   c. held by many people.
   d. firm and uniform.

10. *To plague* someone is to
    a. frighten the person for no apparent reason.
    b. do something to make the person ill.
    c. make the person suffer mentally.
    d. get the person to do something against his or her will.

SPELLING

The Apostrophe

Disregarding or misusing the apostrophe is as serious an error as misspelling the word. Careless writers do not realize that the apostrophe is as much a part of the word as each letter. Because it has only three major uses, the apostrophe is easy to learn and use properly.

I. Contractions. The apostrophe is used in contractions to indicate that a letter or letters have been left out.

it is = it's	have not = haven't	we have = we've
let us = let's	do not = don't	I will = I'll

TRY IT OUT

FORM CONTRACTIONS OUT OF THE FOLLOWING SETS OF WORDS. BE SURE TO USE THE APOSTROPHE WHERE NEEDED.

were + not = ________________	she + is = ________________
you + have = ________________	is + not = ________________
I + am = ________________	we + are = ________________

II. Plurals. To form the plural of a letter of the alphabet, a number, or a symbol, use *'s*.

6's three e's &'s

If the number is written out, use only the *s*.

fours sevens nines

TRY IT OUT

INSERT ANY NECESSARY APOSTROPHES IN THE FOLLOWING SENTENCES.

1. Can you think of a word that contains four es, two ds, and two ns?
2. Although Frank had three 9s and two 6s in his poker hand, he lost to Ed, who had three 10s and two 4s.

III. Possession. To form possessives, first write the name of the possessor—whether it be singular or plural. Then add *'s* to the end of the name. If it already ends in *s*, most writers just add the apostrophe (').

Helen's hat	Dickens' *Tale of Two Cities*
man's fate	the ladies' club
the class' suggestion	two boys' uniforms

To form the possessives of noun combinations, use the apostrophe only after the last noun in the combination.

my sister-in-law's car	the chief of police's remarks

A SPECIAL NOTE: *Do not use an apostrophe with the possessive pronouns: his, hers, yours, ours, theirs, its, whose.*

TRY IT OUT

REWRITE EACH OF THE FOLLOWING PHRASES TO FORM POSSESSIVES USING AN APOSTROPHE.

the movies of the actor ______________________

the games of the children ______________________

the cooking of the mother-in-law ______________________

EXERCISE 8C: Follow the directions for each item.

1. Form contractions out of the following sets of words.

a. here + is = ______________	g. would + have = ______________
b. was + not = ______________	h. what + is = ______________
c. we + will = ______________	i. can + not = ______________
d. you + would = ______________	j. they + are = ______________
e. Helen + is = ______________	k. has + not = ______________
f. does + not = ______________	l. who + is = ______________

m. are + not = ________________

n. I + will = ________________

o. she + is = ________________

p. let + us = ________________

q. must + not = ________________

r. you + are = ________________

s. there + is = ________________

t. will + not = ________________

2. Rewrite each of the following phrases to form possessives using an apostrophe.

 a. the profits of the oil company ________________
 b. the profits of the oil companies ________________
 c. the intelligence of Bob ________________
 d. the prices of today ________________
 e. the complaints of the men ________________
 f. the appetite of the cat ________________
 g. the job of the daughter-in-law ________________
 h. the popularity of rock music ________________
 i. the demands of the union ________________
 j. the demands of the unions ________________
 k. the TV shows of next week ________________
 l. the smile of Barbara ________________
 m. the freshness of the bread ________________
 n. the spirit of the team ________________
 o. the role of Congress ________________
 p. the equipment of the workers ________________
 q. the homework of the student ________________
 r. the homework of the students ________________

3. Insert apostrophes where necessary in the following sentences.

   a. If youre going to become a secretary, youd better remember that "sincerely" contains two es and "concerning" contains two cs and three ns.

   b. Linda Ronstadts album of songs from the 30s and 40s renewed the publics interest in music from the "big band era."

   c. Its the parents responsibility to make sure that they dont buy childrens toys with sharp edges that can cut a youngsters tender skin.

   d. When the temperature is in the 90s, a person shouldnt sit in the sun for too long, for the suns hot rays can cause the bodys heat-regulating mechanism to stop working.

   e. Ive just read that a cats face always has four rows of whiskers, that an elephants diet doesnt include meat, and that the worlds fastest animal is the cheetah.

   f. Isnt it a shame that football players salaries have gotten so high that the teams owners arent able to keep ticket prices at last years level?

The Comma

Although the comma seems to be a troublesome mark of punctuation, you can master it by learning just six principles that cover the great majority of uses. It is also helpful to remember that the comma represents a short pause in speech. However, since not all people pause in exactly the same places, rules must be relied upon for correct usage. Be sure that you have a reason for every comma that you use. If you are not sure that a comma is needed, it is usually wise to leave it out. Use the comma in these cases.

- **I To Separate Items in a Series**
- **II To Separate Two Complete Sentences Joined by *and, but, for, nor, or, so, yet***
- **III To Separate Coordinate Adjectives**
- **IV To Set Off Introductory Material**
- **V To Set Off Interrupters**
- **VI To Set Off Certain Conventional Material**

I. The Comma Is Used to Separate Items in a Series. Each item may be just one word or a whole string of words, but the series must have at least three items.

Patterns for Items in a Series

Patterns: Item 1, Item 2, Item 3

OR

Item 1, Item 2, and Item 3

Examples: The restaurant is small, elegant, expensive.

Three popular professions are data processing, electrical engineering, and drafting.

The convict ran across the yard, climbed over the wall, and escaped to freedom.

The student complained that the course was too hard, that the grades were too low, and that the teacher was too boring.

TRY IT OUT

INSERT ANY NECESSARY COMMAS IN THE FOLLOWING SENTENCES.

1. Scientists can determine a person's sex age and race by examining a single strand of hair.
2. The calf of a blue whale is twenty-three feet long at birth consumes half a ton of milk a day for six months and gains 220 pounds each day.

II. The Comma Is Used to Separate Two Complete Sentences Joined by *and, but, for, nor, or, so, yet.* The two sentences to be joined should be related in thought and of equal importance. (See Chapter Four, page 139, for a more complete discussion of coordination.) It is important to remember that the comma is used only when one of these seven words is being employed to join *two complete sentences.*

Pattern for Sentences Joined by *and, but, for, nor, or, so, yet*

and
but
for
Pattern: Complete sentence, G*nor* W complete sentence.
or
so
yet

Examples: She had prayed he would live, *but* she knew he would die.

She would never forget his face, *nor* would she forget his warm eyes.

A SPECIAL NOTE: If the two sentences are very short, the comma may be omitted. For example: The elephant bellowed wildly and its mate answered.

TRY IT OUT

INSERT ANY NECESSARY COMMAS IN THE FOLLOWING SENTENCES.

1. Lemons have a very sour taste yet they contain more sugar than sweet peaches do.
2. A mayfly lives for only six hours but lays eggs that take three years to hatch.

III. The Comma Is Used to Separate Coordinate Adjectives. An *adjective* describes a noun or pronoun; it makes the meaning of a noun or pronoun more specific. The adjective is usually placed as close as possible to the word it describes. The slot method can be used to identify adjectives. Start with this basic sentence.

That is (a) ______________ thing.

Now let's use some words to test the method.

That is a *new* thing.
That is a *slow* thing.
That is a *popular* thing.

When two or more adjectives are used to modify the same word, the adjectives are coordinate and must be separated by commas.

Pattern for Coordinate Adjectives

Pattern: adjective, adjective noun

Example: bright, colorful shirts

Two tests may be used to determine whether adjectives are coordinate: (1) try to put *and* between them or (2) try to reverse their order in the sentence.

Coordinate Adjectives:	bright, colorful shirts Test 1: bright and colorful shirts Test 2: colorful, bright shirts
Not Coordinate Adjectives:	several colorful shirts Test 1: several and colorful shirts (illogical) Test 2: colorful several shirts (illogical)

TRY IT OUT

INSERT ANY NECESSARY COMMAS IN THE FOLLOWING SENTENCES.

1. The abandoned homeless children wandered the cold rainy streets looking for a warm dry place to rest.
2. Several well-known actors are speaking out against the use of animals in painful laboratory experiments.

IV. The Comma Is Used to Set Off Introductory Material. The introductory material may be just a single word such as *however, therefore, nevertheless,* or *furthermore* . . . or a short expression such as *on the contrary, in fact, for example, on the other hand, in the first place, in general, to tell the truth, of course,* or *in addition.*

Pattern 1 for Introductory Material

Pattern: Introductory word or expression, complete sentence.

Examples: Nevertheless, the world's population will continue to grow. In fact, the world's population will double by the year 2100.

The introductory material may also be a lengthy phrase or a subordinate section. (See Chapter Four, page 144, for a more complete discussion of subordination.)

Pattern 2 for Introductory Material

Pattern: Introductory material, complete sentence.

Examples: During the coldest months of the year, a flu epidemic may spread throughout the nation.

Although an elephant can weigh up to 14,000 pounds, its brain weighs only about 11 pounds.

Revving up the car's powerful engine, the driver waited for the traffic light to turn green.

To feel calm and relaxed, some people take tranquilizers.

TRY IT OUT

INSERT ANY NECESSARY COMMAS IN THE FOLLOWING SENTENCES.

1. To keep your feet warm during the cold winter months you can sprinkle cayenne pepper in your shoes.
2. Before the adoption of the Twelfth Amendment to the Constitution in 1804 the candidate who ran second in a presidential election automatically became vice-president.
3. Although a penny does not buy much of anything these days the U.S. mint still turns out 170 million of them each week.

V. **Commas Are Used to Set Off Interrupters.** An interrupter may be any one of the single words or short expressions that can be used to introduce a sentence. (See rule IV.) Be sure that a comma is placed both *before* and *after* the interrupter.

Pattern 1 for Interrupters

Pattern: Complete, interrupter, sentence.

Examples: The nation is, of course, under the rule of the majority. I believe, however, that the majority is capable of making a mistake.

An interrupter may also be a subordinate section that usually begins with *who* or *which*.

Pattern 2 for Interrupters

Pattern: Complete, *who* OR *which* ~~~~~~~~~~ , sentence.

Examples: Juan, who is worried about pollution, plans to be an ecologist.
The S.S. *Norway*, which is docked at Pier 67, is crippled by a dockworkers' strike.

In Pattern 2, commas are used to surround the subordinate section because the subordination merely adds information about a specific *subject.* In the examples, Juan is a specific man and the S.S. *Norway* is a specific ship. Therefore, the information given in the subordinate section is *added information,* not basic for identification of the subject, and you need to *add commas. No commas* are used to surround the subordinate section when the *information is needed* for basic identification.

Examples: The man who is worried about pollution plans to be an ecologist.
The ship which is docked at Pier 67 is crippled by a dockworkers' strike.

If the *who* and *which* sections were removed from the examples above, we would have no idea which man and which ship are being discussed. Because the subordinate information is needed to clearly identify the subject, commas are *not* used. (See Chapter Four, page 152, for additional discussion of this case of subordination.)

A Special Note: The *who* or *which* and its verb may sometimes be omitted from the subordinate section, but the same rule still applies: If the subordinate section is merely *added information,* then *add commas.* If the subordinate section is needed to identify the subject, then commas are not used.

Examples: Mark, a professional soldier, is a patriotic man.
(Mark, who is a professional soldier, is a patriotic man.)

The lamp sitting on the desk belongs to me.
(The lamp which is sitting on the desk belongs to me.)

TRY IT OUT

INSERT ANY NECESSARY COMMAS IN THE FOLLOWING SENTENCES.

1. Sir Frances Joseph Campbell who was totally blind climbed the highest mountain in the Alps in 1880.
2. The tuatara a New Zealand lizard lives for as long as 300 years.
3. The King Ranch in Texas is in fact larger than the state of Rhode Island.
4. A person who is over six feet tall cannot qualify to become an astronaut in the U.S. space program.

VI. The Comma Is Used to Set Off Certain Conventional Material. Conventional material may consist of dates, addresses, or titles.

April 14, 1996, is my cat's birth date.
My aunt has lived at 24 Oak Street, Austin, Texas 78712, for the last thirty years.
J. T. Racken, M.D., is the President's new physician.

Conventional material may also include numbers.

957,357,268	page 12, line 10
five feet, six inches	Act II, scene iv

Conventional material may also consist of the complimentary close and the opening in an informal letter.

Sincerely yours,	Dear Joe,
Very truly yours,	Dear Uncle George,

A SPECIAL NOTE: In a formal letter, the opening is followed by a colon.

Dear Sir: Dear Mr. Riggs: Dear Ms. Hartley:

TRY IT OUT

INSERT ANY NECESSARY COMMAS IN THE FOLLOWING MATERIAL.

1. Page 93 paragraph 6 of *Natural History* magazine states that the Smithsonian Institution in Washington D.C. has a preserved African bull elephant measuring 13 feet 2 inches in height and weighing 24000 pounds.
2. On February 4 1998 Francis X. Ray M.D. opened his new office at 166-25 Patella Drive Los Angeles California 90069.
3. Dear Professor Young Yours truly Dear Edith

EXERCISE 8D: Insert commas wherever they are necessary in the following sentences. Be prepared to justify the use of each comma or set of commas.

1. Born into slavery George Washington Carver went on to become an outstanding teacher scientist and humanitarian. As director of agricultural research for Tuskegee Institute in Alabama he demonstrated how peanuts could be used to create over 300 different products including flour ink plastics soap linoleum and cosmetics. In addition he used sweet potatoes as the basis for vinegar rubber and postage stamp glue. Dedicated to helping black farmers Carver hoped that his inventions would greatly improve their economic situation.

2. For a period of twenty years a white porpoise nicknamed "Hatteras Jack" guided every ship in and out of the Hatteras Inlet which is off the coast of North Carolina. The amazingly intelligent skillful porpoise would swim around each ship to gauge its size would wait until the tide had reached the proper level and then would lead the vessel safely past the dangerous reefs. After buoys and bells were placed in the inlet Jack apparently realized that his assistance was no longer needed for he disappeared and was never seen in that area again.

3. In August of 1975 W. W. Johnson a 62-year-old retired schoolteacher was walking through the Crater of Diamonds State Park at Murfreesboro Arkansas. Attracted by a sparkling rock on the ground he casually bent over and picked up what turned out to be a flawless 16.37-carat diamond. Now known as the Amarillo Starlight the stone is worth more than $250000.

4. People can die from the bite of a black widow spider. Pigeons and chickens on the other hand eat these deadly insects without even getting sick. Similarly cattle die from eating the New Zealand tutu plant yet goats thrive on it.

5. According to page 121 paragraph 3 of the *Guinness Book of World Records* one of the world's greatest volcanic eruptions took place on the Indonesian island of Krakatoa in 1883. Exploding with the force of 26 hydrogen bombs the volcano wiped out 163 villages killed 36380 people and left a huge crater 1000 feet below sea level. The explosion was so powerful in fact that it was heard clearly 3000 miles away.

6. "Princess Pauline" who was a Dutch midget was the shortest adult person who ever lived. When she was 19 years old she was only 23 inches tall. In contrast Robert Wadlow of Alton Illinois was the tallest person who ever lived. His height reached 8 feet 11 inches when he was 21 years old.

7. The Pilgrims of Massachusetts used a special tool in church a wooden ball attached to a long string on a stick. To awaken someone who fell asleep during a sermon a member of the clergy would swing the stick hitting the person in the head with the wooden ball. Some churches as well as schools and businesses might like to use this tool today.

8. In a small isolated village near Madrid Spain almost every inhabitant has at least six fingers on each hand and six toes on each foot. The result of close intermarriage this deformity is so common in the village that the people are not aware of their own unusual condition but they think that it is the visitors with normal hands and feet who are abnormal.

9. The *Boston Nation* a nineteenth-century Ohio newspaper had pages $7\frac{1}{2}$ feet long and $5\frac{1}{2}$ feet wide. As a result two people were needed to hold the paper in proper reading position.

10. William F. Fry M.D. a California psychiatrist claims that laughing 100 times a day provides as much exercise as 10 minutes of rowing does. Furthermore laughter promotes a sense of relaxation stimulates alertness and may even help to speed healing. Therefore if you are feeling tense or sick you might try reading a joke book or watching a funny movie.

11. Although some people try to escape cold snowy weather by moving to the southern part of the United States they may be in for a surprise. Santa Fe New Mexico for example gets an average of nine inches more snow each year than does New Haven Connecticut.

12. During a heated argument with an Indian a Bolivian cattle herder named José Silva was shot in the face with a 4 foot 2 inch arrow that entered near his temple and emerged near his nose. A doctor recommended immediate surgery but Silva was afraid to undergo the painful dangerous operation. Having grown used to the arrow in his head he decided to leave it where it was. For the remaining 11 years of his life he never complained about the presence of the shaft nor did he ever have even a slight headache.

13. J. Paul Getty the late billionaire spent nearly $42000000 to build a California art museum and he left $1271900000 to maintain it. However he never bothered to visit the museum before he died.

14. Located in Sequoia National Park the General Sherman tree is 272 feet 4 inches tall and is 80 feet in diameter at its base. This tree which is estimated to be over 3000 years old contains enough wood to build 50 six-room houses.

15. Madam Girardelli who was a nineteenth-century Italian performer would begin her act by pouring boiling oil into her mouth. Then after spitting out the oil she might chew on boiling lead until it turned into solid pieces of metal or perhaps she would plunge her hands into the flames of a roaring

fire. Unharmed by these feats Madame Girardelli claimed that she was without a doubt the world's only fireproof person.

16. In Japan gaining entrance to a university practically guarantees a good job after graduation so high school students usually work very hard to prepare for the university entrance test. Indeed most Japanese youngsters do not mind having to go to school 6 days a week for 240 days a year. Eager to increase their knowledge as quickly as possible many students also attend a private "cram school" for several hours each day. Unfortunately only 40 percent of those who take the difficult highly competitive entrance test are accepted into a Japanese university.

17. On December 19 1922 Mrs. Theresa Vaughn was arrested for being married to two men at the same time. During the court hearing however the 24-year-old woman admitted that she actually had 62 husbands most of whom she had married during five years of traveling through Great Britain Germany and South Africa. As everyone in the courtroom listened in a state of shocked silence Mrs. Vaughn explained in a serious down-to-earth manner that she had never divorced any of these men because divorce was socially unacceptable at that time.

18. The stegosaurus was a giant dinosaur that grew to more than 18 feet long and weighed approximately 80000 pounds. Nevertheless its brain weighed only two ounces and was the size of a walnut. To control its huge muscular back legs it had a second brain in its tail. Killed off by the coming of the Ice Age this dinosaur was the largest animal that ever walked the earth.

19. Because the rate of car theft has long been very high in the United States the Bosco Company of Akron Ohio marketed a "Collapsible Rubber Automobile Driver." This dummy which was stored under the car's front seat could be quickly inflated and placed behind the steering wheel. Of course the dummy was supposed to scare away thieves when the car was parked but apparently the invention did not sell well for the company eventually went bankrupt.

20. Scientific research has proven much to everyone's surprise that fish can become seasick. Indeed when fish were kept aboard a ship in the Mediterranean Sea they became just as ill from the huge rolling waves as did any of the human passengers.

EXERCISE 8E: Follow the directions for each item. Be sure to use commas wherever necessary.

1. Write a statement about allergies, using two complete sentences joined by *but*.

   ____

   ____

2. Using coordinate adjectives, describe your best friend.

   ____

   ____

3. Using *when* to begin the sentence, write a statement about one way to avoid being lonely.

   ____

   ____

4. Write a statement about doctors' fees, using a short expression to interrupt the sentence.

   ____

   ____

5. State the address of your school as part of a sentence.

   ____

   ____

6. Write a sentence about a specific make of car you would like to own. Use an interrupter that is a subordinate section requiring commas.

   ____

   ____

7. Use an introductory word or expression to begin a sentence about working mothers.

____

____

8. Complete the following sentence, giving three actions that you believe should be taken.

   High school education could be improved if ____________________

____

9. Write a statement about a blind date, using two complete sentences joined by *and*.

____

____

10. Using *because* to begin the sentence, write a statement about a new law that you think should be put into effect.

____

____

11. Write a sentence about one of your teachers, starting with the person's name and using an interrupter that states the subject that he or she teaches. Do not use the word *who*.

____

____

12. Write a sentence about a particular day that you will never forget. Give the date at the beginning of the sentence.

____

____

13. Describe your bedroom, using coordinate adjectives.

____

14. Write an opening and complimentary close for a letter to the mayor of your town or city.

15. Using at least three items in a series, describe a recent movie you have seen.

16. Using *after* to begin the sentence, write a statement about your favorite weekend activity.

17. Use an introductory word or expression to begin a sentence about credit cards.

18. Write a sentence about one of your parents. Use an interrupter that is a subordinate section requiring commas.

19. Write a statement about rap music, using two complete sentences joined by *so*.

20. Using coordinate adjectives, describe the President of the United States.

 Other Marks of Punctuation

Punctuation not only is necessary but also is extremely useful in adding color and style to your writing.

THE PERIOD

Use after a complete statement.	The campaign was successful.
Use after most abbreviations.	U.S. Mr. etc. B.A.

THE QUESTION MARK

Use only after a *direct* question.	Did the dog bite you? (direct) [not: I asked if the dog bit you. (indirect)]

THE EXCLAMATION POINT

Use after a word, expression, or complete sentence that conveys strong emotion.	Oh! What a surprise! It's an engagement ring!

THE SEMICOLON

Use between two full sentences that are closely related in thought and are of equal importance. (Notice that the sentence following the semicolon does *not* begin with a capital letter.)	Joe is a very poor reader; it takes him three days to read a comic book.
Use between items in a series when the items themselves contain commas.	At the party I met Frank Parks, a bank president; Elaine Warren, a history teacher; and Mimi Carson, a professional singer.

THE COLON

Use after an opening statement to direct attention to the material that follows, which is usually an explanation of the opening statement.	I need the following groceries: ketchup, napkins, and cereal. You made one big mistake: You used a generalization to prove your argument.

Use after the opening of a formal letter, between a title and a subtitle, between numbers indicating chapter and verse of the Bible, and between numbers indicating hours and minutes.

Dear Sir:

Dear Ms. Hernandez:

Taking Action: Writing, Reading, Speaking, and Listening Through Simulation Games

We read Matthew 6:11.

Theresa left at 12:30.

THE DASH

Use to signal a dramatic pause: Use a single dash to emphasize what follows, and use a set of dashes as you would a set of commas. (The dash should be used sparingly in formal writing.)

It was one thing she really needed—a mink toothbrush.

The man walked for hours—as he often did—until it was dark.

PARENTHESES

Use sparingly to set off an interruption that is not as important as the main material.

Thomas Wolfe (1900–1938) wrote *Look Homeward Angel.*
Sailing (not to be confused with cruising) is difficult.

QUOTATION MARKS

In all of the examples below, notice where the quotation marks are placed in relation to the other marks of punctuation. For example, *the commas and the period are always placed to the left of the quotation marks.*

Use to set off the exact words that someone has said when he or she is quoted directly. (Notice that when the wording of a person's statement is changed to form an indirect quotation, you do *not* use quotation marks.)

Susan said, "I will leave tomorrow." (direct)
Susan said that she would leave tomorrow. (indirect)
"I believe," said Peter, "that we are sinking."
"What makes you say that?" gurgled his wife.

Use to set off the titles of stories, magazine articles, short poems, and chapters in books. (The titles of longer works, including books and plays, should be underlined or italicized.)	"The Ugly Truth About Beauty" is one of the essays in this book. The first poem in *Leaves of Grass* is titled "Song of Myself."
Use to set off words that are being used in a special sense.	Health food is "in" today. "Charisma" is a difficult word to define.

EXERCISE 8F: Follow the directions for each item. Be sure to use whatever punctuation is required.

1. Write a direct quotation about snow. Then change it to an indirect quotation.

   Direct: ______________________________

   Indirect: ______________________________

2. Write an exclamation about the current cost of gasoline.

   ____

3. Using fast foods as your subject, write two complete sentences that can be joined by a semicolon.

   ____

   ____

4. Using a dash for emphasis, write a sentence about a recent news event reported in your local newspaper.

   ____

5. Write a brief letter to a store stating your complaint about something you have just purchased. Use three common abbreviations and use marks of punctuation that are appropriate in a letter.

   ____

   ____

   ____

6. Using Thanksgiving as your subject, write two complete sentences that can be joined by a colon.

7. Write a sentence about your favorite beverage, using parentheses to set off an interrupter.

8. Write a direct question about a musical instrument. Then change it to an indirect question.

   Direct: ______________________

   Indirect: ______________________

9. Using clocks as your subject, write two complete sentences that can be joined by a semicolon.

10. Write a sentence about three people in public office, giving each person's name and position. Be sure to use semicolons for clarity.

11. In a complete sentence, list at least three performers who are popular because of physical appearance rather than talent. Use a colon to direct attention to your items.

12. Using direct quotations, present a three-line dialogue between a bank teller and a customer who is having difficulty cashing a check. For each line identify the speaker in a different place in the sentence.

____

____

____

____

____

13. Write a direct question about weather forecasts. Then change it to an indirect question.

Direct: _______________

____

Indirect: _______________

____

14. Use a complete sentence to state the title of a magazine that you like.

____

____

15. Using bubble gum as your subject, write two complete sentences that can be joined by a colon.

____

____

16. Using dashes to set off an interrupter, write a sentence about a household chore you dislike.

____

____

17. Write two complete sentences that can be joined by a semicolon. Use as your subject a sudden urge to eat your favorite food.

____

____

____

18. Using friendship as your subject, write two complete sentences that can be joined by a semicolon. Then rewrite your sentences joining them with one of the seven connectors: *and, but, for, nor, or, so, yet.*

    Using semicolon: ______________________________

    ____

    ____

    Using connector: ______________________________

    ____

    ____

19. In a complete sentence, list at least three of the nation's most serious problems. Use a colon to direct attention to your items.

    ____

    ____

    ____

20. Write a quotation about doctors. Then change it to an indirect quotation.

    Direct: ______________________________

    ____

    Indirect: ______________________________

    ____

EXERCISE 8G: Adding all necessary punctuation and capital letters, create sensible sentences in the paragraphs below. Be sure to include all marks of punctuation presented in this chapter.

although it is considered a complex science astrology can be great fun for most people astrologers believe that an individuals personality is influenced by the position of the planets at the time of his or her birth how well do the following astrological descriptions fit you your family and your friends people born under the sign of Aries March 21–April 20 are doers rather than thinkers if Arians are given their way they will often become dictators they enjoy being the boss and will do anything to maintain their position on the positive side they are builders who act quickly and decisively

Taurus which runs from April 21 to May 20 is the sign of the bull as one would imagine Taureans are stubborn bullheaded and persistent they are slow to think and to act but once they have made up their minds Taureans will refuse to change their points of view moreover people born under this sign are great lovers of beauty and hold one quality above all others honesty

were you born between May 21 and June 20 if so you are a changeable undependable Gemini but you are also a highly creative person with a sharp mind that allows you to understand and act quickly some famous Geminis were John Wayne the film actor George Bernard Shaw the British playwright and Walt Whitman the American poet

the sign of Cancer rules the period from June 21 to July 22 a Cancer also called a Moon Child tends to be overbearing possessive and demanding but these bad qualities are often outweighed by such good qualities as sensitivity generosity and optimism the Cancer is usually heard to say dont worry everything will be better tomorrow

born between July 23 and August 22 Leos are governed by one personality trait they are self-interested to the point of being show-offs and ham actors because they have self-confidence and act on the spur of the moment Leos are never still or quiet they are optimistic and generous in helping others people born between August 23 and September 22 are self-centered Virgos their chief aims are to avoid responsibility and at the same time to achieve selfish goals Virgos have good minds but are often illogical thinkers nevertheless they are thorough about whatever they do perhaps because they keep secrets well Virgos make excellent politicians leaders and diplomats

balance is the key to Libra which governs the period from September 23 to October 22 Librans are emotional romantics who can sometimes lose their self-control they can become impulsive like children when balance is restored Librans become calm and levelheaded at all times they are sympathetic vital people

lustful Scorpios are born between October 23 and November 22 they tend to use great forceful power to control situations in order to reach their major goal in life physical satisfaction with keen minds for support Scorpios seek the ideal life by fighting for every worthwhile cause there can be world peace they insist trust is the answer to everything do you know a driving forceful Scorpio

the Sagittarius November 23–December 21 is driven by conflicting personality characteristics people born under this sign can be stingy and extremely selfish one minute and then without any explanation they can suddenly become generous and openhearted when they are after something they strike quickly get what they want and move on probably the most positive trait that Sagittarians have is their ability to use their clever minds for constructive purposes

Capricorn which runs from December 22 to January 19 is the sign for climbers Capricorns may climb through work or they may climb through illegal means although their methods may vary Capricorns have the drive to climb to the top they can settle for nothing less after reaching the top however they usually ask now what do I do with all of it

anyone born between January 20 and February 19 is an Aquarius he or she is drawn toward public rather than private activity but the nature of the public activity will vary greatly plotting the overthrow of the government the Aquarius shouts liberty equality freedom in contrast an Aquarius might also be a political leader or a humanitarian some famous Aquarians were Adlai Stevenson the American politician Franklin D Roosevelt the President of the U.S. and Douglas MacArthur the American army general

the weakling of the Zodiac is Pisces February 19–March 21 who gets along well with others but tends to agree with the crowd too often indeed such a person is quite content to follow other peoples opinions and actions moreover a Pisces will never succeed because he or she lacks one essential quality the inner drive needed to start new projects but one can admire the fine aspects of a Pisces personality loyalty dependability and adaptability

in his article Practical Astrology John Hutton PhD brings up an important point to remember the heavenly bodies guide us in a general direction he explains beyond that it is up to us to determine the specific path our lives take

EXERCISE 8H: REFRESHER

1. **MAKE ANY CORRECTIONS THAT WILL IMPROVE THE EFFECTIVENESS OF THE INTRODUCTION AND CONCLUSION BELOW.**
2. **PLAN AHEAD BY LISTING THREE MAIN BODY IDEAS.**
3. **CORRECT ANY ERRORS IN VERB TENSE CONSISTENCY.**

How to Be a Good Parent

Introduction

Last July I was walking through a shopping mall parking lot when I spotted a baby girl all alone in a parked car. The baby, who was strapped into an infant seat facing the hot rays of the sun, cried continuously as sweat poured down her forehead and soaked her clothing. I try to open the doors, but they are both locked. So I use one of my shoes to smash a window and rescue the child, who was later treated for dehydration at a local hospital. When the baby's mother finally returns to the car, she seems unaware of the dangerous situation she had created. Such incidents of bad parenting can be stopped completely if people learn the proper skills for raising children. In my essay, I will discuss how to be a good parent.

Main Body I: ______________________________

Main Body II: ______________________________

Main Body III: ______________________________

Conclusion

Of course, since I am not a parent, I did not know very much about this topic. But I think that if all parents follow my suggestions, the nation's young people will grow up to be happy, well-adjusted adults.

SPRINGBOARDS TO WRITING

Using your knowledge of the writing process, explained on pages 14–16, write a paragraph or essay related to this chapter's central theme, *the complex abortion issue,* which is introduced on pages 328–32.

PREWRITING

To think of topics to write about, look at the advertisement and photograph, read the essay, and answer the questions that follow each. If you prefer, select one of the writing springboards below. (All paragraph numbers refer to the essay that starts on page 330.) To develop your ideas, use the prewriting techniques described on pages 17–22.

WRITING A PARAGRAPH *(For help, see the Pointers on page 51.)*

1. Should teenagers be required to get parental approval for an abortion?
2. Demonstrations outside abortion clinics should (should not) be banned.
3. High schools should (should not) give teenagers full birth control information.
4. Agree or disagree: A man should have the legal right to prevent his pregnant wife or girlfriend from having an abortion.
5. In your opinion, when does life begin: at the moment of conception, when the embryo becomes a fetus (at the start of the third month of pregnancy), or at birth? Explain.
6. Should adopted children have the right to know who their biological parents are?
7. Should an unmarried couple choose to have children?

WRITING AN ESSAY *(For help, see the Pointers on pages 54–55.)*

8. Abortions Should (Should Not) Be Legal
9. My Opinion of the Pro-Choice Movement
10. My Opinion of the Right-to-Life Movement
11. Why I Have Mixed Feelings About Abortion
12. My Advice to Someone Who Is Pregnant and Single
13. Answer Anna Quindlen's question: "Do I, with a stable home and marriage and sufficient stamina and money, have the right to choose abortion because pregnancy is inconvenient right now?" (See paragraph 10.)

14. Agree or disagree: Teenage Pregnancies Are a Problem That Affects Our Entire Society
15. The Schools Should (Should Not) Teach Sex Education
16. The Case for (Against) Test-Tube Babies
17. What Makes a Good (Bad) Parent?
18. The Difficulties of Being a Single Parent
19. How I Want to Raise (Am Raising) My Children
20. Agree or disagree with this statement by Pius XI: "However we may pity the mother whose health and even life are imperiled by the performance of her natural duty, there yet remains no sufficient reason for condoning the direct murder of the innocent."
21. Agree or disagree with this statement by Margaret Sanger: "No woman can call herself free who does not own and control her body. No woman can call herself free until she can choose consciously whether she will or will not be a mother."
22. The Alternatives to Abortion
23. Big Families Are (Are Not) a Good Idea
24. The Foster Care System Is (Is Not) Effective
25. The Case for (Against) Premarital Sex

SWANN ©88 THE HUNTSVILLE TIMES

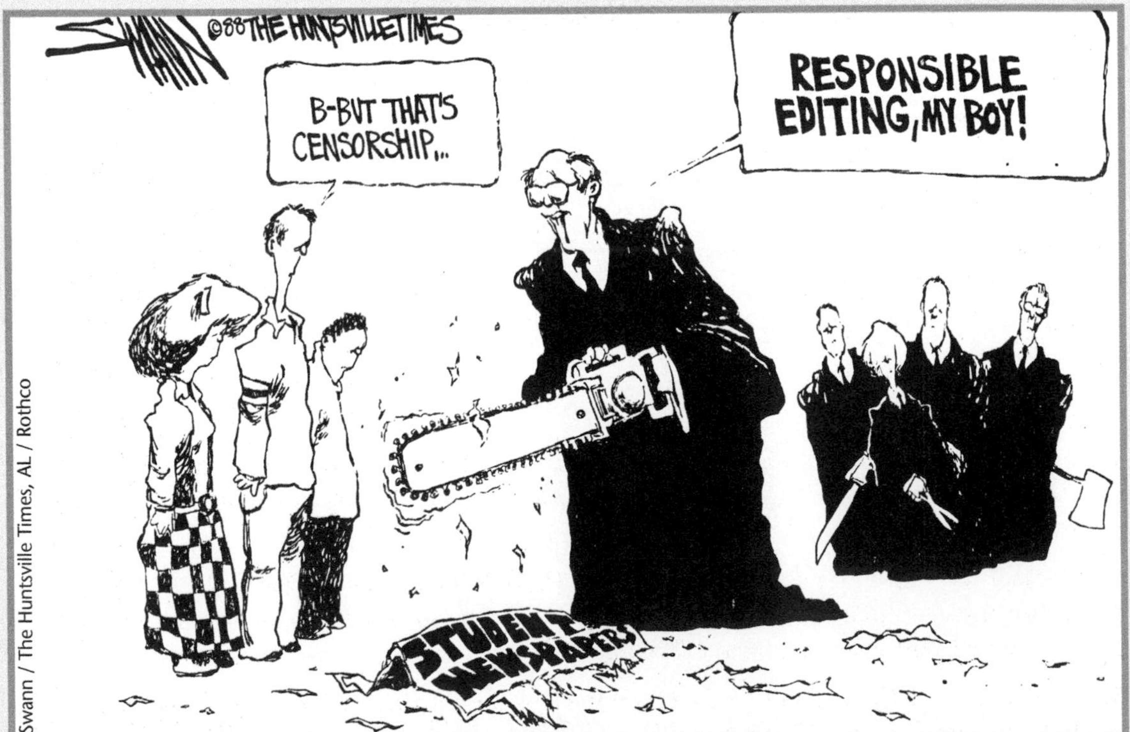

B-BUT THAT'S CENSORSHIP...

RESPONSIBLE EDITING, MY BOY!

STUDENT NEWSPAPERS

Chapter 9

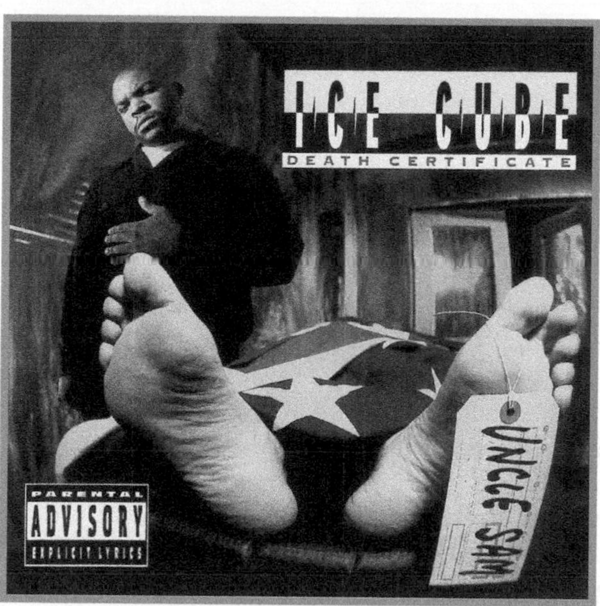

SPRINGBOARDS TO THINKING

For informal, not written, response . . . to stimulate your thinking

1. Read the cartoon at the top of the opposite page. In your own words, what is the cartoon saying? Do you agree or disagree with what it says? Explain.
2. Do you think that movies, rock lyrics, television, and advertisements should be censored to eliminate sex? Explain.
3. Read the cartoon at the bottom of the opposite page. What is its message? Do you think that student newspapers should be censored to eliminate content that teachers and administrators consider improper? Explain.
4. Look at the CD cover above. What do you think is its message? Do you think the cover is in bad taste? Explain. Do you think that CD covers—or song lyrics—should be censored to eliminate offensive material? Explain.
5. Notice the "advisory" label on the CD cover. What is its purpose? Do you think that such labels are a good idea? What is the difference between an "advisory" label and censorship?

Rapping Nasty

James Earl Hardy

(1) Last June, on a steamy Saturday night, the members of 2 Live Crew were doing what they do best—"getting nasty"—in a packed nightclub in Hollywood, Florida. For more than an hour, group members Luther Campbell, Mark Ross, and Chris Wong Won rapped the bawdy tunes that had made them one of America's most popular and controversial rap groups. Behind them two scantily clad female dancers gyrated to the music. Later, as the band's members left the club, they were met by the usual autograph-seeking fans—and the local police. Campbell and Wong Won were placed under arrest. The charge? Performing songs from their best-selling album *As Nasty As They Wanna Be,* which was found to be obscene by a Fort Lauderdale judge just a few days earlier.

(2) The judge's ruling and the band members' arrest were the latest in a series of incidents that many people see as an increasing effort to limit free speech. Protecting 2 Live Crew's right to free speech, they say, is a way of protecting everyone's right to free speech—even if the music is offensive to some people.

(3) The battle over the limits of free speech began almost the moment the Bill of Rights was signed. Difficulty in setting limits often boils down to one question: How do you define obscenity? Former Supreme Court Justice William Brennan, who once favored a limit on obscene speech, says he has given up trying to define the term. As he told *The New Yorker* magazine in March, "If you can't define it [obscenity], you can't prosecute people for it." But others feel that even if words cannot describe it, obscenity does exist. As Justice Potter Stewart wrote in a famous 1964 opinion, "Perhaps I could never succeed in [defining obscenity], but I know it when I see it." The current criteria for obscenity were established in 1973. In the case *Miller vs. California,* the Supreme Court said a work must be "patently offensive" and lack artistic, literary, political, or scientific value to be declared legally obscene.

(4) The judge in the 2 Live Crew case held that *As Nasty As They Wanna Be* lacked any "artistic" value. He cited songs like "Me So Horny" and "Dirty Nursery Rhymes," in which the rappers boast of sexual conquests and describe sexual acts and genitalia in crude and graphic detail. The arrested members of 2 Live Crew face up to a year in jail and a $1,000 fine. The 2 Live Crew leader, Luther Campbell, told *Update* that the album is nothing more than "what comes out of the mouths of men in locker rooms. It's just exaggerated talk about sex, bragging, and being macho. It is meant to be funny, not taken seriously."

(5) But Jack Thompson, a Miami anti-pornography lawyer, wasn't laughing when a Mississippi group called the American Family Association sent him a transcript of the album's lyrics last year. Thompson sent letters and copies of the lyrics to law-enforcement officials in 67 Florida counties and to the governors of the 50 states. He claimed that record-store owners were violating obscenity/pornography laws by selling *Nasty* to children. Broward County deputy Mark Wichner took a tape and transcript to a local judge, who ruled there was "probable cause" to believe the album was obscene under state laws. Law officers brought the judge's decision to the attention of record retailers, who began pulling *Nasty* from their shelves, fearing arrest and fines. The 2 Live Crew then filed suit, claiming their album had in fact not been declared obscene, and the law-enforcement action had been illegal and a form of intimidation. After a three-week trial, Judge Jose Gonzalez Jr. ruled that the album's lyrics appeal to " 'dirty' thoughts and the loins, not to the intellect and the mind."*

(6) Some musicians feel the ruling against 2 Live Crew was bound to happen and that the record industry is partly to blame. In 1985, the Parents Music Resource Center (PMRC) began pushing to have warning stickers placed on record labels of albums whose material was deemed inappropriate for children. Since then, more artists have been criticized for their provocative stage acts (Bobby Brown, Madonna) and controversial lyrics (Guns N' Roses, Public Enemy). "By agreeing [to warning stickers] we were admitting that some of the music was obscene," explains Ice-T, a controversial West Coast rapper. "Once the music was stamped with that label, the door was opened for anyone to come along along and question whether it had a right to be sold or heard by people."

(7) The citizens who live in Broward, Dade, and Palm Beach Counties in Florida know this all too well. They can now be fined and jailed for selling *Nasty* or playing it in public. Judges in two South Carolina counties have also declared it obscene, and officials in other states are trying to force record stores not to carry it. Many record chains have stopped selling *Nasty.* Some continue to sell it, but they request identification from the buyer before they okay the sale.

(8) Campbell says his group was singled out unfairly: "Let's just call it selective prosecution. I could think of a lot of others whose work could be labeled offensive." Holding up a copy of white comedian Andrew Dice Clay's cassette "Dice," he asks with a sly grin, "This isn't obscene? Do you think it is a coincidence that they've gone after a black group producing black music through a black production company? I don't." Armond White, arts editor for the *City Sun,* an African-American weekly based in New York, agrees. Rap music has come under fierce scrutiny by whites who don't understand it, he says. "A lot of

*The United States Supreme Court later ruled that the album's lyrics are not obscene.

parents are afraid because their kids are walking around in Public Enemy T-shirts and listening to 'Fear of a Black Planet.' "

(9) Campbell says the Crew's graphic sexual language is in the black cultural tradition of comedians such as Richard Pryor and Redd Foxx. "We wanted to be known as the Eddie Murphy's of rap," he contends. But the National Association for the Advancement of Colored People (NAACP) has criticized Campbell for associating the group's lyrics with black culture. Michele Moody-Adams, an assistant professor of philosophy at Rochester University, sides with the NAACP. "A culture sustains and supports positive traditions," explains Moody-Adams, who is black. "2 Live Crew's music doesn't speak to the history of black people. It supports the myth that black men are sexually irresponsible, and black women are fair game." While she does not favor censorship, she believes 2 Live Crew's lyrics are "dangerous not only for black people but for all people. How can anyone defend lyrics that dehumanize women, that reduce them to creatures made to satisfy the violent, sadistic sexual fantasies of men?"

(10) Lawyer Jack Thompson, who initiated the campaign against *Nasty*, says that that is the reason for his targeting the group. "I am deeply concerned about the effect such a recording could have on children, and what attitudes [about women] may prevail." Barry Lynn of the American Civil Liberties Union (ACLU) doesn't buy Thompson's argument. "Protecting women and children is one thing; banning a record so that no one has access to it is another. You have an individual deciding what is best for an entire community, and that is dangerous. What one person considers obscene, another may not." Lynn predicts that because of the 2 Live Crew case there will be other recordings brought up on obscenity charges. "We'll probably be defending operas and music from Broadway shows that allude to sex," says Lynn. "Where will it all end?"

(11) No doubt, the major record labels are concerned. Most have been silent throughout the controversy, fearing their own artists may be next. But Atlantic Records doesn't seem to be bothered by all the hype surrounding 2 Live Crew; they have released the group's new album, which speaks directly to the obscenity ruling. The first single and title of the album is called "Banned in the U.S.A.," which borrows from Bruce Springsteen's "Born in the U.S.A." Thompson, who says he doesn't find the albums of Andrew Dice Clay obscene, vows to go after "Banned in the U.S.A." if it "includes trash for lyrics."

(12) Ice-T, though, feels that even if there is such a thing as obscenity, and people like it, it can't be taken away from them. "This should be the bottom line: If you don't like [2 Live Crew], you don't have to listen to them, you don't have to buy their album, you don't have to go see them in concert. And the government and the courts should not be deciding what we can and cannot listen to, what we can and cannot buy, or what 2 Live Crew can rap about. To coin a phrase, they and any other group should have the right to be 'as nasty as they wanna be.' "

READING SURVEY

1. MAIN IDEA

What is the central theme of this essay?

2. MAJOR DETAILS

a. Why were the members of 2 Live Crew arrested in Hollywood, Florida?
b. What did lawyer Jack Thompson do when he saw the lyrics for 2 Live Crew's album?
c. What is Barry Lynn's response to Thompson's argument that 2 Live Crew's album could be harmful to women and children?

3. INFERENCES

a. Read paragraph 11 again. Why isn't Atlantic Records bothered by all the hype surrounding 2 Live Crew?
b. Read paragraph 8 again. Why does Campbell think his group was singled out for prosecution?

4. OPINIONS

a. Read paragraph 12 again. Do you agree with Ice-T that rap groups should have the right to be "'as nasty as they wanna be'"? Why or why not?
b. Do you think either the courts or the government should have the right to prevent the sale of magazines, books, recordings, and music videos that contain strong sexual content? Explain your point of view.

VOCABULARY BUILDING

Lesson One: ***The Vocabulary of Censorship, Part I***

The essay "Rapping Nasty" by James Earl Hardy includes words that are useful when you are discussing censorship.

censorship (paragraph 9)
controversial (1)
bawdy (1)
obscene (1) . . . **obscenity** (3)
offensive (2)
prosecute (3) . . . **prosecution** (8)
crude (4)
graphic (4)
sadistic (9)
initiated (10)

Censorship is the practice of examining publications, movies, television programs, song lyrics, and any other forms of communication in order to remove or forbid anything that is considered objectionable for moral, political, religious, and other reasons.

Censorship is a very **controversial** issue—an issue that stirs up a lengthy, often angry public discussion between people who hold sharply opposing opinions.

People who favor censorship usually do not want the public exposed to anything **bawdy**—anything that includes a sexual message presented in a way that is humorous and lacking in good taste.

People who favor censorship do not want the public exposed to anything **obscene**—anything that is considered disgusting because it goes against accepted standards of proper behavior and is usually intended to be sexually exciting. Examples of an **obscenity** include a remark, act, or event that upsets people who consider it to be in bad taste.

People who favor censorship complain that the lyrics to many of today's songs are **offensive**—so unpleasant and disgusting that they anger and insult people.

People who favor censorship want the government to **prosecute**—to bring legal action against—those who display or sell materials that might be considered sexually exciting. Any such **prosecution** would usually be fought against by writers, artists, and filmmakers who believe in the right to free expression.

People who favor censorship complain that the language used by some comedians is **crude**—lacking in good taste, grace, or sensitivity.

People who favor censorship complain that some song lyrics and some scenes of sex and violence in today's movies are much too **graphic**—shown or described in full and realistic detail to create clear, striking images.

People who favor censorship do not want the public exposed to material that describes the behavior of a **sadistic** person—an extremely cruel person who gets great pleasure from causing pain in others.

People who favor censorship have **initiated**—started or begun—lawsuits against some rap singers.

EXERCISE 9A: Each of the vocabulary words from this lesson is shown below in italics as the word appeared in context in the essay. Write an explanation of each word within the context of the material given. Use your own paper for this assignment.

1. From paragraph 1: "For more than an hour, group members . . . rapped the *bawdy* tunes that had made them one of America's most popular and *controversial* rap groups."
2. From paragraph 1: "The charge? Performing songs from their best-selling album . . . which was found to be *obscene* by a Fort Lauderdale judge just a few days earlier."
3. From paragraph 2: ". . . even if the music is *offensive* to some people."
4. From paragraph 3: "How do you define *obscenity*?"

5. From paragraph 3: " 'If you can't define it [obscenity], you can't *prosecute* people for it.' "
6. From paragraph 4: ". . . the rappers boast of sexual conquests . . . in *crude* and *graphic* detail."
7. From paragraph 8: " 'Let's just call it selective *prosecution.*' "
8. From paragraph 9: "While she does not favor *censorship,* . . ."
9. From paragraph 9: " 'How can anyone defend lyrics that dehumanize women, that reduce them to creatures made to satisfy the violent, *sadistic* sexual fantasies of men?' "
10. From paragraph 10: "Lawyer Jack Thompson, who *initiated* the campaign . . ."

Lesson Two: ***The Vocabulary of Censorship, Part II***

The essay "Rapping Nasty" by James Earl Hardy includes words that are useful when you are discussing censorship.

criteria (paragraph 3)	**scrutiny** (8)
literary (3)	**prevail** (10)
pornography (5)	**banning** (10)
violating (5)	**access** (10)
provocative (6)	**allude** (10)

People who are against censorship point out that it is difficult to establish **criteria** the standards, rules, or tests that would be used to judge the quality of a particular work.

People who are against censorship point out that many excellent **literary** works—works such as books, plays, and other forms of literature—might be considered in bad taste by some people.

People who are against censorship believe that the government should not prevent the sale of **pornography**—publications, photographs, movies, and other forms of communication that are intended primarily to be sexually exciting.

People who are against censorship claim that it would be **violating**—breaking the law of—the First Amendment of the U.S. Constitution, which guarantees freedom of speech.

People who are against censorship claim that the public is not harmed by being exposed to materials that are **provocative**—that are stimulating and that stir up strong feelings, often of a sexual nature.

People who are against censorship do not want books, movies, television shows, and other materials to be under the **scrutiny**—the close, careful examination or study—of a small group of people who will decide what the public can and cannot see and hear.

People who are against censorship argue that the opinion of a small group of people should not be allowed to **prevail**—to win out and have greater strength or influence.

People who are against censorship claim that our democracy will be weakened if the government starts **banning**—forbidding by an official order—materials that displease a small group of people.

People who are against censorship say that only parents should decide whether their children should have **access** to—permission to use or approach—materials that deal with sex and/or violence.

People who are against censorship fear that someday a small group of people might try to prevent the display or sale of materials that merely **allude** to—refer in an indirect way to—sexual topics.

EXERCISE 9B: Using the vocabulary words in this lesson, fill in the blanks.

1. Some people join a health club to have ______________ to a variety of exercise equipment.

2. A ______________ agent helps writers to get their books, plays, and other forms of literature published.

3. The U.S. system of justice is based on the belief that truth will ______________ in the courtroom.

4. The doctor's ______________ speech about mercy killing stimulated the audience to ask many questions.

5. When my wife and children call me "Mr. Stewart," they ______________ to my habit of singing "Do You Think I'm Sexy?" in the shower.

6. The dog owner was fined $25 for ______________ the city's pooper-scooper law.

7. Every year millions of federal income tax returns come under the ______________ of the Internal Revenue Service.

8. I wish my town would pass a law ______________ cars that blast ear-shattering music.

9. The video store operator is arrested for selling ______________ to minors.

10. Early in the semester, the English teacher explained the ______________ she would be using to judge her students' writing.

SPELLING

Plurals

I. Forming Plurals

a. Regular Plurals. A plural is usually formed by adding *s* to the singular word.

matters	sources	groups

If the plural creates an extra syllable, add *es* to the singular.

churches	lunches	kisses

b. *Y* Plurals. If a word ends with a *y* that is preceded by a consonant, change the *y* to *i* before adding endings.

centuries	countries	fallacies

If the *y* is not preceded by a consonant, the *y* is not changed.

monkeys	alleys	turkeys

c. Noun Combinations. If the noun combination is more than one word, add *s* or *es* to the most important word.

mothers-in-law	commanders-in-chief	brigadier generals

If the noun combination is written as one word, add *s* or *es* to the end of the word.

spoonfuls	handfuls	stepsons

d. *O* Plurals. If a word ends with an *o* that is preceded by a vowel, add *s* to form the plural.

radios	patios	rodeos

If a word ends with an *o* that is preceded by a consonant, add *es* to form the plural.

potatoes	heroes	Negroes

A SPECIAL NOTE: Here are some words you frequently see that are exceptions to the above rule. Notice that many of the exceptions are musical terms borrowed from Italian.

sopranos	altos	autos	Eskimos
pianos	solos	tobaccos	dynamos

e. *F* Plurals. Some words ending in *f* or *fe* merely add *s*, whereas some change the *f* or *fe* to *ves*. Because there is no rule for this change, you must learn each word individually and use a dictionary when necessary.

calf—calves
knife—knives
life—lives
roof—roofs
belief—beliefs
safe—safes
self—selves

f. Singulars That Are Plural. Some words have the same form for both the singular and the plural. Notice that most of these words refer to animals, fish, or grains.

deer
sheep
bass
trout
wheat
rye
series

g. Irregular Endings. A few common words have irregular plural endings.

man—men
woman—women
tooth—teeth
goose—geese
mouse—mice
ox—oxen

h. Foreign Words. Many foreign words form their plurals according to the rules of the foreign sources. Some of the plurals you may already know; others you will have to look up in the dictionary.

alumnus—alumni
fungus—fungi
bacterium—bacteria
analysis—analyses
axis—axes
basis—bases
crisis—crises
parenthesis—parentheses
chateau—chateaux

TRY IT OUT

FORM THE PLURALS OF THE FOLLOWING WORDS.

watch ________	quality ________
armful ________	tooth ________
potato ________	crisis ________
life ________	auto ________
sheep ________	sister-in-law ________

II. Proofreading for the Plural *-s* Ending. While working on the first draft of a paragraph or essay, you might be so involved in getting your ideas on paper that you may leave out some word endings, especially the *-s* ending for plurals. If you do tend to forget the *-s* ending when it is needed, then you should use the techniques given in this section when you proofread your writing.

a. As you proofread, watch for marker *words* that introduce either plural nouns or singular nouns.

Marker Words for Singular Nouns
a
an
another
each
every
much
one
that
this

Marker Words for Plural Nouns
all
both
few
many
most
several
some
these
those
two (or any number except one)

In the examples below, notice how the marker words indicate when the plural *-s* ending is and is not needed.

I look forward to *each holiday*.
I look forward to *most holidays*.

TRY IT OUT

FILL IN EACH BLANK WITH AN APPROPRIATE NOUN. BE SURE TO ADD THE *-S* ENDING WHEREVER IT IS NEEDED.

this ______________	every ______________
many ______________	these ______________
nine ______________	another ______________

b. As you proofread, watch for marker *phrases* that introduce plural nouns.

Marker Phrases for Plural Nouns	
one of	none of
each of	a number of
many of	a group of
all of	a pair of
some of	a bunch of
most of	both of

Notice that two of the marker phrases make use of *each* and *one.* When these words are not combined with *of,* they introduce singular nouns; however, when combined with *of, each* and *one* become marker phrases for plural nouns that refer to members of a group of more than one item.

One problem is crime.
One of the *problems* is crime.

A marker phrase can also be expanded so that several words may come between the marker and the plural noun. When you proofread, be sure to look for the noun at the end of the marker phrase.

One of the *problems* is crime.
One of the city's worst *problems* is crime.

TRY IT OUT

FILL IN EACH BLANK WITH AN APPROPRIATE NOUN. BE SURE TO ADD THE *-S* ENDING WHEREVER IT IS NEEDED.

each of my ________________ some of your ________________

a group of ________________ one of the ________________

one ________________ each ________________

both of ________________ all of the ________________

c. Not all plural nouns are introduced by marker words or phrases. Therefore, you need to get into the habit of proofreading slowly, taking special note of each noun in a sentence. Whenever you spot a noun, you should immediately ask yourself if it is supposed to refer to more than one person, place, or thing. If it is, have you used the *-s* ending when necessary? For more proofreading suggestions, see page 135.

TRY IT OUT

INSERT *-S* ENDINGS WHEREVER THEY ARE NEEDED IN THE FOLLOWING SENTENCES.

1. A housefly beats each of its wing about 20,000 time a minute.
2. Most dinosaur lived to be more than 100 year old.
3. Ice cream is one of America's favorite dessert; the average person eats about 23 quart of it each year.

EXERCISE 9C: Form the plurals of the following words.

1. politician ________________
2. brush ________________
3. company ________________
4. brother-in-law ________________
5. echo ________________
6. mouse ________________
7. radius ________________
8. thief ________________

9. class ____________________
10. tablespoonful ____________________
11. donkey ____________________
12. campaign ____________________
13. radio ____________________
14. loaf ____________________
15. box ____________________
16. attorney general ____________________
17. parenthesis ____________________
18. deer ____________________
19. piano ____________________
20. knife ____________________

EXERCISE 9D: Fill in each blank with an appropriate noun. Be sure to add the *-s* ending wherever it is needed.

1. All of the ______________ were gone when I got to class.
2. Most ______________ are not worth what they cost.
3. One of the President's ______________ is missing.
4. The criminal begged for another ______________.
5. Helen sat on a bunch of ______________ by mistake.
6. Some ______________ cheat the consumer.
7. A number of world-famous ______________ make television commercials.
8. These ______________ once belonged to Michael Jackson.
9. Put each of your ______________ on the table.
10. The politician spoke to a group of ______________ last night.
11. Both of your ______________ look weird.
12. The salesperson showed us some of the store's finest ______________.
13. None of my ______________ remembered my birthday.
14. The pair of ______________ split open right on the seam.
15. The comedian told several dirty ______________.
16. This ______________ is better than those ______________.
17. Every ______________ should have at least a few ______________.

18. The overweight plumber ate six ______________ in just ten ______________.

19. Each ______________ takes many ______________ to learn.

20. Many ______________ are dishonest.

EXERCISE 9E: Add the plural *-s* ending wherever it is needed in the following paragraphs. In some instances, you may have to change the spelling of a word before adding the plural ending. If necessary, refer to the rules for forming plurals.

Chang and Eng Bunker certainly had fascinating life. Born in Siam (now Thailand) in 1811, the twin boy were connected at their chest by a thick band of flesh about five inch in length. As they grew up, the twin learned to deal with this physical difficulty so that it did not interfere with their ability to walk or their many daily activity. By the time they reached their teen, the boy had become successful merchant who sold duck egg and peacock feather for a living. Then when the twin were eighteen, a foreign businessman convinced them to make personal appearance in other part of the world. Eventually, their travel brought them to the United State, where they held performance in large town and city. Thousand of curious people paid 50 cent apiece to see "The United Brother" and to ask them question. For an additional $12\frac{1}{2}$ cent, the member of the audience could also buy a pamphlet which included photograph of the twin and all of the important detail of their life.

After several year, Chang and Eng stopped making these appearance because they wanted to be regarded as human being, not as freak. So they became naturalized American citizen and bought a farm in North Carolina. There they tamed wild horse, raised farm animal, and grew wheat, corn, oat, and potato. Then when the brother were 31, they married two Southern sister. Eager to enjoy normal married life, Chang and Eng asked some doctor to separate them surgically. But most of the doctor warned that such an operation would probably kill both of the brother. For the first ten year of their marriage, the two couple lived together, but a growing number of argument finally led to the decision that each of the twin should have his own home. Therefore, the men bought a second farm two mile away and set up a regular schedule which required them to move back and forth between the two farm every three day. Over the year, the two couple produced a total of 21 children, all of them physically normal. The brother lived quiet, happy life until they were 63 year old. Then Chang caught pneumonia and died. Less than two hour later Eng died also, most likely of grief and fright about his own health.

Although there were over 100 reported case of physically joined twin before Chang and Eng were born, they achieved the greatest amount of fame. During their lifetime, story about them appeared in hundred of newspaper and magazine. Indeed, the twin were even used as character in play, poem, and novel. And since the death of these wonder of nature, all physically connected youngster are commonly called "Siamese Twin."

The Unified Essay

A unified essay is one in which all ideas are related and all points link. Many of the skills previously discussed in this book will help you achieve a unified essay. A quick review will illustrate.

Skill Topic	*How It Helps You Achieve a Unified Essay*
Topic Sentence and Paragraph Development	The main idea of each paragraph is clearly stated at its beginning. The rest of the paragraph develops that topic sentence.
Arrangement of Details	Details do not jump around but instead are put in an order that makes sense and flows smoothly.
Paragraph Principles in Essay Writing, and Introductions and Conclusions	The total design of the basic expository essay is five paragraphs. The introduction launches the topic, and the conclusion summarizes it. Each of the three main body paragraphs presents and develops one main idea.

These aids help you in the external plan and design of your essay. Equally important, however, are devices of *internal* unity. Internal unity is achieved with the use of certain words and types of wording that link sentences and even paragraphs more successfully. They are:

Words of Transition

Key Words: Deliberate Repetition

Words of Transition

When moving from one idea or example to the next, you might feel that the change is too abrupt.

Too abrupt:	Loyalty expresses itself in many ways. A grown dog often cannot adjust to having a new owner.
Smoother:	Loyalty expresses itself in many ways. For example, a grown dog often cannot adjust to having a new owner.

To avoid abrupt changes, you can use words of transition. A list of such words is given in a chart on the next page.

When selecting a word of transition, do it with care. Be certain of the type of signal you need—addition, contrast, and so on. Then look through all the words listed in the appropriate signal group until you locate the one most suitable and appropriate for the sentences you wish to connect.

Words of transition should be used sparingly. If you overuse them, your writing will become bulky. Remember that the mind automatically links statements that follow each other. Therefore, you should use words of transition only when they are needed for clarity. As a general, informal rule, a maximum of three or four words of transition should be used in a paragraph of 150 words.

TRY IT OUT

WRITE A COMPLETE SENTENCE BOTH BEFORE AND AFTER THE WORDS OF TRANSITION PROVIDED. BE SURE THAT THERE IS A PERIOD AFTER THE FIRST SENTENCE SO THAT YOU DO NOT WRITE A RUN-ON.

1. *about public transportation:* ______________________

   Therefore, ______________________

2. *about losing weight:* ______________________

   Nevertheless, ______________________

3. *about loneliness:* ______________________

   For instance, ______________________

Words of Transition

Directions: Two steps should be used when you consult this list. First, determine the type of signal you need. Next, select from that signal group the word that is most appropriate to the meaning of your sentences.

Type of Signal	*Words to Use; Signal Group*
To signal an addition	in addition, furthermore, moreover, also, equally important
To signal an example	for example, for instance, thus, in other words, as an illustration, in particular
To signal a suggestion	for this purpose, to this end, with this object
To signal emphasis	indeed, truly, again, to repeat, in fact
To signal granting a point	while it may be true, in spite of this
To signal a summary	in summary, in conclusion, therefore, finally, consequently, thus, accordingly, in short, in brief, as a result, on the whole
To signal the development a sequence	*Value Sequence:* first, second, secondly, third, thirdly, next, last, finally *Time Sequence:* then, afterward, next, subsequently, previously, first, second, at last, meanwhile, in the meantime, immediately, soon, at length, yesterday, today, tomorrow, eventually *Space Sequence:* above, across, under, beyond, below, nearby, nearer, opposite adjacent to, to the left/right, in the foreground, in the background
To signal a relationship	*Similarity:* similarly, likewise, in like manner *Contrast:* in contrast to, however, but, still, nevertheless, yet, conversely, notwithstanding, on the other hand, on the contrary, at the same time, while this may be true *Cause and Effect:* consequently, because, since, therefore, accordingly, thus, hence, due to this, as a result

EXERCISE 9F: Many of the paragraphs written for this book have good examples of the correct use of words of transition. Refer to the following three paragraphs and underline or list all words of transition.

1. Chapter One, page 52, "Some couples who are determined. . . ."
2. Chapter Two, page 76, "To study for an examination. . . ."
3. Chapter Two, page 77, "A street carnival easily draws. . . ."

EXERCISE 9G: Insert an appropriate word of transition in each blank. In some cases, you may decide that no word is needed. Although signal groups are repeated, try to vary the words you select.

1. Some states have strange laws. _______________ in Idaho it is against the law for a person to give someone else a box of candy that weighs more than fifty pounds. _______________ in Alaska it is illegal to look at a moose from the window of an airplane.
2. Birds have very sensitive hearing. _______________ some birds can hear the sound of an earthworm crawling under the grass.
3. Most people think that flowers usually have a beautiful odor. _______________ more than 90 percent of all flowers have either an unpleasant odor or no odor at all.
4. It is easy to determine how far away a thunderstorm is located. _______________ wait for a lightning flash. _______________ count the seconds that pass until you hear the sound of thunder. _______________ divide the number of seconds by 5. _______________ if ten seconds pass between the lightning flash and the thunderclap, the storm is about two miles away.
5. Arnold Rothstein, a famous American gambler in the 1920's, never went out without $100,000 in cash in his wallet. _______________ he was known among gamblers as "The Big Bankroll."
6. Although Hetty Green was a millionaire, she was so tight with money that she would resell the morning newspaper after she had finished reading it.

_______________ John Elwes was worth a fortune, but he was so eager to avoid spending money that he frequently ate spoiled food that others had thrown out and once even ate a dead bird that a rat had pulled from a river.

7. In 1976, a Los Angeles secretary named Jannene Swift actually married a fifty-pound rock. _______________ the ceremony was witnessed by more than twenty people.
8. More than half of all Americans suffer from occasional headaches. _______________ it is not surprising that about 27 million pounds of aspirin are manufactured in the United States each year.
9. Alcohol can irritate the stomach, damage the liver, and destroy brain cells. _______________ drinking large quantities of alcohol is bad for one's health.
10. A drawing of a pyramid appears on the back of the one-dollar bill. _______________ the pyramid is a triangle with a human eye in it. _______________ the pyramid is a banner that proclaims, "Novus Ordo Seclorum" or "A New Order of the Ages."
11. Law schools turn out about 5,000 more lawyers each year than are actually needed by the legal system. ____________________ many parents would still like their children to become lawyers.
12. Blue whales gain weight very quickly. _______________ a young one puts on weight at a rate of 200 to 300 pounds a day.
13. In his best-selling book *How to Make Friends and Influence People,* Dale Carnegie offers three major suggestions for making and keeping friends. _______________ become really interested in others and try to see things from their point of view. _______________ be a good listener, letting others do a good deal of the talking. _______________ praise people as much as possible.
14. We must discourage people from mistreating pets and other animals. ____________________ the federal government should enact laws that provide harsh penalties for those who harm animals of any kind.
15. Americans eat about fifteen pounds of meat per person each month. _______________ the Japanese eat only about eight ounces of meat per person each month.

EXERCISE 9H: Choose three of these five paragraphs to write. Use a separate sheet of paper. In writing these paragraphs, do not overuse words of transition; use them only where needed for clarity.

1. Write a paragraph about the costs involved in spending a day at an amusement park. Use appropriate words of transition that signal examples.
2. Write a paragraph describing the view from your bedroom window. Use appropriate words of transition that signal space sequence.
3. Write a paragraph in which you describe the perfect way to celebrate New Year's Eve. Use appropriate words of transition that signal time sequence.
4. Write a paragraph in which you explain how you are different from either your mother or your father. Use appropriate words of transition that signal the relationship of contrast.
5. Write a paragraph which explains the various reasons why some people smoke cigarettes. Use appropriate words of transition that signal the relationship of cause and effect.

 Key Words: Deliberate Repetition

Ideas can be connected by the deliberate repetition of certain key words. It is best that the word you choose for deliberate repetition be closely related to the main idea of the paragraph or essay. Of course, while such repetition should occur often enough to achieve unity, it should not be overdone.

I. Key Words in a Paragraph. Here is a paragraph that was presented in Chapter One as an illustration of a topic sentence developed by example. Notice how key words are used to create internal unity.

> Some couples who are determined to reveal their individuality are getting married in unusual ceremonies. For example, a couple employed as line workers for the Southwestern Bell Telephone Company exchanged their wedding vows clad in jeans and climbing equipment atop a brightly decorated telephone pole while the justice of the peace shouted instructions from the ground. Elsewhere, a couple dressed in swimsuits were married on the high diving board of a local swimming pool because they felt that swimming was an important part of their lives. Furthermore, one couple was wed at the firehouse where the groom was a fireman because the bride wanted to make their wedding just a little different. Another wedding was held in a 747 jet as it flew over Washington State at an altitude of 10,000 feet. Thus, the wedding ceremony has become another example of how more and more people are showing their individuality today.

TRY IT OUT

REFERRING TO THE PARAGRAPH ABOVE, ANSWER THESE QUESTIONS.

1. What word is deliberately repeated throughout the paragraph? ______________ Why is it, more than any other, a key word? ____

(Continued)

(Continued)

2. What words are used in the paragraph to mean "got married"?

   ____

   Why isn't "got married" merely repeated each time?

   ____

3. What words of transition are used in the paragraph?

   ____

4. What two words are used in both the first and last sentences—but nowhere else—in the paragraph?

   ____

II. Key Words to Link Paragraphs. Paragraphs, as well as sentences, can be linked with the use of key words. Of course, in an expository essay, paragraphs are related to each other as long as they follow the essay pattern presented in Chapter Seven and reviewed in this chapter. However, if you wish to achieve internal unity as well, it is possible to link paragraphs by finding a key word in the final sentence of one paragraph and deliberately repeating it in the opening sentence of the next paragraph. Notice these sentences, which are taken from a five-paragraph expository essay.

Title	*How to Study for an Examination*
The last sentence of one paragraph:	In short, studying for an examination is easier if the student has adequate light and a comfortable study area.
The opening sentence of the next paragraph:	While suitable physical surroundings are important, studying for an examination also calls for a disciplined review of class and reading notes.

TRY IT OUT

REFERRING TO THE SENTENCES ON PAGE 390, ANSWER THESE QUESTIONS.

1. How many times is the word *studying* used? ____________________
2. What other word is deliberately repeated? ____________________
3. How many times is it repeated? ____________________
4. Why are both *studying* and the other word you found key words?

____

If you wish to link paragraphs, it is useful to employ subordination for one or both of the linking sentences. Use the subordinate section to refer to the idea just finished and the independent section to refer to the new idea you are going to discuss. The following is an example of subordination in a linking sentence which opens a new paragraph.

While suitable physical surroundings are important, studying for an examination also calls for a disciplined review of class and reading notes.

You can see that the main idea *just finished* concerns the physical surroundings needed for studying for an examination, and the main idea *being introduced* concerns proper review of class and reading notes.

The use of subordination in sentences that link paragraphs will serve as an extra check for unity: Remember that for correct subordination the two ideas must be *logically related, with one idea more important than the other or one idea closely following the other.* Here is another example.

Although rock music employs intricate sound patterns, country music explores life more directly.

TRY IT OUT

ASSUME THAT THE SENTENCE ON PAGE 391 ENDS ONE PARAGRAPH AND LINKS WITH THE NEXT PARAGRAPH.

1. What would you guess is the topic of the paragraph being closed? ____

   ____

2. What would you guess is the topic of the coming paragraph? ________

   ____

3. Why would this sentence be an appropriate link if used as the first sentence of a paragraph? ____

   ____

Sentence structure other than subordination can be used for linking sentences. In all linking sentences, the pattern is the same. The topic just finished is mentioned first and the topic being introduced is mentioned second. Here are some examples.

A problem closely related to crime in the streets is the increase in drug addiction in today's big cities.

Not only will uncontrolled gambling ruin a person's home life, but it will also seriously threaten a person's job.

In addition to health care, an active social life is important for the elderly.

EXERCISE 9I: Many of the paragraphs in this book are good examples of the correct use of key words. Refer to the following three paragraphs and underline all key words.

1. Chapter One, page 50, "The cockroaches that inhabit. . . ."
2. Chapter Two, page 77, "A street carnival easily draws. . . ."
3. Chapter Seven, page 304, "Many young people who have. . . ."

EXERCISE 9J: For three of the following topic sentences, write a unified paragraph using the deliberate repetition of key words. Although such repetition should occur often enough to achieve unity, it should not be overdone. Use your own paper for this assignment.

1. It is easy to understand why credit cards are so popular.
2. ________________ is the most enjoyable season of the year.
3. Worrying too much is bad for one's health.
4. Many different types of telephones are now available.
5. If men are drafted, women should (should not) be drafted as well.

EXERCISE 9K: For each of the following, you are given the title of an essay and the three main ideas which the essay will cover in its main body paragraphs. Write a linking sentence to start the second main body paragraph and write another linking sentence to start the third main body paragraph.

1. Treasures of the Sea
   Introductory paragraph
   I. food resources
   II. oil resources
   III. unknown natural resources
   Concluding paragraph

   ____

   ____

   ____

2. Major Causes of Divorce
   Introductory paragraph
   I. immaturity
   II. sexual incompatibility
   III. money difficulties
   Concluding paragraph

   ____

   ____

   ____

3. Different English with Different People
   Introductory paragraph
   I. when with friends
   II. when with parents
   III. when with teachers

Concluding paragraph

____

____

____

4. The Problems of the Alcoholic
   Introductory paragraph
   I. at home
   II. at work
   III. with friends
   Concluding paragraph

____

____

____

5. Population Control Is Needed
   Introductory paragraph
   I. our food supply is limited
   II. our supply of natural resources is limited
   III. our space is limited
   Concluding paragraph

____

____

____

EXERCISE 9L: For each of the following, you are given the title of an essay and the three main ideas which the essay will cover in its main body paragraphs. Write a linking sentence to end the first main body paragraph and write another linking sentence to end the second main body paragraph.

1. All Teenagers Should Have a Part-time Job
   Introductory paragraph
   I. affects their personalities
   II. affects their characters
   III. affects their abilities

Concluding paragraph

____

____

____

2. Problems of the Aged
   Introductory paragraph
   I. health problems
   II. money difficulties
   III. psychological problems
   Concluding paragraph

____

____

3. Why People Get Married
   Introductory paragraph
   I. for love
   II. for companionship
   III. for money
   Concluding paragraph

____

____

4. Gambling Can Ruin a Person
   Introductory paragraph
   I. financial ruin
   II. home life ruin
   III. social ruin
   Concluding paragraph

____

____

5. Clothing Is a Big Business
   Introductory paragraph
   I. designer originals
   II. ready-to-wear clothes
   III. make-it-yourself clothes

Concluding paragraph

____

____

EXERCISE 9M: ESSAY ANALYSIS Answer these questions about the essay "Rapping Nasty."

1. In paragraph 1, what words of transition are used to create unity?

   ____

2. In paragraph 2, what words in the first sentence help link that paragraph with the preceding one?

   ____

3. In paragraph 3, what key words are deliberately repeated to create unity?

   ____

4. a. In paragraph 5, what words of transition are used to create unity?

   ____

   b. In the same paragraph, what key words are deliberately repeated to create unity?

   ____

5. In paragraph 7, what word in the first sentence helps to link that paragraph with the preceding one?

   ____

6. In paragraph 9, what key words are deliberately repeated to create unity?

   ____

   ____

7. In paragraph 10, what word in the first sentence helps to link that paragraph with the preceding one?

   ____

8. In paragraph 12, what word in the first sentence helps to link that paragraph with the preceding one?

   ____

EXERCISE 9N: REFRESHER

1. FIND AND CORRECT ANY FRAGMENTS, COMMA SPLICES, AND RUN-ONS.
2. REWORK THE SENTENCES SO THAT THERE ARE AT LEAST THREE EXAMPLES OF SUBORDINATION AND ONE OF COORDINATION.

Does a local school board have the right to ban certain books from the school library? In 1976, the Island Trees School District of New York became divided by bitter disagreements concerning this question. The dispute started when the school board ordered the high school library to remove nine books. That the board claimed were "anti-American, anti-Christian, anti-Semitic, and just plain filthy." The books included such highly respected works as The Fixer, Soul on Ice, and Slaughterhouse Five. With the help of the American Civil Liberties Union, five students challenged the book-banning in court. The case moved through several levels of the justice system then in 1982 it reached the Supreme Court. Where the students' lawyer claimed that the books had been banned for political reasons. He noted, for example, that A Hero Ain't Nothing but a Sandwich had been banned because it said George Washington was a slaveholder. The Supreme Court heard the entire case, it ruled that "local school boards may not remove books from library shelves simply because they dislike the ideas contained in those books," however, the Court did leave open the possibility of removing books for other reasons. When the Island Trees school board heard this decision. It returned the nine books to the library.

This particular case was settled. The debate over school censorship has continued. In recent years, various groups have gone to court to force school libraries to remove such famous books as The Catcher in the Rye and Huckleberry Finn. In some instances, these groups have been successful.

SPRINGBOARDS TO WRITING

Using your knowledge of the writing process, explained on pages 14–16, write a paragraph or essay related to this chapter's theme, *music and censorship*, which is introduced on pages 366–70.

PREWRITING

To think of topics to write about, look at the cartoons and the CD cover, read the essay, and answer the questions that follow each. If you prefer, select one of the writing springboards below. (All paragraph numbers refer to the essay that starts on page 368.) To develop your ideas, use the prewriting techniques described on pages 17–22.

WRITING A PARAGRAPH *(For help, see the Pointers on page 51.)*

1. What is your definition of obscenity? (See paragraph 3.)
2. Agree or disagree: The warning labels now printed on some CD covers are a good idea.
3. Agree or disagree with Michele Moody-Adams, who says that some rap lyrics "dehumanize women, . . . reduce them to creatures made to satisfy the violent, sadistic sexual fantasies of men." (See paragraph 9.)
4. Agree or disagree: Many of today's comedians use too much filthy language in their acts. (See paragraphs 8 & 9.)
5. Agree or disagree with this statement by Potter Stewart: "Censorship reflects a society's lack of confidence in itself."
6. Is the Motion Picture Association's movie rating system useful?
7. Some newsstand operators have been pressured to stop selling magazines that show nudity. Do you agree that such publications should not be sold at newsstands?

WRITING AN ESSAY *(For help, see the Pointers on pages 54–55.)*

8. Do Rap Groups Have a Right to Be "As Nasty as They Wanna Be"? (See paragraph 12.)
9. Why Rap Music Is Terrific (Terrible)
10. Censorship of Books Should (Should Not) Be Permitted in the Public Schools (For a start, see the Refresher on the opposite page.)

11. The Joys of Listening to _____ Music (Fill in the blank with your favorite type of music.)
12. Why I Hate _____ Music (Fill in the blank with a type of music you dislike.)
13. Television Programs Should (Should Not) Be Censored
14. Motion Pictures Should (Should Not) Be Censored
15. Books, Magazines, and Newspapers Should (Should Not) Be Censored
16. Music Videos Should (Should Not) Be Censored
17. Colleges Should (Should Not) Ban Speakers Who Preach Racial Hatred

What did I do all day? I picked up some awesome nose
rings downtown, had soccer practice, ate way too much
candy, and then met up with my friends to get
a ride to the concert, which was ok, but our seats were
really high. You know, Mom, the same old stuff.

[now read every other line]

IT'S NEVER TOO EARLY TO START READING BETWEEN THE LINES.

Your kids live active lives. Maybe too active. Which is why you need to be involved – and listen carefully. Sometimes what they're not saying is as important as what they are. Find out what they're really doing for fun, especially after school; meet their friends, keep track of their social lives, and set reasonable boundaries. These are all ways to show your kids you love them, and help keep them away from drugs. To learn more, call 1-800-MetLife for a free booklet in English and Spanish, *How To Be A Better Parent.*

PARTNERSHIP FOR A DRUG-FREE AMERICA®

Metropolitan Life Foundation

www.metlife.org

Chapter 10

SPRINGBOARDS TO THINKING

For informal, not written, response . . . to stimulate your thinking

1. Look at the photograph above. The two eight-year-old children did all of the damage to their school classroom. When the police arrived, the children said, "We intended to wreck the entire building." What is your reaction to the damage and to what the children said?
2. Do you think this destructive behavior indicates that the children have not been raised properly by their parents? Explain your point of view.
3. Read the advertisement on the opposite page. What is its main message? Is it possible for parents to monitor their children's behavior at all times? Why or why not?
4. If children commit a crime, should their parents be held legally responsible? Should the parents be required to pay for any damage? To pay a fine? To spend time in jail? Explain your point of view.

The Sins of the Parents

Ellen Goodman

(1) A parent was arrested in Los Angeles last week. It happens every day, but not quite like this. Gloria Williams, you see, was arrested for being a parent. More precisely, the thirty-seven-year-old mother of three became the first person accused under a new California law that holds parents responsible when their kids go bad. She is charged with "failing to exercise reasonable care, supervision, protection and control" of a child. The child in question is seventeen years old and an alleged member of a street gang called the Crips. This son is accused of being among those who raped a twelve-year-old girl.

(2) Mind you, if the police are right, Mrs. Williams is no candidate for the Mother's Day Hall of Fame. When they entered her apartment to talk about her son, they found walls covered with gang graffiti instead of rock posters. The photo albums showed members of the family pointing guns. The birthday cake for the eight-year-old was decorated with the gang name.

(3) To this day, the mother, who works for an electronics firm not far from home, insists that her son is no gang member. Perhaps she is blind or blindly loyal or chooses to believe that the Crips are a local Boy Scout troop and the guns are merit badges on the way to becoming an Eagle Scout. Perhaps she does condone her son's gang membership, as the city attorney charges. But the crime she is accused of is a lack of parental control. Let me put it this way: It's ten o'clock at night. Do you know where your seventeen-year-old son is? Sure about that?

(4) The California law was created and passed in the current desperate mood about street gangs and youth, about violence and drugs. In the sociological search for a cause of all these woes, Americans buy one generic label these days. We blame it all on "the breakdown of the family." If the cause is the breakdown of the family, then surely the cure is the repair of the family. Our search for a fix has taken us to many family mechanics. The favorites these days are the ones who believe that the breakdown is caused by a loss of parental authority. Their special low-cost repair would put parents back in the driver's seat. Those who won't take the wheel must be forced into it.

(5) This is the fix-it behind the law that threatens California parents of kids involved in criminal activities with a year in jail and a $2,500 fine. It's the thinking as well behind a Wisconsin law that makes parents financially responsible for the offspring of their teenage children. And it is in part as well the support for laws that require parental consent for abortion.

(6) We are now seeing various attempts to put parents in charge, to shore up authority, to foster at least the image and maybe the reality of a traditional family unit. They are, mostly, efforts to control the behaviors that worry society the most: teenage violence and teenage sex, the yin and yang, the male and female of dangers.

(7) I find this a notable pattern. After all, parents have always been held responsible for the care of their children. They've been held liable for child neglect, for child abuse, for child support. We have always drawn connections between behavior and background. Where did they, we, go wrong? But this current society that knows little about how to restore relationships, that has done less to help parents trying to raise their children in safety and health, has now turned to punishing the failures.

(8) More and more responsibility is passed to parents, even as we worry about their willingness to exercise it. We allow violence on the screen and tell parents to control the dial. We allow drugs on the streets and tell parents to monitor usage. We offer few alternatives to street life and expect parents to keep their kids indoors. We remove communal supports and tell parents to make up the difference.

(9) I don't know about Mrs. Williams's culpability, although if they arrested the mother for her "failure to exercise supervision," why not the absent father? But for every Fagin* figure of a parent, there is another who hasn't given up but, rather, has lost control of a teenager. For everyone who is truly irresponsible, there is another who is overwhelmed, a third who is afraid for her child, a fourth who is afraid of her child. Is that parent now a criminal?

(10) They say that California is the leading edge, the social trendsetter. Now the Golden State has turned the Bible on its head. They've decided that the sins of the sons shall be visited upon their parents.

*Fagin, a character in Charles Dickens's novel *Oliver Twist,* teaches children to be pickpockets.

READING SURVEY

1. MAIN IDEA

What is the central theme of this essay?

2. MAJOR DETAILS

a. According to the author, what do Americans believe is the basic cause of the street gangs, violence, and drug use among today's young people?

b. What laws have California and Wisconsin created to hold parents responsible for their children's behavior?

c. According to the author, in what ways is society partly responsible for the bad behavior of some children?

3. INFERENCES

a. Read paragraph 3 again. What point is the author trying to make with her questions?
b. Does the author think that the new California law is a good idea? Why or why not?

4. OPINIONS

a. Read paragraphs 1–3 again. Do you think that Gloria Williams should have been arrested? Why or why not?
b. What do you think can be done to discourage teenagers from participating in street gangs, violence, and drug use? Explain your point of view.

VOCABULARY BUILDING

Lesson One: The Vocabulary of the Troubled Family

The essay "The Sins of the Parents" by Ellen Goodman includes words that are useful when you are discussing troubled families.

to exercise (paragraph 1)
alleged (1)
condone (3)
desperate (4)
woes (4)
generic (4)
offspring (5)
consent (5)
to shore up (6)
to foster (6)

In a troubled family, parents may fail **to exercise**—to use or put into practice—control over their children.

In a troubled family, children may sometimes be accused of **alleged** crimes—crimes that are suspected but not proven.

In a troubled family, parents may sometimes **condone**—overlook or forgive—their children's bad behavior.

In a troubled family, parents may feel a **desperate**—nearly hopeless—need for help.

In a troubled family, children may suffer from all sorts of **woes**—terrible troubles.

In a troubled family, **generic**—general, not specific, or lacking a brand name—remedies for problems may not help.

In a troubled family, children may have **offspring**—children—of their own.

In a troubled family, children may not always have their parents' **consent**—approval or agreement—for their actions.

In a troubled family, parents may need help **to shore up**—to prop up or support—their control over their children.

In a troubled family, parents may struggle **to foster**—encourage or promote the growth of—a sense of right and wrong in their children.

EXERCISE 10A: For each word in italics, circle the definition that is closest in meaning.

1. If parents *condone* a child's behavior, they will
   a. condemn it.
   b. punish it.
   c. overlook it.
   d. agree with it.
2. *To shore up* a house, you would
   a. raise the roof.
   b. strengthen the foundation.
   c. decorate it.
   d. enlarge it considerably.
3. A family that has many *woes*
   a. has had much good fortune.
   b. contains many children.
   c. is in trouble with the law.
   d. has many troubles.
4. Someone who is *desperate* is
   a. nearly hopeless.
   b. hopeful.
   c. poor.
   d. fearless.
5. If you buy a *generic* drug, you get one that
   a. has a wide variety of uses.
   b. is better than brand-name drugs.
   c. is not as good as brand-name drugs.
   d. has no brand name.
6. Someone who has your *consent* has your
   a. help.
   b. agreement.
   c. disapproval.
   d. cooperation.

7. Your *offspring* would include
   a. your parents.
   b. your brothers and sisters.
   c. your children.
   d. your whole family.

8. *To exercise* power, you would
   a. use it.
   b. prevent someone else from using it.
   c. refuse to use it.
   d. increase it by using it often.

9. An *alleged* criminal is someone who
   a. has committed a crime.
   b. has been found guilty of a crime.
   c. has been accused of a crime.
   d. is not guilty of a crime.

10. If you *foster* someone's well-being, you
    a. wound or injure the person.
    b. serve as the person's parent.
    c. prevent the person from becoming successful.
    d. encourage the person's health and happiness.

Lesson Two: ***The Vocabulary of the Untroubled Family***

The essay "The Sins of the Parents" by Ellen Goodman includes words that are useful when you are discussing untroubled families.

notable (paragraph 7)
liable (7)
neglect (7)
abuse (7)
restore (7)
monitor (8)
alternatives (8)
communal (8)
culpability (9)
overwhelmed (9)

In an untroubled family, parents have a **notable**—worth noticing or remarkable—ability to raise their children.

In an untroubled family, parents usually hold their children **liable**—responsible—for their bad behavior.

In an untroubled family, children do not suffer from **neglect**—lack of proper attention.

In an untroubled family, children do not suffer from **abuse**—mistreatment that may include physical harm and insulting language.

In an untroubled family, there is usually no need to **restore**—renew or rebuild—damaged relationships.

In an untroubled family, parents **monitor**—keep track of—their children's comings and goings.

In an untroubled family, parents offer their children **alternatives**—other choices—to misbehavior.

In an untroubled family, parents may draw strength from **communal**—community—support.

In an untroubled family, parents feel a sense of **culpability**—guilt or blame—for their children's misbehavior.

In an untroubled family, parents are not **overwhelmed**—overcome or overpowered—by the task of raising their children.

EXERCISE 10B: Match each sentence with a vocabulary word from this lesson.

1. Because I am very lazy, I haven't cleaned my house in a year and the grass is a foot high. 1. ____________
2. Overpowered by their emotions, those who had escaped the disaster broke down and cried. 2. ____________
3. Despite all the evidence, the criminal refused to admit his guilt. 3. ____________
4. The lawyer told his client that he would be held responsible for the damage he had caused. 4. ____________
5. Frank can eat 40 hot dogs in 30 minutes. What a remarkable ability! 5. ____________
6. If you want to save money, you will have to begin keeping track of your expenses. 6. ____________
7. A growing number of people are concerned about the mistreatment of circus animals. 7. ____________
8. Everyone turned out for the block party, sharing the gossip and the potluck supper. It was a real community activity. 8. ____________

9. Before making a decision, the school board considered three different plans. 9. ____________________

10. The mayor called in the National Guard to stop the riots and return the city to normal. 10. ____________________

SPELLING

To Split or Not to Split

Some word combinations cause a great deal of confusion because the writer is not sure whether the words should be joined or separated. In some cases, the written form will depend on how the words are used in the sentence. In other cases, it is necessary to memorize the proper spelling.

I. Words That May or May Not Split. Because the spelling of each of these words varies according to its meaning, pay special attention to the definitions given.

already (previously)
The movie had already started when I arrived.

all ready (completely prepared)
We are all ready for the work ahead.

altogether (completely)
My answer is altogether different from yours.

all together (in a group)
The children were all together in the park.

anyone (any person at all)
Anyone can count to a hundred.

any one (one person or thing in a specific group)
Any one of these detergents will do the job.

Note: This also applies to: *everyone—every one; someone—some one*

maybe (perhaps)
Maybe I will join the Peace Corps.

may be (the verb form meaning "might be")
This may be his last public appearance.

II. Words That Never Split

another
bathroom
bedroom
bookkeeper
cannot
downstairs
everything
granddaughter
nearby
nevertheless
northeast
percent
playroom
roommate
schoolteacher
yourself

III. Words That Are Always Split. Because the English language is so changeable, you should rely on an up-to-date dictionary for the current spelling of a word combination. Below are some of the common word combinations that are still written as two words.

a lot
all right
dining room
high school
in fact
in spite
living room
no one

IV. Words That Are Joined by a Hyphen. Because there are no rules to cover all the uses of the hyphen, you should rely on a dictionary whenever you are in doubt. There are, however, a few principles to guide you.

a. Use a hyphen to join compound numbers from twenty-one to ninety-nine.

forty-seven
seventy-eight

b. Use a hyphen (or hyphens) to join two or more words that are combined to refer to the same person or thing.

mother-in-law
cure-all
drive-in
fighter-bomber
court-martial
forget-me-not

c. Use a hyphen (or hyphens) to join two or more words that form a single adjective before a noun.

ten-year-old boy
absent-minded professor
well-known poet
bluish-green eyes
first-rate performance

d. Use a hyphen to join certain prefixes and suffixes to the main word.

co-owner	all-purpose
self-sacrifice	bell-like
ex-president	pro-American

EXERCISE 10C: Underline the correct word or words from the set of words in parentheses. If necessary, consult a dictionary.

Dear Ben:

This is just a quick note to thank you for letting our family use your house while you were away on vacation. Our children had (a lot, alot) of fun swimming in your (thirtyfive, thirty-five, thirty five)-foot pool, and Helen became a (firstrate, first-rate, first rate) cook in your (ultra modern, ultramodern, ultra-modern) kitchen. When I was not using your (woodworking, wood working) tools, I was either watching your color TV or using your pool table. Because it was (some times, sometimes) very hot, (may be, maybe) the biggest blessing was the (air conditioning, air-conditioning, airconditioning). This was a great vacation for (everyone, every one) of us. (In fact, Infact), I (can not, cannot) remember a more enjoyable summer.

We really tried to take excellent care of (everything, every thing) in your house. (Never-the-less, Never the less, Nevertheless), I must apologize for our accidentally damaging your garbage can. It all started when Helen cut (her self, her-self, herself) cleaning up the mess our (sixteenyearold, sixteen-year-old, sixteen year old) son made when he knocked over your (gold fish, goldfish) tank. In my great rush to get Helen to the doctor, I mistakenly shifted your car into "reverse" (in stead, instead) of into "drive," (there by, thereby) causing it to back up through the rear wall of your garage and into the (near by, nearby) (swimming pool, swimmingpool). (However, How ever), don't be concerned! Helen and I are excellent swimmers.

As the car sank to the bottom of the pool, the displaced water started pouring into your (down stairs, down-stairs, downstairs) (play-room, playroom, play room). This unfortunate turn of events caused an electrical short in the house wiring. This was most regrettable since we had been (already, all ready) for an evening of watching television. While we were (all together, altogether) in the (livingroom, living room) having a cold dinner by (candle-light, candle light, candlelight), our (cockerspaniel, cocker spaniel) jumped off the couch knocking over the candle which then scorched the carpet—as well as the house. As (every one, everyone) ran from the flames, the garbage can was knocked over causing the dents. Because Helen and I insist on paying for the garbage can, we have taped a (five dollar, five-dollar) bill to the roof beam that is now stretched across the remains of your (dining room, diningroom) table.

We hope that you and Lavinia are (alright, all right) and that you have found your (well earned, well-earned) trip to the (Northwest, North West) to be an (all together, altogether) rewarding experience. We are (all ready, already) looking forward to (an other, another) vacation at your home . . . if it is (re-built, rebuilt) by next summer.

Your loving (brotherinlaw, brother-in-law, brother in law),

Herb

 Using the Right Word

Errors in some words, more than in others, are often used as yardsticks to measure a person's maturity and level of education. While many such errors are made in everyday speech, they should not be made in formal written English. There are three major yardsticks.

I Comparisons

II Commonly Confused Verbs

III Commonly Confused Expressions

I. Comparisons. When you are comparing two things, never use the superlative form. It is reserved for a comparison of three or more things. For example:

Joe is the older of the two brothers.

Joe is the oldest of the three brothers.

For most short words, form the comparative by adding an *-er* ending and form the superlative by adding an *-est* ending. For most longer words (of three syllables or more), form the comparative by using *more* and the superlative by using *most*.

Positive	*Comparative*	*Superlative*
old	older	oldest
green	greener	greenest
fast	faster	fastest
slow	slower	slowest
beautiful	more beautiful	most beautiful
optimistic	more optimistic	most optimistic
easily	more easily	most easily

Some words have irregular comparative and superlative forms.

Positive	*Comparative*	*Superlative*
good, well	better	best
bad	worse	worst
little	less	least
many, much	more	most

TRY IT OUT

In the following paragraph correct any errors in forming comparisons. Cross out the error and write the correct form directly above it. If necessary, check your answers in a dictionary.

Mexico City has the unusualest combination of sights. In the heart of the city are some of the most newest and modern hotels and office buildings in the western hemisphere. These skyscrapers overlook a ghetto that is probably worser than any in the United States. Begging outside the expensiver restaurants are small children with the leastest amount of education and the most empty stomachs. Even more strange is the sight of one of the city's popularer churches next to a hamburger stand. On the outskirts of the city, the most efficienter factories are just down the road from ancient pyramids, which draw the mostest number of tourists of any attraction in the country. All over Mexico City one finds these combinations of the old and the new, the rich and the poor. One can only guess about which of these two contrasts the visitor finds most fascinating.

II. Commonly Confused Verbs. Certain verb forms may cause confusion because, while they look or sound very much alike, they are really quite different in meaning.

lay, lie

The verb *lay* means to place. (The action is in progress.)

The verb *lie* means to rest. (There is no action.)

lay	*lie*
Please *lay* the book on the table.	The children *lie* on mats.
Yesterday the hen *laid* six eggs.	Yesterday I *lay* in bed all day.
Jack *has laid* out the map.	The dog *has lain* there for an hour.
He *is laying* my coat on the chair.	The deed *is lying* on the desk.

learn, teach

Learn means to gain knowledge.

Teach means to give knowledge.

Professor Higgins tried to teach me biology, but I must admit that I did not learn very much.

leave, let

Leave means to depart from.

Let means to permit or allow.

I will leave for Florida tomorrow if you will let me make the trip.

raise, rise

The verb *raise* means that the subject is making something move upward.

The verb *rise* means that the subject is moving.

raise	*rise*
Raise your hand if you want to speak.	The temperature *rises* during the summer months.
Helen *raised* carrots in her garden.	The sun *rose* through the morning mist.
The teacher *has raised* an interesting question.	The men *have risen* to greet the general.

sit, set

Sit means to be seated.

Set means to place or put.

If you will sit in this chair, I will set the cushion at your feet.

stay, stand

Stay means to remain.

Stand means to be in an upright position.

He had to stay in bed for three days before he was allowed to stand up for a few minutes.

TRY IT OUT

IN THE FOLLOWING PARAGRAPH CORRECT ANY VERB ERRORS. CROSS OUT THE ERROR AND WRITE THE CORRECTION DIRECTLY ABOVE IT.

Yesterday was certainly not my day. As I set down for breakfast, the chair broke and I was soon laying on the floor. Then when I rised from the floor, I bumped my head on the table. My troubles stayed with me in chemistry class, where the professor was trying to learn me how to make acid. After he had demonstrated the process, I insisted, "Leave me do it now!" I mixed the chemicals, lay the stirring spoon on the counter, and then sat the test tube in a metal holder. Suddenly a loud explosion shook the laboratory, and a large black cloud raised from the counter. Yes, I really should have stood in bed yesterday!

III. Commonly Confused Expressions

among, between

Use *among* for three or more things, people, etc.
The club treasury was divided among all ten members.

Use *between* for only two things, people, etc.
What is the difference between an alligator and a crocodile?

amount, number

Use *amount* to refer to the total mass of something.
A large amount of food is wasted every day.

Use *number* to refer to things that can be counted.
A large number of people suffer from a neurosis.

bad, badly

Use *bad* with nouns and generally after verbs that refer to the senses: *look, feel, smell, taste,* and *hear.*
Marsha is a bad cook. I feel bad.

Use *badly* after most other verbs.
Many people drive badly.

can, may

Use *can* to indicate the ability to do something.

My brother can stand on his head.

Use *may* to indicate permission or possibility.

May I leave the room? It may rain.

can hardly (not: can't hardly)

can scarcely (not: can't scarcely)

could hardly (not: couldn't hardly)

could scarcely(not: couldn't scarcely)

I can hardly (not: can't hardly) see straight.

could have (not: could of)

would have (not: would of)

might have (not: might of)

should have (not: should of)

Tony could have (not: could of) done it better.

different from (not: different than)

Neurosis is different from (not: different than) psychosis.

fewer, less

Use *fewer* to refer to things that can be counted.

Fewer jobs are available for unskilled workers.

Use *less* to refer to quantity, value, or degree.

Many people have less education than they really need.

former, latter

Use *former* to refer to the first of two items that have been named.

Use *latter* to refer to the second of two items that have been named.

(If three or more items are referred to, do not use *former* and *latter;* instead use *first* and *last.*)

Las Vegas and San Juan are two popular resorts; the former is in Nevada and the latter in Puerto Rico.

good, well

Use *good* to describe a noun or pronoun only.

Muriel is a good swimmer.

Use *well* to describe a verb only.

She also bowls well.

TRY IT OUT

IN THE FOLLOWING PARAGRAPH CORRECT ANY ERRORS IN USING THE YARDSTICKS. CROSS OUT THE ERROR AND WRITE THE CORRECT FORM DIRECTLY ABOVE IT.

Because Jack always took care of his garden good, people often admired it. Indeed, his flowers could of won prizes in a flower show. To please his friends, each year he planted varieties that were different than those he had used the year before. Last year, for example, he filled his garden with a large amount of roses, zinnias, and carnations. The latter were his favorite type of flower. Placed between all these flowers there was a sign that read: "You can look—but do not pick!" Well, one couldn't hardly blame him for feeling badly when one day he discovered that a thief had visited his garden, leaving behind less flowers than there would be after a tornado. It is no wonder that this year Jack has planted poison ivy.

is when, is where, is that

Never use *when* or *where* to refer to a thing; use *that.*

Awkward: A sonnet is when a poem has fourteen lines.

Corrected: A sonnet is a poem that has fourteen lines.

kind, sort

Never mix singular and plural. Use *this* or *that* with *kind* and *sort;* use *these* or *those* with *kinds* and *sorts.*

This kind of flower is very rare, but those kinds are grown everywhere.

like, as (as if)

Use *like* when no verb appears in the section that follows.

Use *as* (or *as if*) when a verb does appear in the section that follows.

If you do as I tell you, you will look like a movie star.

ought (not: had ought)

People ought (not: had ought) to be honest.

the reason is that (not: the reason is because, the reason is due to, the reason is on account of)

The reason is that (not: because) no one cares.

so, so that

Never use *so* to join two complete sentences when you want to show purpose; instead, use *so that.*

The rocket increased its speed so that (not: so) it could withstand the gravitational pull.

try to (not: try and)

Please try to (not: try and) drive carefully.

used to, supposed to

Never leave out the final *d;* use *supposed to* and *used to.*

Although Jeff was supposed to be a stingy man, he used to spend a good deal of money on clothes.

where, that

Never use *where* to refer to things; use *that.*

I read in the newspaper that (not: where) Mr. Blowhard is running for mayor.

TRY IT OUT

IN THE FOLLOWING PARAGRAPH CORRECT ANY ERRORS IN USING THE YARDSTICKS. CROSS OUT THE ERROR AND WRITE THE CORRECT FORM DIRECTLY ABOVE IT.

It is unfortunate that we are always reading in the newspapers where some parents are upset because their children are taking a sex education class in school. The reason for this concern is because the parents fear that such a class will encourage loose morals. But this will not happen, for the class will be taught by a specially trained instructor who will plan the course ~~so~~ the students will have a complete understanding of the subject. The sex education class is also when the teacher is suppose to try and answer the students' personal questions, those kind of questions which most parents are too embarrassed to answer honestly. Moreover, the teacher will discuss human sexuality in great detail; he or she will no longer stop with a discussion of guppies and puppies like the science teachers use to do. Parents really had ought to give the sex education classes a chance to prove their worth.

EXERCISE 10D: For each item below, write as many fully and interestingly developed sentences as are necessary to follow the directions.

1. Using comparison forms of *sweet*, compare three of your favorite desserts.

   ____

   ____

   ____

2. Using forms of *teach* and *learn*, tell about someone who showed you how to play a particular sport.

   ____

   ____

   ____

3. Using *good, better, best,* compare three enjoyable ways to spend a Saturday night.

____

____

____

4. Using comparison forms of *difficult,* compare three hard courses that you have taken in school.

____

____

____

5. Using *stay* and *stand,* tell about waiting on line in the rain to get tickets for a movie while your friends remained in the car.

____

____

____

6. Using the comparative form of *strong,* compare your strength with that of your best friend.

____

____

____

7. Using *little, less, least,* compare three types of music that you do not care for too much.

____

____

____

8. Using *lay* and *lie,* tell about someone serving you a meal while you are resting in bed.

____

____

____

9. Using comparison forms of *funny,* compare three comedians who make you laugh.

10. Using *bad, worse, worst,* compare three restaurants that you dislike.

11. Using *rise* and *raise,* tell about putting up the American flag as the sun comes up in the morning.

12. Using comparison forms of *interesting,* compare three movies that you have enjoyed.

13. Using *let* and *leave,* tell about someone who allows you to use his or her car while away on vacation.

14. Using *much, more, most,* compare the salaries for three different jobs.

15. Using *set* and *sit*, tell about putting down your books before taking a seat in class.

____

____

____

EXERCISE 10E: Referring to the section on Commonly Confused Expressions, select a word from the choices listed below and fill in the blanks.

Choices:	amount, number	like, as	former, latter
	good, well	bad, badly	can, may
	among, between	fewer, less	

1. Most snakes ______________ live for an entire year without eating any food at all.

2. The country of Tonga once issued a stamp shaped ______________ a banana.

3. Can you tell the difference ______________ a donkey and a pony?

4. Studies show that nonsmokers get far ______________ colds than smokers do.

5. The play was written so ______________ that the audience felt ______________ for the actors.

6. The body needs a small ______________ of copper to help in the formation of red blood cells.

7. A ______________ job not only pays ______________ but also provides an opportunity for advancement.

8. Fish can catch colds just ______________ you and I can.

9. Both soccer and football use eleven players on a team. However, the ______________ is played with a round ball whereas the ______________ is played with an almond-shaped ball.

10. If you are not on a diet, you ______________ have another ice cream cone.

11. The United States is importing ______________ oil now than it did ten years ago.

12. When Eleanor Ritchey died in 1968, she left a $4.5 million fortune to be divided ______________ her 150 dogs.

13. A large ______________ of people are injured each year by falling out of bed.

14. You might be surprised to know that an elephant ______________ swim ______________

15. The durian is an unusual fruit that tastes ______________ but smells ______________ a garbage dump.

EXERCISE 10F: Referring to the section on Commonly Confused Expressions, fill in the blanks.

1. I ______________ hardly believe that mosquitoes are found at the North Pole, but they really are.

2. Most people should try ______________ eat some liver because it is ______________ to contain a great deal of iron.

3. Although sweet potatoes and yams look similar, they are actually quite different ______________ each other.

4. Texas ______________ to be the largest state in the United States, but now the largest state is Alaska, which is almost three times the size of Texas.

5. I read in a magazine ______________ each minute another four handguns are sold over the counter in America.

6. The real-estate agent with 114 empty lots for sale should ______________ advertised the land as "The Greatest Earth on Show."

7. The Biltmore House, a private home in Asheville, North Carolina, is a popular tourist attraction; the reason is _______________ the house contains 250 rooms.

8. You _______________ to learn the Heimlich maneuver _______________ you will be prepared to help if someone chokes on a piece of food.

9. Although most Americans eat only one _______________ of rice, there are actually 15,000 different _______________ of rice growing in the world.

10. Robert Matern _______________ scarcely stand up after he set a world's record by eating 83 hamburgers on May 3, 1973.

11. The most complicated musical instrument is _______________ to be the organ.

12. The pyramids in Mexico are very different _______________ those in Egypt.

13. Iran _______________ to be called Persia.

14. I heard on the radio _______________ a man named Richard K. Brown rode a skateboard at a speed of almost 72 miles an hour.

15. If you had bought a copy of the *New York Times* on Sunday, October 10, 1971, you would _______________ lugged home a 972-page newspaper weighing over seven pounds.

Informal Language

Different language is appropriate for different situations. When you speak, you usually adjust your choice of words and way of talking to suit your audience and the occasion. You might tell a friend, "My old man is a head shrinker," but to a possible employer you would probably say, "My father is a psychiatrist." Your choice of words when you are writing should also suit your audience and the occasion. Thus, the language you use when you write a letter to a close friend will likely be very different from the words you choose when writing an essay.

I. How do you think someone who expects you to be formal would react to the following paragraph?

> If you read the classified ads in the papers, you'll get an idea of what jobs are available now. But it may be a couple of years before you'll be done with school. How'll you know what jobs will be available then? According to this recent report, by 2010 70% of all new workers will be between the ages of 16 and 34. If the U.S. maintains the economic patterns of the last 30 or 40 yrs., these here young people will be competing for some of the following positions. There'll be a demand for college profs. with a Ph.D. in bio. or math. As mass communication systems increase, the television industry and the phone co. will offer many job opportunities, especially in N.Y. and Calif. Because the population will continue to grow, the need for Drs. and other medical personnel will also kind of increase. This here will give you sort of an idea of what jobs will be available for them people with the proper education.

Here are some basic principles to help you rewrite the above paragraph in the formal English usually required in an essay.

Formal Writing Customs. Numbers under 100 usually should be written out in words. When your writing includes numbers both over and under 100, the numerals are generally used to maintain consistency. The % sign should be written out as *percent* after numbers.

Because the pronoun *you* tends to give an informal tone to writing, many writers avoid using *you* when they are writing a formal essay. *Person* or *people* can often be substituted. Other pronouns such as *he, she, we,* or *they* may also be used.

Shortened Forms. Many writers avoid using contractions in formal English whenever possible. However, sometimes a contraction may be necessary to prevent a very awkward-sounding sentence: "Are not the trees beautiful?" would sound much better as "Aren't the trees beautiful?"

Do not use most abbreviations in your academic writing. However, forms such as *Mr., Mrs., Ms., Ph.D., Dr.,* and *Jr.* are permissible when they are used with a person's name. The initials of various organizations may also be used if the organization is usually referred to by its initials. FBI, UNESCO, NASA, VISTA, and GOP are some that are commonly used.

Shortened words such as *phone, photo,* and *ad* are commonly used in everyday speech; however, many writers use the full words when writing formal English.

Adjectives. Most writers avoid using certain informal adjectives in formal writing.

Instead of:	Use:
a couple of	a few
this here	this
that there	that
them ("them people")	those
kind of (meaning somewhat), sort of	somewhat, rather

The adjective *this* can be used with a noun only if the noun has been mentioned before. Therefore, when the noun is mentioned for the first time, *a* or *an* should be used, not *this.*

Confusing: We were driving over the Golden Gate Bridge when suddenly *this* big truck crashed into our car.

Clear: We were driving over the Golden Gate Bridge when suddenly *a* big truck crashed into our car.

TRY IT OUT

REFERRING TO THE YARDSTICKS GIVEN, ON A SEPARATE SHEET OF PAPER REWRITE PARAGRAPH 1 ON PAGE 425 ABOUT FUTURE JOB OPPORTUNITIES, USING MORE FORMAL ENGLISH.

II. How do you think someone who expects you to be formal would react to the following paragraph?

A part-time job doesn't always pan out. I had really banked on getting a job at the local bank because I needed lots of dough so that I could buy a swell set of wheels and take in a movie sometimes. It was a lousy job as a janitor, but it paid plenty of bread. Although the job had sounded like a snap, I goofed it up on the first day. While I was slaving away real hard, I was also getting a gander at all the loot in the vault. I reckoned that there must have been at least a million bucks. Because I wanted to do a mighty good job, I made sure to pick up each scrap of paper and put it through the paper shredding machine. Well, did I flip when I figured out that I had mistakenly shredded a bag containing a lot of checks that were worth over a hundred grand. The next day the bank hired some hot chicks who tried to put the checks back together, but the broads couldn't do it no how. The guy who had hired me was awfully mad and he took it out on me. I was sacked, which didn't bother me. I needed the long green in the worst way, but that banking jazz sure was a drag.

Here are some more basic principles to help you rewrite the above paragraph in the formal English usually required in an essay.

Words of Emphasis. Everyday conversation is filled with many informal words that are used to add strength to a statement. However, formal English also has a wide selection of emphasis words. Most writers choose them when writing an essay.

Instead of:	**Use:**
awfully, mighty, so, plenty, real (used for emphasis)	very, extremely, exceedingly, acutely
in the worst way	very much, acutely, exceedingly
a lot, lots of	a great deal, many
sure (meaning "certainly")	certainly, surely, absolutely, truly
no how	not at all
lousy	bad, terrible, inferior
swell, super, some (used for emphasis)	good, excellent, outstanding, notable, distinguished

Slang. Although slang is often colorful, it should be avoided in writing formal English. Words such as *guy, kid,* and *out of sight* are fine for a conversation with friends, but they rarely fit comfortably into an essay written in formal English. Also, it is more accurate to write *agreement* or *transaction* instead of *deal,* for example. When you are in doubt about whether or not a word is slang, consult your dictionary.

Verbs. Most writers avoid using certain informal verb expressions when writing formal English.

Instead of:	Use:
to figure, to reckon	to suppose, to guess, to think
to bank on	to rely on
to take in a movie	to go to a movie
to take up with	to become friendly with
to take it out on	to release anger at

TRY IT OUT

REFERRING TO THE YARDSTICKS GIVEN, ON A SEPARATE SHEET OF PAPER REWRITE PARAGRAPH II ON PAGES 426–27 ABOUT THE COSTLY MISTAKE.

EXERCISE 10G: Each statement given below might appear as a headline in an informally written newspaper. Rewrite each statement as it would appear in the formal writing of an expository essay. Use normal formal English; do not use very stiff or pompous language.

1. SENATOR BUSTED FOR SKINNY-DIPPING IN POTOMAC
   He's Gonna Get 30 Days in the Slammer

   ____

   ____

   ____

2. DYNAMITE PHISH CONCERT HAS KIDS BOOGYING IN THE AISLES
   Funky Music Really Turns 'Em On

   ____

   ____

   ____

3. THIS FOXY TV ACTRESS BLOWS A WAD OF DOUGH ON SHADY OIL DEAL
   Now She's in Mighty Big Tax Jam with IRS

   ____

   ____

   ____

4. YANKS WALLOP BREWERS IN N.Y.
   Game Was a Drag so Lots of Fans Split

5. A COUPLE OF BIG-TIME LAWYERS GIVE HEAVY ADVICE
   If You Get into a Hassle with the Fuzz, Stay Cool!

6. LATEST PARIS DUDS SURE ARE FAR OUT
   Chicks Dig Dresses Open Down to Belly Button

7. SUCKERS SHELL OUT LOADS OF BREAD FOR PHONY HAIR-GROWING GOO
   Baldies Say It Doesn't Work No How

8. PREZ SACKS OUT AT CLASSY WHITE HOUSE DINNER
   He's in Hot Water with His Old Lady

9. NEW CLUB USING CORNY GIMMICKS & LOUSY FOOD TO MAKE BIG BUCKS
   This Here Hangout's an Awfully Expensive Dump

10. COPS NAB MATH PROF ON COKE CHARGE
Says He Was Framed by Some Rotten Students

11. REAL COOL SCI-FI FLICK OPENS
This Giant Tuna Wipes Out Congress

12. GUY DRIVES AUTO THROUGH FRONT WINDOW OF MARKET TO GET QT. OF MILK
Docs Figure He's Off His Rocker

13. CROOKS RIP OFF 200 GRAND IN JEWELRY HEIST
Private Eye Banks on Finding Them
Hot Rocks for 10% Reward

14. FARMERS KIND OF UPTIGHT CAUSE WATERMELON CROP IS THE PITS
Plants Bugged by a Lot of Insects

15. STUCK-UP JOCK SORRY HE WALKED OUT ON TEAM
Wants to Iron Out Goof in the Worst Way

16. SECRETARY BLOWS THE WHISTLE ON CLASSY RECORD CO. BIGSHOTS
Says Them Guys Made Shady Deals with DJ's

17. OUR ECONOMY'S ON MIGHTY SHAKY GROUND
It'll Take a Big Brain in Wash., D.C., to Get Us Back on Easy Street

18. LIBRARIAN GOES NUTS AND CLOBBERS DUDE UPSIDE HIS HEAD
Victim Gripes: Book Wasn't Really Overdue

19. SMALLTIME BOXER KO'S CHAMP IN FRISCO SLUGFEST
Champ Dumped with a Real Hard Belt to the Kisser

20. PARK AVE. SHRINK SUED OVER HOT NEW BOOK
She Dishes Out Inside Info. About Patients' Hangups

EXERCISE 10H: Using a more formal version of each of the clue words, fill in the crossword puzzle. (If there is more than one word in an answer, do not leave space between words.)

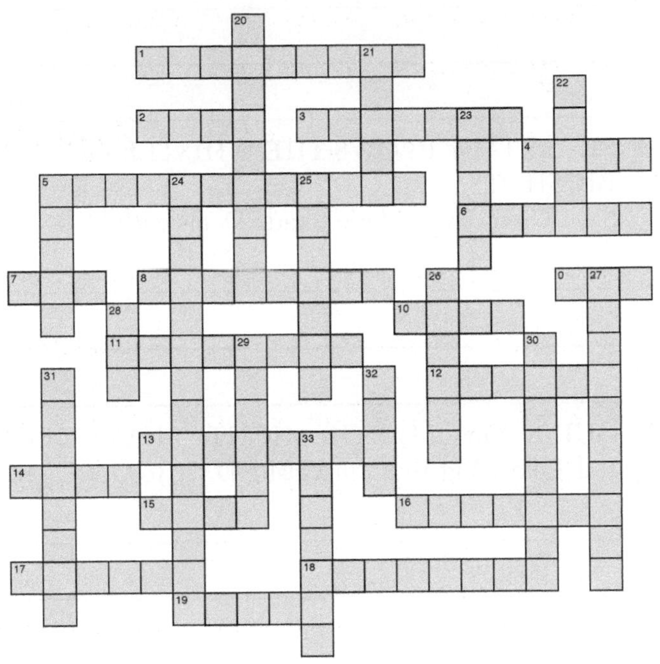

Across

1. I *gotta* get a car.
2. *that there* book
3. gonna
4. *a lot of* people
5. You *goofed!*
6. st.
7. guys
8. in the worst way
9. a *couple of* flowers
10. a *cool* movie
11. no how
12. He is *nuts!*
13. lousy
14. *real* lazy
15. *awfully* hungry
16. I *figure* that I can get a job.
17. can't
18. kids
19. The shoplifter is going to *rip off* some merchandise.

Down

5. a wallet filled with *dough*
20. It *sure* is hot today.
21. I *reckon* that the storm is over.
22. we're
23. *them* boots
24. ads
25. a hassle
26. the cops
27. *play around* with drugs
28. &
29. 30
30. chill out
31. *kind of* expensive
32. He *kicked the bucket.*
33. *bike*

EXERCISE 10I: REFRESHER

1. FIND AND CORRECT ANY ERRORS IN PRONOUN CONSISTENCY.
2. FIND AND CORRECT ANY ERRORS IN VERB AGREEMENT.
3. FIND AND CORRECT ANY SENTENCE FRAGMENTS.

Toughlove, a self-help program for the parents of problem teenagers, offer a strict approach to dealing with adolescents. Started twenty-five years ago by two counselors, the Toughlove movement have grown to include hundreds of local groups throughout the United States, as well as chapters in several foreign countries. At weekly meetings, you are encouraged to set a "bottom line" on your children's behavior. For example, you might set a midnight curfew for your 14-year-old son, who has gotten into the habit of staying out until 6:00 a.m. If the boy ignore the curfew, you would make him stay home for an entire weekend. In a more serious case, Lorraine Bauer were threatened with a butcher knife by her drug-dazed daughter, Diane. After escaping from the family home, Mrs. Bauer called some other members of her Toughlove group. Who immediately came over to take charge of the situation. First, they called several hospitals until they found one that would take Diane that night. Then they offered Diane the "bottom line": If she did not go into the hospital to recover from her addiction. She would have to leave home permanently. Faced with this choice, the girl decided to enter the hospital. However, if she had not decided to go for treatment, she would have had to move out. Taking only her personal belongings and a note listing the names of Toughlove families that was willing to take her in. Although Toughlove's no-nonsense approach may seem harsh, many parents claims that it has enabled them to take control of their own families again.

SPRINGBOARDS TO WRITING

Using your knowledge of the writing process, explained on pages 14–16, write a paragraph or essay related to this chapter's central theme, *the breakdown of the family,* which is introduced on pages 400–403.

PREWRITING

To think of topics to write about, look at the advertisement and the photograph, read the essay, and answer the questions that follow each. If you prefer, select one of the writing springboards below. (All paragraph numbers refer to the essay that starts on page 402.) To develop your ideas, use the prewriting techniques described on pages 17–22.

WRITING A PARAGRAPH *(For help, see the Pointers on page 51.)*

1. Read paragraphs 1–3. Do you think that Gloria Williams deserved to be arrested?
2. Agree or disagree: Many parents do not exercise enough control over their children.
3. Read paragraph 5. Do you agree with the Wisconsin law that makes parents financially responsible for the offspring of their teenage children?
4. Should teenagers be required to get parental approval for an abortion?
5. Does spanking help or harm children?
6. Agree or disagree: All high school students should be required to take a course in parenting skills.
7. As I was growing up, I had too much (not enough) parental supervision.
8. Read the Refresher on page 433. What do you think of the Toughlove program?

WRITING AN ESSAY *(For help, see the Pointers on pages 54–55.)*

9. What Has Caused the Breakdown of Many American Families?
10. How to Help America's Troubled Families
11. What Makes a Good (Bad) Parent?
12. Why Some Young People Belong to Street Gangs
13. I Am (Am Not) Part of a Traditional Family Unit
14. The Difficulties of Being a Single Parent
15. My Mother and Father Are (Were) Good Parents

16. What Can Be Done to Help America's Troubled Teenagers?
17. How Much Control Can a Parent Have Over the Behavior of a Seventeen-Year-Old? (See paragraphs 3 and 9.)
18. The Major Pressures Faced by Teenagers Today
19. I Have (Have Not) Lived Up to My Parents' Expectations
20. How I Want to Raise (Am Raising) My Children
21. Why Some Young People Become Involved in Criminal Activities
22. Parents Should (Should Not) Be Held Responsible for Their Children's Criminal Behavior
23. The Whole Society Is (Is Not) Partly Responsible for the Bad Behavior of Some Children (See paragraphs 7 and 8.)
24. The Major Causes of Teen Violence
25. Teenagers Should (Should Not) Engage in Premarital Sexual Activities
26. How to Discourage Teenagers from Participating in Street Gangs, Violence, and Drug Use
27. Good Alternatives to Street Life (See paragraph 8.)

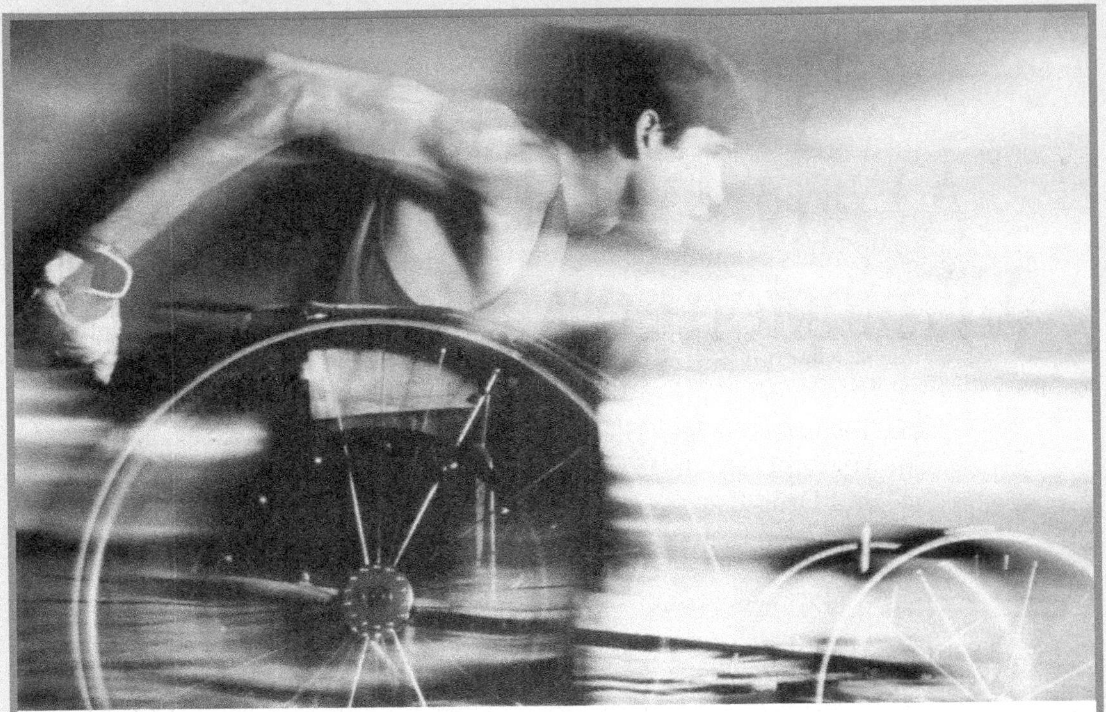

On January 17th, he set a dream in motion.

While you read this ad, marathoner Bill Duff is making an incredible and agonizing journey. He's putting every ounce of his physical and mental endurance on the line to travel 5,000 miles across the United States, propelled only by muscle and determination.

Wheels Across America is his labor of love for The Miami Project. It's his profound contribution to strengthening awareness, increasing support, and furthering progress in finding a cure for paralysis.

Be part of his odyssey. When he wheels through your city, come out to cheer him on. Whether it's in the afternoon, at night, or the first light of dawn.

It's your opportunity to show the world that you're willing to stand up for those who can't. It's also your chance to see a hero.

For more information on when Bill Duff will be visiting your area, please call your local media or 1-800-STAND UP.

The Miami Project

Wheels Across America

Chapter 11

SPRINGBOARDS TO THINKING

For informal, not written, response . . . to stimulate your thinking

1. Read the advertisement on the opposite page. What is Bill Duff's dream? What does the photograph of Bill Duff in action tell you about his attitude toward what he is doing?
2. Do you think Bill Duff is pursuing his dream only to satisfy himself? Explain. Why do you think Wheels Across America chose the words it did for its telephone number?
3. Look at the cartoon above. Would you work two jobs so that you could afford more luxuries in life? Explain.
4. What do you think are the differences between Bill Duff's values and those of Norm in the cartoon? Which values do you admire more? Explain. Which values match yours more closely? Explain.
5. If you had to choose between being rich as a result of working long, hard hours or living on a limited budget and having the freedom to do as you please much of the time, which would you choose? Why?

Money and Freedom

Marshall Glickman

(1) Making money has always been a passion of mine. At the age of twelve, I was a hustling newspaper boy and baby sitter, squirreling away dollar bills in a small red plastic safe that I hid behind my socks. While my brother was out playing basketball, I was devising plans to build my fortune. I cut lawns, delivered pizza, worked in a warehouse and as a security guard. I even had a scheme in college to capitalize on student birth control and sell condoms by mail order. When I left the brokerage house of Shearson Lehman Brothers last June, I was 24 and earning over $200,000 a year. Today I have no job. I'm not unemployed. I'm retired.

(2) "You'd be a good lawyer," my mother always used to say. My mother is a lawyer and college professor who routinely puts in a 60-hour week. She loves the law, loves working, and loves the $350,000 suburban home she and my dad live in. My first career plan *was* to become a lawyer, and I entered Northwestern University as a necessary first step. I hoped to impress Stanford Law by majoring in philosophy. Maybe it was the philosophy, maybe the break from home and the exposure to people of different backgrounds, but I began to question my motivations. I read. I spent my summers traveling—out West, through Europe and Kenya. I met people who had little of the respect for the legal profession that had been bred in me. I began thinking of life as a writer, artist, or adventurer.

(3) In my senior year, partly to relieve the anxiety I felt over my future, I began meditating—first for a half-hour, then up to two hours a day. Zen meditation quieted my scheming mind and taught me to focus on the present. I took the test to enter law school, and my scores were good, within 20 points of what I'd predicted. But I knew I was marching toward a life I wasn't interested in. I fantasized about trekking in the Himalayas, bicycling cross-country, meditating in Kyoto, and writing a novel. But while I spoke bravely about freedom and choice, my suburban upbringing rejected a hand-to-mouth existence on the road. I had the heart of a wanderer but the head of an accountant.

(4) So I postponed my adventures until I could afford them. I wouldn't have a career, I said; I would simply make money—fast. Enough money to make me feel I was a success but not so much that I would get sidetracked. My goal was a nest egg of $100,000, but I promised myself I'd work for only three years, even if I fell short of that. Wall Street seemed the most direct route.

(5) The first months at Shearson were a nightmare. "Hello, my name is Marshall Glickman from. . . ." Slam! Busy signal. Wrong number. To reach 60 people, I had to make 200 to 300 calls a day. I took 15-minute lunches, hired

three college students to help me call, and purchased names and numbers of prospective clients. Each morning I rose at 5:30, meditated for an hour and ran around Prospect Park. As the sun broke through the darkness, I imagined myself in India, in Oregon. All images of a better life had faded by the time I shuffled home from the office at 9:30 P.M., wolfed my dinner and collapsed on the couch with the same half-read book. My eyes burned from staring at the green glow of my Quotron machine.* My neck had a permanent crick from cradling the phone. Three years, I told myself. You just have to hold out for three years. "You're living for tomorrow," said my brother, who is a writer.

(6) Then the market went crazy. Interest rates dropped, and suddenly my phone rang nonstop. The groundwork I had done paid off. I raked in $30,000 to $40,000 a month in gross commissions. By year two, I was the top producer in my office, managing a portfolio of $14 million. Names on my Rolodex included CEO's, television journalists, professional athletes, actors, and a world-renowned architect, not to mention my grandmother. I was a 10-year-old again, successful beyond my wildest dreams, stuffing money into mutual funds and money markets instead of into my little red safe. My meditating dwindled to 20 minutes. I found myself eyeing the price of cars, homes, and exotic vacations. One more good year, I calculated, and I'd double my savings. I'd be a millionaire at 30. Although by now I'd socked away my $100,000, could I walk away while the market was this hot?

(7) I enjoyed the gambling, enjoyed calculating my commissions at the end of each day. I was riding the momentary high, the thrill of the hunt. At the same time, all this unnerved me. I kept reminding myself that Shearson was a means to an end, and I was still committed to that end. Trusting my earlier instincts, I gave notice to my incredulous branch manager two weeks before my third year was up—$135,000 richer. "In another five years you could have been set for life," said my father, who is a businessman.

(8) For weeks after I left Shearson, I didn't know what to say when someone asked me what I did. I weighed the value of each day that passed against what I could have earned if I'd still been working. It was a while before I could pick up a book on a Monday morning without feeling guilty—and poor. Even after I began to travel and those feelings passed, my interest in making money remained. It probably always will. But with $135,000 in the bank and frugal habits, I figure I can continue without working for a long time. I'm going to renovate a house and use the profits to finance a trip to the Orient. I have plans to do some real estate deals, to do some writing, work on a fishing boat in Alaska. It seems possible to do what I want and make some money, too.

(9) Last fall, I pedaled my bike through the Catskill Mountains on the last leg of a trip from Minnesota. At a one-pump station in a town called Big Indian, I

*A Quotron machine is a computer terminal that supplies stock and bond prices as well as other financial information.

called my broker in New York to check on a volatile stock I own. I used to share an office with him. "How's it going, Dave?" I asked. Dave sounded as if he were a soldier reporting bad news from the front. "The market's off 50 points," he moaned. "I'm getting killed." I hung up and chuckled. My worries revolved around saddle sores and flat tires. I climbed back on the bike and felt the sun on my shoulders as the road raced beneath my wheels.

READING SURVEY

1. MAIN IDEA

What is the central theme of this essay?

2. MAJOR DETAILS

a. What probably influenced Marshall Glickman to change his mind about becoming a lawyer?
b. What was the three-year plan that Marshall Glickman decided to pursue?
c. What are Glickman's plans for the future?

3. INFERENCES

a. Read paragraph 2 again. Why did Glickman think that Stanford Law would be impressed if he majored in philosophy?
b. Read paragraph 9 again. Why did Glickman chuckle after speaking with Dave on the telephone?

4. OPINIONS

a. Do you agree with Glickman's decision to retire when he was 24 years old? Why or why not? Would you ever consider doing the same thing yourself? Why or why not?
b. Which is more important to you when selecting a career, the salary or the chance to work at something enjoyable? Explain.

VOCABULARY BUILDING

Lesson One: The Vocabulary of the Financial World

The essay "Money and Freedom" by Marshall Glickman includes words that are useful when you are discussing the financial world.

scheme (paragraph 1) . . .
scheming (3)
to capitalize on (1)
brokerage house (1)
gross commissions (6)
portfolio (6)
CEO's (6)
mutual funds (6)
money markets (6)
dwindled (6)
frugal (8)

People involved in the financial world sometimes have a **scheme**—a carefully arranged and perhaps secret plan of action—for making money. Because some of these people have **scheming** minds, they are always thinking of tricky new plans to try.

People involved in the financial world try **to capitalize on** the very latest financial information in that they try to use this information for their own advantage or profit.

People involved in the financial world sometimes work for a **brokerage house**—a company that buys and sells stocks, bonds, and other investments on behalf of its customers.

People involved in the financial world sometimes earn commissions—percentages of the money they take in on sales. **Gross commissions** are these percentages of money before expenses are subtracted.

People involved in the financial world sometimes help others to put together a **portfolio** or list of specific investments.

People involved in the financial world sometimes have to deal with **CEO's,** chief executive officers, who head companies and thereby provide leadership by making important policy decisions.

People involved in the financial world sometimes buy shares in **mutual funds**—companies that use their stockholders' money to purchase stocks, bonds, gold, or other investments.

People involved in the financial world often put their money in **money markets**—short-term interest-earning loans to banks, large companies, or the federal government.

People involved in the financial world get very upset when the value of their investments has **dwindled** or become smaller.

People involved in the financial world are sometimes **frugal** because they spend money to fulfill only simple needs and are not wasteful.

EXERCISE 11A: Using the vocabulary words in this lesson, fill in the blanks.

1. _______________ help to decide whether their companies should introduce new products or services.

2. A _______________ person saves all of the leftovers from a meal.

3. Voters consider some politicians to be _______________ people because of their tricky and underhanded actions.
4. People put their money in _______________ _______________ to earn interest on their money.
5. When selecting a career, wise people try to _______________ _______________ their talents and interests.
6. If you win a lottery, you may be able to afford to own a stock and bond _______________ worth many thousands of dollars.
7. People invest in _______________ _______________ because they want to buy a range of stocks and bonds that are expected to increase in value.
8. The burglar had a carefully arranged _______________ for stealing all of the gold in Fort Knox.
9. Automobile salespeople usually earn _______________ _______________ in addition to their salaries.
10. When the United States' supply of oil _______________, the price of gasoline rose sharply.
11. When people want to buy and sell stocks and bonds, they usually open an account at a _______________ _______________.

Lesson Two: The Vocabulary of Avoiding Burnout

The essay "Money and Freedom" by Marshall Glickman includes words that are useful when you are discussing ways to avoid burnout.

anxiety (paragraph 3)
meditating (3)
Zen meditation (3)
fantasized (3)
trekking (3)
exotic (6)
unnerved (7)
instincts (7)
incredulous (7)
volatile (9)

People sometimes become **unnerved** by the hectic pace of their lives in that they begin to lose courage, self-control, and the power to act; they may even feel weak and nervous as well. Their tempers become **volatile,** shifting quickly and unpredictably from a calm state one moment to an explosive state the next.

Anxiety takes hold as these people feel uneasy and worry about what might happen in the future. This state of severe physical and mental exhaustion is known as burnout.

Fortunately, recovery from burnout is possible. At first, victims of this condition may be **incredulous,** unwilling or unable to believe what is happening to them. Eventually, however, friends and family members may be able to convince them to slow down. Or the victims may be influenced by their own natural tendencies to behave in a certain way. These **instincts** may tell them that the time has come for a vacation somewhere foreign and often excitingly different and beautiful. Such an **exotic** vacation might involve **trekking**—traveling slowly and with difficulty—through the jungles of South America. On the other hand, some people might prefer to relax on a sandy beach in Hawaii, a scene they have **fantasized** about—daydreamed and had mental images about—for some time. Other burnout sufferers find that the best way to recover is to start **meditating** by closing their eyes and concentrating for twenty minutes or more on a single word or sound. Many people have found that this technique totally relaxes their minds and bodies. Those who practice **Zen meditation,** a form of meditation used by a Japanese religious group, claim that it brings about not only relaxation but also a better understanding of life.

EXERCISE 11B: Each of the vocabulary words from this lesson is shown below in italics as the word appeared in context in the essay. Write an explanation of each word within the context of the material given. Use your own paper for this assignment.

1. From paragraph 3: ". . . partly to relieve the *anxiety* I felt over my future, I began *meditating*. . . ."
2. From paragraph 3: "*Zen meditation* quieted my scheming mind. . . ."
3. From paragraph 3: "I *fantasized* about *trekking* in the Himalayas. . . ."
4. From paragraph 6: "I found myself eyeing the price of cars, homes, and *exotic* vacations."
5. From paragraph 7: "At the same time, all this *unnerved* me."
6. From paragraph 7: "Trusting my earlier *instincts,* I gave notice to my *incredulous* branch manager. . . ."
7. From paragraph 9: ". . . I called my broker in New York to check on a *volatile* stock I own."

SPELLING

Spelling Rule—Dropping the Final E

Many of the words in this essay can be learned easily with the help of this one simple spelling rule.

Words ending in silent *e* usually drop the *e* before a suffix beginning with a vowel and keep the *e* before a suffix beginning with a consonant.

TRY IT OUT

ADD THE SUFFIXES INDICATED TO THE FOLLOWING WORDS.

	-ing	*-ment*	*-able*
move	________	________	________
measure	________	________	________
excite	________	________	________

Here are some examples.

guide + ance = guidance
care + less = careless
decide + ing = deciding

complete + ness = completeness
imagine + able = imaginable
grace + ful = graceful

TRY IT OUT

APPLY THE FINAL *E* RULE TO THE FOLLOWING WORDS.

close + ly = ________
leave + ing = ________
peace + ful = ________

complete + ion = ________
desire + able = ________
propose + al = ________

A SPECIAL NOTE: Here are some words you see frequently that are exceptions to the above rule.

true + ly = truly
argue + ment = argument
notice + able = noticeable

agree + able = agreeable
courage + ous = courageous
canoe + ing = canoeing

EXERCISE 11C: Apply the final *e* rule to these words.

1. combine + ation =
2. place + ment =
3. advertise + ing =
4. courage + ous =
5. guide + ance =
6. definite + ly =
7. create + or =
8. illustrate + ion =
9. rude + ness =
10. fortune + ate =
11. sensitive + ity =
12. hope + less =
13. pleasure + able =
14. freeze + ing =
15. ridicule + ous =
16. bride + al =
17. concentrate + ion =
18. argue + ment =
19. prime + ary =
20. entire + ly =

Parallelism

In math . . . parallel lines run in the same direction and are the same distance apart from each other so that they never meet. Thus, *they correspond or match.*

In English . . . parallelism means that when words express equal or parallel ideas, *they must match or be parallel in form.*

We know that if a car tire goes flat and cannot be fixed, it must be replaced with a tire that is exactly the same size as the other three tires. If a different size is used, the car will sit awkwardly and drive poorly or not at all. Thus it is with sentences: Equal (parallel) ideas must be expressed in matching (parallel) form so that all parts of the sentence work properly.

If you use words that are parallel in form, your writing style can improve a great deal. At times it will be necessary for you to rewrite a sentence so that your word order will be parallel; however, the result will be a more balanced and smoother product. To achieve parallel form in a sentence, be sure to follow these guidelines:

I Words in a Pair or Series Must Match in Form.

II Words That Follow "Set-Up" Words Must Match in Form.

III Words That Go with Pairs of "Set-Up" Words Must Match in Form.

A Special Note: The spelling of the word parallel can be remembered from its meaning: *All* lines are par*all*el (and the double l looks like parallel lines!).

I. Words in a Pair or a Series Must Match in Form.

Nancy likes fishing
and
bowling.

Steve likes to swim,
to fish,
but not
to hike.

Sue wants to be a lawyer
or
a nurse.

Bob neither smokes
nor
drinks.

Notice that the items in a pair or a series can be connected with *and, but, or, nor.*

TRY IT OUT

FILL IN THE BLANKS WITH WORDS THAT ARE LOGICAL AND THAT MATCH IN FORM.

1. When the cowboy hears a banjo, he feels like tapping his toes, ____ ____________________, and snapping his fingers.
2. The lifeguard was ready to jump into the water and to ______________ ____.
3. To stay in business, the storekeeper must fire three employees and ____ ____.

II. Words That Follow "Set-Up" Words Must Match in Form.

"Set-Up" Words			
if	which	the	at
that	could	so that	when
who	a (an)	of	

If we stop trying to participate in government,
if we prefer not to feel pity for others,
and
if we refuse to take risks,
then we are headed for disaster.

TRY IT OUT

FILL IN THE BLANKS WITH WORDS THAT ARE LOGICAL AND THAT MATCH IN FORM.

1. The new parents felt that they had the most beautiful baby in the world and that ____.
2. If he plants his fields on time and if ______________________________, the farmer will harvest a good crop.

Notice that the section that must match in form can start at a few different places. The number of words you decide to match should depend on the emphasis and style you want to achieve. Here are some good ways of writing a parallel sentence.

The pilot told us that the plane would be delayed and that the plane would be crowded.

The pilot told us that the plane would be delayed and the plane would be crowded.

The pilot told us that the plane would be delayed and would be crowded.

The pilot told us that the plane would be delayed and crowded.

Note that the second section of each sentence above started at a different place. As long as the two sections of the sentence are parallel, the second section can start wherever it sounds best in what you are writing. Which way is best? No one way.

TRY IT OUT

FOLLOWING THE MODEL ABOVE, WRITE ALL THE WAYS THE SECOND SECTION OF THIS SENTENCE COULD BEGIN. USE YOUR OWN PAPER FOR THIS ASSIGNMENT.

During the trial, most spectators felt that the defendant was guilty and that the defendant was dangerous to society.

III. Words That Go with Pairs of "Set-Up" Words Must Match in Form.

Pairs of "Set-Up" Words

both	and	not only	but also
either	or	which	and which
whether	or	that	and that
neither	nor	who	and who

David is *both* strong
and handsome.

Bill is a man *who* likes responsibility
and who enjoys a challenge.

The politician liked *not only*
to meet people
but also
to sign autographs.

Neither
blankets
nor
hot drinks
were available to
the storm victims.

TRY IT OUT

FILL IN THE BLANKS WITH WORDS THAT ARE LOGICAL AND MATCH IN FORM.

1. Most married people want their spouses to be both considerate and ______________________________ ______________________________.
2. The old man wanted neither to live with his son nor ______________ ______________________________.
3. Olympic stars are athletes who practice many hours a day and who ______________________________ ______________________________.

EXERCISE 11D: In each of the sentences given, one parallel section does not match in form. Underline that section and rewrite the section, making any changes necessary for correct parallelism. The goal is to make all parallel parts match; in some cases, there is more than one possible form for the sections, and no one form is more correct than another.

1. A good friend is someone to keep your secrets and who stands beside you in hard times.

   ____

   ____

2. The hungry kitten smelled its food and then was running out of the house.

   ____

   ____

3. Whether to balance the government's budget or providing additional funds for the poor was a decision that the President had to make.

____

____

4. Two of the best reasons to travel are the opportunity for meeting new people and to see new places.

____

____

5. The humanoid robot turned corners easily but was falling down the stairs.

____

____

6. When more consumers begin demanding better products and if manufacturers produced higher-quality merchandise, people will be more satisfied with their purchases.

____

____

7. On rainy days, some people like not only to take long naps but also walking in the rain.

____

____

8. The power-hungry dictator usually thinks that war will not be expensive and that victory is easy.

____

____

9. In order to get into the rock concert, the fans were willing to stand in line for hours and paying very high prices for tickets.

____

____

10. Deciding about the need for a diet is easy; to stick to it is difficult.

____

____

EXERCISE 11E: Fill in the blanks with words that are logical and that match in form.

1. Cars would last longer if ______________________ and if ______________________.
2. With a hurricane approaching the seashore community, the residents had to ______________________ and to ______________________.
3. When workers are laid off, they often feel that ______________________ and that ______________________.
4. Neither ______________________ nor ______________________ should be used by anyone who hopes to have good health.
5. Both ______________________ and ______________________ are necessary to prevent crime in the streets.
6. A magician is a person who ______________________ and who ______________________.
7. A good book can be ______________________, ______________________, and ______________________.
8. If you want to succeed in your job, you should ______________________ and you should ______________________.
9. Teachers often have reputations of being both ______________________ and ______________________.
10. Watching the eruption of a volcano is not only ______________________ but also ______________________.

EXERCISE 11F: Using parallelism, write a sentence about each of the following topics. Use as many types of parallelism with as many "set-up" words and pairs of "set-up" words as possible. Do this assignment on your own paper.

1. computer games
2. fear
3. shoplifting
4. football players
5. a great job
6. airplanes
7. influenza
8. horror films
9. supermarkets
10. take-home tests
11. hypnosis
12. T-shirts
13. microwave ovens
14. Jennifer Lopez
15. child abuse
16. greeting cards
17. getting married
18. California
19. TV game shows
20. becoming wealthy

 Misplaced Modifiers

Modifiers are words or groups of words that describe other words.

✔ People who are not married can apply to adopt babies.

In the sentence above, *who are not married* is a modifier that clearly describes *people*. If the modifier is incorrectly placed in the sentence, the meaning changes.

☒ People can apply to adopt babies who are not married.

Because the modifier is misplaced, it now seems to be describing *babies*. In the next example, notice that the misplaced modifier can be just a single word.

☒ The boss almost called Jennifer for five minutes before she answered him.

Because the modifier *almost* is misplaced, the sentence says that Jennifer's boss did not really call her, but she answered him anyway. When *almost* is moved to its correct position in the sentence, the meaning changes.

✔ The boss called Jennifer for almost five minutes before she answered him.

As you can see, a misplaced modifier can make the meaning of a sentence unclear and confusing to the reader. Fortunately, you can avoid this problem easily by following two important guidelines:

I Each Word Must Be Placed As Close As Possible to What It Describes.

II Groups of Words Must Be Placed As Close As Possible to What They Describe.

I. Each Word Must Be Placed As Close As Possible to What It Describes.

The incorrect placement of a word such as *almost, even, just, merely, only,* or *simply* can change the meaning of a sentence.

For example, let's consider the sentence *He said that she was pretty.* When the word *only* is inserted in various places in the sentence, the meaning of the sentence changes completely.

Only he said that she was pretty. *(No one else said it.)*

He **only** said that she was pretty. *(He did not mean it.)*

He said **only** that she was pretty. *(He said nothing else.)*

He said that **only** she was pretty. *(No one else was pretty.)*

He said that she **only** was pretty. *(She was nothing else.)*

He said that she was **only** pretty. *(She was pretty but not gorgeous.)*

TRY IT OUT

INSERT THE WORD *ONLY* IN AS MANY PLACES AS POSSIBLE. EXPLAIN THE MEANING THAT EACH PLACEMENT CREATES.

The police report said that the burglar had been wounded.

____

____

____

____

____

____

____

____

____

A SPECIAL NOTE: Avoid putting a word between the two words in the infinitive form of the verb, such as *to* run, *to* go, *to* be, *to* have, *to* think.

II. Groups of Words Must Be Placed As Close As Possible to What They Describe. Incorrect placement of groups of words can result in illogical—and unintentionally funny—sentences.

☒ We took the broken chair to the carpenter with only three legs.
. . . *a freak carpenter?*

☒ Ted kept a little black book with the telephone numbers of all the girls he had ever dated in his back pocket.
. . . that must have been a big pocket!

☒ The forest ranger spotted a pack of grizzly bears using high-powered binoculars.
. . . bears using binoculars?

TRY IT OUT

EXPLAIN THE MEANING OF EACH SENTENCE AS IT STANDS. THEN UNDERLINE THE GROUP OF WORDS THAT IS INCORRECTLY PLACED IN THE SENTENCE. FINALLY, DRAW AN ARROW TO WHERE THE GROUP OF WORDS BELONGS.

1. The waiter served the chicken in a gorilla suit.
   meaning:
   ____

2. The old car was discovered by the police stuck in the mud.
   meaning:
   ____

3. Some actors are famous for playing comic book heroes such as Christopher Reeve and Michael Keaton.
   meaning:
   ____
   ____

EXERCISE 11G: For each list of words or groups of words, record all the possible logical orders for a sentence. In some cases, there is only one logical order; in other cases, there are more than one. If the latter applies, explain any differences in meaning. Use a separate sheet of paper.

1. treated
   ten
   doctor
   the
   often
   patients
   sick

2. can be
   a writer
   every student

3. different
   come with
   clothes
   many
   Barbie dolls

4. Donald
   his canoe
   frequently
   new rivers
   to explore
   traveled in
5. try to
   its ingredients
   before eating
   find out
   a hot dog
6. live longer lives
   on the average
   married people
7. a bag of popcorn
   scared but smart
   duck
   Muriel
   fed
   to
   a
8. to survive alone
   should learn
   everyone
   in the desert
   how
9. the college
   Alvin, our teacher,
   his son
   at the age of four
   to visit
   invited
10. when walking
    did not bother
    the weather forecasters
    to open their umbrellas
    in the rain

EXERCISE 11H: Find the word or group of words that is not as close to what it describes as possible. Rewrite the sentence with all words correctly placed.

1. Cars are often used by racing car drivers with fiberglass bodies.

____

____

2. I discovered that swifts, which are the world's fastest birds, can fly at a speed of 200 miles an hour reading a book about animals.

____

____

3. Saturday is the most dangerous day of the week to usually drive an automobile.

____

____

4. Ulysses S. Grant was arrested for going over the speed limit on his horse who was the eighteenth President of the United States.

 ____

 ____

5. Terrifying monsters have always been popular with movie fans such as King Kong and Godzilla.

 ____

 ____

6. A large suitcase was seized by two police officers stuffed with marijuana.

 ____

 ____

7. In the fourteenth century, half of the population of the entire earth died from the bubonic plague which was more than 75 million people.

 ____

 ____

8. Sitting proudly behind his desk, the President announced his plan to build a new dam in the Oval Office.

 ____

 ____

9. In 1916, a Pennsylvania inventor named John Andrews made an engine that only ran using water and a secret green fluid.

 ____

 ____

10. The salesman annoyed all of the other passengers in the elevator smoking a big, smelly cigar.

 ____

 ____

11. Such as chicks and bunnies, some Easter presents are not suitable for small children.

 ____

 ____

Dangling Modifiers

A modifier that opens a sentence describes the subject of the sentence.

☑ Climbing the ladder, I struck my head against a branch.

In the sentence above, the modifier *climbing the ladder* describes the subject *I*. If the correct subject is not used, the meaning of the sentence will be confusing and unintentionally funny.

☒ Climbing the ladder, my head struck a branch.

Now the sentence states that my head was climbing the ladder. The modifier is left dangling because it is not describing the subject the writer had in mind.

In each of the examples below, a dangling modifier distorts the meaning of the sentence.

☒ To make new friends, the student lounge is a good place to visit.
. . . a student lounge that makes friends?

☑ To make new friends, you should visit the student lounge.

☒ At the age of four, my parents took me to Puerto Rico.
. . . my parents were four?

☑ At the age of four, I was taken to Puerto Rico by my parents.

☒ Packed into a small can, Emily had trouble removing the sardines.
. . . Emily was packed into a small can?

☑ Packed into a small can, the sardines were hard for Emily to remove.

☒ After leaving the concert, our car would not start.
. . . our car was at the concert?

☑ After leaving the concert, we could not start our car.

A Special Note: To find the subject of an introductory modifier, ask of its verb "Who?" or "What?" The answer is the subject. This subject must be given either in the introductory modifier or in the main sentence.

TRY IT OUT

EXPLAIN WHY EACH OF THE FOLLOWING IS ILLOGICAL.

1. Galloping at full speed, we cheered for our horse to win the race.

   ____

2. Exhausted from a hard day's work, my bed was a welcome sight.

   ____

3. To help prevent tooth decay, sugar should be eliminated from your diet.

   ____

4. While dancing at the club, my house was robbed.

   ____

To correct a dangling modifier, use the logical subject in the main sentence:

After leaving the concert, we could not start our car.

Or rewrite the modifier so that it has its own subject.

After we left the concert, our car would not start.

TRY IT OUT

CORRECT EACH OF THE FOUR SENTENCES IN THE PREVIOUS TRY IT OUT EXERCISE.

1. ______________________________
2. ______________________________
3. ______________________________
4. ______________________________

EXERCISE 11I: Read each sentence given to see if the subject of the introductory modifier is clearly stated. If not, rewrite the sentence employing one of the two correction methods given.

1. After running twenty-six miles in the Boston Marathon, an icy cold glass of beer is especially refreshing.

   ____

   ____

2. To get a college scholarship, your high school grades do not have to be excellent.

   ____

   ____

3. Without any knowledge of modern art, some of Picasso's paintings may seem strange and hard to understand.

   ____

   ____

4. Glowing brightly in the evening sky, we thought they were flying saucers.

   ____

   ____

5. Admiring the beautiful young woman, Dracula became very thirsty.

   ____

6. Known as the Great Emancipator, Abraham Lincoln's birthday is celebrated every year.

   ____

   ____

7. When riding a motorcycle, a helmet should be worn.

   ____

   ____

8. Using a microwave oven, the hamburger was fully cooked in two minutes.

   ____

   ____

9. Bored and lonely, a vacation was just what she needed.

10. Having finished college, it is time to start looking for a good job.

11. To renew a driver's license, an eye test is required in some states.

12. While cleaning out the hall closet, a heavy box fell off the shelf and hit Fran in the head.

13. As a college freshman, many pressures must be dealt with.

14. Before leaving a room, the lights should be turned out.

15. Tired from studying all night, my desk looked like a prison to me.

EXERCISE 11J: Write a complete sentence after each introductory modifier below. Check to make sure that the subject would logically follow the modifier.

Example: While swimming in the Pacific Ocean, *I saw a shark heading in my direction.*

1. After eating six Burger King Whoppers, ____________________

2. To raise children properly, ____________________

3. Upset about the city's crime wave, ____________________

4. Feeling achy and feverish, ____________________

5. At the age of ten, ____________________

6. Shocked by the comedian's filthy jokes, ____________________

7. While studying for the history test, ____________________

8. Before buying an expensive car, ____________________

9. Unable to speak a word of English, ____________________

10. Wearing a low-cut dress to the Oscar Awards ceremony, ____________________

EXERCISE 11K: REFRESHER

1. ADD THE *-D* OR *-ED* ENDING WHEREVER IT IS NEEDED IN THE FOLLOWING PARAGRAPH.
2. FIND AND CORRECT ANY ERRORS IN VERB AGREEMENT.

A study conduct by two psychologists indicate that many of today's young people shares similar attitudes about life. For one thing, they feel cheat because they are inheriting a pollute Earth, a racially divide society, and overwhelming social problems. Indeed, they are worry that America's best years are over. Because they have grown up in a time when almost half of all marriages ends in divorce, they are also afraid of making commitments. As a result, people in their teens and early twenties often prefers to socialize in groups rather than has a steady boyfriend or girlfriend. They usually live longer at home, wait longer to marry, and postpone careers in favor of travel and leisure-time activities. When they are ready to go to work, they tends to avoid low-paying careers such as teaching, nursing, and social work. Instead they choose professions that offers money, power, and a high social standing, for those are the goals their parents has work hard to achieve. On the job, these young people can be difficult to work with; raise in an era of widespread corruption in government and big business, they questions authority and is not especially loyal to the company. If they are not reward quickly with salary increases and promotions, they will immediately start looking for another job. Although they has a strong desire for self-fulfillment, they also has the energy and creativity need to improve life for the next generation.

SPRINGBOARDS TO WRITING

Using your knowledge of the writing process, explained on pages 14–16, write a paragraph or essay related to this chapter's central theme, *money and freedom,* which is introduced on pages 436–40.

PREWRITING

To think of topics to write about, look at the advertisement and the cartoon, read the essay, and answer the questions that follow each. If you prefer, select one of the writing springboards below. (All paragraph numbers refer to the essay that starts on page 438.) To develop your ideas, use the prewriting techniques described on pages 17–22.

WRITING A PARAGRAPH *(For help, see the Pointers on page 51.)*

1. Some people have strange attitudes concerning money.
2. Money brings out the worst in some people.
3. Money can (cannot) buy happiness.
4. I do (do not) "live for tomorrow." (See paragraph 5.)
5. The best (worst) job I ever had was ____________________.
6. I would (would not) like to retire early. (See paragraph 1.)

WRITING AN ESSAY *(For help, see the Pointers on pages 54–55.)*

7. The Perfect Career for Me
8. What to Consider When Selecting a Career
9. My Definition of Success
10. Should People Be Forced to Retire at a Certain Age?
11. The Qualities a Person Needs in Order to Have a Successful Career
12. Is It Possible to Balance a Career and Family Life Without One of Them Suffering?
13. Agree or disagree with this statement by Allan K. Chalmers: "The grand essentials of happiness are: something to do, something to love, and something to hope for."
14. Is It True That the Love of Money Is the Root of All Evil?
15. The Major Goals in My Life
16. How I Expect My Life to Be Different from (the Same as) My Parents' Lives
17. What I Have Learned from Having a Job
18. The Advantages (Disadvantages) of Working for a Year Before Attending College
19. If I Won a Fortune in a Lottery
20. People Do (Do Not) Take Pride in Their Work These Days
21. Are Credit Cards a Good Idea?

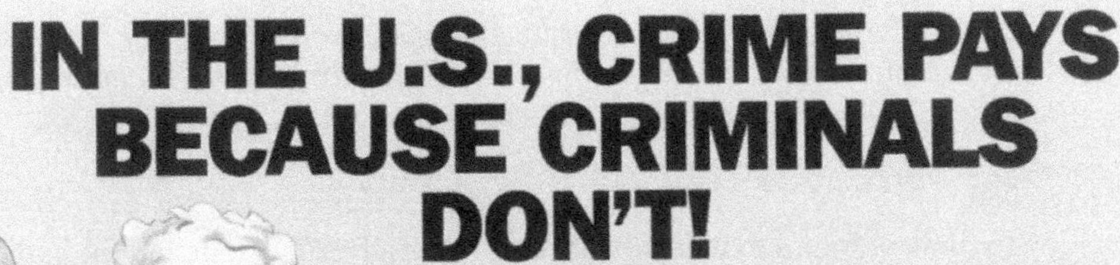

IN THE U.S., CRIME PAYS
BECAUSE CRIMINALS
DON'T!

IN OTHER COUNTRIES THEY DO.

IN ISRAEL:
MANDATORY LIFE IMPRISONMENT FOR MURDER; NO BAIL FOR MURDER SUSPECTS.

IN CANADA:
COMPULSORY LIFE IMPRISONMENT FOR MURDER; 80.6% HOMICIDE CONVICTION RATE.

IN GREAT BRITAIN:
83.5% HOMICIDE CONVICTION RATE;
87.9% ROBBERY CONVICTION RATE;
100% LIFE SENTENCES FOR MURDER.

IN JAPAN:
99.5% VIOLENT CRIME CONVICTION RATE; 98% RECEIVE JAIL TIME; NO PLEA BARGAINING.

IN NEW YORK CITY ALONE:
"THE CHANCE OF A GIVEN FELONY ARREST ENDING IN A PRISON SENTENCE . . . ONE OUT OF 108."

— *From the New York Times*

NATIONWIDE:
". . . FOR EVERY 500 SERIOUS CRIMES, JUST 20 ADULTS AND 5 JUVENILES ARE SENT TO JAIL."

— *From U.S. News & World Report*

GOD HELP AMERICA.

DEMAND PUNISHMENT FOR CRIMINAL BEHAVIOR.
JAIL TIME FOR REPEAT OFFENDERS DETERS CRIME.

National Rifle Association, 1600 Rhode Island Ave., N.W., Washington, D.C. 20036

Chapter 12

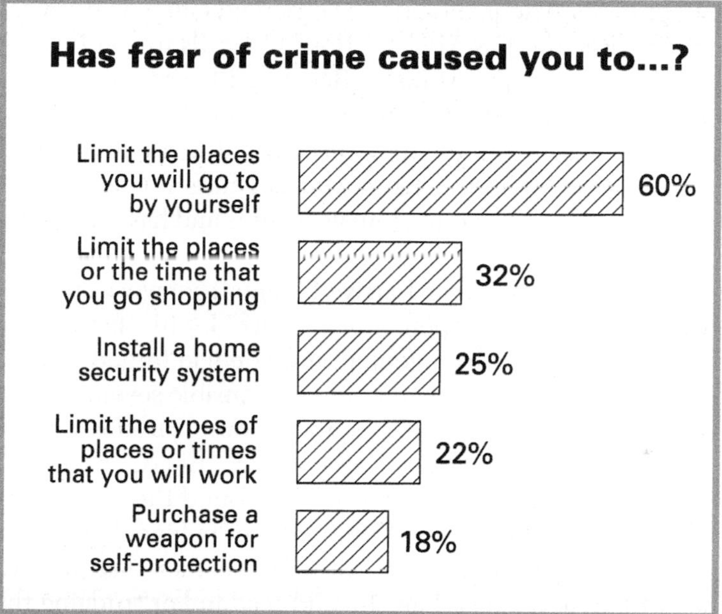

SPRINGBOARDS TO THINKING

For informal, not written, response . . . to stimulate your thinking

1. Read the advertisement on the opposite page. Do you agree or disagree with the headline? Explain. What is your reaction to the statistics listed for the four other countries—and to those for New York City and the entire United States? Explain.
2. Do you agree or disagree with the caption at the bottom of the advertisement? Explain.
3. Read the chart above. It shows the results of a poll conducted for the National Victim Center. The percentages in the chart give the proportion of people who answered "yes" to each question. How would *you* answer each question? Explain your answers.
4. In general, do you think parents today have good reason to be frightened if their children are late coming home from school or other places? Explain.
5. In general, do you think women today have good reason to withhold information from men concerning matters such as the location of "safe houses" for battered wives and communal houses for unmarried pregnant women? Explain.

The Shadow of a Stranger

Wally Lamb

(1) In our area, Michael Ross is a household name. It rides past you on people's bumpers ("Electric Fry Michael Ross"). It calls to you from headlines and editorials about capital punishment. Recently I heard it used as a grim verb by one of my high school students. He was describing to a friend the plot of a movie he had rented: "Then this guy took this girl out to a pond and he Michael Rossed her." Connecticut has convicted Michael Ross for the murders—and in some cases the rapes—of six young female victims and has sentenced him to die in the electric chair.

(2) One day early this year I arrived home from work amid falling snow to find my wife standing at our open door. "What?" I said. "Jared," she answered. "He's 20 minutes late." The arrangement my wife had forged called for Elizabeth and Amy, two of the neighborhood's most responsible seventh graders, to accompany our 6-year-old son on his half-mile route home. Jared is a dawdler by nature and the snow was falling as benignly as confetti. "Relax," I said. "I'll get him."

(3) Elizabeth was absent that day, but I found the other two halfway between home and school. Jared was a hundred feet behind Amy, running up and down a snowbank and so intoxicated with the weather that he was oblivious to me. Though I had never met Amy, I could read in her trudging that combination of indulgence and impatience that marks a good baby sitter. I pulled over to the curb and rolled down the window. "I'm Jared's dad," I told her. "Do you kids want a ride?" She declined for both of them. "Hurry home, then," I said. Driving away, I spotted two other girls about Amy's age on the opposite side of the street. I'd forgotten to roll the window back up, so their raucous heckling was accompanied by a blast of cold air. "Leave her alone, you pervert!" one of them shouted. The friend belly-laughed: "Call the cops! Call the cops!"

(4) It was only then that it dawned on me: Amy's fear as I pulled up to her was the same as my wife's at the front door. To Amy, I was one of those strangers about whom she had been warned: an adult male presumed guilty for survival's sake. I felt disturbed by my son's inaccessibility to me. If I had insisted, I saw now in recalling Amy's expression, she would not have let me have him. "But what if you *were* some sicko?" my wife asked when I told her about all this. She said Amy's handling of the situation made her feel relieved. I looked up to read her face, but her back was to me.

(5) My being the pervert for young girls schooled in the necessity of hostility has made me more cautious. At Stop and Shop, my stomach tightens for the

crying little girl in the produce aisle who has gotten separated from her mother, but I wheel my carriage apologetically, silently, past her. Some woman, I reason, will fix things. My fear of being misconstrued as an abductor overrules my desire to help. Jogging through downtown after hours, I am uncomfortable approaching solitary walking women from behind. I clear my throat, make my steps thud, steer a wide loop out into the road, hoping to avoid surprise. I can detect from their body language just when these women realize I'm behind them: purses are clutched, shoulders curl forward, backs go tense. I'd like to apologize as I pass, but for what? For whom?

(6) Shortly after that snowstorm, my wife received a request to serve on the regional Battered Women's Advisory Board. We shared the feeling that her participation was important—a small, helpful thing; some people doing *something*. "Wish me luck," she said as she went off to her first meeting. At the front door I waved goodbye, then turned back into the house, looking for Jared. He was at the kitchen table drawing peacocks. I pulled up a kitchen chair; I hadn't planned the game I made him play. "What if a strange man drove up to you in a car on your way home from school and said, 'Get in! Your parents are hurt and I'm taking you to the hospital.' What would you do?"

(7) He put down his marker and looked at me. His smoky blue eyes had never been this round. He waited for the answer.

"You don't get in the car," I said.

The drill continued through several variations. The driver's dialogue changed, and he became men we know.

"The guy who shingled Grandpa's roof?"

"I don't get in the car."

"Mr. Andrews down the street?"

"I don't get in the car."

After a while, Jared returned to the peacocks, but I continued to play. He answered without looking up, the game having become too predictable. Whatever my question, he knew the answer. I wish I did. Maybe we've all been Michael Rossed.

(8) The last of the girls that Michael Ross killed was Wendy Baribeault, a student at our high school who was abducted by Ross on the first day of summer vacation in June 1984. I hadn't known Wendy, so her murder was a tragic nonreality for me until the following September when three of her closest friends materialized in one of my senior English classes. They were more three walking open wounds than they were students; they took tests and read assignments and attended proms, going through the motions with zombie-like indifference. "Talk about it," I encouraged them. "Write about your fears and your anger and your friend. Sometimes it helps to put it down on paper and hand it to someone."

(9) Lisa was the first to take my advice. She described how, on the day Wendy's body was discovered, she wrapped herself in her great-grandmother's quilt and stayed curled up in her bed, immobilized. Susan resisted writing until half the school year was over, then one day handed in a 12-page outpouring that sent tears down my face and made me grieve for Wendy in a way I hadn't before. What haunted her, Susan wrote, was what Wendy must have been thinking about her life as the crime was happening, as the end was becoming inevitable.

(10) The following spring I received a letter from Susan, then a college freshman. She was writing, she explained, because it was Wendy's birthday; her friend would have been 19. "For months I shut off the pain when it got to be too much. And by denying myself those emotions, the pain only multiplied. . . . Writing that paper was one of my biggest accomplishments. I've carried it with me to college and read it whenever I'm losing ground." I keep Susan's letter in a box of important papers. What amazes me about it is her impulse to have made of her hurt and fear a present—to have written the letter, affixed a stamp and sent it off despite what the world had taught her. It's one of the rarest gifts I've ever received.

(11) "The Advisory Board is going on a field trip today," my wife tells me, pulling on her coat and hat. "We're going to tour the house they're renovating for the battered women's shelter."

"Where is it?" I ask her.

She gets that look, the one I'd seen on Amy. "I'm not allowed to tell you. It's confidential—one of the rules. The women and their kids have to feel it's safe." At the front door I watch her back out into the street and drive off to her secret place. Every adult male is an adult male stranger.

Reading Survey

1. MAIN IDEA

What is the central theme of this essay?

2. MAJOR DETAILS

a. What incident first made Wally Lamb realize that some people see him as a stranger to be feared?
b. How did Lamb try to help Wendy Baribeault's three close friends?
c. What was the "secret place" that Lamb's wife was going to visit?

3. INFERENCES

a. Read paragraph 5 again. What message are the women sending with their body language?
b. Read paragraph 7 again. What does Lamb mean when he says, "Maybe we've all been Michael Rossed"?

4. OPINIONS

a. Do you agree with Lamb that "every adult male is an adult male stranger"? Explain.
b. What specific actions can be taken to reduce the number of violent crimes committed in the United States?

Vocabulary Building

Lesson one: ***The Vocabulary of a Violent Society, Part I***

The essay "The Shadow of a Stranger" by Wally Lamb includes words that are useful when you are discussing our violent society.

grim (paragraph 1)
benignly (2)
oblivious (3)
raucous (3)
heckling (3)
pervert (3)
hostility (5)
misconstrued (5)
abductor (5)
battered (6)

In a violent society, some people feel that the high crime rate has made life very **grim**—cruel, harsh, and extremely unpleasant.

In a violent society, some people are afraid of any stranger, even one who smiles at them **benignly**—in a gentle, kindly, and harmless way.

In a violent society, people who are **oblivious** to their surroundings—who pay no attention to what is going on around them—can become easy targets for criminals.

In a violent society, some people are afraid of strangers who are **raucous**—making loud and disorderly noises.

In a violent society, some people resort to **heckling**—the use of annoying remarks publicly to embarrass and insult—to scare away a possible criminal.

In a violent society, some people are afraid of being attacked by a **pervert**—a person whose sexual practices are different from what is generally considered normal or proper.

In a violent society, some people openly display **hostility**—active expressions of unfriendliness, anger, or hatred toward others.

In a violent society, some people have been attacked by a person who **misconstrued**—misunderstood or incorrectly interpreted—what they said.

In a violent society, some people are afraid of being attacked by an **abductor,** a person who kidnaps or unlawfully takes away someone by force.

In a violent society, some people are injured by being **battered**—beaten up or struck repeatedly—by a family member or someone else the victim knows.

EXERCISE 12A: Using the vocabulary words in this lesson, fill in the blanks.

1. The comedian refused to allow the audience's ________________ to annoy or embarrass him.
2. In some cities, ________________ between people of different races has led to violence.
3. Last Friday my wife and I both lost our jobs; it was certainly a ________________ day.
4. The ________________ demanded $1 million for the safe return of the kidnapped company chief executive officer.
5. The police broke up the ________________ party because the noise was disturbing the neighbors.
6. The coastline has been ________________ by several severe storms that have uprooted trees, knocked down power lines, and destroyed homes.
7. Students who listen to Walkman radios in class are usually ________________ to what is being taught.
8. The job supervisor insists that his secretary has ________________ his friendliness as sexual harassment.
9. The judge ordered the ________________ to seek psychiatric treatment because his sexual practices were not considered normal.
10. After being awakened by a frightening noise, I was relieved to discover that it was caused by a window shade rattling ________________ in the breeze.

Lesson Two: The Vocabulary of a Violent Society, Part II

Here are more words from the essay "The Shadow of a Stranger" by Wally Lamb that are useful when you are discussing our violent society.

capital punishment (paragraph 1)
forged (2)
dawdler (2)
indulgence (3)
inaccessibility (4)
solitary (5)
indifference (8)
immobilized (9)
inevitable (9)
confidential (11)

In a violent society, some people think that **capital punishment**—the death penalty—is justified for anyone who commits a very serious crime such as murder.

In a violent society, some people are angry because government leaders have not yet **forged**—formed, produced, or shaped—an effective plan for reducing crime.

In a violent society, some people accuse every government leader of being a **dawdler**—a person who wastes time by being lazy or deliberately slow—when fighting crime.

In a violent society, some people feel that light sentences are an **indulgence**—an act of giving in to someone's wishes because of a weak will or an easygoing nature—that encourages criminal behavior.

In a violent society, some people use burglar alarms and bars on windows to guarantee their **inaccessibility**—the state of being beyond reach or unapproachable.

In a violent society, some people prefer a **solitary** existence—being alone—because they fear being attacked if they go out.

In a violent society, some people complain that the police respond to most crimes with **indifference**—an attitude that shows a lack of concern, interest, or feeling.

In a violent society, some people become **immobilized**—unable to move—when they fear being attacked by an approaching stranger.

In a violent society, some people feel that a continued rise in the crime rate is **inevitable**—not avoidable and, therefore, certain to happen.

In a violent society, some people try to protect themselves from criminals by keeping business affairs and travel plans **confidential**—private or secret.

EXERCISE 12B: Using the vocabulary words in this lesson, fill in the blanks.

1. Every day beggars on the street face the ________________ of people who have no interest in helping the poor.
2. During sixteen years of marriage, my husband and I have ________________ a relationship based on love, honesty, trust, and respect.
3. Because the government is deeply in debt, a large tax increase is ________________.
4. The mountain climber was determined to reach the top of Mount Everest because she felt challenged by its ________________.
5. Some experts claim that ________________ stops people from committing serious crimes.
6. Under the Freedom of Information Act, U.S. citizens have the right to see files of information that the federal government kept ________________ for many years.

7. If you want to keep your weight down, then eating a hot fudge sundae is an ________________ you cannot afford.
8. Prisoners who cause trouble may be placed in ________________ confinement, where they must remain alone for several days or weeks at a time.
9. My boss fired me because he said I was a ________________ who wasted too much time making personal telephone calls.
10. Using a tranquilizer dart, the zookeeper ________________ an elephant that needed medical attention.

SPELLING

Spelling Rule—Doubling

Many of the words in Wally Lamb's essay can be learned easily with the help of this simple spelling rule.

When a suffix is added to a word, the final consonant of the word is doubled if the word meets all of these three tests:

1. The suffix begins with a vowel.
2. The word ends with a single vowel followed by a consonant.
3. The word is one syllable or has its accent on the last syllable.

TRY IT OUT

ADD THE SUFFIXES INDICATED TO THE FOLLOWING WORDS.

	-ing	*-ed*	*-ment*
commit	________________	________________	________________
prefer	________________	________________	________________
command	________________	________________	________________

Here are some examples.

begin + ing = begi*nn*ing
hot + est = ho*tt*est
cost + ing = cos*t*ing
drop + ed = dro*pp*ed
forget + ful = forge*t*ful
happen + ed = happe*n*ed

TRY IT OUT

APPLY THE DOUBLING RULE TO THE FOLLOWING WORDS.

sad + en = ____________________
ship + ment = ____________________
permit + ing = ____________________
war + ior = ____________________
drug + ist = ____________________
slip + ery = ____________________
favor + able = ____________________
begin + er = ____________________
insist + ed = ____________________
fit + ness = ____________________
big + est = ____________________
ocur + ence = ____________________

EXERCISE 12C: Apply the doubling rule to these words.

1. bit + en = ____________________
2. chop + ed = ____________________
3. transfer + al = ____________________
4. heat + er = ____________________
5. put + ing = ____________________
6. control + able = ____________________
7. confer + ence = ____________________
8. strip + ed = ____________________
9. thin + est = ____________________
10. open + ing = ____________________
11. rebel + ious = ____________________
12. sharp + est = ____________________
13. forgot + en = ____________________
14. benefit + ed = ____________________
15. run + ing = ____________________
16. win + er = ____________________
17. rob + ery = ____________________
18. beg + ar = ____________________
19. neat + ness = ____________________
20. admit + ed = ____________________

 The Descriptive Essay

Whenever you are engaged in a conversation with a friend, you probably find yourself describing the people, places, and events that have touched your life in some way. You might be describing a weird-looking man you passed in the street, a great restaurant you ate at last night, or a rock concert you recently attended. If the description contains many specific details, your friend should be able to form a clear mental picture of what you have experienced.

Description is also an essential ingredient in an effective piece of writing. For example, in a school course you may be asked to write an essay describing a piece of art, a lab experiment, or the main characters in a novel. To write a good descriptive essay, be sure to follow these guidelines.

- **I Use Sensory Details.**
- **II Use Comparisons.**
- **III Create a Strong Overall Impression, Feeling, or Attitude About the Subject.**

I. Use Sensory Details. Readers should almost be able to see, hear, smell, taste and touch what you are writing about. For example, compare these two descriptions of pizza.

The pizza served at Tony's Pizzeria is good.

The pizza served at Gino's Pizzeria has a thin, crunchy crust smothered with mozzarella cheese and spicy tomato sauce, as well as a generous sprinkling of garlic and oregano.

After reading these descriptions, most people would probably prefer to eat at Gino's because the sensory details create a strong image of delicious pizza.

Before writing a descriptive essay, you should use brainstorming to generate the necessary details. Start by drawing five columns on a wide sheet of paper, and then label each column with one of the senses: sight, sound, smell, taste, touch. Next, try to fill as many of the columns as possible with specific sensory details. This method will encourage you to use several of the senses when you write.

TRY IT OUT

ON YOUR OWN PAPER, DRAW FIVE COLUMNS AND THEN LABEL EACH COLUMN WITH ONE OF THE FIVE SENSES: SIGHT, SOUND, SMELL, TASTE, TOUCH. NEXT, FILL IN AS MANY OF THE COLUMNS AS POSSIBLE WITH SPECIFIC SENSORY DETAILS DESCRIBING YOUR ENGLISH CLASSROOM. FINALLY, COMPARE YOUR DETAILS WITH THOSE GENERATED BY YOUR CLASSMATES.

II. Use Comparisons. Sometimes the most effective way to describe something is to compare it to something that is similar. Notice how the examples below provide strong sensory images.

The filthy dog smelled like a garbage dump.
My sister's voice sounds like the screech of chalk on a blackboard.
The setting sun looked like a scoop of orange sherbet.

TRY IT OUT

COMPLETE EACH OF THE FOLLOWING DESCRIPTIONS WITH A COMPARISON.

1. A cloud looks like ______________________________
2. My toothpaste tastes like ______________________________
3. The music in the dance club sounds like ____________________

III. Create a Strong Overall Impression, Feeling, or Attitude About the Subject. This dominant impression is the general feeling or emotional response that you want the reader to be left with after finishing your essay. The dominant impression gives your essay a focus. Notice how the focus is different in each of the three sentences below.

My home is a very comfortable place to live.
My home should be condemned by the Board of Health.
My home reflects my interests and personality.

Once you have decided on the dominant impression for your subject, you must be careful to develop your essay with only the sensory details that will support that impression. For example, if you are writing about your home being a comfortable place to live, you might describe the tan leather couch with the overstuffed cushions and the red brick fireplace. However, if you are trying to show why your home should be condemned by the Board of Health, you might describe the five-foot-high stack of old newspapers in the living room and the black mold on the bathroom walls.

TRY IT OUT

WHICH OF THE SENSORY DETAILS LISTED BELOW WOULD SUPPORT THE THESIS STATEMENT?

THESIS STATEMENT: MY UNCLE TED IS A VERY STRANGE MAN.

Sensory details:

1. He has a Mohawk haircut.
2. He does volunteer work for the Red Cross.
3. He collects traffic signs and parking meters.
4. He is six feet tall and weighs about 180 pounds.
5. He runs in the Boston Marathon every year.
6. He has a tattoo on his arm that says, “This property is condemned.”

The Pointers for Writing a Descriptive Essay chart on the next page provides some additional guidelines for writing an effective descriptive essay. Following this chart are three model essays.

An essay describing a person

An essay describing a place

An essay describing an object

Be sure to read these essays, for they will help to give you a clear understanding of how to write a good descriptive essay of your own.

POINTERS FOR WRITING A DESCRIPTIVE ESSAY

1. The *introduction* should identify your subject and state your dominant impression about that subject. What is your overall attitude or feeling about your subject?
2. The *main body paragraphs* should include specific details that appeal to the five senses: sight, sound, smell, taste, and touch. The reader should be able to see the person, place or object you are describing.

   If you are describing a *person*, you should include not only a physical description but also a description of the person's character traits as seen through specific actions or behaviors. In addition, you may quote something that the person has said if it provides some insight into the individual's personality.

   If you are describing a *place*, you should describe specific objects found in that place that help to contribute to the dominant impression that you want to create.

   If you are describing an *object*, you should include not only its size, shape, and color but also, if appropriate, the way it sounds, smells, tastes, and feels when you touch it. In addition, describe your emotional reaction to what you are describing.
3. The *order* in which the details are presented should be logical so that the reader will have no trouble creating a clear mental image. The most useful types of order are these:

   Location: You might describe your subject from the top to the bottom, from the right to the left, from the nearest to the farthest, or from the farthest to the nearest.

   Importance: You might start by describing the least important details, move on to the more important details, and then end with the most important details. Or you may reverse this order by starting with the most important details and ending with the least important.

   Time: You might describe what you see as you move through a place, or you might describe changes that occur in your subject over a period of time.
4. The *conclusion* should make clear why you selected the particular subject for your description. In writing this paragraph, you might consider questions such as these: Has this subject had some special importance in your life? Has this subject changed your thinking about some aspect of life? Has this subject given you a better understanding of other people or of yourself? Has this subject influenced an important decision in your life? Does this subject have some special meaning just for you and no one else?

An Essay Describing a Person. The essay below includes not only a physical description of a person but also a description of his character traits as seen through specific actions and behaviors.

Working with Mitch

(1) Mornings, I attend classes at Wyandotte Community College. Afternoons and all day Saturday, I work on the "deli team" at Bargain Planet, a twenty-acre discount store that carries everything from live lobsters to garage-door openers. Quite a few college students take jobs at The Planet because it's only fifteen minutes from campus, and the wages and opportunities for promotion are significantly better than at any of the fast-food chains. However, instead of making the best of a good deal, most of my fellow students use their spare energy complaining about the senior citizen on our team, Mitch Vranich, a 74-year-old retired welder. "The old coot," they call him. I, on the other hand, admire Mitch and consider him my friend. In fact, I have adopted him as a role model.

(2) Mitch is still a strong man, and he is a hard worker. From the time he walks in and replaces his white United Health Plans baseball cap with his orange Planet Deli cap, he keeps busy, often taking on the heavier work that some of the younger team members shamelessly avoid. With his bear-paw hands and his long, muscular arms, he almost flips the eighty-pound cartons of Polish hams from the conveyor onto neat, six-foot-high stacks in the walk-in storage cooler. When he is sorting the five-gallon buckets of potato, macaroni, or bean salad, he jerks them from the floor four at a time, like a weightlifter in training. After six or seven loads, he's puffing a little and his knees make creaking noises as he squats and lifts. "Too much of this," he explains, tapping the aluminum cigar case jutting out of his frayed back pocket like a flagpole. "Bad habit." He always finishes his lunch-meat slicing in half the time it takes other team members and then uses his extra time to "get some exercise," as he puts it, putting heavy cartons and crates of food where they belong. Some of the younger team members think Mitch is trying to show them up, but it looks to me as if he just takes pride in doing a job right and keeping the deli organized. Mitch has self-respect; he won't let his co-workers down.

(3) Whether he is behind the counter taking customers' orders or helping out in the kitchen, Mitch is always sociable. He asks questions and really listens to people's answers. "Windbag" and "know-it-all" are a couple of the kinder terms I have heard applied to him by some team members, but I think Mitch sincerely tries to be helpful. He greets many of the regular customers by name, often advising them intelligently about which meats, cheeses, or salads to purchase. "Ever tried this sausage in spaghetti sauce?" he asks in his gravelly, booming voice. With his tobacco-stained mustache and his shrunken, staring left eye, he won't be photographed for any of Bargain Planet's huge customer service posters, but people often pass up their rightful turn so that Mitch can wait on them. Maybe some of the younger team members resent his popularity with

customers, but I don't see why they are offended by the innocent questions he asks us about our schoolwork, career plans, or leisure-time activities. The man just enjoys a good conversation. As for me, if I am Windexing counter glass or sweeping up shredded lettuce, I look forward to Mitch's whack on my back and "How's the astronomy coming?" It's getting to be a relief when he's on my shift.

(4) Of the many interesting things I've learned about Mitch, the one that surprised and impressed me the most is how well-read he is. On his breaks, even in the winter, he sits in his rusty little pickup in the parking lot poring over a fat paperback, a ballpoint pen propped on his ear. And the books aren't checkout line thrillers, either. He favors classic novels, philosophy, and history, and the pen is for copying passages from them to "meditate on," as he puts it. Sometimes he uses big words, too. The other day, he referred to himself as the "ubiquitous" Serb. I looked the word up when I got home. When he lost most of the vision in his left eye in a bungled cataract operation, he was afraid that he would not be able to read, but luckily one eye is sufficient. Lately, with my two good eyes, I have been trying on Mitch's habit. I read before I go to bed, and at Bargain Planet the next day, I find that ideas from my books do run through my mind. I wonder if I might be "meditating."

(5) I am sure very few of the deli team members even know that Mitch reads a lot, or notice that he uses unusual words now and then. Literacy is not a quality others can actually see in a person. The more I think about it, though, the more I believe that his hard physical labor, his interest in other people, and his serious reading are all part of Mitch's ongoing program of self-improvement. At 74, he is still eager to learn. I would be proud to have people say the same about me when I am his age.

TRY IT OUT

ANSWER THESE QUESTIONS ABOUT THE ESSAY "WORKING WITH MITCH."

1. According to the introduction, what dominant impression of Mitch is the writer trying to create? ____________________
2. According to the body paragraphs, what are the three main reasons the writer admires Mitch? ____________________

   ____
3. In paragraph 2, the writer uses two comparisons to create strong sensory images. What are they? ____________________

   ____
4. According to the conclusion, how has Mitch influenced the writer? ____

   ____

An Essay Describing a Place. In the essay below, the writer has chosen to describe only those objects that help to contribute to the dominant impression of his grandparents' bedroom.

My Grandparents' Bedroom

(1) In the late 1940's, when I was 5 or 6 years old, my parents and I lived with my grandparents in the Williamsburg section of Brooklyn. Although their apartment in this turn-of-the-century building had four and a half rooms, the room I remember most vividly is my grandparents' bedroom, for the warmth and safety of this room played an important role in my understanding of life.

(2) Looking out one of the crystal-clear windows, I was able to see across Grand Street Extension and try to read what was playing at the RKO Republic movie theater. From the other window I could see the rust-spotted fire escape with the huge brown and tan clay jug in which my grandfather would ferment grape juice into wine. The room itself, although appearing gigantic to a tot, was actually quite small. It probably was larger before all of the coats of paint were applied over each other during the almost fifty-year history of the room. The shiny tan paint had a permanent series of smooth cracks in it like the cracks one sees in old oil paintings hanging in museums. The walls looked as if they were covered with lace even before the paint had a chance to dry. The linoleum flooring, with its rich earth tones of browns and greens, seemed perfectly in harmony with nature, despite the fact that it looked shiny and felt cold when I walked on it with my bare feet.

(3) Dark mahogany furniture dominated the room. Each afternoon, though, the sun would bring the wood alive, and the reds would appear lurking in with the browns. On the cream lace cloth that covered the top of my grandparents' dresser was a picture of some dear old relatives who were left behind in the old country. In the center of the dresser was a comb, brush, and hand mirror set, each piece made of tortoise shell and decorated with intricate silver lacework. Only recently did it occur to me why my grandfather, who was a carpenter, built a large wooden cabinet to stand near the door. There was no other closet in the room. Although my grandparents had little of earthly value, my grandfather built a secret compartment into the floor of the cabinet into which he put items such as old photographs, the family's Russian passports, their prized U.S. citizenship papers, and a small sack of soil from the Holy Land. Years later, half of the soil was thrown onto my grandfather's grave and the remaining soil was saved for my grandmother's grave.

(4) To me, the most fantastic piece of furniture in the room was the bed. It had a five-foot-tall mahogany headboard in the shape of a half moon with a wide band of deeply carved cabbage roses running close to the outer edge. The bed looked so big to me that I saw climbing onto it as a challenge. On cold mornings, I would climb into that bed and get between my grandpar-

ents, who were wearing their flannel pajamas and who seemed to be radiating more heat than a blazing fireplace. Although the mattress was soft, it felt as if it had craters, and the bed made a slight sighing sound each time someone moved. Perhaps the most amazing feature of this bed, however, was the great creamy white goose-down comforter that covered us. It seemed to me to be at least as thick as the mattress and twice as heavy. No one ever felt safer or more secure and comfortable than I felt lying there in the warmth between these two loving people. Nothing bad could ever happen to me.

(5) Although I felt completely safe and comfortable in the bed with my grandparents, I somehow knew the feeling could not last forever. As I grew older, the bed, the down comforter—and even my grandparents—seemed to become smaller and smaller. Eventually I realized that the warm, comfortable safety of the bed had to give way to more realistic, mature feelings. It became clear that the warmth and comfort provided a temporary physical safety, and as I grew older and experienced more and more of life, I came to realize that children experience all types of security such as emotional and financial in a physical way. The warmth and softness is all of the safety and security they seem to need. Even now as an adult, when I am overcome with fears and anxieties, I can still close my eyes and return to the comfort and safety of my grandparents' bedroom.

TRY IT OUT

ANSWER THESE QUESTIONS ABOUT THE ESSAY "MY GRANDPARENTS' BEDROOM."

1. According to the introduction, what dominant impression of the bedroom is the writer trying to create? ____________________

   ____

2. What order does the writer use to present the sensory details? ________

   ____

3. In paragraph 4, the writer uses the senses of touch and sound to describe part of the bed. What does he say? ____________________

   ____

4. According to the conclusion, the bedroom helped the writer gain a better understanding of children. What did the writer learn? __________

   ____

An Essay Describing an Object. The essay below includes not only a wealth of sensory details but also the writer's emotional reaction to what she is describing.

My Old Bug

(1) This year's Volkswagens look so shiny and new compared to the '79 model that I still drive. Both models have that ladybug shape, but the new ones have so much headroom that you could put in a loft; mine is a head-conking menace for friends over six feet, two inches tall. They tell me it's time to trade the old clunker in, but what my friends refuse to understand is the value this car has to me. The history of my life is banged, burned, and torn into the body of this old bug.

(2) The outside of the car is a murky underwater kind of greenish-blue that is not normally seen on cars, but it's not the color that makes the paint job odd; it's the texture. Lumpy, grainy, and bumpy, it's what auto body professionals call "orange peel." When I couldn't afford a paint job, my friend J.D. offered to try out his new equipment on my car for free. J.D. went out of the car-painting business two months later; the last I heard, he was driving a truck. A man once pulled up to me in a gas station and said, "Hey, I work on cars. I can fix your paint job for cheap." I politely said, "No," and as he drove off I noticed that his car was patched up with so much Bondo that there was more patch than paint. Even *he* thought my car looked bad. Check out the rusty, crumpled spot in the right rear fender. It came from a roommate backing into the landlord's brand-new deck. My roommate had had a few drinks, but I didn't have the gumption to say, "No, you can't drive my car." Some of my car's flaws remind me of the lessons I've learned.

(3) Under the rear hood is the very loud engine that the old VW's came with. My friends claim that from a block away they can hear my car coming, sounding like a sewing machine hooked up to a megaphone. I don't know much about engines, but I recognize a few crucial parts. Poking up on the left is a metal hoop that looks like a big curtain ring. That's the top of the dipstick, which is used to check the oil. A sweetheart showed me how to check my oil and then patiently taught me how to crawl underneath and drain it when it needed changing. It was a dirty job, but his calm patience made me not mind it. To the right of the dipstick is the carburetor, on top of which are the spark plug wires. The spark plugs work fine most of the time, but unfortunately, the wires are right under a row of open slats in the hood. The slats were made for cooling the engine, but when it rains, they funnel the water inside, shorting out the electrical system—a technical way of saying that the car won't start. Since I can't afford to call a mechanic every time it rains, I keep under the front hood my special mechanic's repair kit: a hair dryer on a long extension cord. When the car won't start, I just find a place to plug in my hair dryer and

dry out the spark plug wires, and the car cranks up. Who else has a car that she can blow-dry?

(4) Finally, there's the inside. The upholstery doesn't match the outside: It's the kind of dull gray-blue that normal cars have, not nearly as interesting as J.D.'s underwater shade. Hanging down from the roof is the piece of headliner that tore loose when I was moving into my first apartment and couldn't afford a moving van; my coffee table wasn't a very good fit for the back seat. The scent of mint air freshener doesn't quite cover up the musty odor of mildew that accumulated before I figured out how to fix the window—with clothespins. When the metal carriage supporting the window glass on the driver's side rusted out, the sweetheart of the oil change helped me reattach it using clothespins and glue. On the passenger's side, the door handle is permanently stuck. The first time it happened was a close call. I was driving my pregnant sister to the hospital while she was in premature labor. Unable to get out on her side of the car, she needed the help of two hospital orderlies to lift her over the steering wheel so that she could get out on my side. My car came close to serving as an emergency delivery room. On the floor next to the foot pedals is a rubber mat with a close-up view of the ground underneath. When the floorboards started to rust out, the resulting gap provided the car with this special backup ventilation system in case the window repair job ever fails. Also on the floor is a whitish line, otherwise known as a water stain, courtesy of a not-so-patient boyfriend who drove us into a swamp on a dare from a smart aleck with a four-wheel drive. Soon after this incident, that particular boyfriend and I parted company.

(5) My image would be so much classier if I had a newer car, one that ran all the time. But my '79 VW isn't just paid for. It carries around in it large chunks of my heart, and its dings and dents are hard-earned reminders of lessons I keep trying to learn. So my friends will just have to keep tucking their heads down, and we'll move furniture in somebody else's car. I'm sentimental. Because memories will always be more important to me than glamour or prestige, I'll continue to drive my old bug just as long as it continues to go.

TRY IT OUT

ANSWER THESE QUESTIONS ABOUT THE ESSAY "MY OLD BUG."

1. According to the introduction, what dominant impression of the Volkswagen is the writer trying to create? ______________________

____

2. What order does the writer use to present the sensory details? ________

____

3. In paragraph 3, the writer uses two comparisons to create strong sensory images. What are they? ______________________

____

4. In paragraph 4, the writer uses the sense of smell to help describe the inside of the car. What does she say? ______________________

____

5. In the conclusion, the writer explains why this car has some special meaning for her. What does she say? ______________________

____

EXERCISE 12D: For each sentence below, write five sensory details that would help a reader form a clear mental image of the subject. Be sure that the details support the dominant impression.

1. My bedroom is a mess.

____

____

____

____

____

2. A McDonald's Big Mac is a tasty sandwich.

____

____

____

____

____

3. The school cafeteria is noisy.

____

____

____

____

____

4. The last time I got sick I felt miserable.

____

____

____

____

____

5. The locker room at the gym is filled with a variety of strong odors.

____

____

____

____

____

6. Sitting in a new car is usually a comfortable experience.

7. The thunderstorm was frightening.

8. My English teacher is (is not) a good-looking person.

9. Being in a movie theater can stimulate all of the senses.

10. A Thanksgiving dinner at my house is usually delicious.

____

____

____

____

____

EXERCISE 12E: Follow the steps below to create a descriptive essay. You may choose one of the topics listed, or you may think of a different person, place, or object to describe.

Topics

a family member
an interesting friend
a teacher you will never forget
your boss
your neighborhood
your workplace
an amusement park
a dance club
a place that makes you feel good
a place that makes you feel horrible
a place that you see every day
an unforgettable place
your most important possession
a car that you have owned
a family photograph
your favorite pet

Steps

1. Select a specific topic for your essay.
2. Create a thesis statement that includes the dominant impression of the person, place, or object you are planning to describe.
3. Draw five columns on a wide sheet of paper, and then label each column with one of the five senses: sight, sound, smell, taste, touch. Next, use brainstorming to fill as many of the columns as possible with specific sensory details.
4. As you read through your lists of sensory details, cross out any details that do not support the dominant impression you want to convey.
5. Decide on a logical order for presenting the details in your essay. Will you use order of location, importance, or time?
6. Think about your conclusion. Why does this topic matter to you? What meaning does it have that you can share with the reader? Keep in mind that your sense of what matters may shift as you write, for good writing often

generates new ideas. However, starting out with a clear sense of your essay's purpose will help you select and organize your details.

7. You are now ready to write the first draft of your descriptive essay.
8. After completing the first draft of your essay, use the revision process described on pages 311–22 to help you achieve a successful descriptive essay.

The Narrative Essay

"Once upon a time. . . ." "Have you heard the story about the guy who . . .?" "You won't believe what just happened to me on the way home from school." Storytelling is one of the most basic forms of human communication. Every culture has stories that go far back into its history, and we are generating our own new stories every day.

In Chapter One, you learned how to use a story or incident to develop a topic sentence into a full paragraph. However, some stories will not fit into a single paragraph because they either are too long or involve a series of related events. These stories need to be told in a narrative essay. Here are some important guidelines for writing an effective narrative essay.

- I **Be Sure That Your Story Contains a Conflict.**
- II **Be Sure That Your Story Has a Point.**
- III **Use the Reporter's Questions to Develop Your Story Fully.**
- IV **Organize the Events of Your Story Logically.**
- V **Be Consistent in the Use of Verb Tenses.**

I. Be Sure That Your Story Contains a Conflict. An interesting narrative always deals with a conflict—a problem, a question, or a struggle between two forces—that is usually resolved by the end of the story. Will I be able to lie to my girlfriend without having her find out? Will I be able to forgive my parents for not telling me that I was adopted? Will I be able to survive a terrifying weekend in jail? Without a conflict, the story will be dull and boring.

II. Be Sure That Your Story Has a Point. The reader won't really care about your story unless it has a point. Did you learn an important lesson from this incident? Did it give you a better understanding of other people or of yourself? Did it change your thinking about some aspect of life? Did it influence an important decision in your life? Answering these questions will help you realize the true significance of your story. In each example below, notice how the writer makes a clear point.

I learned from my first heartbreak not to trust someone else more than I trust myself.

The experience of almost failing my history class broke down my arrogance by showing me how much I didn't know, and it built up my confidence by showing me how ready and able I am to learn.

III. Use the Reporter's Questions to Develop Your Story Fully. Before you start writing the first draft of your narrative essay, do some brainstorming to help you gather the details of your story. As you brainstorm, use the questions that reporters rely on when they write a news story: What happened? When did it happen? Where did it happen? Why did it happen? How did it happen? Who was involved? Answering all of these questions will help you develop your story fully.

Wherever possible, you should use specific details to describe the action so that the reader will be able to form a clear mental image of what happened. You may also include some dialogue that will help to bring the story to life.

TRY IT OUT

THINK OF AN INCIDENT THAT MADE YOU FEEL ANGRY, SHOCKED, OR EMBARRASSED. USE THE REPORTER'S QUESTIONS TO GATHER THE DETAILS OF THE INCIDENT. THEN ADD SPECIFIC DETAILS AND APPROPRIATE DIALOGUE TO HELP BRING THE STORY TO LIFE.

IV. Organize the Events of Your Story Logically. A good story has a rhythm. The reader has a clear sense of *beginning* (the writer is setting the scene for the story), *middle* (the story is getting complicated), and *end* (the story is resolved). In a five-paragraph essay, you can use the introduction to set up the situation, the body paragraphs to work your way through the conflict, and the conclusion to give the reader a sense of why it all matters.

You will find that chronological or time order is often the most effective method to use for arranging the details of your story. You start by telling what happened first, what happened next, and so on.

> I left for the bank with my rent money in my wallet. The subway was crowded, and the conductor kept announcing that we should be patient with the delays. I thought the young man who was crowding up close to me was just getting fresh, but when I got to the bank and opened my purse, my wallet was no longer there.

On the other hand, you may want to use the flashback technique and begin the story at the end.

> It was such a shock. As I was saying to the bank teller that I wanted to make a deposit, I opened my purse. Nothing was there! This is how it all happened. . . .

V. Be Consistent in the Use of Verb Tenses. When you are telling a story or incident that has already happened, be sure to keep all the verbs in the past tense. If the story suddenly shifts to the present tense, the reader will be confused. (For more information on verb tense consistency, see pages 211–13.)

TRY IT OUT

CORRECT ANY ERRORS IN VERB TENSE CONSISTENCY IN THE FOLLOWING STORY.

At about 10:30 last night, I was dragging myself home from work, looking forward to a good night's sleep. As I walked down dark, lonely Prospect Street, I began to hear footsteps behind me. When I look back over my shoulder, I see a tall, shadowy figure in a raincoat. Frightened, I start to increase my pace, but I can hear the person behind me again. He is getting closer. Although I was tired, I began to run as fast as I could. Then the stranger yelled, "Hey, miss! You dropped your umbrella a few blocks back."

The Pointers for Writing a Narrative Essay chart below provides some additional guidelines for writing an effective narrative essay. Following this chart are three model essays.

A narrative essay with a first-person point of view

A narrative essay with a flashback

A narrative essay with a third-person point of view

Be sure to read these essays, for they will help to give you a clear understanding of how to write a good narrative essay of your own.

POINTERS FOR WRITING A NARRATIVE ESSAY

1. The *introduction* should set the scene for your story and should include a thesis statement that explains the major purpose for telling the story. What point are you trying to make by telling this story?
2. The *body paragraphs* should present the story from a particular point of view.

(Continued)

(Continued)

First Person: You speak directly to the reader, using the pronoun *I* throughout the story ("My life changed forever when I . . ."). The first-person point of view creates a personal tone and allows you to express your innermost feelings.

Third Person: An unknown storyteller describes the action ("Mark's life changed forever when he . . ."). The third-person point of view creates a more objective tone and allows the writer to express the inner thoughts of all the participants in the story.

3. The *body paragraphs* should include all of the important information about the story: What happened? When did it happen? Where did it happen? Why did it happen? How did it happen? Who was involved? Wherever possible, describe the action by using specific details that will bring the story to life. You may also include some dialogue that moves the story along and is related to the main point.
4. The *order* in which you tell the details of the story should be appropriate for the major purpose. The most useful types of order for a narrative are these:

   Chronological Order: Chronological or time order describes what happened first, what happened next, and so on.

   Flashback Order: Flashback order often starts by describing what happened last and then moves back in time to describe what happened first, what happened next, and so on.
5. To help the reader follow the story, use appropriate *transitions* that signal time order: *first, second, last, finally, then, next, soon, meanwhile, later, eventually, before, during, after, now, afterward.*
6. The *conclusion* should explain the importance of the particular story. In writing this paragraph, you might consider questions such as these: Did this incident change your thinking about some aspect of life? Did this incident give you a better understanding of other people or of yourself? Did this incident influence an important decision in your life? Does this incident have some special meaning just for you and no one else? What general lesson or observation about life did you gain from this incident?

A Narrative Essay with a First-Person Point of View. The writer speaks directly to the reader, using the pronoun *I* throughout the story. In the essay below, the first-person point of view creates a personal tone and allows the writer to express his innermost feelings.

The Family Secret

(1) I come from a small family, just my parents and one sister, who is sixteen years older than I am. Whenever people wondered why my mother waited so long to have a second child, she would explain that I was a "change of life" baby that God blessed her with when she was in her forties. Perhaps because I came along when my parents were middle-aged, they were especially generous with their love and support, and when I married they quickly accepted my new wife as a member of the family. With all the talk those days about dysfunctional families, I always considered myself to be lucky to have these two wonderful people as parents. Then one day I discovered a long-hidden secret that would tear my family apart.

(2) It all started when my wife and I decided to take a trip to Colombia so that we could introduce our nine-month-old daughter to my wife's family. Because I had never traveled out of the country before, I did not yet have a passport. So I picked up a passport application at the local post office, stopped at a camera shop to have my passport photograph taken, and then went to my parents' home to get my birth certificate. I assumed that my mother had put it away in a safe place, but she said that she had no idea where it was. However, she felt certain that the government would accept my baptismal certificate as proof of my U.S. citizenship. She was wrong. When I took all the paperwork to the post office the next day, the clerk told me that the baptismal certificate would not do. I would have to get a copy of my birth certificate.

(3) The following day I left work a little early so that I could go to the Hall of Records across from City Hall. I filled out the necessary form, handed it in at the appropriate window, and waited until my name was called almost an hour later. As I walked away from the window with my new birth certificate, I started to read it and suddenly gasped. I felt as if I had just been kicked in the stomach. In the space on the document where it asked for the name of the birth mother, there was my sister's name. In the space for the name of the birth father, it simply said, "unknown." Shocked and confused, I stood in the middle of the records office reading this information over and over again for the next several minutes. Then I realized that my body was beginning to shake and tears were welling up in my eyes. To avoid embarrassment, I ran out of the office and down the hall to the men's room, where I hid in one of the stalls until I managed to calm myself down.

(4) After leaving the Hall of Records, I took the subway to my parents' home to clear up my confusion. As the train traveled towards Queens, I told myself repeatedly that the birth certificate had to be wrong. However, when I later

showed the document to my parents, my father immediately said to my mother, "I told you something like this would happen." So it was true! My sister was really my mother; my parents were really my grandparents; my two nephews were really my half-brothers. I quickly exploded with a flood of angry words and then headed for the door as my mother tried to explain that times were different when I was born. Next I headed for my sister's home. When she answered the door, I could tell from the look on her face that she knew why I was there. Instead of inviting me into the house, she came outside. As we walked down the block, she told me that she had become pregnant by a high school boyfriend when she was fifteen years old and that her mother had come up with the solution that was going to be best for everyone. A few years after my birth, my real father died in an automobile accident without ever knowing that he had a son. As we reached the corner, my sister began to cry uncontrollably and I found myself trying to comfort her: "It's okay. It wasn't your fault. You were just a kid."

(5) Since discovering the family secret almost two years ago, I have been trying my best to forgive my parents (or should I say grandparents?) for having made some bad decisions, for not being perfect. But right now we have a very uneasy relationship. I hope that with time I will be able to forgive them, just as I hope that when my daughter grows up, she will be able to forgive me for the mistakes that I have made as a parent.

TRY IT OUT

ANSWER THESE QUESTIONS ABOUT THE ESSAY "THE FAMILY SECRET."

1. In the introduction, what is the writer's thesis statement? ___________

   ____

2. What conflict does the writer deal with in his story? ___________

   ____

3. In the body paragraphs, what order does the writer use to arrange the details of his story? How does the topic of each paragraph contribute to that order? ___________

   ____

4. According to the conclusion, what lesson about life did the writer learn from this incident? ___________

   ____

A Narrative Essay with a Flashback. Flashback order often starts by describing what happened last and then moves back in time to describe what happened first, what happened next, and so on. However, in the essay below, the writer has chosen to start in the middle of his story and then move back in time.

Man Versus Himself

(1) As I leaned up against the cold metal wall, I looked at the seat I was sitting on; it was cold, rusty, and dirty. I then directed my attention to the dark gray, gum-stained floor, which six or seven men were using as a bed. The cell couldn't have been bigger than fifty feet on a side, and there must have been at least twenty people in it. Looking through the cell doors, all I could see through the bars was a brick wall with the inscription "Central Holding Area, NYC Correctional Facility." All I could think was "Hell, I'm in hell!" It certainly did not occur to me at the time that this terrifying experience might teach me something about human behavior.

(2) As a 25-year-old looking back at how it all started, I now laugh at how young and naïve I was at 18. I hated school, I hated my parents, and I had no girlfriend. I thought my life was going nowhere, fast. The only respect I ever received was from my friends. All of them were crazy and angry, just like I was. The only thing that made me happy in those troubled times was graffiti. There was something about putting my name in paint up on a wall that made me feel important. As long as I got to write my name on someone's personal property, I was a happy guy. I wrote on churches, police cars, private homes; it didn't matter what. I went out every night, alone if I had to. I had a following of people who had heard who I was and showed me respect, respect that I felt I needed, earned, and deserved. I swore I would be doing this until the day I died, but I knew that one day I would be caught and that the police were going to enjoy it because I had written on more than ten squad cars, not to mention the precinct itself. I knew the police wanted me, but I didn't want to give them the satisfaction of giving up.

(3) It was now morning in the jail, roughly 6:00 a.m. I had to get arrested on a Friday night; the courts didn't open again until Monday morning. The guards were serving breakfast, if you could call it that. Breakfast consisted of a stale roll with an egg on it and perhaps a slice or two of bacon. I didn't want to eat anyway. The toilet was out in the open where everyone could see. With the guards noisily bringing people in every few hours, I had gotten only an hour of sleep the night before. The last guy they hauled in looked right in my eyes, grabbed me by the back of the head, and banged me right up against the wall. He then threw me off the bench. A few minutes later, a fellow named Brian, who looked as if he had just crawled out of a dumpster, told me that if I didn't fight for what's mine, everyone would take advantage, including him. As much as I thought of myself as a tough guy, I was truly scared.

When Brian asked me how I got in here, I told him it was an armed robbery charge; I lied to him in the hope of gaining some respect. The truth was simple and boring. I was writing on a wall when the police drove by. I would have gotten away if there had been only one squad car, but there were two. From the look on his face, Brian didn't seem too convinced by my armed robbery lie, but he left me alone.

(4) The second night was probably the worst night of my life. The cell stank of urine and God knows what else. Everyone kept staring at me. I think they were contemplating whether or not they wanted to fight me. I must have looked too pitiful to bother with because no one touched me and I actually fell asleep this time. I had continuous nightmares of a cell pressing down on me—like the way I had been squeezing the choices out of my own life. As the last nightmare woke me up, I noticed that I was lying in a puddle of my own sweat. Right at that moment I vowed I would change my life; I just hoped it wasn't too late. I kept pacing back and forth for probably more than an hour, until an inmate ran up to me and threw me against the wall, snarling that my constant pacing was making him nervous. Holding back tears, I stopped pacing and quickly found a seat. I sat motionless for at least seven or eight hours, thinking that the system had forgotten me and that I would be here for the rest of my life. But then a guard opened the cell and called several names, including mine. I was so happy that I ran out the door before anyone else. The guard chained three of us by our ankles and wrists and escorted us to a waiting cell, where I spent one more miserable day before being transported to the courthouse on Monday morning.

(5) You would think that my sentence on top of that experience would have cured me. The judge ruled a misdemeanor crime, punishable by seventy-five hours of community service, which required me to paint over my own graffiti. The police officer who was assigned to watch over me laughed every time I painted my walls over. It didn't bother me though; I figured it was all part of the rehabilitation process. However, the sad thing is that I actually continued to scribble on walls like a baby for another two years after my so-called wake-up call. Every time I put a spray can to a wall, I thought of that dreadful time. I remembered the vow I had made never to write on a wall again, but I continued to do so. Then one morning I woke up, got out of bed, looked in the mirror and said, "That's enough." To this day I have kept that promise. I now have a new life and new friends. I have opened my own business, I have a beautiful girlfriend with aspirations of marriage, and I have a great relationship with my parents. You would think that a terrifying wake-up call would have been enough to frighten me into turning my life around, but it wasn't. It took some time, it took some maturity that must have sneaked up on me when I wasn't looking, and it took some luck to stay alive until that happened.

TRY IT OUT

ANSWER THESE QUESTIONS ABOUT THE ESSAY "MAN VERSUS HIMSELF."

1. In the introduction, what is the writer's thesis statement? ______________________________

2. What conflict does the writer deal with in his story? ______________________________

3. How does the topic of each body paragraph contribute to the logical organization of the essay? ______________________________

4. According to the conclusion, what did the writer learn about himself from this incident? ______________________________

A Narrative Essay with a Third-Person Point of View. An unknown storyteller describes the action. The third-person point of view creates a more objective tone and allows the writer to express the inner thoughts of all the participants in the story.

Quiet Courage

(1) People tend to assume that their actions don't count beyond their own immediate home, school, or job. However, the story of one brave Southern lady demonstrates the difference that the actions of one individual can make. In the early 1950's, Rosa Parks was a seamstress, a wife, and a respected member of the Montgomery, Alabama, National Association for the Advancement of Colored People (NAACP). Outside her immediate community, this simple woman was unknown. Then on December 1, 1955, she took a quiet stand against injustice, a stand that changed the history of the United States.

(2) Rosa Parks' story took place against the background of a rigidly segregated South. Complicated laws regulated every sphere of life, including public transportation. Blacks riding the bus had to pay the driver, then get off and

reenter through the rear door. Drivers sometimes took off before the passengers could get to the back, an insult that Rosa Parks had experienced. Whites sat in the front and blacks in the back. If the white section of the bus was full and another white passenger got on, blacks had to give up their seats and move further back. On December 1, Rosa Parks boarded the bus, paid her fare, and sat down with three other blacks in the fifth row, the first row of the "colored section." After a few stops, the first four rows were filled, with one white man left standing. Since blacks and whites were not allowed to sit in the same row, the driver ordered all four blacks to give up their seats. The other three obeyed; Rosa Parks did not move. When the driver said he was going to have her arrested, she said, "You may go on and do so."

(3) Jailed, she turned to the local chapter of the NAACP for legal assistance. The civil rights movement was in its early days. Civil rights leaders had been looking for a test case to challenge the legality of segregation laws. They were waiting for the right person to be arrested: someone who was respected in the black community, who was willing to face the publicity and harassment of becoming a test case in court, and who was "above reproach." Rosa Parks was the upstanding person that the civil rights lawyers had been waiting for. She also was ready. As an outgrowth of her participation in the NAACP, earlier that year she had received training in nonviolent resistance at the Highlander School in Tennessee, a training center for social change. Following her arrest, Rosa was bailed out of jail by a white civil rights lawyer. With the support of her mother and husband, she quickly agreed to face the pressure that would come with a legal challenge. In a midnight meeting, the Women's Political Council mimeographed 35,000 handbills to be distributed to all black schools the next morning. The message was clear: "We are. . .asking every Negro to stay off the buses Monday in protest of the arrest and trial. . . .You can afford to stay out of school for one day. If you work, take a cab or walk. But please, children and grownups, don't ride the bus at all on Monday. Please stay off the buses Monday." Black ministers delivered the same message from the pulpit that Sunday.

(4) Montgomery was never to be the same. Despite bad weather that Monday, 90 percent of Montgomery's black population stayed off the buses. They either walked or caught a ride with the black cab drivers who stopped at city bus stops and charged just ten cents, the standard bus fare. As the boycott went on, people volunteered to run carpools, and churches bought station wagons, called rolling churches, to help people get to work. The boycott continued into 1956, in spite of harassment. Carpool drivers were arrested for picking up hitchhikers. Ten-cent cab rides were made illegal. Drivers were arrested on petty speeding offenses, and their liability insurance was canceled. Even with these obstacles, the boycott went on for over a year, taking a heavy economic toll on the city of Montgomery. Because the majority of city bus riders were black, white-owned businesses lost customers due to the lack of

transportation. By the end of the boycott 381 days later, many business owners were searching for ways to compromise.

(5) Local people did not have to make the decision; the Supreme Court made it for them. On November 13, 1956, segregation on public buses was ruled unconstitutional. On December 20, federal injunctions forced the Montgomery bus company to follow the Supreme Court's ruling. A news photo taken on December 21 shows Rosa Parks, who had never paid the $14 that she was fined for breaking the bus law, looking out the window of a municipal bus with a white man sitting in the row behind her. Although she was now a famous woman, she was still just an everyday bus rider, an ordinary citizen who had been brave enough to take a stand for what she believed was right.

TRY IT OUT

ANSWER THESE QUESTIONS ABOUT THE ESSAY "QUIET COURAGE."

1. In the introduction, what is the writer's thesis statement? ____________

   ____

2. What conflict does the writer describe in this story? ____________

   ____

3. How does the topic of each body paragraph contribute to the logical organization of the essay? ____________

   ____

4. According to the conclusion, why is this story important? ____________

   ____

EXERCISE 12F: Use the sentences below as the basis for an effective narrative essay. First, arrange the sentences in a logical order for a narrative. Next, eliminate any sentences that are not important for telling the story. Then add dialogue and specific details that will help the reader to visualize what happened. Finally, correct any verb tense errors so that the story is consistently in the past tense.

1. At that moment, I realized that my parents had deliberately locked me out of the house on the coldest night of the winter. How could they do that to me? Did they want me to freeze to death?
2. Fortunately, my friend Mike had his own place and would take me in for the rest of the night. I knew he would still be up because we had left the club at the same time.
3. Mike worked as a salesman in his father's store, the Carpet Emporium, and made a good living. I have known him since the fifth grade when we realized that we shared an interest in old movies.
4. When I was 18 years old, my parents taught me a painful lesson that helped me grow up.
5. One Saturday night as I was getting ready to go out to a club with my friends, my parents reminded me to be home by 1:00 a.m.
6. I argued that the club doesn't really get going until that hour, but my parents refused to listen.
7. While I was at the club, I ran into my old girlfriend, Laura. After talking for over an hour, we decided to give our relationship another try.
8. For several minutes there is no response, but I continue yelling with increasing urgency because of the bitter cold and howling wind. After almost ten minutes, a light finally goes on in my parents' bedroom. By this time, I am frozen.
9. My mother comes to the window, waves at me, and disappears back into the room. Then the light goes out!
10. When I returned home the next morning, I discovered that my parents had unlocked the door. I entered the house quietly, went up to my room, packed up all my belongings, and went back to my friend's place. My mother called me there several times, but I refused to speak to her.
11. At first, I enjoyed staying with my friend, but then I began to discover some of the harsh realities of life. I hated doing all the household chores. Even worse, I wasn't able to find a full-time job that paid enough to cover all my living expenses.

12. After almost a month of this eye-opening experience, I returned to my parents' home. Wiser and more mature, I was now ready to pursue a college education, a fulfilling career, and a better relationship with my parents.
13. As it turned out, I was having so much fun at the club that I lost track of the time and didn't get home until 5:30 a.m.
14. I walk up to the front door and use my key to unlock the bottom lock, but the door won't open because the top lock—the one with the little knob on the inside of the door—had been locked.
15. I start yelling up at the second-floor windows, which are the windows of my parents' bedroom.

EXERCISE 12G: Write a narrative essay describing an incident of some special importance in your life. You may select one of the topics listed, or you may think of a different story you would prefer to tell. Then follow the steps below to create your essay.

Topics

an incident that taught you something about yourself
an incident that taught you something about human behavior
an incident that changed your thinking about something
an incident that affected an important decision in your life
an incident that taught you a bitter lesson
an incident that helped you to grow up
an incident that made you realize how you wanted to live your life
an incident that has changed your relationship with a friend or relative
an incident that made you surprised or disappointed with how you acted
an incident that frightened you

Steps

1. Select a specific topic for your essay.
2. Create a thesis statement that explains the major purpose for telling the story.
3. To gather information for your essay, answer the reporter's questions: What happened? When did it happen? Where did it happen? Why did it happen? How did it happen? Who was involved?
4. To bring your incident to life, add appropriate dialogue, as well as details that appeal to the five senses: sight, sound, smell, taste, and touch.

5. As you read through the information you have gathered, cross out any details that are not important for telling your story.
6. Decide on a logical order for presenting the details of your story. Will you use chronological order or flashback order?
7. Think about your conclusion. Why is this story important to you? What meaning does it have that you can share with the reader? Keep in mind that your answers to these questions may change somewhat as you write, for good writing often generates new ideas. However, starting out with a clear sense of your essay's purpose will help you to select and organize your details.
8. You are now ready to write the first draft of your narrative essay.
9. After completing the first draft of your essay, use the revision process described on pages 311–22 to help you achieve a successful narrative essay.

The Example Essay

In your daily conversations, you probably rely heavily on examples to explain the general statements you make. For example, while you are having lunch with a friend, you start talking about your sister's recent wedding: "The reception was awful. I couldn't wait for it to end." Your friend seems surprised, so you explain: "The roast beef tasted like cardboard, the band was so loud I got a headache, and the hall had no air-conditioning on a really warm night." Because of these examples, your friend now understands why you did not enjoy the reception.

Using examples is also one of the most effective ways of explaining, clarifying, and proving the ideas contained in an essay. In fact, you will most likely find yourself using examples to support the major points in most of the essays you write. To write an effective example essay, be sure to follow these guidelines.

I Be Sure That Your Examples Are Specific.

II Be Sure to Give Enough Examples to Support Your Main Point.

I. Be Sure That Your Examples Are Specific. Specific examples often contain names and numbers as well as images that appeal to the five senses: sight, sound, smell, taste, and touch. Compare the effectiveness of the two examples below, which could be used to support the point that some parents do not try to control their children's behavior.

Vague Example: Recently, in a local restaurant, a little boy was annoying the other customers while his mother ate her sandwich and did nothing to stop him.

Specific Example: Last Tuesday, in a local McDonald's, a little boy about 3 or 4 years old was screaming like a wild hyena and throwing French fries in every direction while his mother munched on her Big Mac and did nothing to stop him.

The specific example is more interesting to read because it creates a strong visual image.

TRY IT OUT

REWRITE THE PARAGRAPH BELOW TO MAKE IT MORE SPECIFIC. ADD NAMES, NUMBERS, AND SENSORY IMAGES TO BRING THE EXAMPLE TO LIFE.

One of the major pressures that a college student faces is time management. For example, I have to get up very early because I have a long trip to school. After getting dressed, I grab some food and rush out the door. After several hours of classes, I rush off to work. By the time I get home at night, I'm a wreck. I have a quick bite to eat and then do homework until really late. When my body finally gives out, I fall into bed.

II. Be Sure to Give Enough Examples to Support Your Main Point. How many examples are enough? That all depends on the point you are trying to make. For some topics, you may be able to support your main point well with one lengthy, highly detailed example in each body paragraph. For most topics, however, you will probably need to develop each body paragraph with at least three or four specific examples. This is especially true when you are trying to convince the reader to agree with your point of view. For example, let's say that you begin a body paragraph with the statement that many advertisements depend on sexual content to sell products. You might support that statement by describing a Calvin Klein Obsession perfume commercial you recently saw on television. If that is your only example, you have not proved that *many* advertisements depend on sexual content; you have only shown that the Calvin Klein commercial does. To prove your point, you would need to give several specific examples.

TRY IT OUT

PROVIDE THREE SPECIFIC EXAMPLES TO SUPPORT THE TOPIC SENTENCE BELOW.

TOPIC SENTENCE: A GOOD FRIEND IS SOMEONE YOU CAN RELY ON WHEN YOU NEED SUPPORT.

SPECIFIC EXAMPLES: ____

____

____

____

The Pointers for Writing an Example Essay chart below provides some additional guidelines for writing an effective essay developed with examples. Following this chart are three model essays.

An essay with one example in each body paragraph

An essay with groups of related examples

An example essay on an academic topic

Be sure to read these essays, for they will help to give you a clear understanding of how to write a good example essay of your own.

POINTERS FOR WRITING AN EXAMPLE ESSAY

1. The *introduction* should provide background information about your topic and should also include a thesis statement that presents the main point you want to make about your topic.
2. Each *body paragraph* may contain one long, detailed example or a group of related examples that support the topic sentence. The examples should use specific names, numbers, and images that appeal to the five senses: sight, sound, smell, taste, and touch.
3. The *order* you use to arrange the examples in each paragraph should be appropriate for the topic. The most effective types of order for an example essay are these:

   Order of Importance: Order of importance generally starts with the least important example, moves to a more important example, and ends with the most important example. It is also possible to reverse this order: start with the most important example and end with the least important one.

   Chronological Order: Chronological or time order describes what happened first, what happened next, and so on. This order is appropriate to use when the examples are incidents.

(Continued)

(Continued)

4. To move smoothly from one example to another, use appropriate *transitions* that signal an example: *for example, for instance, in other words, as an illustration, in particular, also, another, furthermore, in addition, moreover.*
5. The *conclusion* should not present additional examples. Instead it should pull all of your ideas together and remind the reader of the main point presented in your thesis statement. The conclusion may also make a plea for change or draw conclusions from what has been said in the essay. (See Chapter Seven for more information on writing an effective conclusion.)

An Essay with One Example in Each Body Paragraph. The essay below contains one detailed example in each body paragraph. The three examples are actually incidents that the writer has used to prove her main point.

Assigned Risk

(1) I am an assigned risk. That is what my car insurance company calls me; that is how I have been designated by the Department of Motor Vehicles. I have had so many accidents that no insurance company will voluntarily cover me, so the state has assigned an insurance company to take me—a "risky driver"—as a paying customer. However, this situation is definitely not fair, for most of the accidents were not my fault. They were caused by circumstances that were beyond my control.

(2) For example, my first big accident happened because I suffer from allergies. During hay fever season, I was driving down Flatlands Avenue at about thirty-five miles an hour when I suddenly got the urge to sneeze. Although I tried hard to stifle the sneeze, it blew out of me with explosive force. "A-A-Achew!" Now it is a biological fact that it is physically impossible to sneeze and keep your eyes open at the same time. Unfortunately, during the few seconds that my eyes were closed, the driver in front of me stopped quickly when the traffic light turned red. As I opened my eyes, my car smacked right into his trunk and an airbag blasted into my face. Thank goodness no one was hurt. However, I did get a moving violation and my insurance premiums rose sharply. It was not my fault that I had to sneeze.

(3) My next serious accident was not my fault either. I was driving peacefully down a one-way street listening to my favorite tunes and enjoying the warm summer breeze. All of a sudden there was a buzzing in my ear, and an enormous bumblebee was whizzing back and forth in front of my face. I guess

it was attracted by J. Lo's Glow perfume I was wearing that day. To avoid being stung, I jerked my head back and swatted in the direction of the open window, hoping that the bee would fly out. Unfortunately, as I swatted to the left with my right hand, my left hand—on the wheel—jerked to the left also. By the time I regained full control of the wheel, my car had banged against a row of six parked vehicles. When I looked back down the street, I saw that the road was littered with broken side-view mirrors and crumpled door moldings. I felt guilty about all the damage and hoped that the cars' owners would understand my need to protect myself from a threatening bee.

(4) My worst accident happened because I love animals. That is a good quality, not a crime. I was driving—with paranoid carefulness—down a quiet residential street in Brooklyn when the cutest little brown dog darted right in front of my car. I swerved to avoid hitting the animal, lurched up over the curb, and ran into someone's front yard. My car came to an abrupt stop when it hit a tree, which fell over and crashed through the bay window of the house sitting behind it. I tried to explain to the police officer that I had made the right decision by harming things that could be easily replaced rather than by killing an innocent living creature, but he did not seem to follow my logic. The judge didn't either.

(5) After this last accident, the state required me to take a defensive driving course, and my insurance agent informed me that I was no longer in the "good hands" of Allstate. Now I have had to take a second job to pay huge automobile premiums to an insurance company that would rather not cover me in the first place. In addition, my predicament has caused problems with my friends. When they hear that I am an assigned risk, a look of panic crosses their faces and they refuse to get in my car. Why are they so fearful? I am not a dangerous driver; I am not a menace to society. It seems to me that the designation "assigned risk" is one that should not be assigned to me.

TRY IT OUT

ANSWER THESE QUESTIONS ABOUT THE ESSAY "ASSIGNED RISK."

1. In the introduction, what is the writer's thesis statement? ____________

____

2. In the body paragraphs, what examples does the writer provide to prove her thesis? ____________

____

3. What order does the writer use to arrange the examples in her essay?

____

4. In the conclusion, how does the writer restate the main point of her thesis statement? ____________

____

An Essay with Groups of Related Examples. The essay below contains a group of several related examples in each body paragraph. Each group of examples supports the main point of the essay.

The King of the Procrastinators

(1) My mother calls me the king of the procrastinators. I must admit that the first time she used that term I had to look it up in a dictionary. According to *Webster's New World Dictionary*, a procrastinator has a habit of putting off doing something unpleasant until a future time. That certainly describes me. Faced with an unpleasant household chore or schoolwork that needs doing, I will quickly come up with a list of important projects that require my immediate attention.

(2) For example, over a period of several weeks, my mother had been trying to get me to clean up my room, but I always managed to think of something else that I needed to do first. "I can't do it right now, Mom. I've got too many errands to take care of," I'd explain as I ran for the door. Then I'd take my car to get it washed and pick up my dress pants at the dry cleaner so that I would be ready for my date Saturday night. Or I might head for the mall to take advantage of Macy's half-price sale on Dockers and then check out three or four electronics stores for the best deal on a new cell phone. My old one

doesn't have instant messaging, and I really need this feature to make communication with my family and friends easier. My messy room will just have to wait until I get finished with these essential tasks.

(3) I am also good at thinking up reasons for not studying. When my boss at Wal-Mart recently asked me to work on Sunday, I said I couldn't because I had to study for a big history exam. However, when I found myself staring at the thick history textbook that Sunday, I suddenly had second thoughts: "What if my boss fires me because I wouldn't work today? I really need this job." It also occurred to me that I would need some extra money soon to buy my girlfriend a birthday present. She likes gold jewelry, which can be very expensive. After considering my predicament, I called my boss to tell him that I'd be right over. My boss seemed relieved—and so was I.

(4) Although I find studying to be an unpleasant task, it doesn't compare to the anguish I feel when I have to write an essay. That is when my mind goes into overdrive as it searches desperately for a reasonable excuse. Last Friday, for example, I was struggling through the first draft of an essay for my English class when I suddenly realized that I needed to clean up my room. After all, my mother had been complaining for several weeks that if I didn't straighten up the mess soon, "we'll get roaches and rats in the house." I certainly didn't want any creepy critters scurrying across the floor. So the essay would just have to wait. I first tackled the three-foot-high mountain of clothes in front of the bed. I put the jeans on hangers in the closet, folded the shirts neatly and put them in a dresser drawer, and threw the dirty underwear and socks in the hamper. Once all the clothing was taken care of, I decided to go exploring under my bed. There I found an old copy of *Playboy*, a few empty Coca-Cola cans, a half-eaten slice of cold pizza, the remote control for my TV set, and even the P. Diddy CD that I had accused my little brother of stealing. (Sorry, bro.) With the time I spent vacuuming the floor and dusting the furniture, it took me a total of almost four hours to straighten up my room. But it was time well spent because the place looked—and smelled—better than it had in several months, and even housecleaning seemed like fun compared to the blank page staring at me from my desk.

(5) When I finally sat down today to have another go at the essay, my mind immediately went hunting for a new excuse. But my room was clean, my chores were all done, and my boss didn't need me today. At first, I felt trapped. Then I remembered my English teacher's advice to write about something I know really well. I took his advice and, to my amazement, writing this essay turned out to be a rather pleasurable experience. I guess that's because I'm the king of the procrastinators.

TRY IT OUT

ANSWER THESE QUESTIONS ABOUT THE ESSAY "THE KING OF THE PROCRASTINATORS."

1. In the introduction, what is the writer's thesis statement? ____________

   ____

2. In the body paragraphs, what examples does the writer provide to illustrate his thesis? ____________

   ____

   ____

3. What order does the writer use to arrange the examples in his essay?

   ____

4. In the conclusion, how does the writer restate the main point of his thesis statement? ____________

   ____

An Example Essay on an Academic Topic. Like the previous essay, the one below contains a group of several related examples in each body paragraph. This essay, however, uses the examples to develop a topic that might be discussed in a social science course.

Body Language Across Cultures

(1) A businesswoman is nodding her head up and down, but the members of the meeting think that she is saying, "No!" In another situation, a man gives the thumbs up sign to indicate approval, and the fellow next to him wants to fight. Or perhaps two people are standing in conversation, and one person keeps stepping forward as the other keeps stepping back. What is happening? Each of these situations is an example of what can happen when people from two different cultures do not know how to interpret each other's nonverbal communication. Body language differs greatly from one culture to the next; cultural differences in acceptable distances between people, use of eye contact, and interpretation of gestures can cause misunderstanding, confusion, and even hostility.

(2) One way that cultures differ is in the physical "comfort zone" between people. For example, the customary distance for most North Americans and

northern Europeans to stand from each other tends to range from eighteen inches in informal situations to three feet in business settings. For German and Japanese businesspeople, even that three-foot distance may be too close. For southern European, Hispanic, and Middle Eastern people, it may be too far away; their comfort zone is usually eighteen inches or less. These differences can cause all kinds of problems. Two prime areas for difficulty are in business and in love. In business, for instance, Mr. Cirano from Italy may be on the verge of completing a successful business deal with Mr. McIntosh from Scotland. Cirano, however, is standing just a little too close to suit McIntosh. "I'm just not comfortable with this pushy guy. I don't think I could work with him over the long term," thinks the Scot and edges away. "This might be a profitable deal," thinks Cirano as McIntosh sidles away, "but this fellow is a cold fish. Do I really want to be still putting up with him a year from now?" The deal falls apart. Romance can get just as confused. Mary Lou likes Min, but she gives up on the relationship because he keeps such a distance that she thinks he is not interested; Min likes Mary Lou so much that he is being extra careful to show respect. Maria and Heinrich are confused as well. She is not even vaguely interested in him, but she stands so close that he thinks she is trying to attract him. When he responds by putting his arm around her, she is furious at his nerve.

(3) Eye contact can be at least as dangerous as physical distance. In many Latin American, Asian, and Native American cultures, avoiding eye contact, especially with authority figures, is a sign of respect. In Indonesia, prolonged eye contact may be understood as a challenge and can lead to hostility and aggression. In mainstream American culture, on the other hand, not making eye contact is often interpreted to mean that the other person has something to hide and cannot be trusted. Again, these differences can cause trouble. For example, a Native American child learns in her culture that looking an adult in the eye and answering a question directly is a sign of disrespect and a way of showing off. If a teacher does not understand that, the child might be labeled as unmotivated, unresponsive, and maybe even stupid. Romance is another area where problems may arise. Susan's eye contact may be perceived as flirting when she is just being friendly, while Pramoedya's adoring eyes, politely turned away in the Indonesian tradition, may be interpreted as cold.

(4) Hand gestures also can cause an immense amount of trouble. People in some cultures tend to use gestures more than in others. Mediterranean people are especially noted for "talking with their hands." It is the specific gestures, however, that are most likely to lead to misunderstanding. For example, in the United States, twirling your finger near your head can broadcast your opinion that someone is crazy. The same gesture means serious craziness in Japan—but only if you're twirling your finger counterclockwise. If the twirling is clockwise, you are saying the opposite, that the other person is smart. In the United States, "thumbs up" communicates approval; in the

Middle East it is an insulting gesture, and in Japan it means "male." A thumb and forefinger forming an "O" in the United States means "A-OK," but watch out: In southern France, the same gesture means "zero," indicating that the other person is worthless, and in Sardinia it refers to a bodily part and is considered obscene. Imagine what could happen to the successful business deal when the enthusiastic American flashes the Sardinian a delighted "O."

(5) As different cultures come into more and more regular contact, the chances for misunderstanding body language are more frequent. However, the opportunities for learning about each other are multiplying as well. Seminars advise people how to do business across cultures. In addition, we are becoming more familiar with one another's habits in the movies, on television, and increasingly in neighborhoods. Business consultants advise their clients to avoid trouble by following the "two A's": Ask, and be Aware. We would all do well to do the same.

TRY IT OUT

ANSWER THESE QUESTIONS ABOUT THE ESSAY "BODY LANGUAGE ACROSS CULTURES."

1. In the introduction, what is the writer's thesis statement? ______________

   ____

   ____

2. Each body paragraph contains a group of several related examples. What three categories does the writer use to group the examples? ______________

   ____

3. What transitional words and expressions does the writer use to signal examples in this essay? ______________________________

4. In the conclusion, how does the writer restate the main point of her thesis statement? ______________________________

   ____

EXERCISE 12H: This exercise requires you to write an outline for an essay developed with examples. To begin, you first need to decide whether or not you are satisfied with your school. Before making your decision, you might consider the quality of the teachers, the school's facilities, the variety of courses and programs, and the availability of tutoring and other support services, as well as the extracurricular activities. After reaching a decision, write a thesis statement that clearly presents your point of view. Next, for each of the three body paragraphs, write a topic sentence that states one reason for your point of view. Finally, jot down several specific examples to support each reason.

Topic: Why I Am (Am Not) Satisfied with My School

Introduction

Thesis statement: ______________________________

____

Body Paragraph 1

Topic sentence: ______________________________

Specific examples: ______________________________

____

____

____

Body Paragraph 2

Topic sentence: ______________________________

Specific examples: ______________________________

____

____

____

Body Paragraph 3

Topic sentence: ______________________________

Specific examples: ______________________________

____

____

____

Conclusion

EXERCISE 12I: Select one of the topics below as the basis for an essay developed with specific examples. Then follow the list of steps to create your essay.

Topics

My Parents Have (Have Not) Done a Good Job of Raising Me
The Advantages (Disadvantages) of Living Alone
Why Dance Clubs Are Popular
The Best (Worst) Job I Have Ever Had
Telling Lies Can Cause Big Problems
The President Is (Is Not) Doing a Good Job
Television Is (Is Not) Worth Watching
What Love Means to Me
How I Have Changed in the Last Few Years
Why I Would (Would Not) Like to Be a Famous Entertainer

Steps

1. Create a thesis statement that presents the main point you want to make about the topic.
2. Use brainstorming to gather information for your essay. As you brainstorm, ask yourself: What specific examples will help me to illustrate and prove my thesis?
3. As you read through the information you have gathered, cross out any examples that do not clearly support the main point in your thesis statement. Do you have enough examples to prove your point? If not, you will need to do some additional brainstorming.
4. If necessary, revise your examples to make them more specific. Add names, numbers and images that appeal to the five senses: sight, sound, smell, taste, and touch.

5. Decide on a logical order for presenting the examples in your essay. Will you develop each body paragraph with one lengthy example or a group of related examples? What order will you use to arrange the examples: Least to most important? Most to least important? Chronological order?

6. Think about your conclusion. How can you pull all of your ideas together and remind the reader of the main point presented in your thesis statement? Keep in mind that your ideas may change somewhat as you write, for good writing often generates new insights into your topic. However, starting out with a clear sense of your essay's purpose will help you select and organize your examples.

7. You are now ready to write the first draft of your example essay.

8. After completing the first draft, use the revision process described on pages 311–22 to help you achieve a successful essay developed with examples.

The Process Essay

Most of us have a natural desire to learn new skills that will enrich our lives. To satisfy this need, public broadcasting stations offer a variety of programs that teach us how to cook, garden, and do home repairs. If we prefer to receive instruction in printed form, we will have no trouble finding a book to teach us how to paint a picture, invest in stocks and bonds, use a computer, or lose weight. These books and television programs are popular because they each explain a step-by-step process that may help us improve our lives in some way.

The process essay gives you the opportunity to teach a skill, explain how something was done, or describe how something works. To write an effective process essay, be sure to follow these guidelines.

I Use the Introduction to Get the Reader Interested.

II Present All of the Essential Steps in the Process.

III Try to Make the Essay Lively.

I. Use the Introduction to Get the Reader Interested. In addition to stating what the process is, you should explain why it is important. You want to persuade the reader to learn the steps in the process.

TRY IT OUT

FOR EACH PROCESS GIVEN, TELL WHY IT IS IMPORTANT.

1. How to change a flat tire. Why important? ____________________

____

2. How to study properly. Why important? ____________________

____

II. Present All of the Essential Steps in the Process. You should make sure that your directions are complete and specific so that someone who is unfamiliar with the process will be able to perform it successfully. For example, if you are writing an essay about how to prepare for a job interview, you would not be helpful if you merely suggested that the job applicant should dress nicely.

Instead, you should describe the specific clothing that would be appropriate to wear for an interview.

As you give the steps in the process, you should also define unfamiliar terms, offer suggestions, and provide reasons for including certain steps. For instance, if you are writing an essay about how to change a flat tire, you might start by suggesting that the lug nuts should be loosened before the wheel is raised off the ground. Before going on to the next step, you should explain what lug nuts are and why they should be loosened before the wheel is raised.

After you complete the first draft of your process essay, it is a good idea to share it with someone who is unfamiliar with the process. He or she will be able to give you valuable feedback about any information that is missing or unclear.

TRY IT OUT

ON YOUR OWN PAPER, DRAW UP A LIST OF ALL THE STEPS IN A PROCESS THAT YOU KNOW WELL. WHEREVER NECESSARY, ADD SPECIFIC DETAILS, DEFINE UNFAMILIAR TERMS, AND OFFER SUGGESTIONS THAT WILL HELP THE READER TO PERFORM THE PROCESS SUCCESSFULLY.

III. Try to Make the Essay Lively. In addition to providing specific directions, you should try to make the essay lively so that it encourages curiosity and entertains as it teaches. To do more than just recite a recipe or give a dry list of facts and dates, you can try to include one or more of the following—if they clearly relate to the process—(1) an amusing or dramatic incident, (2) an unusually surprising fact, (3) a conclusion that challenges the reader to think and explore further.

TRY IT OUT

THINK OF HOW YOU LEARNED THE SKILLS NEEDED FOR A PARTICULAR JOB OR HOBBY. IF YOU HAD TO WRITE AN ESSAY THAT EXPLAINS HOW THIS PROCESS WAS DONE, WHAT MIGHT YOU INCLUDE TO MAKE IT MORE LIVELY AND INTERESTING?

A surprising fact: ______________________________

____

An amusing or dramatic incident: ______________________________

____

A challenge to think and explore further: ______________________________

____

The Pointers for Writing a Process Essay chart on this and the next page provides some additional guidelines for writing an effective process essay. Following this chart are three model essays.

A *How to . . .* Essay

A *How . . . Was Done* Essay

A *How . . . Works* Essay

Be sure to read these essays, for they will help to give you a clear understanding of how to write a good process essay of your own.

POINTERS FOR WRITING A PROCESS ESSAY

1. The *introduction* should always tell what the process is and why it is important.
2. The *main body paragraphs* should give the parts of the process in an order that is appropriate for the clear and logical presentation of a topic. Time is the most common type of order; it presents what happened first, second, third, and so on. The most useful types of order are these:

The Order (or Its Reverse)	*For Example:*
Importance	How I Lost Ninety Pounds in Six Months Introductory paragraph I. willpower II. dietetic foods III. doctors and drugs Concluding paragraph
Location	How to Clean a Bolt-Action Rifle Introductory paragraph I. the bore II. the breech III. the stock Concluding paragraph
Simple to Complex	How the Atomic Bomb Is Detonated Introductory paragraph I. bomb design II. Uranium-235 III. the implosion chamber Concluding paragraph

(Continued)

(Continued)

Known to Unknown	How the United States Won the Race to the Moon Introductory paragraph I. billions of dollars II. dedicated specialists III. scientific breakthroughs Concluding paragraph
Time	How to Make a Pizza Introductory paragraph I. the proper ingredients II. hands, utensils, and oven III. the masterful combining of ingredients Concluding paragraph

3. To avoid being dull, tease the reader's curiosity with a particularly interesting piece of information or arouse the reader's interest with an amusing or dramatic incident.
4. To achieve a unified essay, use words of transition and the deliberate repetition of key words that tie the parts together.
5. The *conclusion* can challenge the reader to think about the topic and explore it more thoroughly.

The How to . . . Essay. The *How to . . .* type of process essay gives directions which should be clearly stated step by step so that the reader can learn, for example, how to make pizza or how to clean a bolt-action rifle. Here is an example of a *How to . . .* essay.

How to Cope with Stress

(1) You have three midterm examinations next week and a paper due in sociology. To make matters worse, you are scheduled to work an extra six hours at your part-time job, and your car is beginning to make some strange noises. The only bright spot is the big football game this weekend. If you have weeks like this one, you are probably feeling the effects of stress, effects that leave you feeling frazzled and can lead to serious medical problems. Fortunately, stress can be reduced with the help of a simple three-step plan.

(2) The first step to coping with stress is exploring your situation and changing your attitude. What is causing your stress? Like many people, you may have taken on so many activities that you feel overwhelmed. To deal with

this problem, make a list of everything that is contributing to your stress. Then rank each item according to how serious the consequences would be if you did not do it. For example, you need to do well on your midterms, and you need a car to get to school and to work. So as much fun as the football game would be, you should spend the weekend studying and getting your car repaired. If you have trouble ranking the items, show your list to someone who has the objectivity to see a good solution. As you accomplish the things on your list, cross them off. This technique will help you to manage your time more efficiently and will give you a sense that you are in control of your life.

(3) The second step to reducing stress is to begin a program of regular physical exercise. When people are under a great deal of stress, their bodies produce extra adrenalin, which quickens the heartbeat, increases the sugar level in the blood, and slows up or stops digestion. These bodily changes, in turn, cause people to sweat, to have upset stomachs, to feel jittery, and to lose sleep. However, if you exercise vigorously for 20 to 30 minutes a day—run or swim, for example—you will use up the extra energy produced by the high sugar level, and the physical symptoms of stress will probably disappear. Exercise on a planned schedule so that it becomes a habit, and do not exercise too near bedtime so that it does not interfere with sleep. Exercise will calm you and give you a feeling of well-being that will allow you to deal more effectively with your hectic lifestyle.

(4) To reduce stress still further, do mental exercises every day. In a quiet room, sit up straight in a comfortable chair with your feet resting on the floor. Close your eyes and listen to your breathing. Slowly inhale through your nose, hold the breath for several seconds, and then exhale slowly through your mouth. Doing this exercise at least four times should help to relax you. Then with your eyes still closed, visualize a beautiful tropical beach. There you are, floating in the clear blue water. As the gentle current carries you along, you look up at the puffy white clouds crossing the sky. You hear the gentle breeze rustling through the palm trees. You feel calm and peaceful. If you do this mental exercise twice a day for 20 minutes each time, your mind and body will become more relaxed.

(5) Thus, you do not have to be the victim of stress if you follow this three-step plan. First, examine your situation and be realistic about what you can accomplish in the time you have. Then each day find some time in your busy schedule to exercise and take a mental vacation. Consider it the vacation you really need but do not have the time to take. These three steps can help you maintain your health, become more productive at work or school, and enjoy life to the fullest.

TRY IT OUT

ANSWER THESE QUESTIONS ABOUT "HOW TO COPE WITH STRESS."

1. According to the introduction, why is it important to learn how to cope with stress? ____

____

2. According to the body paragraphs, what are the three major steps for coping with stress? ____

____

3. According to the conclusion, why should the reader explore this topic further? ____

____

The How . . . Was Done Essay. The *How . . . Was Done* type of essay describes how something unusual and complicated was achieved so that the reader can learn, for example, how the United States won the race to the moon or how the writer lost ninety pounds in six months. Here is an example of a *How . . . Was Done* essay.

How I Became a Cool Dude

(1) Michelle was the most beautiful girl I had ever seen. Whenever we would run into each other on campus, we would exchange a few words, but I could never get up enough courage to ask her for a date. Then one day I overheard her telling a friend what a nerd I was. A nerd? Until that moment, it had never occurred to me that I might be one. However, that night I forced myself to take a long, hard look in my full-length bedroom mirror. What I saw was a six-foot-tall, 135-pound beanpole with thick horn-rimmed glasses and hair plastered to the sides of his head. Although it was difficult, I had to admit that Michelle was right: I was a nerd. But I realized that I did not have to look that way. Right then and there, I decided that I would use the summer to transform myself into someone Michelle would like.

(2) First, I decided to improve the appearance of my body. I began by drinking protein shakes to put on weight and by working out at a health club to become fit and muscular. This routine yielded great results, for I gained 40 pounds of hard muscle by the end of August. The regular workouts improved my posture too, so that I no longer slouched and walked pigeon-toed. During

the summer, I also shaved off the few scraggly wisps of hair that I called my beard and visited a downtown hair stylist, who cut my hair into the fashionable Tom Cruise look. Next, I went to an optometrist, who replaced those ugly eyeglasses with a pair of blue contact lenses. Then I made an appointment with my dentist to have my stained teeth whitened and to have my two buckteeth filed down. When the Novocain wore off after the procedure, my mouth hurt for three days, but I now had a gleaming smile that Michelle was sure to find attractive.

(3) In phase two of my plan, I changed how I dressed. I traded in my short-sleeved polyester shirts for some tight black DKNY T-shirts to show off my new muscles. In addition, I got rid of the baggy cotton washpants that I had always worn tightly belted above my waist. (It was no wonder that everyone used to call me "Highpockets.") Instead, I bought Calvin Klein jeans and wore them at my hips, a position that I initially found uncomfortable, though the clothes made me feel sexy. Then I got a classic black leather jacket—the kind Keanu Reeves wears—and replaced my basketball sneakers with a pair of Italian loafers. For a final touch, I had my right ear pierced to hold a small gold stud-earring. I had spent all of my savings, but a glance in the mirror told me that I had done the right thing.

(4) In the third phase of my self-improvement program, I learned everything I could about popular culture. I started watching MTV and listening to the Top 40. With deep regret, I found myself ignoring Mozart and Beethoven in favor of Madonna and P. Diddy. I set aside Plato and Aristotle so that I could give my full attention to *Tiger Beat* and *Car and Driver.* I turned my back on my favorite public broadcasting shows so that I would be able to follow the antics of the characters on *All My Children* and *Melrose Place.* As soon as a new Arnold Schwarzenegger or Bruce Willis action film came out, I was in line buying my ticket. Armed with my newly acquired knowledge, I started spending time at Rahar's, the "in" place in town. There I completed my education by learning the latest slang.

(5) Before I knew it, the summer was over. Walking across the campus on the first day of classes, I was both excited and a bit frightened as I worried about everyone's reaction to the new me. My fears vanished quickly, however, when I noticed the approving glances of my fellow classmates. "Cool dude!" someone yelled as I passed. "Cool dude," I repeated softly as my step quickened into a confident stride. Suddenly I spotted Michelle heading right toward me. The look on her beautiful face told me that she was clearly interested. Pausing for a moment, I considered my options and then walked on by. After all, I was a cool dude now—too cool for Michelle.

TRY IT OUT

ANSWER THESE QUESTIONS ABOUT "HOW I BECAME A COOL DUDE."

1. According to the introduction, why did the writer think it was important to become a "cool dude"? ______________________________

____

2. According to the body paragraphs, what three major steps did the writer take to become a "cool dude"? ______________________________

____

3. What method did the writer use to make his introduction and conclusion lively and entertaining? ______________________________

____

The How . . . Works Essay. The *How . . . Works* essay explains, in non-technical language, how scientific and complex processes work so that the reader can learn, for example, how an atomic bomb is detonated or how radio waves are transmitted. Here is an example of a *How . . . Works* essay.

How a Car Works

(1) The average car has about 30,000 individual parts. Thus, your auto mechanic may seem to be speaking a foreign language when he tells you that a particular part in your car needs to be replaced. To make matters worse, the repair always seems to be very expensive. Fortunately, you can avoid costly or unnecessary repairs without having to learn what all 30,000 parts do. In fact, all of the individual parts in a car contribute to three basic functions: creating power, sending that power to the wheels, and controlling the movement of the vehicle. If you understand these three functions, you understand how a car works.

(2) To create the power to move the car, you turn the key in the ignition, which connects to the battery. The battery powers a little motor that begins turning the crankshaft, a twisted rod in the engine. After the first few turns, the power to turn the crankshaft comes from the pistons, which are metal rods that fit snugly inside cylinders. Most cars have either four or six cylinders; some very powerful cars have eight. A device called a fuel injector delivers a mixture of gasoline and air to each cylinder, and a spark plug at the top of the cylinder delivers a spark to create a little explosion that forces the

piston down inside the cylinder. When the car is running, these pistons are constantly going up and down like the horses on a merry-go-round. The bottoms of the pistons are connected to the crankshaft. Therefore, as the pistons go up and down, the crankshaft turns. In addition to creating power, the little gasoline explosions create gases that leave the engine through the exhaust pipe. This pipe contains a catalytic converter, a device that cuts down on the harmful gases that could pollute the air.

(3) Once the pistons begin producing power, it needs to get to the wheels. To make that happen, one end of the crankshaft enters a box of gears called the transmission. When the pistons force the crankshaft to turn, the gears send this rotating motion to the car's front axle that connects the two front wheels. As the axle rotates, the wheels turn and the car begins to move. In some cars, especially older ones, the rotating action of the crankshaft is delivered to the rear axle instead, and the rear wheels make the car move. These cars have a long rod called a driveshaft that comes out of the back of the transmission and runs the length of the car until it connects to some gears in the center of the rear axle. As the crankshaft turns, it makes the driveshaft turn too. With the help of the gears, the driveshaft then turns the rear axle and the wheels.

(4) Once the car is moving, you use three systems to keep it under control: the steering system, the suspension system, and the brake system. Rack-and-pinion steering is the most common steering system. The steering wheel is connected to the steering column, which ends at the center of a long metal bar with teeth. This bar—called the rack—extends between the two front wheels. At the point where the steering column and the rack meet is a little gear called a pinion. When you turn the steering wheel, the pinion gear meshes with the teeth in the rack and moves the bar to the right or the left. Because the rack is connected to the wheels, they then move to the right or the left also. As the car changes direction, the springs and shock absorbers in the car's suspension system help make the ride smooth and steady. When you want to slow or stop the car, you step on the brake pedal. Most cars have disc brakes on the front wheels and drum brakes on the rear wheels; both types of brakes operate by pressing a pad or lining against each wheel with tremendous force until the car stops.

(5) Do you know all about cars now? Certainly not. However, if you understand the basic concepts of how a car works, you will at least be able to ask intelligent questions when your mechanic uses some terms you don't know. Your knowledge will grow with every oil change and rattle and tune-up. Eventually, you will become a better and safer driver behind the wheel and a smarter one when you look under the hood.

TRY IT OUT

ANSWER THESE QUESTIONS ABOUT "HOW A CAR WORKS."

1. In the introduction, what surprising fact does the writer use to encourage the reader's curiosity? ______________________________

____

2. According to the body paragraphs, what are the three basic steps to making a car work? ______________________________

____

____

3. According to the conclusion, why should the reader explore this topic further? ______________________________

____

EXERCISE 12J: For each process essay title given, select the type of order that would be most effective. Then list three major parts of the process by indicating the main idea of each paragraph.

1. How to Break a Bad Habit — Order: ______________
   Introductory paragraph
   I. ______________________________
   II. ______________________________
   III. ______________________________
   Concluding paragraph
2. How to Pick the Right Job — Order: ______________
   Introductory paragraph
   I. ______________________________
   II. ______________________________
   III. ______________________________
   Concluding paragraph

3. How to Avoid Trouble with Your Relatives Order: ______________
   Introductory paragraph

   I. ______________________________

   II. ______________________________

   III. ______________________________
   Concluding paragraph

4. How to Choose a Car Order: ______________
   Introductory paragraph

   I. ______________________________

   II. ______________________________

   III. ______________________________
   Concluding paragraph

5. How to Study for a Test Order: ______________
   Introductory paragraph

   I. ______________________________

   II. ______________________________

   III. ______________________________
   Concluding paragraph

6. How to Stay in Good Health Order: ______________
   Introductory paragraph

   I. ______________________________

   II. ______________________________

   III. ______________________________
   Concluding paragraph

7. How to Choose a Mate Order: ______________
   Introductory paragraph

   I. ______________________________

   II. ______________________________

   III. ______________________________
   Concluding paragraph

8. How to Conserve Energy Order: ______________
   Introductory paragraph

   I. ______________________________

   II. ______________________________

   III. ______________________________
   Concluding paragraph

9. How to Be an Individual Order: ______________
   Introductory paragraph

   I. ______________________________

   II. ______________________________

   III. ______________________________
   Concluding paragraph

10. How to Celebrate a Birthday Order: ______________
    Introductory paragraph

    I. ______________________________

    II. ______________________________

    III. ______________________________
    Concluding paragraph

EXERCISE 12K: Are the following introductions to process essays appropriate? Why or why not? As you evaluate them, refer to the Pointers for Explaining a Process in this chapter, and to the list of Common Errors to Avoid in Introductions and Conclusions in Chapter Seven.

1. *Title:* How Columbus Discovered America

   Introduction

   Did you know that Columbus discovered the land mass later named America when he was looking for a shorter route to the Far East? Finances for his voyage were hard to find, but after an eight-year attempt, Columbus finally convinced Spain to support his venture. Interestingly, although honors were heaped upon Columbus when he discovered the "New World," he died many years later neglected and forgotten. It is always sad when a once-famous person ends his life alone and poverty-stricken.

Question: Appropriate? Why or why not?

____

____

2. *Title:* How to Make a Banana Split

   Introduction

   In this essay I will tell you how to make a banana split. Many ingredients are involved, and I will tell you how to use each one. I am not too good at making banana splits, but I will try to tell you the little that I know about them.

   Question: Appropriate? Why or why not?

   ____

   ____

3. *Title:* How to Make People Hate You

   Introduction

   Making people hate you is not very hard. With some determination, you can learn a few tricks and become an expert. Then you can have all the time you want to be alone and do all the things you want to do by yourself. Of course, if you would like to have the opposite effect on people, this advice can be a guide to what you should avoid in your relationships with other people.

   Question: Appropriate? Why or why not?

   ____

   ____

4. *Title:* How to Run a Farm

   Introduction

   Running a farm is a difficult and often frustrating job, but the satisfaction of working the land can more than make up for the tremendous effort and toil. One thing to keep in mind is that the crops must be planted at the right time.

Question: Appropriate? Why or why not?

____

____

5. *Title:* How to Analyze Doodles

   Introduction

   Doodles can reveal a great deal about the person doing the absentminded scribbling. When people turn to doodling to relax or prevent boredom, the resulting doodle can tell someone who knows how to analyze doodles about the "artist's" personality and basic characteristics.

   Question: Appropriate? Why or why not?

   ____

   ____

EXERCISE 12L: Select one of the topics below as the basis for a process essay. Then follow the list of steps to create your essay.

Topics

How to Prepare a Particular Recipe
How to Find a Job
How to Plan a Party or Wedding
How to Select a Career
How to Study for a Big Exam
How to Be a Good Parent
How to Overcome Shyness
How to Start a Particular Hobby
How to Play a Particular Sport or Game
How to Survive in College
How to Buy a Used Car or Computer
How to Be Successful at Your Job
How to Repair a (an) ________________
How to Take a Good Photograph
How a Particular Holiday Is Celebrated
How a Particular Historical Event Occurred
How a Machine/Piece of Equipment Works

Steps

1. Select a specific topic for your essay.
2. Create a thesis statement that presents the main point you want to make about the process. Why is this process important?

3. Draw up a list of all the steps in the process. Wherever necessary, add specific details, define unfamiliar terms, and offer suggestions that will help the reader to perform the process successfully.
4. To make the essay lively, try to think of an amusing or dramatic incident or an unusually surprising fact.
5. Decide on a logical order for presenting the steps of the process. A process essay is most often organized using chronological or time order.
6. Think about your conclusion. You might emphasize the importance of the process or describe specific situations when it is especially useful. Most important, the conclusion should clearly relate back to your main point about the process. Keep in mind that your sense of what matters may shift as you write, for good writing often generates new ideas. However, starting out with a clear sense of your essay's purpose will help you to select and organize the details of the process.
7. You are now ready to write the first draft of your process essay.
8. After completing the first draft, use the revision process described on pages 311–22 to help you achieve a successful process essay.

EXERCISE 12M: REFRESHER

1. CORRECT ANY ERRORS IN PUNCTUATION IN THE FOLLOWING PARAGRAPHS.

2. INSERT WORDS OF TRANSITION NEEDED TO HELP CREATE UNITY.

Have you ever been punched, slapped, or shoved by someone you were dating. Recent studies indicate that such violent behavior is common among college couples. At Arizona State University, 60 percent of the unmarried upper-class students admitted that they had experienced violence while dating. This physical abuse can take many forms pushing, kicking, beating, or even biting. Some students have been threatened with guns and knives. According to the research, these acts of cruelty often creep into a campus romance because of jealousy over a third person. In other instances, the violent blowups grow out of arguments over sex or drinking. These studies may have overlooked the real reason for the problem stress. Experts point out that many young people are under a tremendous strain brought about by financial educational, and sexual pressures.

Considering the suffering caused by these wild dangerous attacks you may wonder why over half of the students who have been assaulted choose to continue the relationship? One major reason is the fear of loneliness or of losing the status that comes from having a steady date. A study done at Oregon State University revealed that 30 percent of the couples saw physical abuse as a sign of love, and more than one-third felt that hitting actually improved their relationship. These findings indicate that violence and romance will, unfortunately, remain closely linked until young people develop the maturity and self-control needed for a healthy satisfying relationship.

SPRINGBOARDS TO WRITING

Using your knowledge of the writing process, explained on pages 14–16, write a paragraph or essay related to this chapter's central theme, *our violent society*, which is introduced on page 464.

PREWRITING

To think of topics to write about, look at the advertisement and the chart, read the essay, and answer the questions that follow each. If you prefer, select one of the writing springboards below. (All paragraph numbers refer to the essay that starts on page 466.) To develop your ideas, use the prewriting techniques described on pages 17–22.

WRITING A PARAGRAPH *(For help, see the Pointers on page 51.)*

1. Agree or disagree: "Every adult male is an adult male stranger." (See paragraph 11.)
2. If you have ever been the victim of a crime, or if you have ever witnessed a crime, describe exactly what happened.
3. I would (would not) come to the aid of a person being mugged or raped.
4. Some U.S. states and cities now reward a person who comes to the aid of another citizen in trouble. Do you think such a program is a good idea?
5. Agree or disagree with this statement by Mahatma Gandhi: "All crime is a kind of disease and should be treated as such."
6. Answer this question by Robert Emmet Sherwood: "And who are the greater criminals—those who sell the instruments of death, or those who buy them and use them?"

WRITING AN ESSAY *(For help, see the Pointers on pages 54–55.)*

7. How Fear of Violence Affects Society
8. How to Survive in Our Violent Society
9. How to Protect Young Children from Abuse (See paragraphs 3, 6, and 7.)
10. Why Do Some Men Batter Women? (See paragraphs 6 and 11.)
11. What Makes People Turn to a Life of Crime?
12. Should Teenagers Who Commit Serious Crimes Be Given the Same Punishment as Adults Are?
13. A Plan to Reduce Crime in My Community
14. The Case for (Against) Gun Control

15. The Case for (Against) Capital Punishment
16. Today's Television Programs and Movies Do (Do Not) Encourage Violence
17. The Police Are (Are Not) Doing Their Best in Dealing with Crime
18. The Courts Are (Are Not) Firm Enough in Dealing with Criminals
19. Agree or Disagree: Our Prisons Do Not Rehabilitate Criminals

CATHY **BY CATHY GUISEWITE**

WAIT A MINUTE. WHY IS IT MY PROBLEM?? WHY IS THE BURDEN ON ME TO PRESERVE HIS EGO?? JUST TELL HIM NO! SAY NO!!

Chapter 13

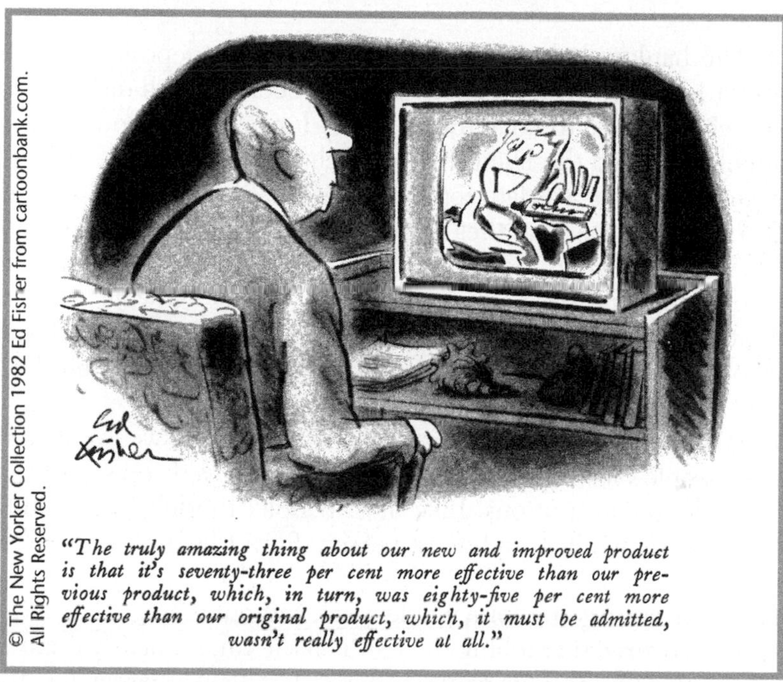

"The truly amazing thing about our new and improved product is that it's seventy-three per cent more effective than our previous product, which, in turn, was eighty-five per cent more effective than our original product, which, it must be admitted, wasn't really effective at all."

SPRING BOARDS TO THINKING

For informal, not written, response . . . to stimulate your thinking

1. Read the cartoon on the opposite page. Should Cathy lie to the fellow or just tell him that she does not want to go out with him? Does she have an obligation to preserve his ego? Explain your answer to each question.
2. What is the underlying message in the cartoon above?
3. What are the major reasons people tell lies? Is lying sometimes appropriate, or is honesty always the best policy? Explain your answer.
4. In general, do you think most people you know personally are honest or dishonest in their dealings with you? In their dealings with stores? In their dealings with the government (paying taxes, applying for unemployment insurance or welfare, etc.)? Explain your answer to each question.
5. In general, do you think that most politicians and government officials are honest? Why or why not?

The Ways We Lie

Stephanie Ericsson

(1) The bank called today, and I told them my deposit was in the mail, even though I hadn't written a check yet. It'd been a rough day. The baby I'm pregnant with decided to do aerobics on my lungs for two hours, our three-year-old daughter painted the living-room couch with lipstick, the IRS put me on hold for an hour, and I was late to a business meeting because I was tired.

(2) I told my client that the traffic had been bad. When my partner came home, his haggard face told me his day hadn't gone any better than mine, so when he asked, "How was your day?" I said, "Oh, fine," knowing that one more straw might break his back. A friend called and wanted to take me to lunch. I said I was busy. Four lies in the course of a day, none of which I felt the least bit guilty about.

(3) We lie. We all do. We exaggerate, we minimize, we avoid confrontation, we spare people's feelings, we conveniently forget, we keep secrets, we justify lying to the big-guy institutions. Like most people, I indulge in small falsehoods and still think of myself as an honest person. Sure I lie, but it doesn't hurt anything. Or does it?

(4) I once tried going for a whole week without telling a lie, and it was paralyzing. I discovered that telling the truth all the time is nearly impossible. It means living with some serious consequences: The bank charges me $60 in overdraft fees, my partner keels over when I tell him about my travails, my client fires me for telling her I didn't feel like being on time, and my friend takes it personally when I say I'm not hungry. There must be some merit to lying.

(5) But if I justify lying, what makes me any different from slick politicians or the corporate robbers who raided the S&L industry? Saying it's okay to lie one way and not another is hedging. I cannot seem to escape the voice deep inside me that tells me: When someone lies, someone loses.

(6) What far-reaching consequences will I, or others, pay as a result of my lie? Will someone's trust be destroyed? Will someone else pay *my* penance because I ducked out? We must consider the *meaning of our actions.* Deception, lies, capital crimes, and misdemeanors all carry meanings. *Webster's* definition of *lie* is specific:

1. a false statement or action especially made with the intent to deceive;
2. anything that gives or is meant to give a false impression.

A definition like this implies that there are many, many ways to tell a lie. Here are just a few.

The White Lie

(7) The white lie assumes that the truth will cause more damage than a simple, harmless truth. Telling a friend he looks great when he looks like hell can be based on a decision that the friend needs a compliment more than a frank opinion. But, in effect, it is the liar deciding what is best for the lied to. Ultimately, it is a vote of no confidence. It is an act of subtle arrogance for anyone to decide what is best for someone else.

(8) Yet not all circumstances are quite so cut and dried. Take, for instance, the sergeant in Vietnam who knew one of his men was killed in action but listed him as missing so that the man's family would receive indefinite compensation instead of the lump-sum pittance the military gives widows and children. His intent was honorable. Yet for twenty years this family kept their hopes alive, unable to move on to a new life.

Facades

(9) We all put up facades to one degree or another. When I put on a suit to go to see a client, I feel as though I am putting on another face, obeying the expectation that serious businesspeople wear suits rather than sweatpants. But I'm a writer. Normally, I get up, get the kid off to school, and sit at my computer in my pajamas until four in the afternoon. When I answer the phone, the caller thinks I'm wearing a suit (although the UPS man knows better).

(10) But facades can be destructive because they are used to seduce others into an illusion. For instance, I recently realized that a former friend was a liar. He presented himself with the right looks and the right words and offered lots of new consciousness theories, fabulous books to read, and fascinating insights. Then I did some business with him, and the time came for him to pay me. He turned out to be all talk and no walk. I heard a plethora of reasonable excuses, including in-depth descriptions of the big break around the corner. In six months of work, I saw less than a hundred bucks. When I confronted him, he raised both eyebrows and tried to convince me that I'd heard him wrong, that he'd made no commitment to me. A simple investigation into his past revealed a crowded graveyard of disenchanted former friends.

Ignoring the Plain Facts

(11) In the sixties, the Catholic Church in Massachusetts began hearing complaints that Father James Porter was sexually molesting children. Rather than relieving him of his duties, the ecclesiastical authorities simply moved him from one parish to another between 1960 and 1967, actually providing him with a fresh supply of unsuspecting families and innocent children to abuse. After treatment in 1967 for pedophilia, he went to work, this time in Minnesota. The new diocese was aware of Father Porter's obsession with children, but they needed priests and recklessly believed treatment had cured him. More children were abused until he was relieved of his duties a year later. By his own admission, Porter may have abused as many as a hundred children.

(12) Ignoring the facts may not in and of itself be a form of lying, but consider the context of this situation. If a lie is *a false action done with the intent to deceive,* then the Catholic Church's conscious covering for Porter created irreparable consequences. The Church became a co-perpetrator with Porter.

Stereotypes and Clichés

(13) Stereotype and cliché serve a purpose as a form of shorthand. Our need for vast amounts of information in nanoseconds has made the stereotype vital to modern communication. Unfortunately, it often shuts down original thinking, giving those hungry for truth a candy bar of misinformation instead of a balanced meal. The stereotype explains a situation with just enough truth to seem unquestionable.

(14) All the *isms*—racism, sexism, ageism, et al.—are founded on and fueled by the stereotype and the cliché, which are lies of exaggeration, omission, and ignorance. They are always dangerous. They take a single tree and make it a landscape. They destroy curiosity. They close minds and separate people. The single mother on welfare is assumed to be cheating. Any black male could tell you how much of his identity is obliterated daily by stereotypes. Fat people, ugly people, beautiful people, old people, large-breasted women, short men, the mentally ill, and the homeless all could tell you how much more they are like us than we want to think. I once admitted to a group of people that I had a mouth like a truck driver. Much to my surprise, a man stood up and said, "I'm a truck driver, and I never cuss." Needless to say, I was humbled.

Out-and-Out Lies

(15) Of all the ways to lie, I like this one the best, probably because I get tired of trying to figure out the real meanings behind things. At least I can trust the bald-faced lie. I once asked my five-year-old nephew, "Who broke the fence?" (I had seen him do it.) He answered, "The murderers." Who could argue?

(16) At least when this sort of lie is told it can be easily confronted. As the person who is lied to, I know where I stand. The bald-faced lie doesn't toy with my perceptions—it argues with them. It doesn't try to refashion reality; it tries to refute it. *Read my lips.* . . . No sleight of hand. No guessing. If this were the only form of lying, there would be no such thing as floating anxiety or the adult-children of alcoholics movement.

(17) These are only a few of the ways we lie. Or are lied to. As I said earlier, it's not easy to entirely eliminate lies from our lives. No matter how pious we may try to be, we still embellish, hedge, and omit to lubricate the daily machinery of living. But there is a world of difference between telling functional lies and living a lie. Martin Buber once said, "The lie is the spirit committing treason against itself." Our acceptance of lies becomes a cultural cancer that eventually shrouds and reorders reality until moral garbage becomes as invisible to us as water is to a fish.

(18) How much do we tolerate before we become sick and tired of being sick and tired? When will we stand up and declare our *right* to trust? When do we stop accepting that the real truth is in the fine print? Whose lips do we read this year when we vote for president? When will we stop being so reticent about making judgments? When do we stop turning over our personal power and responsibility to liars?

(19) Maybe if I don't tell the bank the check's in the mail I'll be less tolerant of the lies told to me every day. A country song I once heard said it all for me: "You've got to stand for something or you'll fall for anything."

Reading Survey

1. MAIN IDEA

What is the central theme of this essay?

2. MAJOR DETAILS

a. What happened when the author tried going a whole week without telling a lie?
b. What types of lies does the author describe?
c. According to the author, what will eventually happen if our acceptance of lies continues?

3. INFERENCES

a. Read paragraph 7 again. Why is a white lie "a vote of no confidence"?
b. Read paragraph 14 again. What point is the author trying to make when she describes her experience with a truck driver?

4. OPINIONS

a. Read paragraph 5 again. Do you agree with the author's statement that "When someone lies, someone loses"? Explain your point of view.
b. Read paragraph 8 again. Do you agree with the sergeant's decision to list one of his men as missing? Why or why not?

Vocabulary Building

Lesson One: The Vocabulary of Lying, Part I

The essay "The Ways We Lie" by Stephanie Ericsson includes words that are useful when you are discussing lying.

confrontation (paragraph 3)
to justify (3)
indulge (3)
travails (4)
hedging (5)
deception (6)
misdemeanors (6)
frank (7)
facades (9)
plethora (10)

People who lie may want to avoid a **confrontation**—an unfriendly face-to-face meeting—with others.
People who lie often try **to justify**—to prove or show to be right—their behavior.
People who lie may think of themselves as honest people, even though they **indulge** in—give in to a desire for—dishonest behavior.
People who lie may suffer **travails**—pain and suffering—because of their lies.
People who lie may try to protect themselves by **hedging**—making unclear statements or refusing to give a direct answer to a question.
People who lie are engaging in some kind of **deception**—dishonesty or trickery.
People who lie may think that lies are only **misdemeanors**—minor crimes or offenses.
People who lie may be afraid to make a **frank**—open and honest—remark.
People who lie often put up **facades**—false fronts—to meet other people's expectations.
People who lie may make a **plethora**—an oversupply or overflow—of excuses for their lies.

EXERCISE 13A: Using the vocabulary words in the lesson, fill in the blanks.

1. The crime the boys committed was only a ________________.
2. The voters wished the candidate would stop his ________________ and answer the question.
3. The President tried to ________________ his lie by saying that he wanted to protect the nation.
4. We all put up ________________ to keep others from seeing who we really are.
5. The people suffered terrible ________________ during the war.
6. Honesty, not ________________, is the best policy.
7. The frightened child told a ________________ of lies in hopes of avoiding punishment.

8. My advice is not to ______________ in overeating; you'll regret it immediately.
9. The reporter asked the voters to be truthful and give their ______________ opinions of the politician's behavior.
10. Sometimes a ______________ between those who disagree helps settle a problem.

Lesson Two: The Vocabulary of Lying, Part II

The essay "The Ways We Lie" by Stephanie Ericsson includes more words that are useful when you are discussing lying.

stereotypes (paragraph 13)
clichés (13)
omission (14)
obliterated (14)
humbled (14)
to refute (16)
embellish (17)
to lubricate (17)
to shroud (17)
reticent (18)

People who are dishonest may form **stereotypes**—oversimplified images or mental pictures—of those who are different from themselves.

People who are dishonest may rely on **clichés**—overused or unoriginal ideas or expressions—when they do not want to tell the truth.

People who are dishonest hope that others will not question the **omission** of—the failure to include or mention—some facts.

People who are dishonest know that the truth can be easily **obliterated**—wiped out or erased without a trace.

People who are dishonest are not usually **humbled**—reduced in pride and self-respect—by their need to tell lies.

People who are dishonest may try **to refute**—to prove to be wrong—statements that they know are true.

People who are dishonest are often tempted to **embellish**—to add imaginary details to—the truth.

People who are dishonest often tell small lies **to lubricate**—to smooth over or reduce difficulty in—their relationships with others.

People who are dishonest often tell lies **to shroud**—disguise or hide—unpleasant truths.

People who are dishonest may become **reticent**—silent or unwilling to speak—when they are caught in a lie.

EXERCISE 13B: Using the vocabulary words in the lesson, fill in the blanks.

1. The cigarette manufacturer made a large donation to the political party to _______________ his relationship with lawmakers.
2. Forgetting to tell me about the accident was a serious _______________.
3. The student's essay was filled with many overused _______________.
4. The doctor was _______________ about discussing the patient's condition with anyone but a family member.
5. The lawyer intends to _______________ the charges against her client.
6. Members of minority groups often become the victims of negative _______________.
7. The normally proud baseball team was _______________ by the enormous loss.
8. The parents' joy _______________ their anger when the runaway child was found.
9. The inexperienced job applicant was tempted to _______________ his qualifications.
10. Because of our pride, we tend to _______________ our shortcomings from others.

SPELLING

Prefixes and Suffixes

Are you ever unsure of whether to use one or two *l*'s in *generally* or one or two *s*'s in *misspell?* The following principles concerning prefixes and suffixes will help you to avoid this type of confusion.

When the prefix ends with the same letter that begins the main part of the word, be sure to include both letters.

When the suffix begins with the same letter that ends the main part of the word, be sure to include both letters.

TRY IT OUT

CREATE A NEW WORD BY JOINING EACH PREFIX OR SUFFIX WITH ITS MAIN WORD.

ideal + ly = _______________ mean + ness = _______________

ir + regular = _______________ il + legal = _______________

un + necessary = _______________ over + run = _______________

Here are some examples.

dis + satisfied = di*ss*atisfied
inter + racial = inte*rr*acial
mis + state = mi*ss*tate
im + moral = i*mm*oral
ir + relevant = i*rr*elevant
il + logical = i*ll*ogical

TRY IT OUT

CREATE A NEW WORD BY JOINING EACH PREFIX OR SUFFIX WITH ITS MAIN WORD.

cruel + ly = ______________
ir + resistible = ______________
dis + appoint = ______________
un + natural = ______________
definite + ly = ______________
over + ripe = ______________

EXERCISE 13C: Fill in the missing letters in each word, using either one or two of the letters indicated. If necessary, refer to the list of common prefixes and suffixes in Appendix II.

1. *r* i ___ esponsible
2. *n* drunke ___ ess
3. *r* i ___ eplaceable
4. *s* mi ___ pelling
5. *s* di ___ appear
6. *l* accidenta ___ y
7. *n* u ___ eighborly
8. *r* inte ___ action
9. *s* di ___ illusioned
10. *r* inte ___ eaction
11. *r* ove ___ ated
12. *n* u ___ acceptable
13. *l* i ___ igitimate
14. *n* kee ___ ess
15. *s* mi ___ inform
16. *r* inte ___ elationship
17. *m* i ___ ature
18. *s* di ___ agreeable
19. *r* ove ___ ule
20. *l* i ___ iterate

 The Comparison/Contrast Essay

We frequently use the skills of comparison and contrast to help us make decisions and understand the world around us. Should I buy the Honda Accord or the Toyota Camry? Do I want to major in accounting or nursing? Do I want to eat lunch in the school cafeteria or at the local diner? Should I drop Jennifer and start dating Carol? To make these decisions, we compare two things to see how they are similar, and we contrast them to see how they are different.

In an essay, you can use comparison and contrast either to persuade or to inform. For example, you might write an essay comparing football and rugby to persuade the reader that one sport is better than the other. Or your purpose for writing the essay might be to give the reader a better understanding of the British sport of rugby by comparing it to football. To write an effective comparison/contrast essay, be sure to follow these guidelines:

- **I Select Two Subjects That Are Related in Some Way.**
- **II Write a Thesis Statement That Includes Your Purpose for Writing the Essay.**
- **III Use Several Specific Points of Comparison to Support Your Purpose.**
- **IV Organize the Points of Comparison in a Logical Way.**

I. Select Two Subjects That Are Related in Some Way. If the two subjects do not have enough in common, you will find it impossible to write an effective comparison/contrast essay. Dogs and cats can be compared because they are both pets; traditional film cameras and digital cameras can be compared because they are both used to take photographs. However, airplanes and cell phones cannot be compared because they are not related in any way. At the same time, if you select two subjects that are very similar, the points you make will be obvious and your essay will be boring.

TRY IT OUT

FOR EACH SUBJECT GIVEN BELOW, THINK OF A SECOND SUBJECT THAT COULD BE PAIRED WITH IT IN AN EFFECTIVE COMPARISON/CONTRAST ESSAY.

1. my mother and ______________________
2. the best date I've ever had and ______________________
3. shopping malls and ______________________

II. **Write a Thesis Statement That Includes Your Purpose for Writing the Essay.** The thesis statement for a comparison/contrast essay should identify your subjects, state the main point you want to make about them, and indicate whether you are comparing or contrasting them (or both). Notice how the thesis statements below fulfill all three requirements.

The Honda Accord and the Toyota Camry are both excellent automobiles, but they differ in a number of important ways.

Although Las Vegas and Atlantic City both rely on gambling as the major attraction, Las Vegas is a better place to visit.

TRY IT OUT

USING ONE OF THE SUBJECT PAIRS YOU CREATED IN THE PREVIOUS TRY IT OUT, WRITE A THESIS STATEMENT THAT COULD BE USED IN THE INTRODUCTION OF A COMPARISON/CONTRAST ESSAY.

III. **Use Several Specific Points of Comparison to Support Your Purpose.** On a sheet of paper or on your computer, make two columns, one for each of your subjects. Then in the left-hand column, jot down a list of points and details that you might want to make about Subject A. Next, read each point on your list, asking yourself: How does Subject B compare on this point? Jot down the answer to that question in the right-hand column. For example, if you are comparing VCR's and DVD players, you might start by indicating in the left-hand column that the picture produced by a VCR tends to be a little blurry. How do DVD players compare on that point? In the right-hand column, you would note that the picture produced by a DVD player is much sharper.

After completing your two lists, cross out any points that do not clearly support the purpose of your essay. If you are not left with enough points of comparison to support your thesis statement, you will need to do some additional brainstorming. Finally, add specific facts, examples, and descriptive details to develop each of your points. These details will help the reader understand the similarities and differences you are discussing. For instance, in the essay comparing VCR's and DVD players, you might explain that while VCR's fill the television screen with 400 lines of information at one time, DVD players fill the screen with 800 lines of information. As a result, the picture is so highly detailed that it is possible to see single hairs on an actor's head.

TRY IT OUT

ON YOUR OWN PAPER, BRAINSTORM TWO LISTS OF POINTS OF COMPARISON THAT COULD BE USED TO SUPPORT THE THESIS STATEMENT YOU WROTE FOR THE PREVIOUS TRY IT OUT. THEN ADD SPECIFIC FACTS, EXAMPLES, AND DESCRIPTIVE DETAILS TO DEVELOP EACH POINT.

IV. Organize the Points of Comparison in a Logical Way. You may organize the points in a comparison/contrast essay in one of three ways: point by point, subject by subject, or a combination of the two. To use point-by-point organization, make a point about Subject A and then discuss that same point about Subject B. Then make a second point about Subject A, followed by a discussion of that point for Subject B. Continue to move back and forth between the two subjects until you have presented all of your points. Let's say that you use point-by-point organization to present three points in one body paragraph. The pattern of organization would be AB, AB, AB. Once you start using point-by-point organization, be sure that you continue to discuss the subjects in the same order until you complete the paragraph. If you change the pattern of organization within a paragraph, the reader may find it difficult to follow the discussion.

To use subject-by-subject organization, make all of your points about Subject A and then go on to make all of your points about Subject B. If you are presenting three points, the pattern of organization would be AAA, BBB. When you are using subject-by-subject organization, be sure to cover the same points for both subjects in the same order.

Which of the two patterns of organization should you use when you are writing a comparison/contrast essay? That all depends on what you want to emphasize. Use point-by-point organization if you want the individual details to stand out. Use subject-by-subject organization if you are more interested in emphasizing the larger picture.

TRY IT OUT

LOOK THROUGH THE LIST OF POINTS OF COMPARISON THAT YOU CREATED FOR THE PREVIOUS TRY IT OUT. DECIDE ON THE MOST LOGICAL WAY TO ORGANIZE THE POINTS. WHICH POINTS BELONG TOGETHER IN THE SAME PARAGRAPH? WHICH METHOD OF ORGANIZATION WOULD BE MORE EFFECTIVE FOR EACH PARAGRAPH: POINT BY POINT OR SUBJECT BY SUBJECT?

The Pointers for Writing a Comparison/Contrast Essay chart on the next page provides some additional guidelines for writing an effective comparison/contrast essay. Following the chart are three model essays.

A comparison/contrast essay using point-by-point organization

A comparison/contrast essay using subject-by-subject organization

A comparison/contrast essay combining point-by-point and subject-by-subject organization

Be sure to read these essays, for they will help to give you a clear understanding of how to write a good comparison/contrast essay of your own.

POINTERS FOR WRITING A COMPARISON/CONTRAST ESSAY

1. The *introduction* should include a thesis statement that identifies your subjects, states the main point you want to make about them, and indicates whether you are comparing or contrasting them (or both). You should also try to spark the reader's interest by using one of the methods described on pages 303–304 of Chapter Seven.
2. The *body paragraphs* should be developed with several points of comparison that clearly support your thesis. Each point should include specific facts, examples, and descriptive details to help the reader understand the similarities and differences you are discussing. To present a balanced discussion, be sure to give an equal amount of coverage to both subjects.
3. The *order* you use to arrange the points of comparison in each paragraph should be appropriate for the topic. The most effective types of order for a comparison/contrast essay are these:

   Point by Point: To use point-by-point organization, move back and forth between your two subjects, maintaining the same order throughout the paragraph. Compare Subject A and Subject B on the first point, on the second point, and so on. (AB, AB, AB).

   Subject by Subject: To use subject-by-subject organization, present all of your points about Subject A and then go on to present all of your points about Subject B. (AAA, BBB).
4. To move smoothly from one point to another, use appropriate *transitions* that signal comparison and contrast: *similarly, likewise, in like manner, in contrast, however, but, still, nevertheless, yet, on the other hand, on the contrary, at the same time, although this may be true.*
5. The *conclusion* should refer back to the main point of your thesis statement and should make a final comment or observation about the similarities and/or differences you have discussed in your essay.

A Comparison/Contrast Essay Using Point-by-Point Organization. The writer of the essay below uses point-by-point organization because he wants to emphasize the individual points he makes about the United States and Nigeria.

Different Cultures, Different Customs

(1) When I left Nigeria and came to the United States at the age of 20, I found that Americans had some amazing ideas about African culture. Some Americans asked me peculiar questions: "Do Africans live in trees?" "Do they

wear clothes?" "Do they have automobiles?" Because these were really weird questions, I had to give the real picture of my country and Africa at large. In Nigeria we wear clothes, we have automobiles, and we live in houses like the people in the United States. In those ways our cultures are alike. However, the cultures of Nigeria and the United States are very different from each other in many ways, especially in aspects of courtship, marriage, and the raising of children.

(2) Courtship is one major difference. In the United States when two people love each other, as long as they are at least 18 years of age, they can get married whether the parents approve or not. In Nigeria, if the couple decide to get married without the parents' permission, the parents could curse the marriage, and it is strongly believed that the parents' curse could prevent the couple from having children or keeping a job. In the United States, a couple can go out together and visit each other's apartments without the family being there. During courtship in Nigeria, an unmarried couple cannot go out alone together or visit each other's apartments. If they are going to get married in the near future, then they can visit each other's families during courtship and develop a relationship with other members of both families. During these visits, the girl's father might interview the boy and ask questions about his family background, his education, his job, and his sense of responsibility. The major question is: Why do you want my daughter for your wife? It is the boy's job to convince the father that he can provide for the girl and will never hurt her. In more recent times, it is considered good if the boy can help his future wife to get a job so that she can help support her younger brothers and sisters. In addition, the boy pays a dowry, a very large sum that he has to give the bride's family for the privilege of marrying their daughter. Even if the parents do not insist on the dowry, the uncles and aunts usually do because they know that some members of the family become rich when the dowry is paid.

(3) After courtship, marriage is also different. In both countries nowadays, it is usual for both the man and the woman to have a job. In the United States, if the woman has a higher-paying job, that makes her the breadwinner in the house, while sometimes the man takes over the woman's domestic duties. In the Nigerian marriage, the man has more right to everything in the house, and he is the breadwinner even if the woman earns more in her job. It is a taboo in Nigeria for a man to take over a woman's domestic duties. Although the divorce rate is very high in the United States, it is not in Nigeria because the woman has to put up with every kind of domestic situation; she has vowed in the church to remain a good wife in all conditions. The overwhelming thing is that in the United States a divorced man might have to leave the house to the woman and the children, and then he has to live somewhere else. This has never happened in Nigeria. A woman cannot take a family issue to the court for public hearing. It would be like "painting the family name black" or "rubbing the family name in swamp." In Nigeria, the family issues remain within the house and would never be taken to court.

(4) Raising children is another distinct factor of cultural difference between the United States and Nigeria. It is very common to put young children in a day-care program in the United States because both parents work. In Nigeria, there are very few day-care centers because most parents leave their children in the care of friends or neighbors, who are like part of the extended family. Material things are also handled differently. In the United States many parents try to satisfy their children's wants no matter what the cost or the effects of satisfying the desire. Some children in the United States get anything they want whether the parents like it or not because the children are capable of threatening the parents if they are not satisfied. In Nigeria, the parents buy only what they want for the child. The child has no choice as far as the parents are concerned. If the child rejects anything from a parent, he or she gets whipped because it is a sign of disrespect to the parent. American parents could not emulate the Nigerian parent because American law prohibits beating the child; however, beating is not unusual in Nigeria. If the parents are not home, the neighbors have permission to administer the whipping, and when the parents get home they may add on their own beating because the child has embarrassed the family.

(5) Although the cultures of Nigeria and the United States are very different from each other, they have both been good for my mental growth. As I have learned more and more about my new culture, I have adapted easily to the many wonderful aspects of American life. At the same time, I still honor my heritage by continuing to practice the best Nigerian customs. Because I can now use the valuable traditions of two countries, I consider myself lucky to be a Nigerian American.

TRY IT OUT

ANSWER THESE QUESTIONS ABOUT THE ESSAY "DIFFERENT CULTURES, DIFFERENT CUSTOMS."

1. In the introduction, what is the writer's thesis statement? ____________

   ____

2. In paragraph 4, what are the three main points of comparison? ______

   ____

3. In the conclusion, how does the writer restate the main point of his thesis statement? ____________________________

   ____

A Comparison/Contrast Essay Using Subject-By-Subject Organization. The writer of the essay below uses subject-by-subject organization because he is more interested in creating an overall impression than he is in emphasizing all of the details.

To Box or to Ban

(1) "One . . . two . . . three . . . four . . . (get up!) . . . five . . . six . . . seven . . . (Get Up!) . . . eight . . . nine . . . (GET UP! GET UP!) . . . TEN! The winner!" One man can't get up from the floor of the ring; the other man wins. A sport that is based on one contestant beating up the other one, according to the American Medical Association (AMA) and the American Academy of Neurology (AAN), should not be allowed. Supporters of boxing, however, believe that the medical establishment's position unfairly discriminates against boxing and that those who want to box have a right to enter the ring. Voices on both sides of the argument are passionate. The AMA and the AAN call for boxing to be banned in the United States; boxing advocates believe that boxers have a right to their sport and that banning it would be a violation of that right.

(2) The most obvious issue in the controversy is boxing deaths. Twenty-four-year-old Robert Benson, for example, collapsed into a coma following a ten-round draw and died five days later without regaining consciousness; his was one of six boxing deaths in the year 2000. Statistics on boxing deaths vary wildly; one source reports 30 professional boxing deaths between 1979 and 2002, and another lists 114. Records of amateur boxing indicate 7 deaths between 1993 and 2002 and 19 since 1982. "There is absolutely no way you can make boxing safe," according to the AAN. Boxing advocates, however, argue that boxing is no more dangerous than many other sports that are not being attacked by the medical establishment. Football is statistically twice as deadly. For six sports, the following fatality rates have been reported per 100,000 participants: horse racing, 128; skydiving, 123; mountaineering, 51; motorcycle racing, 7; college football, 3; boxing, 1.3. The other sports are not in danger of being banned, argue boxing supporters. Why pick on us?

(3) Death, however, is not the only health issue involved. Brain and spinal cord injuries can damage a boxer for life. In a 1970s study, neurosurgeons throughout Britain were asked about the number of post-traumatic brain-damage patients they had treated. They responded: 12 jockeys, 5 footballers, 2 rugby players, 2 wrestlers, 1 parachutist, and 290 boxers. The AMA has estimated that perhaps 15 percent of professional boxers per year suffer brain damage. There is some evidence suggesting that boxing can be a cause of Parkinson's disease, as in the sad case of Mohammad Ali. The AMA and AAN believe that such a level of irreparable damage should not be tolerated. Yet boxing advocates argue that to ban boxing would create an even greater health risk. With boxing legal, the sport is regulated, there are regular health checkups, and boxers receive immediate medical attention in the ring. If the sport were banned, they argue, it would go underground, and none of these safeguards would exist. "If the AMA would like boxing to take place in bars and backrooms where there's no medical supervision, then they're going to

have deaths," states the president of the American Association of Professional Ringside Physicians. Furthermore, supporters of the sport argue, boxers make the free choice to fight with full knowledge of the risks. Dr. Robert Cantu, noting that our society has tolerated such extreme risks as Evil Knievel's canyon jumping and the *X-Games* on ESPN, points out, "We serve society for the better by working to make those sports safer." Responsible regulation rather than banning is the best policy, he suggests.

(4) A third issue is the ethics of boxing. Boxing opponents claim that it is a brutal, barbaric practice that should not be allowed in a civilized society. The AMA states that "all forms of boxing are public demonstrations of interpersonal violence" and that the goal of the sport is to render the opponent completely helpless. Boxing critics believe that it is the job of a civilized society to ensure that such behavior is not allowed. Boxing advocates, on the other hand, argue that boxing is not a form of interpersonal violence but rather a sport of controlled aggression. There are rules, and the sport is refereed. The goal is not harm to the opponent; the goal is to win, which is more often accomplished by outsmarting the opponent and winning points than by knocking him out. Skill, not violence, is at the heart of the sport.

(5) The argument goes on. It was in 1972 that the AAN first proposed that boxing be abolished, and agreement has not even begun to be reached. The stakes are high. Lennox Lewis and Mike Tyson each pocketed approximately $25 million for their 2002 heavyweight title bout; the fight, which was broadcast to 1.8 million homes, generated $103 million in pay-per-view revenues. The star power of fans like Sylvester Stallone and Bruce Willis attracts coverage by popular programs such as *Entertainment Tonight* and *Access Hollywood.* Should boxing be banned? With so much money and glamour attached to the sport, it is unlikely that agreement will be reached any time soon.

TRY IT OUT

ANSWER THESE QUESTIONS ABOUT THE ESSAY "TO BOX OR TO BAN."

1. In the introduction, what is the writer's thesis statement? ____________

   ____

2. What three major points does the writer discuss in the body paragraphs?

   ____

3. In the conclusion, what final observation does the writer make about boxing? ____

   ____

A Comparison/Contrast Essay Combining Point-By-Point and Subject-By-Subject Organization. The writer of the essay below uses both methods of organization for a topic that might be discussed in a social science course.

Why Don't You Understand Me?

(1) "Honey, let's stop and ask for directions." "Hey, I've got the map. I can figure it out." "Sweetheart, we've been going around in circles for two hours." "Aha, here's Route 37. Let's try this way." Guess which of the speakers is a woman and which is a man. We each have made our own informal observations of the way women and men communicate. Researchers who study language patterns confirm our casual hunch that men and women indeed communicate differently. According to some studies, men's and women's patterns of conversation are so different that men and women might as well be citizens of two different countries speaking two different languages.

(2) These studies indicate that men's and women's communication patterns have two very different purposes. Men tend to see the world as a battleground for a constant negotiation of one-up/one-down. Life is a contest to preserve independence and avoid failure, and the purpose of conversation is to maintain one's status in that contest. Women, on the other hand, tend to see the world as a network of connections. For them the underlying purpose of communication is intimacy and connection. Conversation is a negotiation for closeness, support, and mutual understanding. Because men and women operate out of such different purposes, the result is very different patterns of conversation in both public and private interactions.

(3) In public situations, the differences between men's and women's conversational patterns show up in several ways. One is joke telling. Men are much more likely than women to tell jokes in group situations where there is an audience of four or more in the group. Men most often tell their jokes to other men but will also tell them to mixed groups or to women. Women, who are stereotyped as not being joke tellers at all, are more likely to tell jokes in groups containing only women and no more than three listeners. Gossip is another area of difference. Men prefer to talk about physical things such as cars, events such as sports, or public institutions such as business or politics. Women tend to be much more interested in the personal details of people's lives. Although men often stereotype women as being gossipy and catty about other people, researchers studying women's conversation have found that when women gossip they are not usually mean and critical. Gossip is rather a way of establishing closeness and enjoying the daily ups and downs of social life. Men and women also differ in terms of boasting. Men are more likely to talk publicly about their successes and accomplishments. Women have been socialized to believe that it is rude and inappropriate to brag in public. They are much more likely to act modest and not to put their accomplishments forward.

(4) Differences in men's and women's conversational styles not only show up in public situations; they are evident in private as well. How many times have you seen a cartoon of a man absorbed in reading the newspaper or watching television and a woman trying to get his attention? Although men often talk more than women in public situations, they are likely to talk less at home. Because men tend to see conversation as a way of preserving independence and status in a competitive world, they are likely to want to come home and take a rest from it. Women, on the other hand, see home as the perfect setting for the personal connection of one-to-one conversation. Who wants to watch the ballgame when you can talk about your day? In private talk, men and women also differ in their approach to problem solving. If someone is having difficulties, men are likely to offer advice and propose solutions. Women are more likely to show sympathy and understanding. "I don't want advice," a woman might say, "I just wanted you to know." Men use conversation as a mode for giving information; women use it to establish connection.

(5) These differences between men's and women's conversational styles can lead to the feeling of being misunderstood and even to conflict. However, just as it is possible for people from different cultures to learn enough about each other to be able to communicate, it is also possible for men and women to become aware of each other's differing styles. By acknowledging their differences and making an extra effort to understand, both men and women can reduce conflict and increase the opportunities to enjoy and, yes, even understand one another.

TRY IT OUT

ANSWER THESE QUESTIONS ABOUT THE ESSAY "WHY DON'T YOU UNDERSTAND ME?"

1. In the introduction, what is the writer's thesis statement? ____________

____

2. What three major points does the writer discuss in the body paragraphs?

____

3. What method of organization does the writer use in each body paragraph? ____

4. In the conclusion, what final observation does the writer make about her topic? ____

____

EXERCISE 13D: This exercise requires you to write an outline for a comparison/contrast essay. To begin, you need to select two restaurants that you know well. They might be fast-food restaurants, local diners, or fancy places that serve gourmet food. Then write a thesis statement that indicates which of the two restaurants you think is the better one. Next, for each of the three body paragraphs, write a topic sentence that states one main area of comparison: the quality of the food, the variety of food on the menu, the cost, the environment, or the service. Finally, to support each topic sentence, jot down three specific points that compare and/or contrast the two restaurants.

Introduction

Thesis statement: ______________________________

____

Body Paragraph 1

Topic sentence: ______________________________

Points for Subject A	*Points for Subject B*
____________	____________
____________	____________
____________	____________

Body Paragraph 2

Topic sentence: ______________________________

Points for Subject A	*Points for Subject B*
____________	____________
____________	____________
____________	____________

Body Paragraph 3

Topic sentence: ______________________________

Points for Subject A	*Points for Subject B*
__________	__________
__________	__________
__________	__________

Conclusion

EXERCISE 13E: Select one of the topics below as the basis for a comparison/contrast essay. Then follow the list of steps to create your essay.

Topics

your neighborhood several years ago and your neighborhood now
your views on an important issue and those of a parent, bother, sister, or friend
who you were several years ago and who you are now
writing an essay by hand and writing it on a computer
true love and puppy love
living in a city and living in the suburbs
going to an out-of-town college and going to a local college
high school education and college education
soap operas and real life
library research and Internet research
two places you have lived
two weddings or parties you have attended
two popular singers, actors, athletes, or politicians
two cars, computers, or other machines
two friends
two views on a controversial issue
two teachers you have had
two careers or fields of study
two religions

Steps

1. After selecting a specific topic, decide on the purpose for your essay. Is your purpose to persuade or to inform?
2. Create a thesis statement that identifies your subjects, states the main point you want to make about them, and indicates whether you are comparing or contrasting them (or both).
3. On paper or on your computer, draw up a two-column list of similarities and differences. Next, cross out any points that do not clearly support the purpose of your essay. If you do not have enough points of comparison to support your thesis statement, do some additional brainstorming.

4. Add specific facts, examples and descriptive details to develop each of your points. These details will help the reader understand the similarities and differences you are discussing.
5. Decide on a logical order for presenting your points of comparison. Will you arrange the points using point-by-point organization or subject-by-subject organization? Or will you use both methods?
6. Think about your conclusion. What can you say to remind the reader of your thesis? What final comment or observation can you make about the similarities and differences? Keep in mind that your ideas may change somewhat as you write, for good writing often generates new insights into your topic. However, starting with a clear sense of your essay's purpose will help you select and organize your points of comparison.
7. You are now ready to write the first draft of your comparison/contrast essay.
8. After completing the first draft, use the revision process described on pages 311–22 to help you achieve a successful comparison/contrast essay.

The Classification Essay

Classification is the process of separating people, things, or ideas into different groups or categories. We constantly rely on classification to help bring order into our lives. For example, we organize our clothing so that all our underwear is in one drawer and our shirts are in another. When we go into a supermarket, we find all the fresh produce together (usually near the entrance), while all the meat is at the back of the store and the dairy products are grouped in refrigerator cases that line one side. Classification, then, helps us when we are hunting for something, whether it is a clean shirt or a quart of milk.

In a classification essay, you have the opportunity to divide your topic into different categories so that the reader will have a better understanding of the subject matter. In addition, you might offer a fresh way of thinking about the topic, or you might even try to persuade the reader to agree with your point of view. To write an effective classification essay, be sure to follow these guidelines:

I Divide Your Topic into Categories Based on a Controlling Principle.

II Write a Thesis Statement That Includes Your Purpose for Writing the Essay.

III Present the Categories in a Logical Order.

I. Divide Your Topic into Categories Based on a Controlling Principle. The controlling principle is the rule you are following for selecting the categories. Let's say, for example, that you want to write a classification essay about jobs. If you decide to classify jobs by salary, your categories might include low pay, average pay, and high pay. Or you might prefer to classify jobs by the educational background required: high school, college, and graduate school. You could also classify jobs by using one of these controlling principles: the work environment, the degree of difficulty, the hours, or the amount of danger. Each of these principles would yield a different set of categories. The point is to choose a controlling principle that supports your purpose for writing the essay. Then be sure to divide your topic into categories on the basis of that single principle.

TRY IT OUT

WHICH CATEGORIES WOULD BE APPROPRIATE FOR THE CONTROLLING PRINCIPLE GIVEN BELOW?

Topic: Cars *Controlling Principle: Cost*

Categories: 1. foreign made
2. expensive
3. convertible
4. moderately priced
5. fuel efficient
6. economy

II. Write a Thesis Statement That Includes Your Purpose for Writing the Essay. The thesis statement should identify your topic and reveal the controlling principle you have used to select your categories. In addition, an effective thesis statement explains why these categories are important. Why are you discussing them? What is the main point you are trying to make? Compare the effectiveness of the two thesis statements below.

There are three major types of digital cameras.

Before you buy a digital camera, you need to know about the three major types: cameras for beginners, cameras for more advanced users, and cameras for professional photographers.

Both thesis statements identify the topic and the controlling principle: three major types of digital cameras. However, the second thesis statement is more interesting because it includes the purpose for writing the essay and even names the three categories.

TRY IT OUT

REVISE THE THESIS STATEMENT BELOW SO THAT IT INCLUDES THE PURPOSE FOR WRITING THE ESSAY AND PERHAPS EVEN THE THREE CATEGORIES.

There are three major types of pollution in my city.

III. Present the Categories in a Logical Order. Chronological order may work well when one category happens before another. For example, if you are discussing three types of wedding based on the time of day when they occur, your categories might be morning weddings, afternoon weddings, and evening weddings. However, the best method of organization for most topics will be least-to-most order. To use this method, you start with the category that is the "least" and end with the category that is the "most." You might move from the least important to the most important, from the least unusual to the most unusual, from the least annoying to the most annoying, from the least popular to the most popular, or from the least expensive to the most expensive. The idea is to end with the most memorable category.

TRY IT OUT

AFTER SELECTING A TOPIC GIVEN BELOW, CHOOSE AT LEAST THREE USEFUL CATEGORIES BASED ON THE CONTROLLING PRINCIPLE. THEN ARRANGE THE CATEGORIES IN A LOGICAL ORDER. USE YOUR OWN PAPER FOR THIS ASSIGNMENT.

Topics: movies, TV shows, music, books, magazines

Controlling Principle: favorite types

The Pointers for Writing a Classification Essay chart below provides some additional guidelines for writing an effective classification essay. Following the chart are three model essays.

A classification essay about restaurant customers

A classification essay about pets

A classification essay on an academic topic

Be sure to read these essays, for they will help to give you a clear understanding of how to write a good classification essay of your own.

POINTERS FOR WRITING A CLASSIFICATION ESSAY

1. The *introduction* should include a thesis statement that identifies your topic, reveals the principle you have used to select your categories, and explains why these categories are important. The introduction may also name the specific categories you plan to discuss.
2. When you select the categories, be sure that they meet three criteria:

   All of the categories must be based on the same controlling principle.

   Each category must be different from the other categories so that they do not overlap.

   All of the categories must clearly support the main purpose of the essay.

(Continued)

(Continued)

3. The *body paragraphs* should be developed with specific examples, incidents, and descriptive details that illustrate each category. Use comparison and contrast to show the ways in which the categories are similar and the ways in which they are different. The goal is to make each category clear and understandable to the reader.
4. The *order* in which the categories are presented should be logical. Chronological order may work well when one category happens before another. However, the best method of organization for most topics will be least-to-most order.
5. To move smoothly from one category to another, use appropriate *transitions: the first, the second, the third, the last, the next, the final, one, another, the least important, more important, the most important.*
6. The *conclusion* should refer back to the main point of your thesis statement and should make a final comment or observation about the categories you have discussed in your essay. Why is it important for the reader to know about these categories?

A Classification Essay About Restaurant Customers. In the essay below, each category is supported with several specific examples that clearly show how the three types of customer differ from one another.

My Worst Customers

(1) Waiting on tables at the Silver Moon Diner has a few advantages. On a busy weekend, I can pocket decent tips, and every semester the boss allows me to readjust my hours so that I can work around my changing school schedule. Of course, the job has its share of disadvantages too, like dealing with a grouchy chef and carrying heavy trays loaded with food. However, the real trial is having to wait on difficult customers, most of whom fall into one of three categories: royalty, undecideds, and scavengers.

(2) The customers who act like royalty want what they want, and they want it right now. They don't want their scrambled eggs hard or soft: "Make them firm, but a little on the runny side." If the chef is unable to make sense of those instructions to their exact pleasure, those eggs get sent straight back. Some complain that the orange juice doesn't taste fresh-squeezed. Nowhere on the menu does it claim that we squeeze the oranges; those customers need to go to the juice bar down the block. "My silverware doesn't match." "This

plate has a crack"—a hairline crack on the bottom side. What was she doing looking under the plate? "My soup is too hot; my ice cream is too cold." I'm surprised no one has asked for a shoeshine yet. To make matters worse, these "royal" customers show no appreciation for all the service they demand; they never say "please" or "thank you," and their tips wouldn't pay for a cup of coffee.

(3) While the royalty know exactly what they want, the undecided customers are a problem because they don't know what they want. Everyone else at the table is ready to order, but that one "undecided" simply can't make up her mind. As a result, I will have to return to that table several times during the next ten to fifteen minutes to see if she has reached a decision. After much agonizing, she will finally say, "I think I'd like the roast beef with potato pancakes." Then the person sitting next to her orders corned beef and cabbage, and she immediately wants that instead. She is satisfied with that choice until I bring her order just as the man at the next table gets his plate of beef stew. Suddenly that is what she really wanted all along. "I'm sure you wouldn't mind taking this back," she says ever so sweetly, as if I have nothing else to do. These people never expect to be charged for their flip-flopping choices, and they monopolize a table twice as long as anybody else, which of course means that I only make half as many tips.

(4) The third type of annoying customer is the scavenger. Scavengers want to pay for one meal and walk out with three. They will ask for a doggy bag even if there are only two French fries left on the plate. Then just about everything on the table will disappear into that doggy bag: the little packets of sugar and Sweet'n Low, the leftover bread and rolls, the bottle of ketchup, and even the radishes, carrots, and celery from the relish tray. One of the weekend regulars goes so far as to ask for a second basket of rolls when he is done with his meal. Into his knapsack they go. On occasion I have even seen a knife or a spoon slide into a customer's pocket. To complete the meal, scavengers will be sure to stop at the bowl of mints by the cash register. Ignoring the little spoon sitting on top of the mints, these people will grab a fistful of candy before they leave the diner. I have learned not to expect tips from the scavengers. They are so busy snatching up for themselves that they are not about to leave something for me.

(5) All of these—the royalty, the undecideds, and the scavengers—are so intent on what they want that the fact that I am a human being seems to escape them. I would like to see these people wear my uniform for a day and find out what it feels like to wait on customers like themselves. Maybe the Waiter for a Day plan would change their demanding, flip-flopping, and hoarding ways. At the very least, they might learn to give waiters some consideration and a decent tip.

TRY IT OUT

ANSWER THESE QUESTIONS ABOUT THE ESSAY "MY WORST CUSTOMERS."

1. In the introduction, what is the writer's thesis statement? ____

2. What principle does the writer use to classify her customers? ____

3. In the conclusion, how does the writer refer back to her thesis statement? ____

A Classification Essay About Pets. In the essay below, the writer uses classification to provide guidance to readers who might be interested in getting a pet.

Pets and Their People

(1) It has been said that over a period of time, people come to resemble their pets physically. Perhaps it is more true to say that pet owners choose pets that fit their personalities and meet their needs. There is a pet for every personality, and with few exceptions they fit into three basic categories: low-maintenance pets, trophy pets, and human substitutes.

(2) Those who like the idea of a pet but not the bother will choose from the low-maintenance division. For people who aren't home much, who regard a pet as a home accessory or who reject the idea of grooming, walking, or caring for anything requiring more personal attention than a plant, the ideal pet is a goldfish or a small lizard. (Hamsters and white mice, while easy to care for, thrive on interaction and as such are pushing the limit.) These pets are able to entertain themselves and require feeding once a day at most. They are small and portable, and therefore easy to bring to a friend's home in case of last-minute out-of-town jaunts. Because they tend not to live long, low-maintenance pets are not recommended for those who become emotionally attached to their pets (see "human substitutes" below). Also, it is best not to name these short-lived creatures, as it is hard to be casual about flushing George or Veronica down the toilet, even if it is only a neon tetra.

(3) Hobbyists, enthusiasts, and men who want to impress women will often choose a trophy pet. A trophy pet can range from the enviable (a pedigreed cat, a show dog, or a racehorse, for example) to the decidedly different (a venomous snake, a miniature pig, an exotic talking bird, or a deadly insect). Often, trophy pets have special requirements, which can include expensive trips to the dog

parlor or the need to swallow a live rabbit every week. In addition, trophy pets tend to attract a great deal of attention, as anyone who has ever walked down the street with a boa constrictor wrapped around his waist will attest. Therefore, a trophy-pet owner should be someone who enjoys the limelight and does not mind devoting a great deal of time and money to that end.

(4) Finally, for those people who feel lacking in their personal relationships—no children, no spouse, not enough friends—the "human substitute" is the ideal pet. Dogs and cats are the most popular choices because they are affectionate, trainable, and emotionally needy. However, it is not unusual to behold the "substitute" kind of pet owner speaking affectionately to a turtle or even a piranha. Psychologists might call this projection; these pet owners would insist that they are bonding with their animal companions. (Don't call them pets!) I have known a few such pet owners to take this behavior to the extreme. A childless friend of mine has had a series of professional photographs taken of her Yorkshire terrier. This in itself is not so unusual . . . except that the dog was dressed for the occasion, in a clown suit. Of course, there are dangers inherent in such extreme emotional attachment. If—as in the case of one over-60 couple I know—you regard a rodent as the grandchild you never had, you may be devastated when little Corky, having lived out his healthy hamster lifespan of three years, goes to that big cedar chip pile in the sky.

(5) If you are thinking about getting a pet, ask yourself what kind of person you are. Do you enjoy independence and spontaneity in your life? Do you want to attract a partner or a crowd? Do you have a great deal of love to give, or do you just need a friend? As the old saying goes, there is a lid to every pot, and it's just as true that there's a bird, a beast, or a bug that's just right for you.

TRY IT OUT

ANSWER THESE QUESTIONS ABOUT THE ESSAY "PETS AND THEIR PEOPLE."

1. In the introduction, what is the writer's thesis statement? ____________

   ____

2. What principle does the writer use to classify the pets? ____________

   ____

3. According to the conclusion, why is it important for the reader to know about these pet categories? ____________

   ____

A Classification Essay on an Academic Topic. The two previous essays were developed using personal experiences and observations. This essay, however, uses research to develop a topic that might be discussed in a social science course.

Youngest, Oldest, In Between?

(1) Who was the baby of your family? Was the oldest one bossy? Was the youngest one spoiled? Or maybe you were the only child with no one to beat you up and no one to pick on. Children know that their position in the family makes a difference. Psychologists who study birth order agree. They describe three types of personalities that tend to correspond with the birth order positions of firstborn, middle child, and youngest child.

(2) Firstborns are the children of new parents who often want to do everything right and imagine that they can raise a perfect child. Thus, it is no surprise that firstborn children tend to have high expectations of themselves. Typical firstborns are perfectionists and high achievers. They tend to work in an orderly way and pay careful attention to detail. They carry out tasks in a logical way and do not give up. With only adults as their first role models and no siblings to play with, they are likely to be serious and studious. As a result, firstborns are frequently "A" students. Often seeking approval from others, they tend to accept authority and shy away from making trouble or taking risks. Only children, because they have no younger siblings, are classified by psychologists as a special case of firstborns with many of the same traits. Firstborns and only children are often strong leaders. Of the first twenty-three astronauts sent into outer space, twenty-one were either firstborns or only children.

(3) Middle children live in a world between the firstborns and the babies. They do not have the advantage of being in charge or of being the little cute one. Caught in the middle, they tend to be the mediators and peacemakers, the ones who can see both sides of a conflict and who knock themselves out trying to get everyone to agree or to like each other again. They also tend to be loyal and generous friends. Because they spend their childhood trying to catch up with the older one, middle children are often very competitive. The advantage of being the middle child is that Mom and Dad have had a little more experience and are more relaxed. The disadvantage is not getting as much attention as the older one got. It is common for a family to have three photo albums jam-packed full of pictures of the first child, fifteen photos of the second child, and three of the third. Because of their experience growing up as the ones in between, middle children tend to make good diplomats and good managers who are able to take responsibility for getting others to work together well.

(4) The baby of the family is everyone's darling. Youngest children tend to be charming and manipulative; they are good at getting people to do what

they want. Because everyone wants to play with the youngest child, he or she often turns out to be sociable, affectionate, humorous, playful, and full of ideas. Unlike their careful oldest siblings, youngest children are not afraid to question authority or take risks. They are also not the perfectionist workers that the older ones are; they may be dreamy and absentminded rather than practical. Last-borns tend to be attracted to occupations that are people oriented. Good salespeople are often the youngest of their family.

(5) These descriptions are general tendencies, not rules. Everyone probably knows someone who fits one of these types perfectly and someone else who seems to blow the theory to bits. However, even though they are not watertight, theories of birth order can be useful tools. They can give us insight into ourselves as we try to understand who we are and why we behave the way we do. An understanding of birth order theory also can help parents support the positive qualities and discourage the negative ones associated with each birth order position. Consider your own experience; do the theories offer insight to you?

TRY IT OUT

ANSWER THESE QUESTIONS ABOUT THE ESSAY "YOUNGEST, OLDEST, IN BETWEEN?"

1. In the introduction, what is the writer's thesis statement? ______________

____

2. What method of organization does the writer use to present the three categories? ____

3. According to the conclusion, why is it important for the reader to know about these categories of birth order? ______________________

____

____

EXERCISE 13F: Divide each topic below into three categories that could be used to develop a classification essay. The controlling principle has been provided for each of the first five topics. You will need to choose a controlling principle for the remaining topics.

1. Topic: students

   Controlling principle: main reason for attending school

   Categories: ______________________________

   ____

   ____

2. Topic: music

   Controlling principle: types that appeal to young people

   Categories: ______________________________

   ____

   ____

3. Topic: daydreams

   Controlling principle: subject matter

   Categories: ______________________________

   ____

   ____

4. Topic: TV watchers

   Controlling principle: how frequently they watch

   Categories: ______________________________

   ____

   ____

5. Topic: parties

   Controlling principle: main purpose

   Categories: ______________________________

   ____

   ____

6. Topic: friends

   Controlling principle: ______________________

   Categories: ______________________

   ____

   ____

7. Topic: restaurants

   Controlling principle: ______________________

   Categories: ______________________

   ____

   ____

8. Topic: cable television stations

   Controlling principle: ______________________

   Categories: ______________________

   ____

   ____

9. Topic: parents

   Controlling principle: ______________________

   Categories: ______________________

   ____

   ____

10. Topic: clothing styles

    Controlling principle: ______________________

    Categories: ______________________

    ____

    ____

EXERCISE 13G: Select one of the topics below as the basis for a classification essay. Then follow the list of steps to create your essay.

Topics

teachers	neighborhoods	Web sites
co-workers	TV reality shows	dates you have had
junk food	shoppers	sports fans
advertisements	music videos	politicians
college courses	mail	gossip
graffiti	heroes	people in a dance club
bosses	weddings	eaters
neighbors	video games	vacations
home furnishing styles	your strengths	your weaknesses

Steps

1. After selecting a topic, choose at least three useful categories based on the same controlling principle.
2. Create a thesis statement that identifies your topic, reveals the principle you have used to select your categories, and explains why these categories are important.
3. For each category, jot down specific facts, examples, incidents, and descriptive details that will help the reader understand the category. In addition, be sure to explain how this category is different from the others.
4. Decide on a logical order for presenting your categories. Least-to-most order is often the most effective way to arrange the categories.
5. Think about your conclusion. What can you say to remind the reader of your thesis? What final comment or observation can you make about the categories you have discussed in your essay? Why is it important for the reader to know about these categories? Keep in mind that your ideas may change somewhat as you write, for good writing often generates new insights into your topic. However, starting with a clear sense of your essay's purpose will help you select and organize your categories.
6. You are now ready to write the first draft of your classification essay.
7. After completing the first draft, use the revision process described on pages 311–22 to help you achieve a successful classification essay.

The Cause/Effect Essay

Almost every day we use cause/effect analysis to help us examine the events that touch our lives. Why did I buy a car that I can't really afford? What caused the stock market to plunge 500 points today? Why are my parents getting a divorce? When we ask questions like these, we are searching for causes or reasons. At other times, we are more concerned with the effects or results of a particular action. If I get a part-time job, how will that affect my life? Will taking a vitamin supplement be good for me? What will be the effects of the President's new tax plan? By examining the causes or effects of an event or action, we hope to make better decisions and improve our understanding of the world around us.

In an essay, you can use cause/effect analysis either to inform or to persuade. For example, you might write an essay discussing the major causes of violence to give the reader a better understanding of this problem. Or you might write an essay discussing the major effects of violence to persuade the reader that we need stricter gun control laws. To write an effective cause/effect essay, be sure to follow these guidelines:

I Do Not Oversimplify.

II Do Not Mistake Coincidence for a Cause/Effect Relationship.

I. Do Not Oversimplify. Because most events are complicated, they usually have several causes and effects. Be careful not to fall into the trap of writing about only the most obvious ones. For instance, in the last few years, many Internet companies have gone bankrupt. The obvious cause is the lack of customers for the companies' products and services. However, if you examine this trend more closely, you might uncover a number of underlying causes: poor advertising, uninteresting products and services, the inefficient delivery of goods and services, and the lack of sufficient funding. To avoid oversimplifying, always search for at least three different causes or effects.

TRY IT OUT

WHY DO PEOPLE GET MARRIED? IN THE SPACES BELOW, JOT DOWN AT LEAST SIX CAUSES, INCLUDING SOME THAT MAY NOT BE OBVIOUS.

____

____

II. Do Not Mistake Coincidence for a Cause/Effect Relationship. You cannot assume that an earlier event caused a later event. Notice how this mistake creates faulty logic in the example below.

After Matthew gets wet in a rainstorm, he frequently comes down with a cold. This proves that getting wet causes colds.

The fact that Matthew frequently comes down with a cold after getting wet is a coincidence. Colds are caused by viruses, not rainstorms.

Similarly, you cannot assume that two events have a cause/effect relationship merely because they happen at the same time.

At about the same time that rock-and-roll was introduced in the United States, the country began to experience a noticeable increase in crime. Therefore, rock-and-roll causes crime.

The fact that these two events happened at about the same time does not prove that they are related in any way. Crime is a complex issue that has a great many causes.

TRY IT OUT

FOR EACH ITEM BELOW, EXPLAIN WHY A CAUSE/EFFECT RELATIONSHIP HAS NOT BEEN ESTABLISHED.

1. Last week my mother prayed that she would win the state lottery, and yesterday she won $10,000. This proves that prayer really works.
2. I suddenly had the feeling that my brother was in trouble, and at that precise moment, he called me from jail. I must have special mental powers.

The Pointers for Writing a Cause/Effect Essay chart on the next page provides some additional guidelines for writing an effective cause/effect essay. Following the chart are three model essays.

An essay that focuses on causes

An essay that focuses on effects

An essay that focuses on causes and effects

Be sure to read these essays, for they will help give you a clear understanding of how to write a good cause/effect essay of your own.

POINTERS FOR WRITING A CAUSE/EFFECT ESSAY

1. The *introduction* should include a thesis statement that identifies the topic, states your main point about it, and indicates whether you are writing about causes, effects, or both. To spark the reader's interest, the introduction may also explain why it is important to learn about this topic.
2. The *body paragraphs* should be developed with specific facts, examples and reasons that clearly explain each cause and/or effect. This evidence should prove that the cause/effect relationship you are discussing is correct.
3. The *order* you use to arrange the causes or effects should be appropriate for the topic. The most effective types of order for a cause/effect essay are these:

   Order of Importance: Order of importance generally starts with the least important cause or effect, then moves to a more important one, and ends with the most important one. Using this order will leave the reader with a strong final impression. It is also possible to reverse this order: start with the most important cause or effect and end with the least important one.

   Chronological Order: Chronological or time order discusses what happened first, what happened next, and so on. This order is appropriate to use when you want to show the order in which the causes occurred or the way in which one effect led to another and then another.
4. *Transitions* will help you establish clear relationships between the ideas you are discussing. Some transitions help signal causes while others help signal effects.

   To Signal Causes: *one cause* (*reason*), *another cause* (*reason*), *the first cause* (*reason*), *the second cause* (*reason*), *the third cause* (*reason*), *the most important cause* (*reason*), *because, since*

   To Signal Effects: *one effect* (*result*), *another effect* (*result*), *the first effect* (*result*), *the second effect* (*result*), *the third effect* (*result*), *the most important effect* (*result*), *as a result, therefore, thus, consequently*
5. The *conclusion* should refer back to the main point of your thesis statement and should make a final comment or observation about your topic. Why is it important for the reader to understand the cause/effect relationship you have discussed in your essay?

An Essay That Focuses on Causes. In the essay below, the writer uses many specific facts and examples to illustrate each cause.

Why I Joined a Street Gang

(1) After discovering education in jail, Malcolm X wrote, "I still marvel at how swiftly my previous life's pattern slid away from me, like snow off a roof. It is as though someone else I knew of had lived by hustling and crime." That is how I feel now about my former life as a gang member. I am in college now, studying computer architecture, building a new life that is not about violence and fear. The evidence of my old life, though, is still with me. The woman next to me in class last night asked about the skull tattooed on my arm. I am neither proud of it nor ashamed. It is simply evidence of a history that cannot be erased. She asked me why in the world a smart fellow like me would join a gang. I told her that, growing up the way I did, there were all kinds of reasons for me to turn to a gang.

(2) My home life wasn't much. My father left when I was too young to remember him. I don't even know what he looks like; my mom tore up all the pictures. I guess my mom loved me, but she was never around enough for me to know for sure. She worked in a factory all day and in a restaurant half the night, so how was she going to know what her kid was getting into? The little bit of raising that I got came from my brother, who was eight years older than I was. He was already into the life of the streets by the time I started school. Since he was the only role model I had, I wanted to be like him. I wanted the tough swaggering walk, the tattoo and buzz cut, the black leather jacket, the Harley-Davidson motorcycle that made so much noise that everyone had to notice. Even though my brother made sure I had the food and clothes that I needed, he was out with his friends most of the time, so home was a pretty lonesome place.

(3) I was lonely at home, and I was lonely at school too. I matured late. When I was 13 years old, I was only five feet, three inches tall and weighed about 120 pounds. I was always the puniest kid in the class, even smaller than some of the girls. I got kicked, poked, shoved, knocked down, and picked up so that I could be knocked down again. Teachers liked me because I was a quick learner, so that made things even worse. "Teacher's pet" and "kiss-up" were some of the nicer things that kids called me. By the time I got to the eighth grade, I had learned to cover up my smarts, and my brother had taught me how to use my fists to defend myself. Determined to prove that I was no longer a nerd, I started to get into trouble in the ninth grade. I didn't hesitate to punch out anyone who picked on me or even gave me a dirty look. When a teacher accused me of starting a fistfight in the hallway, I cursed him out and was suspended for a week. About halfway through the eleventh grade I got involved in a knife fight in the boys' locker room. That was when the school kicked me out, and the neighborhood gang took me in. They liked that I wasn't afraid of a fight, and I liked that they treated me like family. I was finally getting the attention and acceptance that I had craved for so long.

(4) Being in the gang also gave me the material things I had never been able to have as a kid. We controlled the drug sales in the neighborhood, and the money flowed fast. Now I had a Rolex watch, gold chains, and a closet full of designer clothes that were a lot better than what the kids who used to pick on me had. I also bought a Total Gym, an expensive exercise machine that I saw Chuck Norris advertising on a TV infomercial. With the help of this equipment, my body started to fill out with solid muscles. Suddenly I had girls throwing themselves at me like I couldn't believe, especially after I paid cash for a red Chrysler Sebring convertible with a Bose sound system that could be heard from two blocks away. Now I had money for a powerful computer and could go back to learning things, this time in the secrecy of my own room where no one would accuse me of being a nerd. I thought I had it all.

(5) Then a few of the gang members got killed, and my best buddy went to jail. I quickly realized that I could wind up just like my friends—either dead or behind bars. So I decided to put my Brooklyn street life behind me, and I went to live with my Aunt Alma in Bayside, Queens. With her support and encouragement, I managed to pass the GED on my first try and then enrolled in a community college. At school I am starting to see that I can have friendships based on something besides insane loyalty that is held together by nothing stronger than fear and loneliness. Some people would judge me harshly for things that I did in the past, but at the time I was just trying to survive in the only way I could figure out. I was a lonely kid with no one to help me find other choices. I am happy that those days are over now.

TRY IT OUT

ANSWER THESE QUESTIONS ABOUT THE ESSAY "WHY I JOINED A STREET GANG."

1. In the introduction, what is the writer's thesis statement? ____________

   ____

2. What are the writer's three major causes for joining a gang? ________

   ____

   ____

3. In the conclusion, what observations does the writer make about his life as a gang member? ____________________________

   ____

An Essay That Focuses on Effects. In the essay below, the writer uses brief incidents to illustrate each effect.

Cell Phone Hell

(1) Maybe I'm strange or behind the times, but I just don't "get" cell phones. I can understand having one for roadside or family emergencies, but other than that, I simply don't understand the need to communicate verbally twenty-four hours a day. An ever increasing portion of the population obviously disagrees with me: Many people would no sooner walk out of the door without their cell phones than without their clothes. However, cell phones have other effects besides mere convenience. These little gadgets have changed our quality of life in a number of ways, some of which are not always for the better.

(2) First, cell phones in their role as grown-up pacifiers have created a whole generation of people who never have to say "good-bye." Those who are insecure about their relationships or their jobs can now be in constant touch. Have you ever walked down the street behind someone who is loudly phoning his beloved to say, "Hi sweetheart, I'm about a half-block away from home; I'll see you in a minute. Love you too!" Please . . . it's not as if he's calling to see if he can pick up a quart of milk on the way. Similarly, cell phones enable the workaholic who can't be away from the office for ten minutes without checking in. I once worked with a woman who would call me about our projects while sunning herself at the beach. Before the days of cell phones, these people had to take an occasional break from each other; now they have a way to never, never let go.

(3) A second effect of cell phones is the almost nonstop disturbance of the peace. People who use cell phones seem to think that the person at the other end is hard of hearing. This creates shouting matches in the most inappropriate places. On a recent elevator ride, I was conversing with a friend when a man got in on another floor, speaking in that broadcasting mode peculiar to cell-phone users. It became a contest of escalating voices to see whose conversation would be heard. No one could really hear much of anything in the racket that resulted. Even worse, the last time I went to a movie, a girl sitting near me answered her ringing cell phone during the film and then proceeded to give the caller a summary of the plot. When other members of the audience began to yell at her to shut up, she responded with, "Shut up yourself!" The shouting match continued until an usher escorted the girl out of the auditorium several minutes later. By that time, I had missed the most important scene in the film.

(4) Finally, cell phones have brought about an end to what we used to know as privacy. No matter where we are, we're stuck hearing other people's business, which is broadcast as if it were our business too. I have heard cell phone accounts of the most intimate details of people's lives, from their stock portfolios to their love lives. In a restaurant I heard a woman talking on a cell phone with someone who seemed to be her husband ("Have you fed the kids?"); she informed the caller that she was having dinner with her mother, all the while

smiling slyly at the person sitting across from her, who happened to be a man. Public transportation is at least as bad as restaurants. The last time I rode a bus, my newspaper reading was disrupted by a cell phone conversation that began with a young woman's complaint about her future mother-in-law's interference with her wedding plans, moved on to the fact that she didn't want to make the mother-in-law angry because the woman was very rich, and concluded with the revelation that this was the real reason she was marrying the guy in the first place. I deeply and sincerely did not care to know all that.

(5) There was a time when I could go to a movie or browse the stacks at my favorite bookstore and know that I could leave behind the world of insistently ringing phones for awhile. Those days are gone, my friends. We as a society are compelled to talk, talk, talk all the time, and cell telephones are the instruments of our addiction. We can run, but we cannot hide from a wireless world that can't bear the concept of disconnection.

TRY IT OUT

ANSWER THESE QUESTIONS ABOUT THE ESSAY "CELL PHONE HELL."

1. In the introduction, what is the thesis statement? ________________

____

2. According to the writer, what are three major effects of cell phone use?

____

____

3. In the conclusion, what final observation does the writer make about cell phone use? ________________________________

____

An Essay That Focuses on Causes and Effects. In the essay below, the writer deals with both causes and effects in each body paragraph.

What Is the Best Parenting Style?

(1) When your mother said, "Wash the dishes," did you jump to do it because you knew you had to? Could you get away with arguing back? Or did you just ignore her? Obedience and control are practiced differently from one family to the next. Psychologists who study families have found that the way authority is carried out in the home has a strong effect on the way children develop.

(2) In some homes, parenting is based on strict authority. Rules are firm, and not following them will lead to punishment. Obedience, not independent judgment, is expected from children. So, for example, if a child wants to question a rule, the answer might be "Because I said so." The most important values in this type of home are respect for authority, hard work, and traditional, orderly ways of doing things. Children's impulses are seen as something to be disciplined and controlled through parental power. Research suggests that the consequence of this style is that children have a clear sense of order; they are good at taking directions and following the rules. However, they tend to lack confidence. Not having learned to trust their own judgment, they are often lost without someone else to tell them what to do. They are not used to taking risks or independent responsibility. For example, they might be more comfortable playing a board game with clear rules than inventing an adventure with pirates and stolen treasure. Other children may see them as withdrawn or unfriendly when they really just lack confidence.

(3) In homes in which the parents are highly permissive, the children tend to develop very differently. With this style of parenting, a high priority is placed on allowing children to follow their impulses. They have freedom to regulate their own behavior and express themselves spontaneously. Few demands or responsibilities are placed on them. The parent may want to be a friend more than an authority figure. There are not many rules, and if a child questions a rule, the answer might be, "Good question. Let's talk about it." The child may even be invited to participate in setting up the rules. The relationship is based on reasoning rather than power. The result of this style tends to be children who are friendly and confident because they are used to having adults treat them as equals. However, because they are not used to being disciplined, they often lack self-control. These children might be great at inventing a creative game but not so good at sticking with it if they are not winning or if the sand castle keeps washing away. While they may create interesting projects, they might not be so good at cleaning up afterward. Although children from permissive homes are often charming, they are likely to lose their tempers when their desires are not met; they are used to having their way.

(4) A different kind of personality is encouraged in homes where parenting is both firm and loving. In these homes, the parents set clear and consistent limits for their children; they explain their rules and encourage discussion and even disagreement. If a child wants to question a rule, the response might be, "What will you do to show me that you can handle more freedom?" These parents believe that it is their responsibility to give their children direction, but that it should be given in a way that the child can understand. The child is given the maximum independent responsibility that he or she can handle. Children are encouraged to explore, but to do so within clear boundaries. "Yes, you can build a model airplane, but not in the living room. And everything has to be cleaned up and put away by 9:30." Thus, both reasoning and parental power are part of the equation. Parenting style

research indicates that children raised in these homes tend to be self-confident about their ability to accomplish tasks and meet challenges. They are not afraid to try something new, and they have the self-discipline to follow through even when the task becomes frustrating. These children handle responsibility well because they are used to being held accountable for their actions. They also tend to do well socially. Because they were allowed to express their emotions but not allowed to rule the household with their feelings, they are able to regulate their emotions in a mature way. Some studies suggest that these children are most likely to be successful.

(5) Although many other factors such as gender, culture, and the child's temperament also contribute to a child's development, parenting style is a powerful influence. Both research and common sense suggest that firmness, reasoning, and love are all critical to healthy development. The most positive results are achieved when children receive a rich balance of all three.

TRY IT OUT

ANSWER THESE QUESTIONS ABOUT THE ESSAY "WHAT IS THE BEST PARENTING STYLE?"

1. In the introduction, what is the thesis statement? ____________________

   ____

2. According to paragraph 2, children who are raised in homes with strict authority are often lost without someone else to tell them what to do. What caused the children to develop in this way?

   ____

3. According to paragraph 3, the children of highly permissive parents often lack self-control. What caused the children to develop in this way?

   ____

4. According to paragraph 4, what are the effects of parenting that is both firm and loving? ____________________

   ____

   ____

5. In the conclusion, what observation does the writer make about parenting styles? ____________________

   ____

EXERCISE 13H: For each topic given below, provide three causes or effects as indicated.

1. Topic: a sharp increase in the number of overweight children

   Causes: ______________________________

   ____

   ____

2. Topic: the popularity of TV reality shows

   Causes: ______________________________

   ____

   ____

3. Topic: deciding to start an exercise program

   Causes: ______________________________

   ____

   ____

4. Topic: getting a college education

   Causes: ______________________________

   ____

   ____

5. Topic: more Americans getting married later in life

   Causes: ______________________________

   ____

   ____

6. Topic: having a car

   Effects: ______________________________

   ____

   ____

7. Topic: alcohol abuse

   Effects: ______________________________

   ____

   ____

8. Topic: shyness

   Effects: ______________________________

   ____

   ____

9. Topic: teenage parenthood

   Effects: ______________________________

   ____

   ____

10. Topic: not getting enough sleep

    Effects: ______________________________

    ____

    ____

EXERCISE 13I: Select one of the topics below or one of the topics in Exercise 13H as the basis for an essay that focuses on causes, effects, or both. Then follow the list of steps to create your essay.

Topics

an important decision or change in your life	divorce
a serious problem in your community	drug abuse
the popularity of the Internet	stress
dropping out of school	teenage marriage
moving to the United States	getting a job
the popularity of a certain public figure	becoming addicted to television

Steps

1. After selecting a topic, brainstorm a list of causes and/or effects that you could use to develop your essay.

2. Create a thesis statement that identifies the topic, states your main point about it, and indicates whether you are writing about causes, effects, or both.
3. Jot down specific facts, examples, and reasons that clearly explain each cause and/or effect. This evidence should prove that the cause/effect relationship you are discussing is correct.
4. Decide on a logical order for presenting the causes and/or effects. Will you arrange them using order of importance or chronological order?
5. Think about your conclusion. What can you say to remind the reader of your thesis? What final comment or observation can you make about your topic? Why is it important for the reader to understand the cause/effect relationship you have discussed in your essay? Keep in mind that your ideas may change somewhat as you write, for good writing often generates new insights into your topic. However, starting with a clear sense of your essay's purpose will help you select and organize the causes and/or effects.
6. You are now ready to write the first draft of your cause/effect essay.
7. After completing the first draft, use the revision process described on pages 311–22 to help you achieve a successful cause/effect essay.

The Definition Essay

In writing an essay that constructs a definition, you have the opportunity to approach a subject with more thoroughness and spirit than the efficient, short dictionary definition has. A definition essay presents your personal understanding of the topic by explaining what it means to you.

Usually a definition essay is constructed so that it will have the effect of stimulating thought and providing a fresh approach to a topic. This type of essay is always written for a specific purpose. This chapter includes examples of three popular types of definition essays.

An essay written to suggest a new or enlarged way of looking at something

An essay written to illustrate and comment on an aspect of human nature, society, and so on

An essay written to clarify an existing practice and perhaps to present a new plan of action

To write an effective definition essay, be sure to follow these guidelines:

I Break Your Topic into Parts That Can Be Clearly Understood.

II Try to Avoid the Obvious.

III Use a Variety of Techniques to Develop Your Definition.

I. **Break Your Topic into Parts That Can Be Clearly Understood.** These parts may be aspects, characteristics, or qualities. For example, in a five-paragraph essay describing the perfect teacher, the main body paragraphs would present three important qualities that might be used to define the person.

TRY IT OUT

FOR EACH TOPIC BELOW, JOT DOWN THREE ASPECTS, CHARACTERISTICS, OR QUALITIES THAT COULD BE USED TO DEVELOP A DEFINITION ESSAY.

an ideal date	*democracy*	*generosity*
____________	____________	____________
____________	____________	____________
____________	____________	____________

II. Try to Avoid the Obvious. For example, if you are writing a definition of love, you might immediately think of the relationship, often sexual, between a man and woman. But you could present a fresher approach to the topic if you considered other types of love:

parent for child	dictators for their power
person for God	person for learning
person for money	scientist for science
child for a pet	person for country
animal for its master	person for self

TRY IT OUT

LIST EIGHT POSSIBLE WAYS OF LOOKING AT THE QUESTION: WHAT IS FEAR? TRY TO INCLUDE SOME TYPES OF FEAR NOT OFTEN THOUGHT ABOUT.

________________ ________________

________________ ________________

________________ ________________

________________ ________________

III. Use a Variety of Techniques to Develop Your Definition. You might be tempted to develop your definition by relying heavily on synonyms, other words that have a similar meaning. However, you should also try to use a variety of definition techniques to help the reader see your topic in a new way. One of the more popular techniques is negation; you define a word by explaining what it is not. For instance, if you are trying to define punk rock, you might explain how it is different from other forms of rock music.

In addition, you can expand your definition by using some of the techniques found in the other essay types described in Chapters Twelve and Thirteen. Specific examples will make the definition of an abstract term such as *love* seem more concrete. A short narrative will draw the reader into your topic. Explaining a process will show how an aspect of your topic works. To expand and clarify your definition further, you might also use classification, comparison/contrast, and cause/effect.

TRY IT OUT

SELECT ONE TYPE OF FEAR THAT YOU LISTED IN YOUR ANSWER FOR THE PREVIOUS TRY IT OUT. USE SYNONYMS, NEGATION, EXAMPLES, AND SOME OF THE OTHER DEFINITION TECHNIQUES TO EXPAND YOUR TOPIC INTO AN EXTENDED DEFINITION. USE YOUR OWN PAPER FOR THIS ASSIGNMENT.

POINTERS FOR WRITING A DEFINITION ESSAY

1. The *introduction* should state what is being defined. You should avoid using a dictionary definition because it provides too narrow a start (and because it is a technique vastly overused by students). The introduction might consider such questions as "What or whom does it affect?" "Why is it significant?" "When did it take place?" when such questions are appropriate for the subject being defined.
2. The *main body paragraphs* should break what is being defined into its major parts. A separate paragraph should be devoted to each of these major parts. If what you are defining is

   . . . *an object*, such as an automobile, the parts are concrete;

   . . . *an idea*, *person*, or *place*, such as love, President Lincoln, or Cape Canaveral, the parts can be things that are not concrete because they concern abstract ideas such as spirit and feelings.

3. The *parts that you select* will reflect your judgment, point of view, and major purpose, such as
   a. to suggest a new or enlarged way of looking at something.
   b. to illustrate and comment on an aspect of human nature, society, etc.
   c. to clarify an existing practice and perhaps present a new plan of action.
4. The *order* in which the selected parts are presented should be clear and logical. Look back at the Pointers for Explaining a Process on pages 518–19 for a more complete explanation of those orders: by importance, by location, from simple to complex, from known to unknown, and of time.
5. If your definition seems too shallow, try to enrich your perception of the subject. Try thinking about your subject in terms of
   a. its physical properties (through all five senses: sight, touch, hearing, smell, taste).
   b. its uses—and dangers.
   c. its effect on: people, history, attitudes, etc.
   d. what it is not.
6. Whenever possible, illustrate with specific examples, facts, or incidents. A definition that merely recites synonyms goes around in circles because it avoids being specific.

An Essay Written to Suggest a New or Enlarged Way of Looking at Something. In the definition essay below, the writer offers a fresh view of what a home is.

Home

(1) What is "home"? Picture Mom and Dad and their children sitting down to dinner together in the evening. Afterwards, Mom helps her teenage daughter, Betty, with her math homework while Dad plays checkers with his 10-year-old son, Jason. Maybe the family watches television for a little while before bedtime. On the weekends, perhaps they have friends and relatives over for a cookout. This may be the traditional picture of home—a place of security and friendly gatherings—but it is not a very typical picture today. For many Americans, home has now become a place to sleep, to work, and to store things.

(2) These days Americans of all ages lead such hectic lives that home is often little more than a place to sleep and change clothes. Family members see each other in passing; they seldom share activities, let alone a daily meal. In the morning, Mom and Dad rush off to work at 7:30 and the children leave for school a half hour later. At 3:30, Betty goes directly from school to her part-time job at Burger King. After returning to an empty house, Jason goes out to play for a while and then eats dinner alone. When his parents arrive home at 6:30, he is in his bedroom doing his homework. When Betty comes in the door a few hours later, she yells a quick hello to her parents, grabs some leftovers from the refrigerator, and heads for her room to eat and relax. Because the family members have different schedules, they have little chance to spend time with each other.

(3) Adults who do spend time at home today are usually there because it has become their workplace. Government studies estimate that as many as one-third of all American workers perform some or all of their work-related activities at home. Computers, fax machines, scanners, and other new technology allow many kinds of work to be done anywhere. Using electronic mail and telephone conference calls, a textbook editor at home in California can communicate with her boss in New Jersey as easily as if they were across the hall from each other. To avoid the lengthy commute to Lower Manhattan, a Wall Street stockbroker can use his home computer to keep in touch with clients, track stock prices, and place buy and sell orders. Instead of traveling from town to town selling her gift baskets, a woman in Evanston, Illinois, can advertise her products on the Internet and fax brochures to her customers. Of course, when these people work at home, they may be physically present, but they are not available to their families. The office door is closed.

(4) Finally, today's American home is a storage place for things. Couples who work hard feel that they deserve designer clothes, expensive furniture, sophisticated exercise equipment, and the latest electronic devices. Thus, if all the family members happen to be home at the same time, they are

frequently preoccupied with their possessions. While Mom is in her bedroom working out on her treadmill, Dad is in the living room watching an action film on his big-screen home theater complete with surround sound speakers. At the same time, Jason is in his room playing Mortal Kombat on his Sony PlayStation, and Betty is in her room trying on her new Donna Karan jeans while listening to Celine Dion on her CD player. The family members are involved with things rather than with each other.

(5) Home used to be a refuge from the harsh outside world, a place where people could receive the love, comfort, and support of concerned family and friends. As many Americans became increasingly interested in acquiring material possessions, their homes turned into way stations, business offices, and storage places. Today's American home may be filled with wonderful things, but it has lost its true purpose.

TRY IT OUT

ANSWER THESE QUESTIONS ABOUT THE ESSAY "HOME."

1. According to the introduction, what is the traditional picture of home?

   ____

   ____

2. According to the body paragraphs, what are the three main purposes for today's home? ______________________________

   ____

3. What specific examples are used to develop paragraph 3? __________

   ____

   ____

4. According to the conclusion, does the writer think that today's American home is better than the traditional one? ____________________

   ____

An Essay Written to Illustrate and Comment on an Aspect of Human Nature, Society, and So On. Often this is done by the construction of a definition of an event, a person, or a place. Here is an essay that comments on an aspect of society.

Who Are the Homeless?

(1) Last year a group of teenagers in New York City poured gasoline on a homeless man sleeping under a bridge and then set him on fire. As he wildly beat at his clothes and screamed in pain, they laughed and watched him burn to death. This complete lack of respect for a homeless person is extreme but, in truth, many Americans view the homeless as nothing more than worthless alcoholics and drug addicts living off of society. Perhaps we might begin to make a sincere effort to help the homeless if we better understand who they really are.

(2) One large group of homeless people consists of "throwaway children," the thousands of teenagers each year who are forced to leave their homes because of family conflicts or physical abuse. Sara, a 16-year-old girl from Indianapolis, Indiana, is a typical throwaway child. After being sexually abused by her stepfather, she complained to her mother, who took no action whatsoever. Angry and frightened, Sara packed a suitcase of clothing, took $85 from her mother's purse, and ran away from home. She hitchhiked to Los Angeles, California, where she was unable to find a job to support herself. Even fast-food restaurants would not hire her because she lacked a permanent address. When her money was gone, she began begging on the streets and sleeping in a local park. Growing tired of this existence, Sara eventually turned to prostitution on the Sunset Strip. There she has joined hundreds of other homeless teenagers who regularly sell their bodies to pay for food, clothing, and a cheap room somewhere. According to the U.S. National Network of Runaway and Youth Services, Sara is just one of the more than 2 million throwaway children now living on the nation's streets.

(3) An even larger group of homeless people consists of the mentally ill. Since the 1970's, doctors have increasingly relied on drugs to treat mental illness. Instead of being hospitalized indefinitely, patients have been sent home with prescriptions. In many instances, however, these people have ended up on the streets because they did not have family members who were willing to provide emotional or financial support. Dennis, a 42-year-old man from New York City, found himself in that exact situation. When Dennis was 19, he was diagnosed with schizophrenia, a mental illness that caused him to withdraw into a fantasy world of his own. After being hospitalized for twenty-two years, he began to improve with the help of a new medication. Because his parents were no longer living, he was sent to live in a group home for mentally ill people. A few weeks later he ran away after being threatened by one of the other patients. Dennis now survives by eating in soup kitchens and sleeping in doorways; when the weather turns cold, he spends time in the city's subway stations and bus terminal. Without his medication, he is beginning to lose hold of reality again. The government estimates that approximately one-quarter of all the homeless are mentally ill people like Dennis.

(4) By far the largest group of homeless people consists of families with children. In recent years, many companies have downsized their operations or have moved their factories out of this country to save on labor costs. Although the companies' stockholders may have benefited, the companies' workers have not. For example, May and Joe Kalson lost their jobs when General Motors closed its factory in Tarrytown, New York. After their unemployment insurance ran out, they went on welfare for a while, but the payments did not cover all of the living expenses for themselves and their two teenage sons. When the Kalsons could no longer afford to pay the rent on their small apartment, they piled all of their belongings into their old Chevy and headed for Detroit in search of work. But the automobile factories there had no job openings. While the Kalsons have waited for that situation to change, May has managed to find some work cleaning other people's houses, and Joe has occasionally found work as a day laborer. Their first night in Detroit the family stayed in a homeless shelter, where some of their clothing was stolen while they slept. The Kalsons now sleep in their car. According to the U.S. Conference of Mayors, over half of all the homeless people in this country are families like the Kalsons.

(5) The throwaway children, the mentally ill, and the homeless families are not the only people who are forced to live on the streets. Other groups include the elderly, Vietnam veterans, recent immigrants, people with physical disabilities, and former convicts. Although alcoholics and drug addicts must also be included, the majority of homeless people are decent, law-abiding citizens who, through no fault of their own, have found themselves living in poverty. Unfortunately, they are part of a society that respects the wealthy and looks down on the poor. When we are able to show respect and consideration for the poor, we will begin to deal effectively with the problem of homelessness in America.

TRY IT OUT

ANSWER THESE QUESTIONS ABOUT THE ESSAY "WHO ARE THE HOMELESS?"

1. According to the introduction, why is it important to understand who the homeless are? ______________________________

____

2. According to the body paragraphs, what are the three major categories of homeless people? ______________________________

____

3. What order is used to present the three major categories of homeless people? ______________________________

____

4. In the conclusion, the writer comments on an aspect of society. What does he say? ______________________________

____

An Essay Written to Clarify an Existing Practice and Perhaps to Present a New Plan of Action. Often this type can persuade the reader. Here is an essay that clarifies existing practices in the Japanese school system and then presents a new plan of action for the American school system.

American Schools Should Take a Lesson from Japan

(1) It is a widely accepted fact that many of America's schools are doing a poor job of educating the nation's young people. Research studies indicate that about 30 percent of American high school students drop out before graduating. In some high school systems, fewer than half of the students who enter ever graduate. We should not be surprised, then, that one in four Americans is illiterate—unable to read and write at the most basic level. What can be done? American schools should take a lesson from Japan, where strict rules of behavior, very demanding school schedules, and high academic standards have produced nearly 100 percent literacy.

(2) Because Japanese schools use numerous rules to encourage good student behavior, the schools may seem a bit like military academies. From first grade through the senior year of high school, the students are required to spend 15 to 30 minutes a day cleaning the building, taking out the garbage, and removing graffiti. Because the students have to clean up any mess they

make, they tend not to make a mess in the first place. Most schools also require students to wear uniforms and do not permit wristwatches, hair ribbons, dyed hair, perfume, jewelry, makeup, or anything else that could set one student apart from another. Although students occasionally break these rules, Japanese teens are not as rebellious as American young people. As a result, the hallways in a Japanese school are safe and the classes are orderly.

(3) The Japanese school schedule is long and demanding. A typical high school day begins at 8:00 in the morning. The students spend almost 90 percent of the day studying serious academic subjects such as history, math, and science; the schools place much less emphasis on classes such as music, art, and physical education. School lets out at 6 P.M. after extracurricular activities in which most students participate. Then students return home, eat dinner, and do two or three hours of homework before bedtime. Students also go to school every other Saturday morning. In addition, at age 13 most young people begin attending three hours of "cram school" three nights a week. A "cram school" is private school that teaches thinking skills and further reinforces material taught in the public schools. During summer vacation, which is only six weeks long, teachers assign homework so that students will not forget what they have learned.

(4) The school schedule needs to be this demanding because students must be prepared to meet the high academic standards established through a national testing program that begins in early childhood. National tests determine which preschool, elementary school, high school, and—most important of all—which university an individual attends. Indeed, teenagers who fail a few of these tests may not have the opportunity to go to a university at all. Without this advanced education, these young people will never be able to rise to important positions in Japanese society. Instead they will most likely spend their lives in low-paying jobs as servants or factory workers. As a result, Japanese students are under intense pressure to do well on these tests. The teenagers themselves call the high school years "examination hell." Today, a growing number of private schools are taking students who are unable to cope with the pressures of the Japanese educational system.

(5) Of course, it would not be desirable to create these pressures in the American educational system. However, other features of the Japanese system would be worth copying. For example, if American students were required to clean schools and obey the rules of proper behavior, perhaps they would gain the self-discipline and sense of responsibility needed for academic achievement. Making the school year longer would give students more time to learn the basics needed to succeed in American society. Raising academic standards and requiring students to work harder would help to improve the nation's literacy rate. If these changes were put into place in America's schools, the high school graduation rate would probably increase significantly, and more of our young people could look forward to a happy, productive future.

TRY IT OUT

ANSWER THESE QUESTIONS ABOUT THE ESSAY "AMERICAN SCHOOLS SHOULD TAKE A LESSON FROM JAPAN."

1. According to the introduction, why should we "take a lesson from Japan"?

____

____

____

2. What three major aspects of the Japanese school system are defined in the body paragraphs? _______________________

____

____

3. In the conclusion, what plan of action does the writer present? _______

____

____

____

4. Has the writer persuaded you to agree with her plan of action? Why or why not? _______________________

____

____

EXERCISE 13J: The parts listed for each of the definition essays given are too shallow for the scope and purpose of the title given. Referring to the Pointers for Writing a Definition Essay, tell why the definition is shallow and then list parts that would be more appropriate for the title.

1. Beauty Can Mean Many Things

	Revised Parts
Introduction	Introduction
I. nice face	I. _______________
II. good build	II. _______________

III. pretty clothes	III. ______________
Conclusion	Conclusion

Why shallow? ______________

2. The Rushed Life of a College Student

	Revised Parts
Introduction	Introduction
I. getting to class on time	I. ______________
II. using the library	II. ______________
III. meeting new people	III. ______________
Conclusion	Conclusion

Why shallow? ______________

3. Life Is Not Fair

	Revised Parts
Introduction	Introduction
I. Things don't always work out.	I. ______________
II. We all have some bad luck.	II. ______________
III. The "bad" comes with the "good."	III. ______________
Conclusion	Conclusion

Why shallow? ______________

4. A Good Friend Is a Treasure

	Revised Parts
Introduction	Introduction
I. A good friend is rare.	I. ______________
II. A good friend is hard to find.	II. ______________
III. Loneliness is a sad feeling.	III. ______________
Conclusion	Conclusion

Why shallow? ______________

5. What Does Being "Intelligent" Mean?

	Revised Parts
Introduction	Introduction
I. smart	I. ______________

II. high I.Q.	II. ____________________
III. learns quickly	III. ____________________
Conclusion	Conclusion

Why shallow? ____

6. Living in the Suburbs Is Better Than Living in the City

	Revised Parts
Introduction	Introduction
I. good shopping facilities	I. ____________________
II. good recreational facilities	II. ____________________
III. good cultural facilities	III. ____________________
Conclusion	Conclusion

Why shallow? ____

7. TV Advertisements—An Insult to the American Public

	Revised Parts
Introduction	Introduction
I. Ads are frequent.	I. ____________________
II. Ads interrupt good programs.	II. ____________________
III. Ads try to sell products.	III. ____________________
Conclusion	Conclusion

Why shallow? ____

8. San Francisco—A Tourist's Treasure

	Revised Parts
Introduction	Introduction
I. its history	I. ____________________
II. how to get there	II. ____________________
III. who lives there	III. ____________________
Conclusion	Conclusion

Why shallow? ____

9. Success Cannot Be Measured by Money Alone

	Revised Parts
Introduction	Introduction
I. Money is not everything.	I. ____________________

II. Success means more than wealth. II. ____________________

III. Successful people I know. III. ____________________

Conclusion Conclusion

Why shallow? ____________________

10. A Knowledge of Psychology Is Helpful in Everyday Life

Revised Parts

Introduction Introduction

I. id I. ____________________

II. ego II. ____________________

III. superego III. ____________________

Conclusion Conclusion

Why shallow? ____________________

EXERCISE 13K: Construct a definition for each topic given. First, decide on a purpose for your definition. Next, select the parts that should be discussed in order to achieve your purpose.

1. Topic: wastefulness

Your purpose: ____________________

Parts selected: I. ____________________

II. ____________________

III. ____________________

2. Topic: a good job

Your purpose: ____________________

Parts selected: I. ____________________

II. ____________________

III. ____________________

3. Topic: a car

Your purpose: ____________________

Parts selected: I. ____________________

II. ____________________

III. ____________________

4. Topic: happiness

   Your purpose: ______________________________

   Parts selected: I. ______________

   II. ______________

   III. ______________

5. Topic: your mother or father

   Your purpose: ______________________________

   Parts selected: I. ______________

   II. ______________

   III. ______________

6. Topic: a newspaper

   Your purpose: ______________________________

   Parts selected: I. ______________

   II. ______________

   III. ______________

7. Topic: diets

   Your purpose: ______________________________

   Parts selected: I. ______________

   II. ______________

   III. ______________

8. Topic: your school

   Your purpose: ______________________________

   Parts selected: I. ______________

   II. ______________

   III. ______________

9. Topic: good music

   Your purpose: ______________________________

   Parts selected: I. ______________

   II. ______________

   III. ______________

10. Topic: maturity

    Your purpose: ____________________

    Parts selected:

    I. ____________________

    II. ____________________

    III. ____________________

EXERCISE 13L: Select one of the topics below or one of the topics in Exercise 13K as the basis for a definition essay. Then follow the list of steps to create your essay.

Topics

courage
responsibility
guilt
selfishness
self-confidence
jealousy
security
frustration
freedom
prejudice
patriotism
laziness
respect
common sense
good manners
street smarts
peer pressure
inner strength
a good parent
a nerd
a hero
an optimist
a pessimist
a sports fanatic
a control freak
a type of music
a type of movie

Steps

1. Write a thesis statement that identifies your topic and provides a brief standard definition as a starting point. The thesis statement may also indicate why your extended definition might be interesting or important to the reader.
2. Break your topic into three aspects, characteristics, or qualities that can be clearly understood.
3. Jot down specific examples that will illustrate and clarify each aspect, characteristic, or quality.
4. To develop each aspect further, use some of the other definition techniques: negation, narration, process, classification, comparison/contrast, and cause/effect.
5. Decide on a logical order for presenting the aspects of your definition. Order of importance is often the most effective method for arranging the aspects. However, a different order may also work well: location, simple to complex, known to unknown, or time.
6. Think about your conclusion. What can you say to remind the reader of your thesis? What final comment or observation can you make about your

extended definition? Why is it important for the reader to know what this topic means to you? Keep in mind that your ideas may change somewhat as you write, for good writing often generates new insights into your topic. However, starting with a clear sense of your essay's purpose will help you to select and organize the aspects of your definition.

7. You are now ready to write the first draft of your definition essay.
8. After completing the first draft, use the revision process described on pages 311–22 to help you achieve a successful definition essay.

The Argument Essay

Most people would like to have reasonable, well-thought-out opinions on many of the subjects that are of major concern in life. Intelligent opinions should be based on evidence that is factual and logical. Such opinions, however, should not be rigidly unchangeable; if an argument presents either new evidence or a new approach to already known evidence, people should be open-minded enough to change their opinion.

When you argue an opinion, your purpose is to tell the reader *why* you have your opinion and to persuade the reader to agree with you. To support your argument, you may use personal experiences as well as facts and other specific evidence gathered from research. This chapter includes examples of three types of argument essays.

An argument essay based primarily on personal experience

An argument essay based on both personal experience and research

An argument essay based primarily on research

To write an effective argument essay, be sure to follow these guidelines.

I Select a Topic You Feel Strongly About.

II Consider Your Opponent's Position.

III Answer Your Opponent.

IV Build an Argument That Is Logical.

V Use Devices That Will Add Impact to Your Argument.

VI Support Your Position with Information Supplied by an Expert.

VII Support Your Opinion with Facts and Specific Evidence Rather Than with Personal Judgments and Emotional Reactions.

I. Select a Topic You Feel Strongly About. If you do, you will probably find it easier to build a forceful and convincing argument.

II. Consider Your Opponent's Position. Analyzing your opponent's point of view before you begin writing will help you clarify your own thinking on the issue and will help you construct a more persuasive argument.

III. Answer Your Opponent. If possible, state your opponent's position in your essay and then point out the flaws in that argument. By doing so, you will not only weaken your opponent's argument, but you will also show the reader that you have considered all sides of the issue. When responding to an opponent, be sure to maintain a respectful tone. Calling your opponent "a jerk" or "a crazy idiot" is likely to turn the reader against you. Concentrate on attacking the argument, not the person.

IV. Build an Argument That Is Logical. In particular, be careful not to form a generalization based on a single experience you may have had. For example, it would not be logical to suggest that people should avoid using credit cards because you once had trouble paying your credit card bills. To create a logical argument, you would have to show that many other people have had a similar problem. (For more information on logic, see Appendix I: Critical Thinking—Logic.)

V. Use Devices That Will Add Impact to Your Argument. Some of the methods you can use when planning an effective argument can be borrowed from the other types of expository essays discussed in chapters 12 and 13.

a. To support an opinion, include a dramatic incident that illustrates the main point.
b. To explain an opinion, describe the process of how something is, was, or might be.
c. To clarify an opinion, construct a clear definition of a key term or concept.

VI. Support Your Position with Information Supplied By an Expert. However, before using this information, ask yourself two questions: First, is the person an expert on the subject you are discussing? Movie stars frequently speak out on social issues such as poverty and capital punishment. Although these people have a right to state their opinion, they are not experts who have studied the issues in great detail. Second, does the expert have anything personal to gain by providing this information? For example, you might question the accuracy of a study showing the health benefits of drinking wine if the research was paid for by the wine industry.

VII. Support Your Opinion with Facts and Specific Evidence Rather Than with Personal Judgments and Emotional Reactions. A fact is something that can be clearly measured or observed; specific evidence is something that comes from a recognized authority such as an encyclopedia, a book, or a person who is an expert on the subject you are discussing.

TRY IT OUT

SELECT WHICH OF EACH SET IS A FACT.

1. ______ a. In 1776, a person with an income of $4,000 a year was considered to be very wealthy.

   ______ b. If every American household earned at least $20,000 a year, the country's problems would be solved.

2. ______ a. Grizzly bears are mean, ugly animals.

   ______ b. A grizzly bear can run as fast as a horse.

3. ______ a. The average American consumes about one ton of food and drink each year.

   ______ b. The average American consumes too much food and drink each year.

POINTERS FOR WRITING AN ARGUMENT ESSAY

1. The *introduction* should lead into the reasons for your opinion. This can be done by
   a. stating your opinion at the outset.
   b. giving an appropriate incident that will clearly illustrate and give impact to your opinion.
   c. asking a provocative question that will stimulate thought on the subject of your opinion.
2. The *full statement of your opinion* should appear where it has the most impact. This can be done in the introduction, main body, or conclusion.
   a. If your opinion is in the introduction, all reasons given must relate directly back to your basic position and the conclusion should include a restatement of your opinion.
   b. If your opinion is in the main body, it should smoothly follow the device used in the introduction.
   c. If your opinion is in the conclusion, it should not come as a surprise; all the reasons presented must build to the inevitable climax or conclusion.

(Continued)

(Continued)

3. The *support for your opinion* should be based on facts, examples, authorities, and other specific evidence. This support must be strong enough to stand on its own. The reader should be able to form an intelligent opinion from the evidence you have presented; you should not have to insist that you are correct.
4. Your argument should be logical. Refer to Appendix I for a more complete discussion of logic so that you will be reminded not to make errors such as oversimplification, generalization, and attacking the person.
5. For impact, try these argument techniques:
   a. To illustrate:
      . . . use a dramatic incident.
      . . . explain the process of how something was, is, or might be.
   b. To clarify:
      . . . give a clear definition of a key term.
      . . . ask an organizing question to give focus.
      . . . anticipate an objection by stating it and then answering it.
   c. To dramatize:
      . . . give the dangers of the present system.
      . . . make a comparison to something else.

An Argument Essay Based Primarily on Personal Experience. Argument essay topics that are assigned for in-class writing can usually be developed well with personal experience and observations. Here is an example of an argument essay that relies heavily on the writer's experiences.

The Pause That Refreshes

(1) In a traditional college education, students go to school semester after semester, taking courses that will broaden their knowledge and help them achieve specific career goals. When the students have accumulated enough credits, they fulfill their dream of being awarded a college diploma. These days, however, many students are finding graduation day to be the beginning of a time of struggle and confusion, for they finish school owing money and wondering what they are going to do now that they are in the real world. These students would have benefited from taking a one-year break in their college education so that they could go to work full time. Interrupting college to work for a year can help pay college expenses, set a person on the right career path, and provide opportunities to develop the maturity to do well in college.

(2) Taking a year off to work can make the difference between leaving school debt-free and leaving with a huge student loan to pay off. College tuition can run anywhere from $1,500 a year for a public institution to $15,000 a year for some private schools. Room and board can add $3,000 to $5,000; books and laboratory fees can add another $500 to $1,000 a year. Then there are the usual day-to-day expenses: transportation, a haircut, a new pair of shoes, or a ticket for a Rolling Stones concert. I was fortunate when I started college because my parents were able to pay part of my tuition. But I still needed to work 20 to 30 hours a week delivering pizzas. Although the job covered the rest of my expenses, my college studies suffered. At the end of my freshman year, I was disgusted with my grades and tired from my hectic schedule. So I dropped out of school and went to work full time. When I returned to college a year later, I had saved enough money so that I didn't have to work to support myself; instead I could put all of my time and energy into studying.

(3) Taking time off to work during the college years can also help a student decide on the right career. For example, because I was good in math, I always thought I wanted to be an accountant. But after working as an accountant's assistant for a few months, I realized that I would go crazy looking at hundreds of little numbers on a computer screen all day. After an argument with my boss, I left this job and soon found another one doing general office work for a stockbroker. When I heard about all the money that brokers can make, I became very interested. But then I saw how the young brokers had to make "cold calls" to strangers to sell stocks and bonds; they were on the telephones from early morning until late at night, and if they didn't meet their quotas, they were fired. That wasn't for me! I quit this job after I found a new one at an animal shelter. Because I had never had pets, I was surprised when I discovered that I loved working with the animals. In fact, I didn't even mind having to clean out their cages. I was especially interested in watching the veterinarian give shots, treat sick animals, and deliver kittens and puppies. As a result of this work experience, I have returned to school to study veterinary medicine. With this specific career goal in mind, I find that I am now much more motivated to work hard at my studies.

(4) Finally, taking a year off to work can help a student develop the maturity needed to do well in college. My parents were upset when I decided to drop out of school because they were concerned that I might not return to finish my education. But they didn't have to worry. Indeed, working made me realize that I needed a college degree to get a good-paying job. In addition, I gained a new sense of responsibility that stayed with me when I returned to school. I was fired from my job at the accounting firm because I frequently showed up late and did my work carelessly. I guess I was partying too much at night. Having learned my lesson, I settled down and took my next job seriously. I cut out the partying during the week so that I could make it to work on time, and I did whatever my boss told me to do to the best of my ability.

Now that I'm back in college, I don't cut classes unless I'm really sick, and I hand in all of my assignments when they are due.

(5) As I move from class to class, I meet many students who remind me of the way I used to be. They have money problems and are drifting through college with no career goals in mind. These students should think seriously about taking a temporary leave of absence to go to work. Working a year may just be the pause that refreshes. When they return to school, they will most likely get more out of the time and money that go into earning a college degree.

TRY IT OUT

ANSWER THESE QUESTIONS ABOUT THE ESSAY "THE PAUSE THAT REFRESHES."

1. What is the writer's full point of view as stated in the introduction?

___

___

2. Are the writer's three reasons well supported with specific evidence?

___

___

3. In paragraph 4, the writer responds to his parents' objection. What does he say? ___

___

4. In the conclusion, where does the writer restate his point of view?

___

___

5. Do you find the writer's argument persuasive? Why or why not?

___

___

An Argument Essay Based on Both Personal Experience and Research. The most effective way to develop many argument essay topics is with a combination of both personal experience and research. Here is an example of that type of essay.

The Case Against Fast-Food Restaurants

(1) Burger King sells 710 million Whoppers a year, enough to circle the Earth almost three times. KFC cooks so many chickens every year that if they were laid head to toe, they would reach the moon. McDonald's opens at least 1,000 new restaurants a year, and Subway, a fast-growing sandwich chain, is opening 25 restaurants a week. Fast food is currently a $95 billion industry. Do most Americans like fast food? They certainly do! But is fast food good for Americans? No, it isn't. Americans should avoid eating at fast-food restaurants because the meals are unhealthy, the food is often carelessly prepared, and the environment is unpleasant.

(2) Fast-food meals are unhealthy because they are high in calories, fat, and sodium. For example, a Big Mac, a large order of French fries, and a large Coca-Cola contain a total of 1,320 calories, 53 grams of fat, 1,390 grams of sodium, and 86 grams of sugar. The government recommends that the average person's daily diet should contain no more than 2,000 calories, 60 grams of fat, and 2,400 grams of sodium. One Big Mac meal, then, provides two-thirds of the daily calorie requirement and contains almost 60 percent of a person's daily allowance of sodium and over 80 percent of the daily allowance of fat, most of which is saturated fat—the kind that clogs the arteries. Would chicken be a healthier choice? A KFC Original Recipe chicken breast and drumstick contain 490 calories, 27 grams of fat, and 1,080 grams of sodium. Although the chicken may have a slightly better calorie count, the meal is still unhealthy. The nutritional information provided by Burger King, Wendy's, and other fast-food chains reveals a similar pattern: Many of the foods are loaded with high levels of fat and sodium that are not good for the health. High fat intake can lead to heart disease and cancer, and sodium can raise blood pressure and contribute to overweight. Granted, fast-food restaurants now serve salads, but who goes to McDonald's to order a salad?

(3) Another problem with fast food is that it is often carelessly prepared. Although fast-food restaurants have detailed rules about how the food should be cooked and served, former employees admit that these rules are sometimes ignored. Most fast-food employees are inexperienced young people, and, especially during the busy times of the day, they are under a great deal of pressure. If a hamburger patty falls on the floor, the cook may just pick it up and put it on a bun. When the French fries are done cooking, they are salted—or perhaps oversalted—with no regard for the proper amount of seasoning. Worse, during a slow time of the day, employees may play pranks. Probably the best known is spitting on the hamburger before putting on the top of the bun and then laughing about the "special sauce."

(4) Finally, many fast-food restaurants offer an unpleasant atmosphere for eating an enjoyable meal. During the rush hours, customers first have to wait in long lines to order the food and then have to search for an empty table. Because these restaurants are frequently understaffed, food wrappers,

beverage cups, and used napkins may be left on the tables for long periods of time. When a worker eventually arrives to clean up the mess, he or she removes the litter and wipes the table with a wet rag that does little more than smear the dirt all over the surface. Before sitting down in a booth, customers had better check the seat for a blob of ketchup or a small pool of soda that could stain their clothing. As people eat their food, they are annoyed by screaming children who are running around the restaurant while their parents finish their meal. At the same time, teenagers at a nearby table are bouncing up and down to the music blasting from their boom box. Meanwhile, other customers stand by the tables waiting to get a seat.

(5) In spite of this unpleasant environment, fast-food restaurants are more popular than ever because they offer convenient meals to Americans who are caught up in today's hectic lifestyle. However, people should realize that they are paying a heavy price for eating in these restaurants, for most of the food is unhealthy and may be poorly prepared. Instead of eating in a fast-food restaurant, people would do better to eat at home, where a delicious home-cooked meal can be prepared quickly and eaten in a relaxing atmosphere.

TRY IT OUT

ANSWERS THESE QUESTIONS ABOUT THE ESSAY "THE CASE AGAINST FAST-FOOD RESTAURANTS."

1. What is the writer's full point of view as stated in the introduction?

 ____

 ____

2. Are the body paragraphs developed with personal experience or research?

 Paragraph 2: ______________________________

 Paragraph 3: ______________________________

 Paragraph 4: ______________________________

3. In paragraph 2, the writer responds to an opponent's point of view. What does he say? ______________________________

 ____

4. In the conclusion, the writer makes a comparison. What does he say?

 ____

 ____

5. Do you find the writer's argument persuasive? Why or why not?

 ____

 ____

An Argument Essay Based Primarily on Research. Some argument essay topics require a good deal of research for support. In most instances, this research will include information gathered from books and articles in the library and from materials supplied by professional organizations. In addition, the research may include interviews with experts in the field. Here is an example of an essay that is based primarily on research.

Doctors Are Worth Every Penny They Charge

(1) Almost everyone complains about how much doctors charge. According to the American Medical Association, the average fee for an office visit for an established patient is $65 and for a new patient, $120. A full medical checkup costs about $300 with all the laboratory tests. A patient who needs surgery can expect to pay the surgeon about $1,200 for an appendectomy, $4,500 for a hip replacement, and as much as $10,000 for a heart bypass. Are these fees high? Yes, but people need to consider the larger picture. Doctors are entitled to collect high fees because of their many years of expensive training, the enormous cost of maintaining their practice, and the stressful nature of their work.

(2) Before doctors are ever allowed to practice, they receive at least thirteen years of intense and expensive training. After four years of college and four years of medical school, the graduates typically owe about $85,000 each in student loans. Then these new doctors begin a two-year internship at a hospital, where they may work twenty-four-hour shifts as part of exhausting eighty-hour weeks under the close supervision of other physicians. Next they do a three-year residency in a hospital where they specialize in one area such as internal medicine, pediatrics (children's medicine), or dermatology (skin diseases). Some specialties require even longer residencies. Heart surgeons, for example, must do an eight-year residency. Although interns and residents are paid, their pay covers only basic living expenses. Meanwhile, the interest on student loans continues to grow. In other words, most doctors are 32 to 36 years old before they can begin to practice, and most carry a huge debt.

(3) They not only have to pay off this debt but must also cover the costs of running their medical practice. Two of the largest costs are an average of $20,000 for the office rent and $55,000 for the office payroll. Other expenses include about $8,000 a year for office equipment and supplies, $5,000 a year for laboratory and medical equipment, and $5,000 a year for drugs and medical supplies. Malpractice insurance costs tens of thousands of dollars a year, although some doctors such as bone specialists and brain surgeons pay as much as $150,000. When all of these expenses are added up, the average yearly cost of running a practice comes to at least $120,000. Few other professions carry overheads this high.

(4) To make matters worse, doctors must cope with a great deal of stress in their work. The hours are long and irregular; doctors work an average of sixty hours a week. A typical doctor begins the day by visiting hospitalized patients at 6:00 A.M. Office visits usually run from 8:30 A.M. to 4:30 P.M., and then the doctor returns to the hospital to consult with another physician or to see a patient admitted through the emergency room. After eating a quick dinner, the doctor will probably spend the evening catching up on paperwork or reading professional journals to stay up to date on the latest medical advances. In the course of a week, the doctor will see as many as 140 patients. At each of

these 140 meetings, he or she has to make difficult decisions concerning the patient's health. A wrong diagnosis or treatment can end both the patient's life and the doctor's career. Thus, no allowance can be made for normal human error. Is it any wonder that doctors have extremely high rates of heart disease and suicide?

(5) Considering the years of training involved, the enormous cost of running a practice, and the long, stressful hours that doctors work, people should gladly pay their fees. It takes tremendous intellectual and physical stamina, self-discipline, and dedication to be a doctor. The demands of the profession are great, and so the rewards should be great as well.

TRY IT OUT

ANSWER THESE QUESTIONS ABOUT THE ESSAY "DOCTORS ARE WORTH EVERY PENNY THEY CHARGE."

1. In the introduction, the writer begins to answer her opponents. What does she say? ______________________________

____

2. In paragraph 2, what process does the writer describe? ______________________________

____

3. Where might the writer have gotten the information contained in this essay? ______________________________

____

4. In the conclusion, the writer summarizes her argument in one sentence. What does she say? ______________________________

____

5. Do you find the writer's argument persuasive? Why or why not?

____

____

EXERCISE 13M: Read each of the following statements carefully. Label each either *fact* or *opinion.*

________ 1. The famous Washington, D.C., cherry trees were a gift from the mayor of Tokyo in 1912.

_______ 2. "Sanka" comes from the French phrase *sans caffeine,* meaning "without caffeine."

_______ 3. The giant panda is a cuddly, adorable animal that everyone loves to admire.

_______ 4. Colleges should provide day-care services for the children of adult students.

_______ 5. Elvis Presley owned eighteen television sets.

_______ 6. Benjamin Franklin campaigned unsuccessfully to have the turkey declared our national symbol.

_______ 7. The White House has 132 rooms.

_______ 8. All politicians are corrupt.

_______ 9. While hanging by his heels forty feet above ground, the magician Harry Houdini escaped from a straitjacket.

_______ 10. John F. Kennedy was a handsome man.

_______ 11. Responsible for saving thousands of lives during World War II, a carrier pigeon was given a medal by the Lord Mayor of London.

_______ 12. Virginia has the perfect climate.

_______ 13. Robins get drunk if they eat the red berries of the Florida holly bush.

_______ 14. When glass breaks, the cracks move at the speed of almost a mile a second.

_______ 15. Reading the daily newspaper is an important habit for good citizens to develop.

_______ 16. Everyone knows the correct way to change a tire.

_______ 17. The Rockies are the most beautiful mountains in the world.

_______ 18. Cranberries were one of the first crops exported from the American colonies.

_______ 19. It is hard to tell the difference between a fact and an opinion.

_______ 20. At one time, most barbers were also surgeons.

EXERCISE 13N: For each item given below, first explain why the evidence does not support the opinion effectively. Then suggest what type of evidence would be effective.

1. ***Opinion:*** Gun control laws should be enacted in all fifty states.

Evidence: The National Rifle Association (NRA) claims that the Second Amendment to the Constitution guarantees the right of all Americans to carry guns. However, those NRA people are just a stupid bunch of gun-toting lunatics who don't know what they are talking about. A national gun control program is needed to reduce the high rate of violence in the United States.

Why isn't this evidence effective? ______________________________

____

What type of evidence would be effective? ______________________________

____

____

2. ***Opinion:*** Animals should not be used for medical experiments.

Evidence: Cats and dogs are adorable, cuddly creatures that can provide us with love and companionship. Unfortunately, some scientists are so coldhearted that they don't mind using these innocent animals for medical experiments. How can these people not realize that what they are doing is wrong? If we are truly a civilized society, then we should not allow animals to be used in horrible scientific experiments.

Why isn't this evidence effective? ______________________________

____

What type of evidence would be effective? ______________________________

____

3. ***Opinion:*** Gambling should be legalized in all fifty states.

Evidence: Some people are concerned that legalized gambling may have negative effects on society. However, Jack Pott, the president of the Easy Aces Gambling Casino in Las Vegas, claims that gambling is a highly enjoyable form of entertainment that does not harm anyone. Mr. Pott has been in the gambling business for over thirty years, so he certainly knows what he is talking about.

Why isn't this evidence effective? ______________________________

____

What type of evidence would be effective? ______________________________

____

4. ***Opinion:*** Living alone is not a good idea.

Evidence: People who live alone run a high risk of having their homes broken into while they are out. In the twenty-one years that I lived with my family, no one ever tried to rob our home. But six months after I moved out on my own, my apartment was burglarized and over $3,000 of valuable possessions were stolen. My experience proves that it is safer to live with other people.

Why isn't this evidence effective? ______________________________

____

What type of evidence would be effective? ______________________________

____

5. ***Opinion:*** Sex education should be an essential part of the public school curriculum.

Evidence: High school sex education classes should provide students with specific birth control information. In a recent interview, Academy Award–winning actress Meryl Hunt said that it is important for schools to teach teenagers how to protect themselves while having sex. She feels so strongly about this issue that she plans to discuss it on all the television talk shows.

Why isn't this evidence effective? ______________________________

____

What type of evidence would be effective? ______________________________

____

6. ***Opinion:*** The death penalty should be abolished.

Evidence: The federal government should outlaw capital punishment. It is upsetting to think that in many states it is legal to kill someone who has been convicted of murder. Even if the person is guilty, it is still wrong to take a human being's life. The death penalty is not the solution to our nation's high crime rate. That is why our enlightened society should abolish capital punishment.

Why isn't this evidence effective? ______________________________

____

What type of evidence would be more effective? ____________________

____

EXERCISE 130: Select one of the topics below as the basis for an argument essay. Then follow the list of steps to create your essay.

Topics

Single People Should (Should Not) Be Allowed to Adopt Children
A Gay Couple Should (Should Not) Be Allowed to Marry
Is Marriage Going Out of Style?
Should Gambling Casinos Be Legalized in All Fifty States?
Sports Superstars Are (Are Not) Worth the Enormous Salaries They Receive
Watching Television Is (Is Not) a Waste of Time
All Animals Do (Do Not) Have Rights
Does Society Pressure Young People to Grow Up Too Quickly?
UFO's Do (Do Not) Exist
Life As Shown on Television Is (Is Not) Realistic
People Do (Do Not) Have a Responsibility to Care for Their Elderly Parents
Can a Man and a Woman Have as Close a Friendship as Two Men or Two Women Can Have?
Prostitution Should (Should Not) Be Legalized
The Case for (Against) Doctor-Assisted Suicide for Terminally Ill Patients
Should an Unhappily Married Couple Stay Together for the Sake of Their Children?
Does the Law Offer More Protection for Criminals Than for Victims?

Steps

1. After selecting your topic, jot down several reasons that will support your point of view. In addition, jot down the reasons why some people may not agree with your point of view. If necessary, do some research in the library or on the Internet to make sure that you have not overlooked any major reasons.

2. Look over your two lists of reasons. Has your point of view changed at all? When you feel sure that your point of view is correct, you are ready to write your thesis statement. Your thesis statement should identify your topic and indicate your position on it.

3. Jot down facts, examples, dramatic incidents, statements by authorities, and other specific evidence to support each reason for your point of view. If

necessary, do some additional research in the library or on the Internet to find strong evidence.

4. Next, jot down any flaws that you see in your opponent's position. Why are the people who disagree with your point of view wrong?
5. Decide on a logical order for presenting your reasons. Order of importance is often the most effective method to use; start with your weakest reason and end with your strongest.
6. Think about your conclusion. What can you say to remind the reader of your thesis? What conclusions can you draw based on the evidence you have given in your essay? What specific actions would you like the reader to take? Keep in mind that your ideas may change somewhat as you write, for good writing often generates new insights into your topic. However, starting with a clear sense of your essay's purpose will help you to select and organize your reasons.
7. You are now ready to write the first draft of your argument essay.
8. After completing the first draft, use the revision process described on pages 311–22 to help you achieve a successful argument essay.

EXERCISE 13P: REFRESHER

1. Find and correct any comma splices and run-on sentences.

2. Make any necessary corrections in punctuation and capitalization.

A group of milwaukee teenagers known as the 414's has broken into more than sixty business and Government computer systems in the United States and Canada. Using home computers and devices that allow computers to send information over the telephone lines the 414's have managed to gain entry to the computerized records stored at such locations as Los Alamos National Laboratory, Security Pacific National Bank in Los Angeles, and New Yorks Memorial Sloan-Kettering Cancer Center. Officials at Sloan-Kettering revealed that some accounting information had been erased from their computer's memory but that the patients therapy records had not been touched. Executives at many of the companies that have had computer break-ins have refused to reveal the exact nature of the damage, in fact, some companies have not reported computer crimes at all for fear of the bad publicity.

Why have the teenagers been committing these illegal acts? For the 414's, breaking into a computer is like climbing a mountain, both of those activities offer an exciting challenge that ends with the thrill of accomplishment. In addition, the 414's do not share society's view of morality. As one of the computer hobbyists has stated, Philosophically, we don't believe in property rights. According to this philosophy, the information stored in a computer is not private property it belongs to anyone who has enough skill to uncover it. However, most computer experts insist that these break-ins are not merely harmless games they are actually dangerous destructive crimes.

SPRINGBOARDS TO WRITING

Using your knowledge of the writing process, explained on pages 14–16, write a paragraph or essay related to this chapter's central theme, *lying*, which is introduced on page 534.

PREWRITING

To think of topics to write about, look at the cartoons, read the essay, and answer the questions that follow each. If you prefer, select one of the writing springboards below. (All paragraph numbers refer to the essay that starts on page 536.) To develop your ideas, use the prewriting techniques described on pages 17–22.

WRITING A PARAGRAPH *(For help, see the Pointers on page 51.)*

1. One little lie can cause a big problem.
2. Describe a type of lie that Stephanie Ericsson has not discussed.
3. Read paragraph 7. Should you tell a friend that "he looks great when he looks like hell"?
4. Read paragraph 8. Should the sergeant have told the family of the dead soldier that he was killed in action?
5. Read paragraphs 11 and 12. Do you agree with Stephanie Ericsson that "the church became a co-perpetrator with Porter"?
6. Explain why a particular stereotype is not true. (See paragraph 14.)
7. I am (am not) good at making up excuses.
8. Agree or disagree with this statement by Pierre Corneille: "One ought to have a good memory when he has told a lie."

WRITING AN ESSAY *(For help, see the Pointers on pages 54–55.)*

9. Why People Tell Lies
10. My Many Facades
11. Honesty Is (Is Not) Always the Best Policy
12. Agree or disagree with Stephanie Ericsson's statement: "I discovered that telling the truth all the time is nearly impossible." (See paragraph 4.)
13. Agree or disagree: "When someone lies, someone loses." (See paragraph 5.)
14. Is Honesty a Rapidly Vanishing Value in American Society?
15. Most Politicians Are (Are Not) Liars
16. How Lying Harms Society
17. The Government Does (Does Not) Tell Us the Truth
18. Why People Like to Gossip
19. Agree or disagree with this statement by Samuel Butler: "Any fool can tell the truth, but it requires a man of some sense to know how to lie well."
20. Agree or disagree: "Our acceptance of lies becomes a cultural cancer that eventually shrouds and reorders reality until moral garbage becomes as invisible to us as water is to a fish." (See paragraph 17.)

APPENDIX I

Critical Thinking—Logic

An essay—even one with proper grammar—will not be successful if it is built on faulty reasoning. You must think and write clearly, giving effective evidence to support well-thought-out ideas.

I. As you read the following paragraph about the draft, pay close attention to the reasoning used to build the argument.

> I wholeheartedly disagree with Senator Claghorn's proposal to establish a universal national draft. The stupidity of the plan is apparent when one considers that the senator has been divorced three times and is now being sued for back alimony payments by his last wife. In addition, our enemy Fidel Castro uses this draft system in Cuba, which makes me wonder if perhaps the senator is a Communist sympathizer. Instead of drafting fine young men, the government should send all of the convicted murderers to fight our wars. After all, these criminals like to kill people. This would be the democratic thing to do in the home of the free and the land of the brave.

Analysis. The writer of this paragraph seems to have some strong feelings about his subject, but, unfortunately, he gives no proof to support his argument that a universal national draft is a bad idea. The senator's marital troubles may indicate that he is not a good marriage risk, but these problems certainly have no bearing on the worth of the man's idea. Instead of discussing the plan, the writer prefers to **attack the person** who proposed it.

The writer then reasons that the plan cannot be any good because our enemy already uses it. We may have ideological differences with Fidel Castro, but that does not mean that everything Cuba does is necessarily bad. **Guilt by association** is being used to destroy the proposal.

The counterproposal will not hold up under examination because, while it may be true that some murderers enjoy committing their crimes, it is ridiculous to assume that this is true of all killers. Thus, it is a **generalization** to say that all convicted murderers like to kill people.

Even if it were true that all murderers like to kill, too many questions have not been considered in formulating this new proposal: Can murderers be trusted in the armed forces? Is there a moral argument against such a plan? When dealing with a complex problem, you need to analyze and examine your subject from many points of view before coming to any conclusions. The writer, who has created a plan based only on his own personal feelings, is guilty of **oversimplifying** his solution.

The writer ends his argument by carefully linking his own proposal with democracy, freedom, and bravery—words that have good connotations for Americans. With the same purpose in mind, the writer identifies Senator Claghorn's plan as communistic, a term that has negative connotations. Thus, the writer has tried to **feed our prejudices.**

TRY IT OUT

THE FOLLOWING PARAGRAPH IS BUILT ON SOME OF THE SAME CONFUSED THINKING THAT HAS JUST BEEN DISCUSSED. FIND THE ERRORS AND LABEL EACH WITH ITS APPROPRIATE NAME. ON A SEPARATE SHEET OF PAPER, EXPLAIN WHY IT IS WRONG.

The taking of vitamin C will protect the American people from catching the dreaded common cold. Doctors obviously agree with this because they always tell people who have colds to drink a great deal of orange or grapefruit juice, both of which are filled with health-giving vitamin C. Dr. Arthur Mometer, who conducted a research study on vitamin C, claims that the vitamin neither prevents nor cures colds. However, his claim cannot be true because he is a money-hungry quack who was recently found guilty of not paying all of his taxes. His sister, Annie Mometer, was just arrested for practicing medicine without a license. Therefore, the federal government should ignore Dr. Mometer's findings and should force all food manufacturers to add large quantities of vitamin C to their products. If this is done, Americans will be forever free of the menace of the common cold.

II. As you read the following paragraph about college life, pay close attention to the reasoning used to build the argument.

> College students should concentrate on having a good time and should never pay attention to intellectual growth. Studying too much can lead to serious consequences. Just last week R. T. Zank, the school bookworm, suffered a nervous breakdown right after his chemistry final. However, Sammy Swinger, the handsome football quarterback who never opens a book, is sure to succeed because he is so well liked.

Analysis. The writer of this argument makes his first error in logic when he indicates that there are only two alternatives: A student spends all of his or her time either studying or having a good time. But there are other courses of action that have not been mentioned. For example, a student may spend part of the time studying and part of the time socializing. The situation is not as black and white as the writer's **either-or argument** would have us believe.

The story of R. T. Zank proves only that the writer is not a very clear thinker. It is highly doubtful that studying was the sole cause of Zank's nervous breakdown. If the writer had explored the case, he probably would have discovered that Zank had some serious personal problems. Thus, a **false cause** is being used to prove the argument.

The case of Sammy Swinger falls apart under examination because the writer does not supply the proper evidence to prove that the football player will succeed. The fact that Sammy is well liked does not mean that he will be successful. **Irrelevant evidence**—that is, evidence that has no logical relationship to the topic—should not be used to back up an argument.

TRY IT OUT

THE FOLLOWING PARAGRAPH IS BUILT ON SOME OF THE SAME CONFUSED THINKING THAT HAS JUST BEEN DISCUSSED. FIND THE ERRORS AND LABEL EACH WITH ITS APPROPRIATE NAME. ON A SEPARATE SHEET OF PAPER, EXPLAIN WHY IT IS WRONG.

Loud, wild rock music is ruining the morals of today's young people. For example, my nephew, Eddie, stole a car right after attending a rock concert. Even more shocking is the fact that since the introduction of rock music to the United States, the juvenile crime rate has risen steadily each year. It is clear, then, that if rock music is not banned in this country, young people will eventually destroy the American way of life.

III. As you read the following paragraph about cigarette smoking, pay close attention to the reasoning used to build the argument.

> Cigarette smoking is certainly not harmful to health. My grandfather began smoking cigarettes when he was 11 and he lived to be 95. My Uncle Jim, who smokes four packs of cigarettes a day, is a healthy seventy-two. In addition, Mike Marvel, the ace baseball player, says that Puffo Cigarettes make him feel relaxed and refreshed before a big game. Besides, everybody smokes cigarettes, so smoking can't be wrong.

Analysis. The writer of this paragraph uses two examples to try to prove that cigarette smoking is not harmful to health. These illustrations may help clarify the argument, but they are **inadequate evidence** because they do not prove the writer's case. Two men are not representative of the millions of people who smoke. A reputable research study using a much larger sampling would be adequate evidence to convince the reader.

The writer then makes the mistake of citing a baseball player's comment as added proof. Whenever an authority is used, one must decide if the person is an authority on the subject of the essay. Mike Marvel may know a good deal about baseball, but he does not know any more about cigarette smoking than anyone else. One might also wonder if the authority had any hidden motives for making his statement. In this case, the baseball player endorsed Puffo Cigarettes because he was being paid. Therefore, he certainly was an **inappropriate authority.**

The writer ends his argument with yet another poor attempt at proving his opinion. Although a good many people do smoke cigarettes, it is a ridiculous generalization to claim that everybody does. It is more accurate to limit the statement by saying that many people smoke cigarettes. In the same way, strong words such as *never* and *always* usually have to be reduced to *sometimes* and *often.* It is important to limit an **unqualified statement** to make it more accurate.

Even if it were true that everybody smokes cigarettes, this fact still would not prove that smoking is not harmful to health. One hundred fifty years ago many people believed that slavery was a good thing, but that did not mean it was. The **everyone-is-doing-it argument** does not prove anything, for even the majority can be wrong.

TRY IT OUT

THE FOLLOWING PARAGRAPH IS BUILT ON SOME OF THE SAME CONFUSED THINKING THAT HAS JUST BEEN DISCUSSED. FIND THE ERRORS AND LABEL EACH WITH ITS APPROPRIATE NAME. ON A SEPARATE SHEET OF PAPER, EXPLAIN WHY IT IS WRONG.

Television programs have never been as good as they are today. *The Eaton and Chilada Show,* the popular cooking program, and *Branches,* the drama series based on a family tree, have both won Peabody Awards for excellence. Also, Anne Tenna, the program director of the United Broadcasting Network, announced that the quality of today's television programs is much higher than it used to be. This must be true because everybody watches so much television nowadays.

IV. As you read the following paragraph about flying saucers, pay close attention to the reasoning used to build the argument.

If flying saucers do exist, they might be dangerous to our society. Thus, we should be afraid of flying saucers, if there are such things, because they could do a good deal of harm to the people of Earth. Peter, my next door neighbor, claims that he doesn't consider flying saucers dangerous. In fact, he says that he would enjoy riding in a flying saucer from another planet because he loves to ride in airplanes. Personally, I do not think that flying saucers are a danger because I do not think they even exist; after all, I have never seen one.

Analysis. The writer begins by presenting the logical statement that flying saucers might be dangerous if they really exist. But instead of immediately trying to prove his statement, he merely uses new words to repeat the same argument in the next sentence. Because the reader is just being led in a monotonous circle, this error is called **circular reasoning.**

Peter is also an illogical thinker. When Peter compares riding in a flying saucer with riding in an airplane, he forgets that, although the vehicles might be somewhat similar, there are probably some very big differences between the two. Things that are being compared must be similar in all major aspects or the result is a **false comparison.**

The argument falls apart completely with the concluding statement that flying saucers do not exist because the writer has never seen one. It is invalid to argue that something does not exist because one has **no personal knowledge** of it.

TRY IT OUT

THE FOLLOWING PARAGRAPH IS BUILT ON SOME OF THE SAME CONFUSED THINKING THAT HAS JUST BEEN DISCUSSED. FIND THE ERRORS AND LABEL EACH WITH ITS APPROPRIATE NAME. ON A SEPARATE SHEET OF PAPER, EXPLAIN WHY IT IS WRONG.

All dangerous criminals should be locked up in prison for life to prevent them from doing more harm to society. Because innocent citizens must be safeguarded, thieves, murderers, and rapists should never be released from prison. We should not put these violent criminals back on the streets only to commit more outrageous crimes. I have certainly never heard or read about an ex-convict who did not eventually commit another serious theft or assault and end up back in prison. Indeed, dangerous criminals, like other dangerous animals, should be kept in cages forever.

EXERCISE IA: Analyze each of the following statements for its soundness of reasoning. Use your own paper for this assignment.

1. You can't teach an old dog new tricks.
2. Because Edna has a good sense of humor, she will make an excellent art director.

3. Marlon Brando, the famous movie actor, says that the United States government owes the American Indians a great deal of land.
4. Everybody else drinks liquor, so why shouldn't I?
5. Psychiatry is absolutely useless because I have never known anyone who was helped by it.
6. One of Tom's good friends was just arrested for shoplifting. I didn't think Tom was that kind of person.
7. A garbage collector should make as much money as a doctor makes. After all, they both provide services that are vital for public health.
8. If all doctors were completely honest, medical treatment would be less costly.
9. Parents should never punish their children. Otherwise, their children will not love them.
10. Honesty is always the best policy.
11. Members of the Wandering Prune rock group sing very poorly because it is widely known that they take narcotics.
12. If you have had a college education, you are sure to get a good job. My three older brothers, all of whom graduated from Kalamazoo University, are now executives for large corporations.
13. The nations of the world must pass laws to control population growth so that there will be enough food for the people who now go to bed hungry. Because so many people are starving in the world, each country should enact legislation that will limit the birth rate.
14. You should buy United States savings bonds to uphold the red, white, and blue. In addition to saving money, you will be showing your patriotism as a red-blooded American.
15. Many colleges all across the nation are closing. This proves that people are not as interested in education as they used to be.

APPENDIX II

Common Prefixes and Suffixes

A *prefix* is a syllable which, when added to the beginning of a word, affects its meaning.

A *suffix* is a syllable which, when added to the end of a word, affects its meaning.

Being familiar with the most common prefixes and suffixes can help you to increase your vocabulary and improve your spelling.

Common Prefixes

meaning	*AGAINST*	
anti-	antiballistic	
contra-	contrary	
meaning	*MORE THAN*	
extra-	extraordinary	
hyper-	hypersensitive	
super-	superpatriotic	
ultra-	ultraconservative	
meaning	*THE NEGATIVE*	
dis-	disagree	
il-	illegal	
im-	immoral	
in-	inadequate	
ir-	irresponsible	
mis-	mistake	
non-	noninvolvement	
un-	unhappy	
For numbers	*meaning . . .*	
HALF:	semi-	semicircle
ONE:	uni-	uniform
ONE:	mono-	monologue
MANY:	poly-	polysyllable
For place	*meaning . . .*	
BEFORE:	ante-	anteroom
BEFORE:	pre-	predate
AFTER:	post-	postscript

BACK:	re-	return
BACK:	retro-	retrofire
UNDER:	sub-	submarine
ACROSS:	trans-	transplant
BETWEEN:	inter-	interpersonal
INSIDE:	intra-	intravenous

meaning	*SELF*
auto-	autograph

meaning	*POOR, POORLY*
mal-	malnutrition

Common Suffixes

noun meaning	*ACT OF*
-tion	segregation

noun meaning	*STATE OF*
-hood	adulthood
-ment	estrangement
-ness	kindness
-ship	friendship
-tude	solitude
-dom	freedom

adjective meaning	*ABLE TO BE*
-able	comfortable
-ible	compatible

adjective meaning	*FULL OF*
-ate	fortunate
-ful	tactful
-ous	pompous
-y	gloomy

adjective meaning	*WITHOUT ANY*
-less	penniless

verb meaning	*TO MAKE, TO PERFORM*
-ate	integrate
-ify	unify
-ize	computerize

EXERCISE IIA: To determine the correct prefix for a word, you will often have to consult the dictionary. In this exercise, however, the correct prefix is supplied. Form the following words.

Using the prefix		*Form*	
1.	un	not truthful	1. ________________
2.	il	not logical	2. ________________
3.	semi	half civilized	3. ________________
4.	post	date it after	4. ________________
5.	non	not athletic	5. ________________
6.	in	not decent	6. ________________
7.	anti	against the freeze	7. ________________
8.	uni	one sphere	8. ________________
9.	im	not possible	9. ________________
10.	dis	not appear	10. ________________
11.	hyper	excessively active	11. ________________
12.	sub	below the conscious	12. ________________
13.	ir	not rational	13. ________________
14.	mal	functioning poorly	14. ________________
15.	mis	not understood	15. ________________

EXERCISE IIB: For each word below, give a general definition. (If you are unsure of a meaning, consult your dictionary.) Next, briefly explain how the prefix influenced the word's meaning.

1. autobiography: ________________________________
2. retrorocket: ________________________________
3. supernatural: ________________________________
4. prehistoric: ________________________________
5. transform: ________________________________
6. monogamy: ________________________________
7. polygamy: ________________________________

8. reconcile: ____________________
9. ultrahigh (frequency): ____________________
10. intrastate (highway): ____________________
11. interstate (highway): ____________________
12. extrasensory: ____________________
13. contradiction: ____________________
14. antechamber: ____________________

EXERCISE IIC: Construct each word by referring to the list of common suffixes and, if necessary, to the dictionary.

1. noun: state of being happy ____________________
2. noun: act of flirting ____________________
3. noun: state of being a child ____________________
4. adjective: full of fortune ____________________
5. adjective: able to agree ____________________
6. adjective: without any worth ____________________
7. verb: to make ideal ____________________
8. verb: to make beautiful ____________________
9. noun: state of being an apprentice ____________________
10. noun: state of being contented ____________________
11. adjective: full of wind ____________________
12. adjective: able to deduct ____________________
13. noun: state of being solitary ____________________
14. noun: state of being a serf ____________________
15. adjective: full of thanks ____________________
16. adjective: full of courage ____________________
17. verb: to make originally ____________________

APPENDIX III

Spelling Demons

A

absence
absolutely
accident
accommodate
acquaintance
across
actually
adequately
adolescent
advertisement
afraid
against
alcohol
allowed
all right
ambitious
among
analyze
another
answer
anticipate
apologize
apparently
appearance
appreciate
approach
appropriate
approximately
architect
argument
arrangement
article
assassination
assignment
assistance
association
athlete
atmosphere
attempt
attendance
attitude
average
awkward

B

background
basically
beautiful
beginning
behavior
benefit
business

C

campaign
candidate
career
carefully
category
certainly
character
children
chocolate
cigarette
circumstance
citizen
clothes
column
comfortable
commercial
committee
competition
completely
conquer
conscience
conscious
continually
convenient
cooperation
counselor
courtesy
criticize
crowded
cruel
curiosity

D

decision
definitely
definition
dependent
description
desperate
develop
difference
difficult
dilemma
disappear
disappoint
disastrous
discipline
discourage
discussion
disease
division
doesn't
doubt

E

easily
eighth
eliminate
embarrassed
emphasis
emphasize
encourage
engineer
enormous
enough
enthusiastic
entirely
environment
equipment
especially
evaluate
eventually
everything
exaggerate
excellent
exercise
existence
expensive
experience
experiment
explanation
extremely

F

familiar
fascinating
favorite
February
finally
financial
foreign
fortunately
forty
forward
frequently
frustrated
fulfill
function
furthermore

G

genuine
government
governor
grammar
grateful
guarantee
guard
guidance
guilty

H

height
hundred

I

imaginary
immediately
impossible

independence
individual
influence
instructor
intelligent
interest
interfere
introduce
island

J

jealous
jewelry
judgment

K

knowledge

L

laboratory
lawyer
length
library
license
likelihood
likely
literature
loneliness
luxury

M

magazine
maintenance
maneuver
manufacture
marriage
maybe
mechanic
medicine
minimum
minutes
missile
mortgage
muscle
mysterious

N

necessary
neighborhood
ninety
nuclear
nuisance

O

obstacle
obviously
occasional
occurred
official
operator
opinion
opportunity
opposite
organization

P

paid
parallel
paralyze
particularly
patience
peculiar
performance
permanent
persuade
philosophy
physical
picture
pleasant
poison
politician
pollution
population
possession
possibly
practically
practice
prefer
preparation
presence
previously
privilege
probably
problem
procedure
proceed
profession
professor
propaganda
psychology
pursue

Q

qualification
quantity
quarter
questionnaire

R

realize
recognize
recommend
religious
remember
repetition
representative
require
responsibility
restaurant
rhythm
ridiculous

S

sacrifice
safety
satisfied
schedule
science
secretary
separate
several
severely
signal
significant
similar
since
sincerely
situation
sophomore
source
speech
straight
strategy
strength
strictly
studying
substantial
substitute
subtle
succeed
success
sufficient
surgeon
surprise
survive
suspicious
symbol

T

taught
technique
temperature
tendency
themselves
theory
therefore
thought
together
tomorrow
tragedy
truly
twelfth

U

university
unnecessary
unusual
usually

V

vacuum
valuable
vegetable
violence

W

Wednesday
weird
where
writing
wrong

Index

A

B

C

D

E

F

G

Q

R

S

T

U